One Third of a Nation

I see millions of families trying to live on incomes so meager
that the pall of family disaster hangs over them day by day . . .
I see one third of a nation ill-housed, ill-clad, ill-nourished.

FRANKLIN D. ROOSEVELT

One Third of a Nation

LORENA HICKOK REPORTS ON THE GREAT DEPRESSION

EDITED BY

Richard Lowitt and Maurine Beasley

UNIVERSITY OF ILLINOIS PRESS   Urbana Chicago London

Frontispiece: Photograph by Dorothea Lange, FSA

Library of Congress Cataloging in Publication Data

Hickok, Lorena A
    One third of a nation.

    Includes index.
    1. Depressions — 1933 — United States.
2. United States — Economic conditions — 1918–1945.
I. Lowitt, Richard, 1922-   II. Beasley, Maurine
Hoffman.   III. Title.
HC106.3.H518   338.5'42   80-25905
ISBN 0-252-00849-9

Contents

*Unless otherwise indicated, all communications are addressed to Harry L. Hopkins; the state or city within brackets refers to the subject matter of the letter.

The Unsung Heroes of the Depression[1]

Lorena Hickok

To the "chiselers" and the "shovel-leaners" who have been living on the taxpayers' money these last four years this story is humbly dedicated.

It is their story, as they themselves told it — sometimes desperately, sometimes with quivering lips, sometimes only by the patient, bewildered expression in their eyes — to one who traveled up and down the country as confidential observer for the man who was charged by their Government with the job of seeing that they did not starve.

Four years ago, to the writer, they were not really people at all. They had no faces. They were just "the unemployed." Muffled figures, backs curved against the wind, selling apples on the street corners of New York. One's friends made jokes about "unemployed apples." Grimy hands thrusting needles and wilting gardenias through your cab window when you were halted in cross-town traffic, while you wondered if you ought to buy them, or if it was "just another racket." Old bundles of rags, presumably soaked in that mixture of water and wood alcohol that the cops called "smoke," sleeping endlessly around rubbish fires along the East river.

"What I want you to do," said Harry Hopkins in July, 1933, "is to go out around the country and look this thing over. I don't want statistics from you. I don't want the social-worker angle. I just want your own reaction, as an ordinary citizen.

"Go talk with preachers and teachers, businessmen, workers, farmers. Go talk with the unemployed, those who are on relief and those who aren't. And when you talk with them don't ever forget that but for

1. In 1937 Hickok wrote this chapter as a draft introduction to a projected book on her experiences as an investigator for Harry L. Hopkins and his Federal Emergency Relief Administration. She sent it to Kathryn Godwin, Hopkins's secretary, appending the note: "This is that introductory chapter. It will need a lot of changes, of course, and it may not be all. But it will give you an idea. — L.A.H."

the grace of God you, I, any of our friends might be in their shoes. Tell me what you see and hear. All of it. Don't ever pull your punches."

First, a sickening trip on a blistering July morning through Washington's notorious slums, "the Alleys."[2] Then, to Philadelphia. Down into West Virginia and Eastern Kentucky. A month in up-state New York and New England. Two weeks in New York City. Six weeks—and 7,000 miles in an old Chevrolet—in the Dakotas, Nebraska, Iowa, and Minnesota. Down through the Tennessee Valley. Two weeks among the beet sugar workers in Colorado. The Imperial Valley in California, where a thermometer in the car registered 126 degrees Fahrenheit. * * * Fayette county, Pennsylvania, during a coal strike. Aroostook county, Maine, during potato harvest. Bottineau county, North Dakota, just before the first blizzard. * * * Wheeling, West Virginia, when smoke began pouring out of the stacks at the steel mills. Miami, Florida, when the tourists began to come back. * * * Pineville, Kentucky, when relief was cut off. Sioux City, Iowa, when CWA came in. Toledo, Ohio, as WPA was starting. * * * Back and forth, up and down the country. By motor, by train, by plane. A three-year Odyssey through every man's land—and no man's land.

One by one, sometimes bold, sometimes hesitant, sometimes demanding, sometimes faltering, they emerged—individuals. People, with voices, faces, eyes. People with hope. People without hope. People still fighting. People with all courage squeezed out of them. People with stories.

There was the Negro woman in Philadelphia who used to walk eight miles every day over the scorching pavements just on the chance of getting, perhaps, a little cleaning to do, at 10 cents an hour.

There was the chauffeur in New York who, on the day before he reported for the first time to work as a laborer on a park project, stood about for hours watching how the other men handled their picks and shovels, so he would "get the hang of it and not feel so awkward."

There was the little Mexican girl, aged 6, in Colorado, who said, sure, she'd worked "in the beets" two Summers already and, yes, sometimes she did get pretty tired.

There was the young musician, who said: "For a few weeks it isn't so bad for a man and his wife and baby to get along on $4.80 a week, paying $3 of it out for rent. But when it runs into months, and you can't see anything ahead, you get damned discouraged."

There was the WPA worker in Erie, Pa., proud as Lucifer because he had developed into "a darned good asphalt man" while working on relief and WPA projects.

There were those unemployed miners' wives in Scotts Run [West

2. This report must have been made orally to Hopkins. Her first written report is dated August 6, 1933, and covers her trip to Pennsylvania.

Lorena Hickok and Eleanor Roosevelt (with Paul Person, governor of the
Virgin Islands), in the Caribbean, March 1934.

Lorena A. Hickok, ca. 1945.

Virginia], who instinctively liked and trusted the tall, slender lady with the warming smile and soft, lovely voice who drove up to their homes in an old Ford one Summer day—and found out later that she was the President's wife.

There were those little boys who refused to go to school in Houston, Texas, wearing the trousers of terribly conspicuous black-and-white-striped ticking that had been given them, because everybody would know they were on relief.

There were those two small boys, a year or so later, in Salt Lake City, who were overheard boasting about whose father had been on relief longer.

There was the small town woman in Iowa who spent part of her husband's first CWA check for oranges, because she hadn't tasted any for three years.

There was the architect who said he didn't mind working on a road as a day laborer because "at least my children can tell the teacher their father is working. They don't have to say what he's doing."

There was the farm woman in South Dakota who had a recipe for Russian thistle soup and said, "It don't taste so bad, only it ain't very filling."

There was the boy of 20 who limped wearily into his home in a Baltimore suburb one Autumn night in 1934 after having walked nearly 20 miles down into the center of the city and back, "just stopping at every place and asking if they didn't need somebody to work—at anything."

There were those plucky, resourceful people in Lansing, Michigan, who set up a cooperative, issued scrip to a farmer in return for some vegetables, and, when the farmer turned it over to an undertaker in part payment for his wife's funeral, redeemed it by painting the hearse.

There was that little man with the Charlie Chaplin mustache and mothy black velour hat set at a pathetically jaunty angle on his grizzly-grey Paderewski haircut, standing in slush up over his ankles, with his trousers wet half way to his knees, patiently and clumsily pecking away with a shovel he didn't know how to use, out at Floyd Bennett airport [Brooklyn] one raw day last February.

There was the former business executive who said: "It's our wives who resent the pretty young girls they send out as visitors. Suppose you were my wife—and I'll bet you are thanking your lucky stars you're not—run down, without any decent clothes, looking ten years older than you ought to look. How would you like it if some smooth-faced young girl, nicely dressed, all made up, with powder on and lipstick, and pink fingernails, came into your house, sat down on the edge of a chair, and began to ask you a lot of personal questions? You'd want to throw something at her, wouldn't you? The contrast is just too painful, that's all. Couldn't they send middle-aged men, maybe? Then the neighbors might not guess, either. They might think they were just peddlers."

There was the unemployed fur-worker in Pittsburgh who said: "Lady, you just can't know what it's like to have to move your family out of the nice house you had in the suburbs, part paid for, down into an apartment, down into another apartment, smaller and in a worse neighborhood, down, down, down, until finally you end up in the slums."

There was that woman in her late thirties, with the thin, sensitive face, in Bakersfield, California, who said timidly: "I can talk to you about this now, because we aren't on relief any more. * * * It's this thing of having babies. You've got no protection at all. You don't have any money, you see, to buy anything at the drugstore. * * * And there you are, surrounded by young ones you can't support. And always afraid. * * * All you have is a grocery order. I've known women to try to sell some of their groceries to get a little money to buy the things they need at the drugstore. But if they catch you at it, they take you off relief. Maybe they wouldn't if they really knew what you wanted the money for, but most women don't like to talk about those things to outsiders. * * * You understand, don't you? I'm not asking for anything for myself. My husband is working now. We're not on relief any more. * * * I suppose you can say the easiest way would be not to do it. But it wouldn't be. You don't know what it's like when your husband is out of work. He's gloomy all the time and unhappy. You haven't any money for movies, or anything to take his mind off his troubles. You must try all the time to keep him from going crazy. And many times — well, that is the only way."

One by one, they come and go. Not all of them saints, by any means. And not all of them, by any means, dishonest or lazy or hopeless. Thousands of them in the last three years have "come back," have found jobs as industry revived, have moved out of the crowded flats where they were living with relatives, have paid up their debts. Perhaps — and it is to be hoped that this is so — many of them have even forgotten that there ever was a Depression! And thousands of them have not found jobs, perhaps never will. A reviving industry, with the best of intentions, cannot immediately absorb such a load as piled up in this country during the black years. The young, the physically fit, the mentally alert first are called and should be. The man over 40, the untrained, the weak, for many of these there may be no future at all. They must remain, to the ends of their lives, in the ranks of the tattered legion of the economically damned.

"Chiselers" and "shovel-leaners" who have been living on the taxpayers' money these last four years — this is their story. And to them it is dedicated, in all sincerity and humility.

Preface

Forty-eight years ago Lorena A. Hickok began traveling around the United States as chief investigator for Harry L. Hopkins, administrator of the Federal Emergency Relief Administration. Her job: To prepare confidential reports on conditions in the United States, as the administration of Franklin D. Roosevelt grappled with the problems associated with providing relief to the victims of the Great Depression. Specifically, Hickok examined the effects that the programs Hopkins directed were having on Americans. With the exception of four reports, her letters on what she saw have been available to interested researchers for many years, but there has been no published edition of these letters for the general public. Our chance meeting in the summer of 1979 at the Franklin. D. Roosevelt Library in Hyde Park, New York, provided the impetus for this project, which now brings to the readers Hickok's superb reports on life in America in 1933 and 1934.

Hickok make our task somewhat easier than expected because she identified most of the people she encountered in her travels. Where she did not do so, she either expected Hopkins to know the individual or neglected to secure full identification owing to the pressure or haste under which she worked. Our difficulties in identifying individuals were largely confined to problems stemming from the second category. While we have identified most individuals, we have not been successful in every instance. Moreover, where Hickok did not identify a person beyond his or her job description, we made no effort to provide the name of the individual.

Deleted material is noted in the usual manner by three dots. However, occasionally Hickok in her reports included dots that served as a transition to another point she wished to make. In these instances, to distinguish from editorial deletions, three asterisks (* * *) have been used.

Material deleted from the reports usually consisted of repetitious sentences or paragraphs, reiterations of what was discussed in an earlier report, or what the editors viewed as excessive detail pertaining to administrative aspects of local or state relief programs. Our focus was on

Hickok's broad and brilliant survey of general conditions in every state, city, community, or project she visited in 1933 and 1934. In addition, because Hickok usually wrote her reports under pressure late at night, misspellings and slight inconsistencies occasionally appeared. Since these reports are not literary documents, we have corrected these mistakes and changed inconsistencies without so noting in the document.

This edition of her reports ends with the year 1934. While we include almost the entire set of her reports to Hopkins, we are printing only a few of the letters to Eleanor Roosevelt, using them to supplement material sent to Hopkins or to round out the picture of conditions in a particular state or community. Some of these letters Hickok had excerpted before putting them with her papers. Hickok sent about 120 reports to Hopkins, while she conducted a daily correspondence with Eleanor Roosevelt. The first ten boxes of her papers contain approximately 2,300 of Roosevelt's letters to Hickok from 1933 and 1962. However, there are no more than 50 letters from Hickok to Roosevelt during the 17 months (August 1933–December 1934) covered in these reports. As noted below, Hickok visited and traveled with Eleanor Roosevelt during these months and often stayed in the White House, so she had no need to write letters. Also, many of the letters Hickok wrote to Roosevelt during this period are believed to have been destroyed.

The final item consists of a report dated January 1, 1935. Here Hickok reviewed the state of the economy with regard to various industries and sections of the nation and assayed what had been done and what still needed to be done. This lengthy report is based on material found in her previous reports as well as those of other field investigators.

All but four of the Hickok reports are to be found in boxes 67 and 68 of the Harry L. Hopkins Papers, and another set can be found in boxes 11 and 12 of the Lorena Hickok Papers. Both are on deposit at the Franklin D. Roosevelt Library in Hyde Park. Four reports, which Hickok wrote from various cities in Georgia in 1934—those from Athens, January 11; Augusta, January 14; Jesup, January 16; and Moultrie, January 23—are available only in the Hickok Papers. The draft prospectus for a book Hickok thought about writing—"The Unsung Heroes of the Depression"—is in box 12 of the Hickok Papers. The letters to Eleanor Roosevelt that we used are located in boxes 1 and 2 of the Hickok Papers.

The photographs that illustrate these reports are intended to convey visually what life was like for some Americans during the Depression. Although many of the photographs were taken after Hickok visited these areas, they nevertheless reflect the kinds of conditions and the devastation and deprivation that people experienced during the early and mid-1930s.

We acknowledge the assistance of several individuals in the preparation of this book. Dr. William L. Emerson, director of the Franklin D. Roosevelt Library, helped us decide on the main title and also to search for pictures with which to illustrate Hickok's letters. We thank Richard L. Wentworth, director of the University of Illinois Press, for his encouragement and support. Susan L. Patterson, a severe yet sympathetic editor, by her penetrating queries and skillful reading of the manuscript, greatly improved it. Jean Seaburg prepared the index. Laurie Helmers and Barbara B. Crandall, who typed the manuscript, did an excellent job. We are indebted to Mary Alice Cousin for her assistance with the research for photographs.

Finally, we both have benefited from awards granted us by the Eleanor Roosevelt Institute and by the Research Councils of our respective universities, Iowa State University and the University of Maryland, College Park.

Richard Lowitt, *Iowa State University*
Maurine Beasley, *University of Maryland*

Introduction

Harry L. Hopkins had one of the toughest assignments in the early New Deal. He headed the greatest organized effort ever made in the United States to relieve nationwide distress. As federal relief administrator, he was responsible for doling out to the unemployed and the needy $500,000,000 allocated by Congress in May 1933 to help the states meet their most pressing relief needs. Half of this sum was available to the states on the premise that for every dollar provided by the Federal Emergency Relief Administration (FERA), three dollars of public money from all sources would be spent. The other $250,000,000 served as a discretionary fund that Hopkins allocated to states whose needs were so great and whose funds were so depleted that they could not meet the matching provisions. Congress in the following sessions increased the funding, and Hopkins who insisted that he was "spending to save" (the title of the volume he published in 1936 delineating his experiences as head of the FERA) proved himself a remarkably adept and creative administrator whose handling of huge amounts of federal funds with a relatively small staff (751 on June 20, 1934) was accomplished with dispatch and efficiency.[1]

So concerned was Hopkins with the plight of the unemployed and so capable an administrator did he prove himself that by 1934 he was burdened with other important and related assignments: administrator of the Surplus Relief Corporation and of the Civil Works Administration (CWA). The former attempted to provide material subsistence, largely in the form of surplus foodstuffs, to the needy, while the latter created jobs to provide the worker with wages. This was a marked improvement over work relief, where the individual's paycheck was deter-

---

1. Fred S. Hall, ed., *Social Work Yearbook 1935* (New York, 1935), 151. As of June 30, 1934, $1,340,760,934 had been allocated from public funds, exclusive of wages paid by CWA. Local governments supplied 20 %; states, 16 %; and the federal government, 63 %. Ibid., 521. An excellent overview of Hopkins's career during the New Deal years can be found in Searle F. Charles, *Minister of Relief: Harry Hopkins and the Depression* (Syracuse, N.Y., 1963).

mined by a social worker evaluating a client's needs. CWA and after 1935 the Works Progress Administration (WPA) provided jobs and eliminated the social worker and the connotation of being on relief.

When Hopkins in the spring of 1933 joined the New Deal, as he noted in 1936, "the well had gone completely dry for one out of every six families in the land."[2] About four million families were destitute, and responsible estimates cited anywhere between twelve and eighteen million people in need. Hopkins used the latter figure and claimed in June 1933 that in some counties 90 percent of the people were seeking help; in some states he cited a figure of 40 percent.[3] Although the magnitude of the crisis was overwhelming, Hopkins was as well prepared for his assignment as an individual could be. In 1931 Franklin Delano Roosevelt, as governor of New York, organized the Temporary Emergency Relief Administration (TERA), the prototype of FERA and the first state agency of its type. TERA provided relief for over one million New Yorkers, and Hopkins became its head in March 1932, after acting as its executive secretary. He came to this post from the field of social work, serving when Roosevelt called upon him as director of the New York Tuberculosis and Health Association. A man of deep human sympathies, a hard-working and driving administrator, Hopkins was blessed when he came to Washington, D.C., in that he did not inherit, as did cabinet members, an established bureaucracy but was free to pick and choose personnel. Since there were no precedents and since relatively little had been done on any level of government or industry to provide protection against the distressful conditions that were becoming overwhelming for millions of Americans, Hopkins was able to innovate, experiment, and put ideas and concepts into practice more quickly than other New Dealers who had to cope with established, tradition-laden bureaucracies. In addition, since FERA was regarded as a temporary organization, it was exempt from civil service requirements, giving Hopkins more leeway and flexibility in recruiting.

Entering upon his assignment, Hopkins faced the immediate and stupendous task of setting up machinery, of providing federal participation in an area regarded as the domain of state and particularly local agencies that had previously handled the bulk of the work involved in administering relief. It was the local official who investigated relief clients, determined need, administered work-relief projects, distributed funds, and performed numerous other supervisory and administrative chores. Hopkins, in accord with his congressional man-

2. Harry L. Hopkins, *Spending to Save* (New York, 1936), ix.
3. Ibid., 99. Hopkins's remarks can be found in the *Proceedings of the National Conference of Social Work: Detroit, 1933* (Chicago, 1933), 65–71. In September 1934 it was estimated that about 4,000,000 families were on relief. Hall, ed., *Social Work Yearbook 1935*, 521.

date, accepted this structure, and local relief activities were supervised by state emergency relief administrations which, in turn, were subject to federal guidelines designed to provide a standard of uniformity and an assurance of honesty in the use of disbursed funds. By insisting that only public agencies should dispense public funds, Hopkins departed from previous American relief practice. As a result, hordes of social workers and public-spirited citizens, hopelessly grappling with massive needs through private organizations strapped for adequate resources, joined the public payroll and staffed the state and local agencies now responsible for relief. Since a large portion of these people were women, they came to play a significant part in the apparatus Hopkins directed. Women headed and staffed both state and local agencies. They were top administrators as well as fieldworkers and played a tremendously important, and hitherto largely unrecognized, role in ministering to human needs and suffering early in the New Deal. Many were personally known to Hopkins, but he had little to do with their selection. Most were chosen by state and local officials willing, owing to the crisis, to cast aside possible prejudices and accept professionally trained women for positions of increased responsibility in handling desperate people and huge sums of money. Some proved inept; others were remarkably effective in coping with and comprehending the predicament of people in situations not of their own making and also in recognizing that race, religion, and political affiliation should be irrelevant in determining need.

Since relief investigators had to determine the need of individuals, they had to probe into peoples' lives, intrude upon their private miseries, and add to their ordeal by further embarrassment and humiliation. In facing the facts of poverty and becoming hardened but not calloused to them, some officials gained insights and understandings that when relayed to Hopkins helped him convince Congress, the president, and others of the human dimensions of the Great Depression and of the need for both remedial and corrective action.[4]

Immediate decisions facing relief officials involved the allocation of funds for food, rent, utility payments, household supplies, and clothing. Available funds were usually insufficient, and families had to go without minimally desirable allocations. Because of inadequacies of substance, Hopkins was concerned about the ways in which relief was extended: either in kind, by orders on local merchants, or through a cash allowance. But most desirable, and the way that CWA operated, was through full wages for work, with no strings attached as to how the wages should be spent. CWA, however, was not created until November 1933, and it never totally displaced other forms of relief, such

4. Local administrators were state relief officials not on the federal payroll. See the story on relief in *Time*, Feb. 19, 1934, 11–13.

as commissaries providing weekly supplies of groceries or other items some official decided were good or necessary for unemployed recipients. While the commissary added to the woes of neighborhood retailers, the grocery order, another form of relief, listed specific items the recipient could secure in a neighborhood store. More beneficial and less humiliating was the granting of cash, allowing the individual and the family to determine how the sum of up to about $30 a month would be spent. Cash relief, aside from work relief, was the most desirable form of relief and favored by Hopkins. But local and state officials made these basic decisions, and Hopkins tried to supplement allocations through the distribution of agricultural surplus commodities when available.

While he recognized the immediate necessity of direct relief, Hopkins also understood that millions of unemployed were anxious to work for their livelihood and avoid the stigma of charity, of first being pitied and then scorned. Moreover, throughout the country the unemployed were organizing and protesting against what they considered the indignity of public charity. Communists played a significant role, one only now beginning to be fully comprehended by historians, although Hopkins, as this volume illustrates, was acutely aware of the role they were assuming among the unemployed.

To put workers reduced to idleness, whether on relief or not, back to work President Roosevelt by executive order on November 9, 1933, created CWA, the first federally operated work program, under authority granted him in the National Industrial Recovery Act (NIRA). Intended primarily as a short program to aid the unemployed during the coming winter and until the projects supported by the Public Works Administration (PWA), which was directed by Harold L. Ickes, the secretary of the interior, could be fully launched, CWA speedily put over four million people to work. By January 1934 these workers, half from relief rolls and half from the ranks of the unemployed, were on payrolls. To accomplish this feat required an administrative setup that Hopkins had been putting together since he arrived in Washington with the advent of the New Deal. It extended into more than 3,000 counties, and its staff worked frantically in the beginning. Pay scales for different regions of the country were devised with different categories of workers paid at different wage levels. The staff Hopkins initially recruited now assumed new duties, and additional personnel were added to assist first in launching and then in winding down the CWA program. Joining relief workers were engineers, economists, lawyers, and other professionals as Hopkins's organization assumed new tasks outside the range of his previous experience. In all CWA expended over $800,000,000 on 180,000 projects and was discontinued at the end of March 1934. Three quarters of this amount, it was estimated, went as wages to otherwise unemployed individuals.[5]

In addition to these heavy duties Hopkins assumed responsibility, under a provision in the Emergency Relief Appropriations Acts of 1933 that granted FERA authority to allocate funds to states to assist "needy persons who have no legal settlement in any state or community," for launching a program of transient relief. In January 1933 it was estimated that there were approximately 1,500,000 homeless persons in the United States. Not all were on the road. Many would be cared for by other programs, such as the Civilian Conservation Corps (CCC). Nevertheless, there were almost 300,000 transients — families and single men and women — who received assistance under this program. Here, too, Hopkins was moving in unchartered waters with a Division of Transient Activities assisting in the establishment of varied projects and camps to aid transients in ways other than the prevailing ones of providing them with food in a soup kitchen, a night in jail, and encouragement to move on.[6]

Another problem, a serious and unanticipated one, arose for Hopkins before 1933 ended. In May Congress approved an agricultural program, the Agricultural Adjustment Act (AAA), in the face of mounting agricultural discontent, especially in the Midwest, where violence had erupted and a farm strike was threatening to spread throughout the region. The legislation went into effect too late to benefit farmers during the 1933 crop year. In addition, the National Recovery Administration (NRA), created in June and under the aegis of the dynamic and volatile Hugh S. Johnson, was approving codes for various industries that provided, among other things, for price fixing. The result was that farmers would have to pay higher prices for many consumer items at a time when no federal program was assisting them directly. Thus, with agricultural prices at rock-bottom and no farm program functioning, hard-pressed farmers, facing a severe winter that would be followed by the most acute drought in American history, quickly came into the ken of Hopkins and the organizations he headed.

Unlike the unemployed urban dweller who sought the means to purchase or secure the things he needed and who, when employed, did not use what he made, the farmer in distress was threatened with both the loss of his job and his capital — land, machinery, and livestock — at one and the same time. His situation in 1933 was already desperate. By the end of that year as many as one million farm families were on relief rolls. And FERA employees in the farm states quickly gained an

5. Hall, ed., *Social Work Yearbook 1935*, 152, 520.
6. In January 1934 expenses of $1,858,509 were incurred for transient activities; in July they amounted to $3,125,129. Ibid., 500.

understanding of the human dimensions of the farm problem. Partly because of the severe drought and partly because many farmers no longer worked their own land and lacked machinery, livestock, and seed, by February 1935, despite AAA payments and the functioning of many agricultural programs, 733,000 farm families were still on relief rolls.[7]

To help the farmer in distress Hopkins set up a Rural Rehabilitation Division in the FERA, which had its counterpart in the state organizations. Relief administrators quickly learned that the American farmer was almost as diverse as the American worker. Owners, tenants, sharecroppers, and farm laborers had needs and problems different than those of unemployed urban dwellers, and their circumstances varied throughout the country.

Rural rehabilitation under FERA sought to accomplish three things: first, if possible, to help the farm family become self-supporting; second, if this was not possible, to relocate the family so that its members could maintain or reconstruct their life patterns in a more suitable setting; and third, to locate stranded industrial workers on a cooperative basis in a rural or semirural setting with the paramount goal of self-sustainment. Plans were devised to assist farm families involved with these programs through state Rural Rehabilitation Corporations that involved loaning farmers money under a carefully devised schedule.

A severe drought, an unpredicted calamity, added to Hopkins's woes in the summer of 1934. FERA had to assist thousands of farm families not previously on relief rolls. Congress helped through an appropriation of $525,000,000 for drought relief, a portion of which was made available to FERA. Most of these programs were later conducted in conjunction with other agencies or were assumed by them. Nevertheless, FERA purchased over four million acres of land in its attempt to ameliorate distress caused by continued abuse of unproductive lands.[8]

The root of the farm problem centered about the dilemma of the surplus, with overproduction enhanced in part by improved technology and declining overseas and domestic markets. This was owing to worldwide competition and changing dietary and work patterns that reduced consumption of many staple agricultural items. The Federal Surplus Relief Corporation, chartered in October 1933 — with Hopkins on its board of directors — distributed more than $94,000,000 worth of surplus commodities, chiefly foodstuffs, fuel, and blankets, by July 31, 1934.[9] Surplus commodities were secured either through direct purchase or by donation from AAA. Distribution of these items to the needy was made into work relief, thereby providing jobs for some unemployed

7. Hopkins, *Spending to Save*, 140.
8. Ibid., 150; Hall, ed., *Social Work Yearbook 1935*, 520–21.
9. Hall, ed., *Social Work Yearbook 1935*, 152.

individuals. Most important were the corporations's endeavors in the distribution of canned meat secured from drought-destroyed cattle and sheep purchased by the AAA in the summer of 1934. During its first two years the corporation functioned as a virtual subsidiary of FERA.

Responsible for these various programs — FERA, CWA, and those dealing with transients, farmers, and surplus distribution — Hopkins, before the WPA (which reorganized their operations and focused more heavily on work than relief) went into effect in March 1935, was one of the most harried and harassed of New Dealers.[10] Opening and expanding new areas of federal involvement, besides causing some confusion and duplication, created multitudes of problems and situations demanding Hopkins's attention and required that he know what was happening in the vast domain of his concerns. These concerns penetrated every community, city, and county in the United States. He had to provide data of all kinds to the public through the press and to the president and the Congress as well. Since the agencies and programs he directed did not operate in a vacuum, Hopkins had to know, for example, what programs other New Dealers were launching, what governors in the states were doing, and how citizens throughout the land were coping. To assist him in keeping abreast a division of Research, Statistics, and Finance in FERA secured data from staff handling state programs. And almost immediately Hopkins was deluged with statistical reports pertaining to the number of families and individuals receiving relief, as well as to the sums of money being spent. In effect Hopkins was drowning in a sea of statistical data. And he was gaining little insight and hence understanding of the human dimensions of the situation the various agencies and programs he supervised were encountering.

To remedy this concern Hopkins, by the summer of 1933, decided to send investigators out into the country to report directly to him. Lorena A. Hickok, an experienced newspaperwoman and a friend of Eleanor Roosevelt, was the first and the ablest of the investigators. Her assignment was to tour some of the worst afflicted areas of the country and to report fully and frankly on conditions, to present him with the unvarnished truth. In the course of her travels throughout the summer and fall of 1933 and all of 1934, she visited every part of the country except the Northwest, and her reports comprise most of the documents edited for this volume.

In concrete and specific terms Hickok gave Hopkins what he most wanted and needed: a picture of the human aspects of the crisis situation, including the impact of various programs on individuals in dif-

10. A Woman's Work Division and a program for providing aid to cooperatives and self-help associations for the barter of goods and services were also within Hopkins's purview, but these were developed only on a limited scale.

ferent states, regions, and communities. To go along with mounds of statistical data tabulated in Washington, Hopkins received from Hickok invaluable reports that allowed him to comprehend more fully the scope of his responsibilities and the dimensions of his problems because her reports continually suggested and noted conditions and circumstances requiring further examination. In addition, they gave Hopkins some insight into the thinking of men and women in all walks of life throughout many parts of the United States. With these reports Hopkins and, at times, the president secured more exact knowledge and details about conditions than did the officials, including governors, within whose jurisdiction a particular situation existed. Moreover, for present-day readers these reports make abundantly evident observations presented in the course of this introduction; namely, the prominent role Communists played in working with the unemployed and the significant role of women in administering programs under Hopkins's jurisdiction. Time and again it was women serving in an administrative capacity who gave Hickok her best and clearest insights into particular local situations. The reports also indicate the racial tensions engendered by New Deal programs that provided uniform wage scales or relief grants without consideration of prevailing mores in the South and Southwest, which had placed blacks and Hispanics on lower levels than their white or Anglo counterparts. The dilemmas posed by this situation whereby blacks and Hispanics could secure more money on relief than by toiling as a peasant class, while middle-class whites besides losing their jobs also lost their status, posed problems for Hickok which she poignantly related to Hopkins. In doing so she also indicated at times her inability to view the situation objectively. Her biases and prejudices as well as her lack of historical perspective occasionally overcame her usual factual reporting.

She derived her information, as she explained in a report to Hopkins in November 1935 (when she was no longer on regular assignment but was focusing more on the political situation affecting relief programs and the forthcoming presidential campaign in specific states), by "driving about, stopping in all sorts of places, talking with all sorts of people. There is hardly a type of person I haven't talked with — and at length. Relief officials, WPA officials, state officials, county and city officials, business people, professional people, politicians, both state and local, so-called civic leaders, clergymen, labor leaders, teachers, farmers, relief clients on WPA projects. Newspapermen, too, almost everywhere — political writers, editorial writers, men who cover business and finance, men who cover the relief story. Certainly if there is any better way to get a cross-section of public opinion in this country, I don't know it."[11]

11. Hickok to Hopkins, Nov. 3, 1935, Box 11, Lorena Hickok Papers, Franklin
     D. Roosevelt Library, Hyde Park, N.Y.

Hickok's reports provided Hopkins — and now provide the reader — with an excellent cross-section of public opinion at a time when the New Deal was getting under way and FERA was the chief agency focusing on the plight of the unemployed. They also presented — and still present — a graphic view of conditions in the United States at the height of the Great Depression. Indeed, possibly the only reporting to rival Hickok's on the human side of the Great Depression would be some of the periodical pieces that Edmund Wilson wrote in 1930 and 1931 and collected first in *The American Jitters* (New York, 1932) and then as part II of the volume, *The American Earthquake* (Garden City, N.Y., 1958).

Although FERA was not officially liquidated until June 30, 1938, the year 1935 marked a transition from federal emergency relief to a federal works program and the launching of a system of social security. Hopkins's role and needs changed, and he called on Hickok only for limited and specific assignments after 1934. The reports in this volume end in 1934 and do not reflect either Hopkins's or Hickok's changing roles and new assignments. Hickok's next job, worked out after consultation with both President Roosevelt and Hopkins, took her to Michigan, where she spent three weeks sizing up the administrative side of various New Deal programs, particularly as they related to Roosevelt's political situation, which was regarded as precarious. Her contacts now were largely with government officials on all levels, and her concern was with trying to establish better communications among them. No longer was she reporting on the conditions of people afflicted by the impact of depression, drought, and dust. Nor was she discussing the effect of programs on these people. Her emphasis was on internal tensions and difficulties, and her overall focus was to help make the New Deal function more effectively, thereby insuring Roosevelt's triumph in the 1936 election.

II

Lorena Hickok was the product of what she referred to as "the Golden Age of Individualism." In an introduction to an unfinished autobiography she wrote, "Americans were still pioneers, frontiersmen, in their outlook when I was born over a creamery in rural Wisconsin on March 4, 1893. It was our national philosophy that each individual American could go as far as his ability and determination would take him."[12]

In a sense her life lived out that dream. From that humble beginning in East Troy, Wisconsin, the daughter of a traveling buttermaker, she became the confidante of Eleanor Roosevelt, lived in the White House as Mrs. Roosevelt's guest, and earned recognition for her journalistic ac-

12. Foreword, unfinished autobiograhy, p. 1, Box 14, Hickok Papers (hereafter cited as unfinished autobiography).

complishments. As a child she displayed unusual determination, in spite of frequent beatings from a tyrannical father, who horsewhipped her puppy, threw her kitten against the barn, and drove her mother to bouts of weeping. She wrote years later, "Never once did he whip me — and the whippings grew progressively more severe as I grew older — when I didn't mutter, inaudibly behind my gritted teeth: 'You wouldn't dare do this to me if I were as big as you are.' "[13]

After her mother died in the dingy village of Bowdle, South Dakota, where her father's trade had taken the family, Hickok was told to leave home. At fourteen, she began work as a hired girl, staying with nine different families in the next two years. Finally a saloonkeeper's wife felt sorry for her and sent her to live with her mother's cousin, Ella Ellie, in Battle Creek, Michigan.[14]

Under the cousin's guidance she finished high school and enrolled at Lawrence College, Appleton, Wisconsin. Unable to get along with sorority members, she clerked in a grocery store so she could pay for meals off-campus and avoid eating in the college dormitory. Flunking out at the end of her freshman year, she returned to Battle Creek and started work as a $7-a-week cub reporter for the Battle Creek *Evening News*, meeting trains and collecting "personals." Following a second unsuccessful try at Lawrence, she landed a job on the *Milwaukee Sentinel*, determined to emulate the success of Edna Ferber as a Milwaukee reporter.[15]

Hickok experienced the customary sex discrimination of her period, but she learned to surmount it. As she explained, "When I first went into the newspaper business I had to get a job as a society editor — the only opening available to women in most offices. Then I'd build myself up solidly with the city editor by volunteering for night assignments, get into trouble with some dowager who would demand that I be fired, and finally land on the straight reportorial staff, which was where I had wanted to be from the beginning."[16] This was the path she followed at the *Sentinel*, where she provoked the ire of the grande dames of the Schlitz brewery family.

In 1917 Hickok got a job on the *Minneapolis Tribune*, but she yearned for adventure in Europe. Hoping to join the Women's Legion of Death, a group fighting in the tangled maze of the Russian Revolution, she headed to New York. There she was fired after a month as a reporter on

13. Chap. 1, "The Making of an Introvert," unfinished autobiography, pp. 6–7.
14. Chap. 2 (untitled), unfinished autobiography, pp. 2, 24–25.
15. Outline, unfinished autobiography, p. 1. See also John P. Broderick, "An Interviewer Interviewed," unpublished article, n.d., p. 2, Box 14, Hickok Papers.
16. Foreword, unfinished autobiography, p. 2.

the *New York Tribune* and resorted to police work—patrolling parks to rescue young women from amorous soldiers and sailors. Unable to get to Russia, she returned to Minneapolis.

Trying college once again, Hickok enrolled at the University of Minnesota while doing rewrite on the *Tribune*. But she ran afoul of a dean of women who tried unsuccessfully to make her live in a dormitory. Her college career ended as she rose to become *Tribune* Sunday editor and then chief reporter—with by-line—under managing editor Thomas J. Dillon.

Hickok called Dillon "The Old Man" and gave him credit for teaching her "the newspaper business, how to drink, and how to live."[17] For six years under Dillon she covered assignments rarely given to women in those days—politics, the visit of "a rather frowsy Queen of Rumania," and sports, interviewing, among others, Knute Rockne and Red Grange. Her fame as a feature writer spread as she focused on personalities varying from Woodrow Wilson to circus performers. It prompted a male journalism student at the University of Minnesota to interview her on her own career. He described her as "good-natured, overweight, erratic, and the cleverest interviewer in this section of the country." "I have lots of experience interviewing people," Hickok told him. "One time I slept with a murderess. There was only one empty bed, so she and I slept together."[18]

Hickok also touched on the handicap of being a woman: "The best job in a newspaper office is of course the managing editorship and you seldom see a woman getting a job like that."[19] Yet she painted a dismal portrait of women reporters including herself:

I always think of the woman journalist type as a sour individual, a kind of disillusioned being, with the "Listen girlie" manner, and mannishly dressed. Something like myself, is the type, I guess, only I don't dress mannishly. Then there's another sort of woman journalist—the office flirt variety. That sort is rather messy, coming into the office and disrupting all the organization of the reporting staff. On the whole, I like them better than the first type. The first is just awful. Then there are exceptions that can't be classed in either of these groups—they're the best, I think.[20]

In 1926 Hickok was stricken with diabetes and left Minneapolis. She went to San Francisco for a year to regain her health and to try unsuccessfully to become a writer. When her money ran out, she decided to tackle the heights of American journalism.

This time she was ready for the rough-and-tumble world of New York

17. Outline, unfinished autobiography, p. 2.
18. Ibid.; Broderick, "An Interviewer Interviewed," pp. 1, 3, Box 14, Hickok Papers.
19. Broderick, "An Interviewer Interviewed," p. 4, Box 14, Hickok Papers.
20. Ibid.

City. First came a year on the Hearst tabloid, the *Daily Mirror*. Then in 1928 she became one of the first women to be hired by the Associated Press (AP). At first she was restricted to features because women were regarded as unable to handle hard-news stories. As she complained bitterly in a letter to another newspaperwoman, "The newspaper business is allright for a woman who is contented to write nothing but features without any news in 'em or — better still — syndicated stuff, which pays a helluva lot better than newspaper work, straight anyway. . . . But if you're built as I am mentally, temperamentally, nervously, or however you want to put it, and you don't get any kick out of it except the thrill that comes out of working on *news* — real, honest-to-gawd stories — then it's just hell."[21]

Soon she vanquished male competitors and advanced to by-lined reporter status, covering the top news stories. She became "part of the horde of New York newspaper reporters and photographers that would sweep down on some defenseless little town unfortunate enough to be the scene of a good murder, [a] trial, a page-one divorce story." As she described it, "We were a wild, boisterous, cynical, unmannerly crew. Only the bootleggers loved us."[22]

Ishbel Ross, one of the first historians of women journalists, credited Hickok with "achieving standing with the AP that no other woman has matched." Described as "a big girl in a casual raincoat with a wide tailored hat, translucent blue eyes and a mouth vivid with lipstick," she fit the image of a hard-boiled reporter. Covering the same beats as men reporters — straight politics, political corruption trials, sensational murders — she repeatedly wrote by-lined stories for the AP national wire.[23]

Her toughest assignment was the Lindbergh baby kidnapping story. During a blizzard she crawled on hands and knees around the Lindbergh house to peer in the windows and check out an unfounded rumor that the baby had been returned. Afterwards she was sick for six weeks but kept working. Earlier, hot on the trail of the kidnapper, she and a photographer had come within yards of the shallow grave where the baby's body eventually was discovered by a truck driver. For the rest of her life she mourned missing out on what would have been a tremen-

---

21. Hickok to Bess Furman, n.d., Box 26, Bess Furman Papers, Library of Congress, Washington, D.C.
22. Chap. 7, "The Lindbergh Kidnaping Story," unfinished autobiography, pp. 3-4.
23. Ishbel Ross, *Ladies of the Press* (New York, 1936), 204. See also memo from JMK (unidentified AP editor) to Kent Cooper (AP general manager), Feb. 6, 1931, Box 18, Hickok Papers.

dous scoop. "Things happened to me on that story that shouldn't happen to any reporter," she noted.[24]

Hickok's life switched direction when she was assigned to cover Eleanor Roosevelt during her husband's first campaign for president in the fall of 1932. The two women had become acquainted in 1928 when Hickok was assigned to the Democratic National Committee headquarters in New York City and Mrs. Roosevelt was involved in her husband's campaign for governor. But it was not until the presidential campaign that the friendship bloomed. As Hickok accompanied Mrs. Roosevelt on train trips, frequently her sole companion, Mrs. Roosevelt, initially shy and cool, turned to Hickok for a confidante.[25]

After the election Hickok's AP stories helped introduce the new first lady to the American public. They presented her as an independent-minded woman determined to remain "plain, ordinary Mrs. Roosevelt." Hickok's coverage of Mrs. Roosevelt ended on Inauguration Day, after she had made history as the first reporter to conduct an on-the-record interview with a first lady in the White House.[26]

The next day Hickok returned to her job in New York, but the two women remained in close contact, exchanging letters on a daily, and sometimes twice-daily, basis. They also talked frequently on the telephone. But Hickok's friendship with Mrs. Roosevelt strained her relationship with the AP. During the campaign Hickok violated professional standards of objectivity by clearing all stories on Mrs. Roosevelt with either her or Louis Howe, a former newspaperman and Roosevelt's chief advisor. On one occasion her pay had been slashed when she withheld a story at Mrs. Roosevelt's request. In addition, she had become an unofficial press advisor to Mrs. Roosevelt, making arrangements for her to hold women-only press conferences in the White House.[27]

24. Chap. 7, "The Lindbergh Kidnaping Story," unfinished autobiography, pp. 6–9.
25. Lorena A. Hickok, *Reluctant First Lady* (New York, 1962), 7–11.
26. AP dispatch from New York, Nov. 9, 1932, Box 14, Hickok Papers. Hickok, *Reluctant First Lady*, 49, 103–7; Eleanor A. Roosevelt, *This I Remember* (New York, 1949), 78; Bess Furman, *Washington By-Line* (New York, 1949), 150–51. For an assessment of the relationship between Eleanor Roosevelt and Hickok during the 1932 campaign, see Maurine Beasley, "Lorena A. Hickok: Journalistic Influence on Eleanor Roosevelt," *Journalism Quarterly*, 57 (1980): 281–86.
27. Hickok to Malvina Thompson (Mrs. Roosevelt's secretary), July 23, 1949, Box 17, Hickok Papers; Bess Furman's diary entry, dated Jan. 26, 1933, Box 1, Furman Papers; Furman, *Washington By-Line*, 153; Ruby A. Black, "Covering Mrs. Roosevelt," *Matrix*, Apr. 1933, 3–4, 6, 16; Joseph P. Lash, *Eleanor and Franklin* (New York, 1973), 480; Roosevelt, *This I Remember*, 102.

Finally Hickok felt she had to choose between her friendship with Mrs. Roosevelt and her loyalty to the AP. She left in June 1933, after months of agonizing over the decision. One factor was Mrs. Roosevelt's encouragement to try other endeavors. "Hick, my darling," Mrs. Roosevelt wrote, "wouldn't the AP let you write for a magazine?" She urged Hickok to seek a higher-paying job: "I want you to be happy in your work, but I want you to be free from this worry over finances."[28]

After resigning Hickok became the chief investigator for Hopkins, traveling throughout the nation to observe relief programs. No doubt the job was arranged through Mrs. Roosevelt. Before beginning work, Hickok accompanied Mrs. Roosevelt on a month-long, off-the-record vacation. Rejecting even a Secret Service escort, the two drove alone through New England and eastern Canada. The next summer they drove together through the western United States.[29]

In her new post Hickok used her journalistic skills and contacts to prepare confidential reports on relief efforts across the country. Her findings were dispatched to Hopkins in detailed reports that often reiterated some of the information she sent to Mrs. Roosevelt in daily letters as well as copies of the reports. Although the reports were detailed, the material was presented in a breezy, irreverent style, free from cant and bureaucratic jargon, and was informative, entertaining, and readable. Often Hopkins and Mrs. Roosevelt passed on her findings to the president, who gave them close attention, according to contemporary observers. Mrs. Roosevelt wrote Hickok that "FDR finds your reports most interesting," and she noted on one occasion that "FDR told me he wished your reports could be published. He is hard to please,

28. Hickok to Thompson, July 23, 1949, Box 17, and Eleanor Roosevelt to Hickok, Apr. 3 and Apr. 20, 1933, Box 1, Hickok Papers. The relationship between Hickok and Roosevelt came to public attention in 1979 after their voluminous correspondence, numbering some 3,000 letters, was opened to researchers at the Franklin D. Roosevelt Library. Unfortunately, interest has focused on the nature of the letters exchanged by the two for a period of more than thirty years. The language suggests that the two may have had a lesbian relationship, although this allegation is denied by members of the Roosevelt family. The controversy over this aspect of their friendship has obscured the historical importance of the letters. See Deidre Carmody, "Letters by Eleanor Roosevelt Detail Friendship with Lorena Hickok," *New York Times*, Oct. 21, 1979, 34, and Henry Mitchell, Megan Rosenfeld, and Arthur Schlesinger, Jr., "Eleanor Roosevelt and the Styles of Friendship," *Washington Post*, Oct. 23, 1979, C1–2, 4. See also Doris Faber, *The Life of Lorena Hickok: E.R.'s Friend* (New York, 1980), 91–110 passim. See, too, Beasley, "Hickok: Journalistic Influence," for another meaningful view of the relationship between the two.

29. Eleanor Roosevelt to Hickok, June 14, 1933, Box 1, Hickok Papers, and Hickok, *Reluctant First Lady*, 119–31, 158–61.

too, and he always asks me if I've anything to read him from you."[30]

Acquiring with Mrs. Roosevelt's aid a car nicknamed "Bluette," replaced with a temperamental successor called "Stepchild" after an accident in Arizona, Hickok drove across vast expanses of the United States from 1933 to 1936, making fact-finding tours through thirty-two states. She employed the same techniques she had used as a reporter, chiefly interviews and personal observation. And at night she sat in uncomfortable hotel rooms, frequently exhausted, typing out what were in effect mini-essays on Depression conditions. Through her work she brought human misery home to high Washington officials from some of the nation's hardest hit places. Although her work necessarily contained some facts and figures pertaining to unemployment and relief, it also contained another dimension. Like the good reporter she had been, she looked for human interest stories and vignettes on victims of the Depression.[31]

If Hopkins had been skeptical of Hickok's ability to earn her then respectable salary of $6,000 annually, his doubts soon were allayed. With her years of journalistic experience, Hickok proved able to analyze a community within hours of arriving in town. Hopkins discovered that her reports provided a wealth of intelligence, enabling him to bridge the gap between Washington and local relief programs. Almost as soon as she returned from her first trip to coal fields in Pennsylvania, West Virginia, and Kentucky, he sent her to New York and on to Maine.

After New England Hopkins dispatched Hickok to the Midwest during a crucial period of agrarian unrest — at a time when drought, dust storms, and grasshopper invasions had wiped out crops, particularly in the Dakotas. Against this background political opponents attacked the New Deal's thus far feeble efforts in assisting agriculture. Leaders of the Farm Holiday Association insisted that Secretary of Agriculture Henry A. Wallace guarantee a net annual income for farmers, and the governor of North Dakota called for a massive embargo on wheat until prices advanced.[32]

Gravely concerned about this situation, Hopkins instructed Hickok to telegraph her first reports, which he sent on to Howe at the White House and to other policy-makers. The administration paid close atten-

30. Hickok, *Reluctant First Lady*, 134; Eleanor Roosevelt to Hickok, Sept. 6 and Nov. 12, 1933, Box 1, Hickok Papers. See also Charles, *Minister of Relief*, 140, and "News and Comment from the National Capital," *Literary Digest*, Nov. 18, 1933, 12.

31. See Foreword for a proposed book of edited reports, attached to a letter from Hickok to Kathryn Godwin (Hopkins's secretary), Nov. 21, 1936, Box 12, Hickok Papers.

32. Theodore Saloutos and John D. Hicks, *Agricultural Discontent in the Middle West: 1900–39* (Madison, Wis., 1951), 479–80.

tion. On a copy of Hickok's report from Minot, North Dakota, appears a handwritten notation indicating that President Roosevelt himself telephoned the head of state relief to speed up delivery of emergency supplies after reviewing her account of destitution there.[33]

The midwestern trip took Hickok back to the scenes of her own childhood. Her return brought no nostalgia, only gratitude that she had moved away. As a product of the Midwest, she understood its people and places and realized that farmers were reaching the limits of their endurance by the vagaries of both weather and economic policy. Her reports appraised the strength of Communists and others who were taking advantage of the critical situation and the New Deal's early inability to cope with it.[34]

As a self-made individual, Hickok was proud of her white-collar status and empathized with relief recipients from a similar stratum of society. When Hopkins gave her instructions to "go around the country and look this thing over," he told her not to worry about getting statistics or "the social-worker angle." He sent her out to "talk with the unemployed, those who are on relief and those who aren't, and when you talk with them don't ever forget that but for the grace of God you, I, any of our friends might be in their shoes."[35]

Hickok found this easy to do as long as she was traveling in parts of the country with which she was familiar. But, since she was neither a profound thinker nor an educated social critic, Hickok revealed her bigotry toward minority groups when Hopkins sent her to the South in January 1934. For the first time she encountered uneducated, rural blacks and was fed tales as to how dangerous it was for a white woman to travel alone in rural areas. Uncertain how to react, she quickly reiterated the vicious racism of those with whom she first came in contact. After meeting more moderate officials, she eliminated extreme comments from her later reports. Her prejudices toward minority groups also permeated her remarks on Indians and Hispanics. Traveling through the West in the spring of 1934 she wrote that Mexicans would be "perfectly contented" to stay on relief for the "rest of their lives," theorizing that the "Indian in them certainly wouldn't make them ambitious."[36] After visiting an Indian reservation in Nebraska, she de-

33. Telegrams, Hopkins to Hickok, Oct. 26 and Oct. 27, 1933, Box 11, Hickok Papers; notation on report of Hickok to Hopkins, Nov. 1, 1933, Box 67, Harry L. Hopkins Papers, Franklin D. Roosevelt Library.
34. Reports of Hickok to Hopkins, Nov. 6 and Nov. 10, 1933, Box 67, Hopkins Papers.
35. Foreword for proposed book of edited reports, attached with letter of Hickok to Godwin, Nov. 21, 1936, Box 21, Hickok Papers.
36. Report of Hickok to Hopkins, May 4, 1934, Box 68, Hopkins Papers.

scribed the inhabitants in stereotypic terms doing a stump dance.[37] Yet in many reports Hickok depicted individual members of minority groups as hard-working victims of profit-hungry businesses and stingy employers.

In her travels Hickok tried to minimize her relationship with Washington. She avoided publicity, refused interviews, and tried to talk to "just average people" without telling them she was reporting directly to Hopkins. In advance of her visits to local relief operations, Hopkins routinely wrote officials that Hickok was not coming to interfere with their programs but to "learn from all sources the picture of our relief activities throughout the United States." As part of her reporting, she hunted up old newspaper contacts, persuading reporters in San Francisco, Los Angeles, New York, and Salt Lake City to send her confidential reports on local conditions. Repeatedly she advised Hopkins of administrative failure due to politics or incompetency, exploding in one report, "Texas is a Godawful mess."[38]

Her findings played a part in Mrs. Roosevelt's direct efforts to remedy conditions in the desolate mining towns of West Virginia. When she read Hickok's description of the misery near Morgantown, in the fall of 1933, Mrs. Roosevelt drove there alone to meet Hickok and to tour the area with her. Soon Mrs. Roosevelt made arrangements for impoverished families to move into a new subsistence farming community called Arthurdale. Although the resettlement did not work out as expected, the effort helped establish Mrs. Roosevelt's reputation as a leading humanitarian.[39]

Aware that Hickok's ego needed the reinforcement no longer provided through by-lined news stories, Mrs. Roosevelt praised her reports repeatedly. After Hickok had been on the road for a year, Mrs. Roosevelt assured her that "Mr. Hopkins said today that your reports would be the best history of the depression in future years." Occasionally she told Hickok rather enviously that "your job is more stimulating then mine," a reference to her dislike of a steady round of handshaking and tea-pouring. She also tried to keep Hickok from getting emotionally involved in the plight of the poverty-stricken. When

37. Report of Hickok to Hopkins, Nov. 3, 1933, Box 67, Hopkins Papers.
38. Reports of Hickok to Hopkins, Apr. 11 and Sept. 3, 1934, July 18, 1936, Box 68, Hopkins Papers. For an example of the kind of letter Hopkins wrote to local relief officials, see Hopkins to Harry Greenstein (administrator for unemployment relief in Maryland), Oct. 23, 1934, Record Group 69, Records of the Federal Emergency Relief Administration, National Archives, Washington, D.C.
39. Hickok, *Reluctant First Lady*, 136–41; Lash, *Eleanor and Franklin*, 520–50. See also report of Hickok to Hopkins, Aug. 16–26, 1934, Box 68, Hopkins Papers.

Hickok berated herself for failing to donate $200 to finance an appeal for a penniless youth facing execution in Colorado, Mrs. Roosevelt replied, "You mustn't agonize so over things. . . . your giving the $200 would have been useless."[40]

In March 1934, Hickok accompanied Mrs. Roosevelt at her request on a special mission to inspect poverty in the Caribbean. This time they were joined by four newspaperwomen, Bess Furman of AP, Ruby A. Black of United Press, Emma Bugbee of the New York *Herald Tribune*, and Dorothy Ducas of International News Service. The group toured Puerto Rico and the Virgin Islands, and Hickok reported at length to Hopkins on chronic problems in Puerto Rico.

President Roosevelt himself authorized Hickok's assignment in the spring of 1935 as a confidential investigator for the National Emergency Council. In actuality it was a political post—to determine the popularity of the New Deal in advance of the 1936 election. Hickok's early prognostications proved inept: she predicted Roosevelt would be in serious trouble.[41]

By this time Hickok's health had begun to fail, due to diabetic tendencies, travel fatigue, and obesity fueled by fondness for rich food and drink. In their correspondence Mrs. Roosevelt chided her about the need to stay on a diet and to avoid liquor: "If I have stopped the drinking of too much corn liquor I probably have increased your chances for health in the next few years and hangovers can't have added much to the joy of life."[42] Dining provided Hickok one of her few pleasures during the grueling ordeal of constant travel. Writing Mrs. Roosevelt of her last "real meal in New Orleans," she lauded it as "memorable": "two gin fizzes, some kind of a marvelous shrimp concoction known as shrimp Arnaud, pompano baked in a paper bag, potatoes souffle, a pint of sauterne, crepes Suzette . . . and black coffee."[43]

Hickok worried over being dependent on Mrs. Roosevelt. Living in the White House between trips as Mrs. Roosevelt's guest, Hickok complained: "I'm really on relief, myself," to which Mrs. Roosevelt replied, "You might say it's rather luxurious relief."[44] A *Time* magazine article infuriated Hickok, describing her as a "rotund lady with a husky voice" and "baggy clothes" and implying that she owed her position solely to Mrs. Roosevelt.[45] She exploded in a note to Hopkins's secretary: "I love Mrs. Roosevelt dearly—she is the best friend I have in the world—but

40. Eleanor Roosevelt to Hickok, Dec. 7, 1933, and June 25 and Sept. 1, 1934, Box 1, Hickok Papers.
41. Reports of Hickok to Hopkins, May 27 and Nov. 3, 1935, Box 68, Hopkins Papers.
42. Eleanor Roosevelt to Hickok, Nov. 22, 1933, Box 1, Hickok Papers.
43. Hickok to Eleanor Roosevelt, Apr. 9, 1934, Box 1, Hickok Papers.
44. Hickok, *Reluctant First Lady*, 155.
45. *Time*, Feb. 19, 1934, 12.

sometimes I do wish, for my own sake, that she were Mrs. Joe Doaks of Oelwein, Iowa."[46]

Hickok left Hopkins's employ in 1936 and depended on Mrs. Roosevelt's help in locating other jobs. She was a publicist for the New York World's Fair from 1937 to 1940 and executive director of the women's division of the Democratic National Committee from 1940 to 1945, living at the White House during World War II. Her last employment was with the New York Democratic State Committee from 1947 to 1952.

Partially blind, Hickok moved to Hyde Park, New York, in the 1950s to be near Mrs. Roosevelt. Together they co-authored a book, *Ladies of Courage* (1954) on women in politics, and Hickok wrote a biography of Mrs. Roosevelt, *Reluctant First Lady* (1962), as well as books for young people. She barely had enough to live on, and Mrs. Roosevelt aided her repeatedly.[47] Hickok remained a resident of Hyde Park until her death in 1968.

From 1933 to 1936 she interviewed thousands of Americans on relief, perhaps more than any other one individual. Capturing both the bitterness and heroism of ordinary Americans caught in economic catastrophe, her letters and reports represent an unmined treasury for social historians. As vivid and fresh today as they were almost a half century ago, Hickok's reports reflect the human side of the Great Depression. Hickok was not an economist, a statistician, or a political scientist. Hers was the training and quick savvy of the newspaper feature writer able to sniff out a story and make it touch the hearts of thousands of readers.

Her experiences caused her to change her own views on economic independence as she witnessed the need for people "to look to their government for the common necessities of life." Toward the end of her life she lamented what she considered the loss of American individualism: "I am pretty certain that had I been turned loose at the age of fourteen, in the world as it is today in America, to beat my way around earning a precarious living as an untrained domestic servant, the welfare agencies, the social workers, the psychiatrists, and the juvenile court would have nabbed me. . . . The chances are I'd have been sent away somewhere to be trained to be a good servant."[48] She also mourned the end of her newspaper career: "I was just about the top gal reporter in the country. . . . God knows, I've had the conceit taken out of me plenty in the years since. Being a newspaper reporter was the only thing I ever was really good at."[49]

46. Hickok to Godwin, Feb. 18, 1934, Box 68, Hopkins Papers.
47. Interview with the Reverend Gordon Kidd, retired rector of St. James' Episcopal Church, Hyde Park, N.Y., by Maurine Beasley, Apr. 12, 1979.
48. Foreword, unfinished autobiography, pp. 3–4.
49. Hickok to Thompson, July 23, 1949, Box 17, Hickok Papers.

One Third of a Nation

To Harry L. Hopkins

[Washington, D.C.] August 6, 1933

Dear Mr. Hopkins:

Since we have not discussed as yet the form my reports to you are to take, I'm going to give you the first one in the form of a letter, telling you where I've been and what I've heard this last week. . . .

On the whole, I have encountered little dissatisfaction with the way the relief is administered or with its adequacy — which is rather surprising considering the fact that in some cases it is pitiably small. In Philadelphia I heard nothing but praise. Even David Schick, the left-wing Socialist, whose chief complaint was that it wasn't uniform — that in some counties it was good and in some counties not so good — said he thought it was being handled excellently in Philadelphia, and that Philadelphia ought to be taken as a model for the rest of the state. Dave Fernsler, the Associated Press man in Harrisburg, said there had been a good deal of politics mixed up in it a few months ago and some scandals, but he thought that situation had now cleared up pretty much. The Philadelphia Record has gone out and investigated complaints that they received and has usually found that there was little justification. The Northampton county Republican chairman thinks there ought to be more "made work," but blames the lack of it on local politicians "who haven't any imaginations." Governor [Gifford] Pinchot and Miss Mary Wright, Eric Biddle's[1] secretary, who sees the people who come into state headquarters with kicks, think that there is too much of a tendency on the part of those actually in contact with the unemployed to treat them as they would the indigent — "problem cases" — they encounter while with private agencies in normal times. Miss Wright cited the case of a woman in Harrisburg whose relief, she said, was cut off on grounds of moral turpitude because she happened to be living rent-free — and those on relief get no rent allowance in Pennsylvania — with an unmarried couple! She said she interceded, and that they finally agreed to pay the woman half the relief to which she was entitled! I have not myself encountered that attitude. The case workers and supervisors I've seen would be more inclined to lean over backwards in the opposite direction. And anyway they're too busy to stop and make "problems" out of

3

their cases. In Media I met a supervisor who, with one assistant, has had as many as 800 families to look after at one time, and who has spent days and nights trying to figure out how to get relief to people who need it and won't ask for it. She is giving cash, out of a fund from a private agency, to some of her exceptionally high class people — a lawyer and his family, for instance, and a husband and wife both of whom are university graduates — to spare them the humiliation of presenting food orders at the grocery, and she has gone to the greatest amount of trouble imaginable to keep secret the fact that they are getting relief.

The chief dissatisfaction seems to be with the kind of relief, rather than with its adequacy or the way in which the recipients are treated. Food orders are not popular. Among the recipients I've heard complaints ranging all the way from the common one that the grocers "short-weight" them and that they themselves could do better if they had the cash and could "shop around" to that of members of the Unemployed League that receiving food orders makes them feel like "charity cases." Most of the people I've interviewed outside the Relief Administration are opposed to them, and so are many of those in the Administration. The feeling seems to be that every American should have the right to earn the money he gets for relief, receive it in cash, and spend it as he sees fit. "These people aren't children," you hear over and over again. "They're honest, self-respecting citizens who, through no fault of their own, are temporarily on relief. The vast majority of them have always managed their own affairs, can be trusted with cash — however little they're going to get to live on — and should be." You've no doubt heard the arguments on the other side many times — that they wouldn't spend it for food, and that food is more necessary than shelter, etc. One old Negro in Philadelphia did volunteer the statement that, while he and his wife could undoubtedly get along better if they had cash instead of food orders, many of his race were so irresponsible that it was better for them to have food orders, and that, therefore, he and his wife didn't feel like complaining!

The rent situation is bad, of course, as it apparently is everywhere. Everybody worries about it — the people on relief, the people administering relief, and the poor landlords. In the hope of getting some ideas, I went to see Oscar I. Stern, president of the Realty Board in South Philadelphia, where a great majority of those on relief live. It's a sad tale — thousands of landlords have lost their property for non-payment of interest and taxes. They've been having sheriff's sales at the rate of 1,300 a month in Philadelphia, but that, of course, includes homeowners who have lost their homes. His only suggestion was that landlords whose tenants, on relief, cannot pay rent be exempt from taxes, on the ground that they are already being heavily taxed for relief, but he observed that this would be almost impossible to accomplish. He

4

sent me over to the Philadelphia Real Estate board, where, one afternoon each week, landlords come in and tell their troubles. Unfortunately, it was a very hot afternoon, and the place closed up early, so there was no one there when I arrived. There is a good deal of "squatting," in smaller communities as well as in Philadelphia, in abandoned houses, so bad that no one who could raise a cent to pay rent would ever live in them. The condition of some of these places is frightful. On the other hand, in Delaware county, some of the unemployed have moved out into the houses on abandoned farms, have fixed them up, and are raising gardens and chickens, and getting along quite well. One woman told me that, even if — or when — her husband did get employment, they were going to stay right there until they got "a little ahead." In Philadelphia I ran into an Italian landlord who owned two houses in which were living five families beside his own, all of whom were on relief and none of whom had paid any rent for many months. Since his rents were his sole income, and that was wiped out, he had applied for relief, but had been turned down. The case worker told me she suspected his tenants of sharing their food orders with him — and that she was certainly *not* going to make any investigation! Up in Northampton county I ran into cases where unemployed tenants went out voluntarily and worked out the landlord's taxes on county roads, thereby keeping him from losing his property and earning a little of their rent.

There is developing in Pennsylvania a sort of union of the unemployed — the Unemployed Council, apparently entirely under Communistic influence, and the Unemployed League, for the most part more moderate. I've heard all sorts of reports on them. At Allentown, for instance, they went out and picketed relief recipients engaged on "made work." Dr. Charles R. Fox, burgess of the little factory town of Northampton, where they've been having strikes, said the secretary of the League there told him the Unions were paying members of the League to act as pickets! They are making membership drives, holding ice cream festivals to get money for their organizations, and drawing up demands. One of them, the Bethlehem local, was actually represented at the hearing on the Steel code, by a preacher, who presented their code, including a provision that no steel company executive should be paid more than $50,000 a year. I had a long talk yesterday with John G. Ramsaye, secretary of the Unemployed League for Northampton county. . . . I found him to be a rather moderate, sane sort of person, whose ideas on relief were not so different as that from those of many of the people who are administering it. One of the League's chief complaints, he said, is against food orders — "which make us feel like charity cases." He suggested the possibility of trying everybody out on cash and then putting those back on food orders who demonstrated they were unable to handle cash. When I asked Governor Pinchot today what he thought of the idea, he said it would increase the burden of investigation too much, and I suppose it would make that load a lot heavier. "All of us, whether we're radical, or whether, like us, we don't go along with the Reds," Ramsaye said, "have pretty much the same ideas about relief." He said the chief trouble in the more radical groups was over food orders — that the men who refused to do the "made work" would be perfectly willing to do it if they could get cash for it. "We'd like to feel that we were earning our way instead of working for food orders that are handed out to us as though we were charity cases," he said. Ramsaye was willing to concede that the relief budget presented in their program . . . might be a bit high, but he implied they were willing to compromise if only they could get a hearing.

It seems to me that these organizations of the unemployed can cause plenty of trouble if they are not handled properly. Ramsaye, for instance, is right on the fence just now, ready to jump either way. He and his crowd might go completely "red," or they might go the other way and perhaps be of some help in running the show. People like Ramsaye wouldn't ordinarily be "reds" at all. Ramsaye himself is a steel worker, likes his work when he has any, and earnestly believes in President Roosevelt's program. His only resentment seems to be against "fellows like Eugene Grace[2], who gets a bonus of $163,000 while the Community chest has one Hell of a time raising $163,000 for unemployment relief." Ramsaye believes there should be more "made work" — for cash relief. "There are lots of things we could do around here," he said. "We could fix up the river fronts. We could plant trees. We could repair buildings. There's plenty to do, and I'd like to know why they don't have us do some of those things, and give us a little cash for it, instead of those food orders. We'd all be better off and feel more like human beings."

Curiously enough, the Republican county chairman says exactly the same thing! From him I got the impression that the unemployed in that part of the country are in perhaps even a worse frame of mind than Ramsaye would indicate. "If they're not in a fighting mood, they're getting hopeless," he said. "Some of them are getting so they just accept relief and never look forward to living any other way. They started off by fighting it — they'd nearly starve before they'd accept it. Gradually they're getting used to it. They'll never be any good any more, many of them." He added: "If I were broke and starving, I don't believe there's a case worker in the country who could make me accept one of those damned food orders."

In my own visits, I've seen the other side of the picture, too. In Philadelphia, for instance, I ran across two Negresses, mother and daughter, who walk eight miles every day to earn, by doing cleaning and washing, a little money to pay toward their rent. They get 10 cents an hour for their work — when they get any!

6

You said you were interested in finding out how long this thing is going to last. Nobody I've talked to can see any let-up. In the first place, it's generally conceded that the amount of relief per family has got to be increased. Food prices have gone up something like 30 per cent. While I was in the office in Harrisburg Tuesday, a little grocer came in to see if something couldn't be done to make it possible for families on relief who were trading with him to get an extra allowance for coal oil, which they use for cooking. In his neighborhood the food orders amount to 75 cents per person. He and I sat down and tried to figure up how much food you could buy per week for—say, $1.50. We didn't get very far.

Another problem now presenting itself is what to do about the debts of these people as they go back to work. Some of those families owe as much as $1,000 in unpaid grocery bills, back rent, doctor bills, and so on. In some cases they owe money to their employers—rent for company houses, for instance—and some employers are grabbing it right out of the first pay checks. Ramsaye, for instance, got back on part time at the Bethlehem steel plant recently. He and his case worker figured out that he should get along on his earnings, and he was taken right off relief. But out of his first check, the company held back $8 he owed for fuel. He had to go back on relief. He said that he and the men in his organization felt that some adjustment must be made so that employers couldn't do that sort of thing. I actually saw yesterday one pay check for 8 cents! The man had $2.08 coming to him, but the company held back $2. Ramsaye's idea is that people on relief should not be held responsible for debts, such as rent, they have incurred while on relief, but that debts they incurred before they went on relief should be paid. "Only they'll have to give us time," he said. While there is a good deal of re-employment, with the result that large numbers of cases are being dropped, I believe many of them will have to come back. Yesterday I went to see some people who had voluntarily had themselves taken off the rolls six weeks ago. The man had got a job working on the roads. The job lasted five weeks. He managed to pay up $32 in personal taxes—last year and this year—paid a month's rent, the first rent he had paid since the beginning of 1932, and, of course, bought food. Now the job is finished, and, said his wife, "We hate it, but I'm afraid we're going to have to go back on relief." These people don't want to be on relief. They loathe it. The percentage of those who call up and announce that they have jobs and don't want any more food orders is truly impressive. But if their jobs don't last, or if they are expected to pay off their bills right away, what are they going to do? The Republican county chairman puts it this way: "What's the use of going back to work if you're worse off than you were before?"

I doubt if you'll ever find time to read all this. Perhaps it isn't what you want at all. Well, the only way to find out is to try one out on you.

I've probably gone too much into detail. That, I suppose, is because it's all new to me and therefore, to me, terribly important and extremely interesting. . . . Only don't tell me to leave it *all* out, please, because I like this job. Believe me, it's absorbing! . . .

1. Pennsylvania administrator for Federal Emergency Relief Administration [FERA].
2. President of U.S. Steel Corporation.

To Harry L. Hopkins

REPORT   Field: Pennsylvania, August 7–12 [1933]   Inclusive

After two weeks in Pennsylvania, I came out with the impression that the unemployed problem, together with labor troubles where jobs are opening up, may result in a good deal of disorder within the next few months.

The administration of relief to the unemployed of course enters the picture as a stabilizing influence, where it is well and fairly adequately distributed, and as a most disturbing influence where it is not. A Catholic bishop, whose diocese includes Pittsburgh and the bituminous coal mine area in which strikes have been in progress, said:

"Inadequate though it may be, the emergency unemployment relief has been and is the most stabilizing force we have. The Pennsylvania board may run out of funds this fall and may be unable immediately to get more. If this happens, the Federal government will have to put up the money, or — well, God help us all!"

Our chief trouble in Pennsylvania is due to politics. From the township to Harrisburg, the state is honeycombed with politicians all fighting for the privilege of distributing patronage, and the professional relief staffs who have gone in to reorganize the distribution have put up a superb fight against terrific odds.

One of the most powerful lobbies at Harrisburg, I was told, is the poor directors'[1] lobby. There is no doubt that, in the distribution of relief, a majority of the poor directors had a grand chance to make use of patronage — and did. Most of them are being deprived of this by the professional staff, and they are fighting mad. They are conducting constantly an under-ground campaign against us. With the removal of the poor directors, patronage is being eliminated from the relief picture. It hampers us seriously in another way, however. One of our staff in Fayette county told me that 75 percent of the men employed on state highways, under the public works program, got their jobs through political influence, and that it was practically impossible for a man on the relief rolls to get one of those jobs.

There is no doubt either that, with the rise in food prices — in some instances 50 percent, I am told — relief allotments per person and per family in Pennsylvania are pitifully inadequate. Governor Pinchot himself recognizes this fact and said something must be done about it. The Federal policy is much more liberal than that of the Pennsylvania Emergency Relief Board or the county committees, in some cases even less generous than the state board.

The Federal Emergency Relief Administration is not in a position to dictate, however, because the state of Pennsylvania is putting up the money. Federal policies cannot be enforced. The amount of relief distributed is up to the county committee. The county committee gets its money from the state board. The state board has to appeal to the Legislature, and the Legislature is afraid of the taxpayer. There is a $20,000,000 bond issue for unemployment relief going before the voters in November. I am told it may be defeated. Incidentally, a poll tax in Pennsylvania undoubtedly will prevent the majority of the unemployed from voting!

The fact that the county Emergency Relief Committees, made up of leaders of the community, decide what the allotments per person and per family in each county will be, makes for a good deal of unevenness. For instance, the towns of Scottdale and Everson are in different counties, but there is only a river between them. The allotments in one county were more generous than they were in the other, and there were demonstrations by the unemployed in one town because the people on the other side of the river were getting more than they were. . . .

In the whole situation in Pennsylvania, politically, from the labor standpoint, and among the unemployed, the Federal government is hugely important. Although the politicians are fighting for patronage rights, you seldom hear the average man say, "I'm a Republican," or, "I'm a Democrat." What they do say is: "I'm for the President." And then: "If he doesn't make a go of this, a lot of people are going to be surprised, that's all." It is the tremendous popularity of the President that undoubtedly brings the Federal government so prominently into the picture. The soft coal miners, for instance, seem to have no faith at all in anyone save the President. They carried his picture in their picket lines and in their little parades — with the American flag and queer little bands made up of saxophones and accordions — when they went back to work. Stuck up in a window of the home of a miner who had been out of work and nearly starving on inadequate relief for more than a year, I saw a newspaper clipping, apparently out of an advertisement, of the President's picture and a Blue Eagle. The people on relief generally

9

seem to have that same feeling about him. The state government they ignore. They look to the Federal government for aid and are inclined to hold the Federal government responsible when it is not forthcoming. And as I said before, the Federal government cannot control the situation because the state is supplying three-fourths of the money.

All this, it seems to me, puts the President, the Federal Emergency Relief Administration, and the Federal government as a whole in a pretty difficult and serious dilemma.

Another difficulty is the apparent lack of interest on the part of the average citizen — who is the taxpayer — in unemployment relief. It's hard to get them to talk about it all. If they do, they are generally disapproving. "Those fellows don't want to work," they say and cite instances where a man on the relief rolls was offered a job for a day or two and turned it down. What they don't understand is that the unemployed have learned that accepting one of those temporary jobs takes them off the relief rolls, and that the clerical work involved is apt to keep them off long after the money they earned on the job may have run out. This is no criticism of the administrators, but there is bound to be some delay getting a man back on the relief rolls after he has been removed. Therefore, you can hardly blame a man for not wanting to run the risk of being cut off the relief rolls for a job that may last a day or so and pay him two or three dollars. Another kick from the taxpayer is that there isn't enough "made work." They say, "Those fellows ought to be made to work for what they're getting." And: "There are plenty of things they could do toward fixing things up, that would be giving us something for our money." This subject will be taken up later in the report.

The most nagging problems in connection with relief administration in Pennsylvania seem to be: The rise in food prices, which has made the relief inadequate; "that rent situation," as our people usually refer to it; a lack of medical supplies; and a lack of clothing. . . .

The present allotment, members of the Pittsburgh unemployed organizations told me, will not permit the purchase of soap or any sort of cleaning materials. In many cases, they said, families who once lived comfortably in decent neighborhoods are crowded into quarters almost uninhabitable and alive with bed bugs. Mattresses and pillows have become so filthy and vermin infested that they've had to burn them and now sleep on newspapers spread out over the bed springs, with bundles of newspapers for pillows.

Pennsylvania of course pays no rents, except one month in cheaper quarters if a family has been evicted. The result is that, in the larger cities especially, families move about every six months — always into more crowded, less desirable quarters, in less desirable neighborhoods. You have the spectacle of a family with half grown children having started in a comfortable, detached house in the suburbs now living in one room in the slums — a room alive with bed bugs. The effect on the children is terrible, too, the unemployed point out. . . .

The idea that government, by giving the unemployed as in Pennsylvania only food orders, which deprives them even of the choice whether or not to pay their rent and cut down on their food, is actually placed in the position of conniving with them to beat the landlord seems a bit bizarre. . . .

Clothing for the unemployed in Pennsylvania has apparently been given largely — if not entirely — by private agencies. They are running out of clothing now. The Red Cross, I was told, is now down to the point where it is giving out only cloth — and sometimes without thread or buttons. There is a crisis developing over the lack of shoes. School opens early in September, and practically everywhere I went I heard the cry, "Our children must have shoes, or they can't go to school." Incidentally, I found one man re-soling shoes for his family with pieces of automobile tire.

In Scottdale, a Catholic priest — whose worried eyes still haunt me — begged for medical supplies. Incidentally, the Catholic priests in some of those towns represent almost the last bulwark against riot and disorder among the unemployed. This man told me he had done everything he could to keep the people in church as much as possible — in order that he might not lose his hold with them. He was deeply worried. He said he had exhausted his credit and the credit of the parish at the drugstore. . . .

The lack of "made work" seems in many instances to be due to lack of imagination and resourcefulness. One drawback is that many communities are so broke that they can't raise the money for the supplies. In one town I visited — a town of 2,000 population, with 97 percent of the population on relief — the streets were in an appalling condition. The streets are township roads and, as I understand it, could be improved with "made work." I remarked on this, but someone replied, "Yes, but you see the town is so poor that it had to turn off its water supply a few weeks ago. If there had been a fire, the whole place would have burned up. And of course that town couldn't raise the money for paving, even if the labor was free." On the other hand, when I told the executive director of a neighboring county about it, he replied: "That shouldn't stop them. I've paved streets by taking old bricks, smoothing out the foundation, and putting them back again. That didn't cost anything." Possibly someone could go into some of those communities and show them what "made work" is and how cheaply, in many instances, it could be provided. . . .

The most difficult towns in which to launch made work programs are the mining towns where the company owns all the property. A mining town is in a sense a transient town. The life of the average mine is, I believe, about 25 years. This being true, and the companies owning the whole town, anyway, there naturally isn't much community spirit in those towns. "Why, I'd be razzed to death," one man told me, "if I went to one of those towns and said, 'Come on, boys, let's make a park!'"

I still feel, as I felt a week ago, that vast numbers of the unemployed in Pennsylvania are "right on the edge," so to speak—that it wouldn't take much to make Communists out of them. The Communists most decidedly are not friends of the government. They openly say they hope the Administration program will fail. They want bloodshed. They say so themselves.

Apparently they have had much to do with the organization of the unemployed. The chairman of the unemployed organization in Indiana county put it this way: "The Communists came in there and tried to organize us. Well, we organized and then kicked them out." In Westmoreland county they have lost control of the organization. In a recent election the Communist candidate for head of the organization got only six votes. But that's due largely, I think, to the personality and courage of the executive director. He said he learned afterwards that the members of the organization had planned to beat him the first time he attended one of their meetings. They are now working with him and getting along pretty well.

The people who go into these organizations it would seem to me are the people most worth saving. They've still got some fight in them. Any of your relief workers will tell you there's much more hope of getting people like them back to normal than there is in the case of people who have become apathetic. The radical group in Pittsburgh have worked out a system of investigation of their own — and they investigate the case workers, too. . . . The organizations are growing—how fast I was unable to determine — and in many cases they are being formed with the encouragement and cooperation of the labor unions. You'll find men belonging to both organizations.

The thing they seem to want first of all is recognition. The group from Indiana county told me that therein lay the real cause of the disturbance there. They had been trying for six months, they said, to get the county relief committee to meet with them and, after the executive director had made an engagement for them to meet with the committee, and the committee failed to show up, they simply exploded.

In Pittsburgh, the executive director has taken them right in and is working with them. Committees from the unemployed organizations meet with his board once a month. He meets with them once a week himself. And he has set up a system of appeals — with the organizations appealing from the decision of the case worker to the supervisor and from the supervisor to himself. It is true that the Pittsburgh group turned out to be more vociferous in its demands than any other I had

12

met, but the executive director expressed the opinion that there would be more difficulty than there now is if he hadn't recognized them. The man who headed the committee I saw there is apparently respected and liked by the staff at relief headquarters. . . .

Of the inadequacy of the relief, the Pittsburgh group were especially bitter. In Northeastern Pennsylvania and up around Scranton I heard relatively few complaints about inadequacy. I have since decided that perhaps these were the apathetic sort about whom the social workers are worried. In Scranton I was told there were very few kicks because whatever they are getting now is far far ahead of what they were getting under the old poor director system. Families of five in that regime were given as little as $8 a month!

Of course there are continuous kicks against the food order system. As one of the Pittsburgh unemployed put it, "Does a man's status change when he becomes unemployed, so that, while he was perfectly able to handle money while he had a job, he can't be trusted with it when he's out of work?" The Pittsburgh organization has suggested use of scrip — giving them their allotments in scrip instead of as a food order, since they apparently can't have cash. . . .

Our relief policy in the coal strike area apparently didn't make anybody very happy. The miners kicked because, in cases where they had earned credit at the company stores, this was regarded as "resource," and relief was withheld. They said the company stores told the investigators they had earned credit when they did not. They kicked some about the delay in getting relief at the start, too. Governor Pinchot's secretary thought the relief staff were too "hard-boiled" about granting relief in the cases of miners with earned credit at the company stores, said they had no idea of the seriousness of the situation, and thought they should give in to some of the more insistent. The staff took the attitude that it was up to the state board to assume the responsibility for breaking down their rules, and refused to do it without authorization from Harrisburg. The Governor's secretary said he thought the state could very well afford to throw in $100,000 to help pacify the miners, but the reply of the staff was, "How are we going to get $100,000 to pacify your agitators when we can barely get enough to feed our regular clients?" There was some bitterness over this. The coal operators, who pay most of the taxes — in one township the school tax last year was $250,000, with the coal companies paying $208,000 of it — naturally felt that they were being forced to feed their enemies. And the small business people, professional men, and so on felt that, by feeding the strikers, we were only prolonging the strike.

I can see little indication of any great decline in the relief load in Pennsylvania this winter. It is a little early to tell, but it seems to me that figures indicating a decline may be deceptive. Factors entering in are:

the debt loads of the people going back to work — something apparently will have to be done to prevent creditors, especially when the creditors happen to be their employers, from jumping in and grabbing off so large a portion of their earnings that they haven't enough left to live on; the fact that many of the jobs, under the public works act, for instance, are not permanent; the fact that, even under the codes, there still won't be any too many jobs; and the fact that those who have the hardest time getting jobs are men from 40 years old on. A man of 45, for instance, is apt to have a large family, half grown, and to need more generous relief allotments than a younger man with small children and not so many of them. The number of unemployed may decrease, but those left behind are going to need more adequate relief, and they are the people with large families.

One of the bright spots in Pennsylvania was the garden program. . . . I visited some of the gardens — including a backyard garden in a mining town where the soil, so far as I could see, consisted almost entirely of coke ashes! Even the men living in the abandoned coke ovens at Latrobe had gardens — pathetic little patches of tomatoes and cabbages. By and large, the happiest and most contented people I saw were those working in the gardens, but — as an Italian in Scranton, who had that week been awarded the pennant for having the best garden, wistfully said:

"I'd rather have my job back in the mines than be doing this."

1. County officials responsible for relief until county boards of assistance were established in 1937.

To Harry L. Hopkins

REPORT   Field: West Virginia, August 16–26 [1933]   Inclusive

Major Francis W. Turner, West Virginia state relief administrator, I found to be a most resourceful person, with a broad, sympathetic and, it seemed to me, intelligent attitude toward the whole relief show. He is also a fighter. He would have to be a fighter — and a resourceful fighter, too — to handle the situation in that state. And I have the feeling that he is doing a good job.

His major difficulties are financial and political. The financial problem is extremely serious. The chief of the Associated Press bureau in Charleston told me that West Virginia's new tax laws will apparently cut the state's income by $15,000,000 in 1933. He seemed to think that about the only source for any considerable increase in revenue would be a cigaret tax, but he doubted such a law would ever pass in the Legislature, so powerful is the lobby of the tobacco interests.

The money the state is putting up against the $1,000,000 we are sending down there in September is not of course actually relief money. As I understand it, men are to be taken off the relief rolls and put to work on county highways, maintenance of which is being taken over by the state, and paid out of $1,800,000 set aside for that maintenance. And most of the jobs will be temporary, throwing the men back onto the relief rolls when they get through. In addition, each county is setting aside a certain sum and has agreed to take over the widows and orphans and normally unemployables from the relief rolls and take care of them out of that money. Ohio county, for instance, in which Wheeling is located, is setting aside $32,000. Miss May Maloney, state relief field representative in that district, thinks the counties should be made to furnish the state emergency relief administration lists of all the people they are helping and to what extent. "Otherwise," she said, "mark my words, the politicians will grab every cent of it."

And so the whole financial set-up in West Virginia doesn't look any too encouraging. And in the meantime, the relief there is pretty skimpy. A family in West Virginia is supposed to get $15 a month. Because of shortage of funds, they've been getting $10. And several counties — I know this was true in Mingo and Ohio counties — had run out of funds August 26, with no more available before September 1. Miss Maloney, temporarily stationed in Wheeling, took her last relief money — borrowed, as I understand it, from another county where the case load had dropped unexpectedly [August 25], bought flour with it, and distributed it among her people. And that was all they were to get for a week. Major Turner said $1,000,000 will be far from adequate in West Virginia for the month of September. Schools are opening in September, and, on top of his regular food problem, he'll have a widespread demand for clothing. . . .

The political interference with relief is just about as bad in West Virginia as it is in Pennsylvania. About the whole relief and labor situation, Major Turner made a remark which, I think, sums it up pretty well:

"Here you've got our whole civilization built on rotten foundations that are about to give way — and a lot of damned fool capitalists and petty politicians fiddling away while the thing collapses!"

Major Turner, for instance, although he had been on the job for some time had not, up to August 26, been actually appointed state relief director for West Virginia. On one pretext or another the governor has held it up. Naturally, it hampers him somewhat. . . .

The county directors are of course hampered all the time. "It's the local politicians who make our job tough," the director in Mingo county told me. Miss Mabel Sutherland, director in Logan county, said the same thing. All the little petty politicians are trying to get their fingers into the pocketbook. Patronage is a serious nuisance.

For instance, Major Turner remarked as we were driving to Wheeling Friday that he was going back to Charleston the next day to "commit political suicide" in his home town. He is himself a Democrat. Most of the members of his lay board and the majority of the county court, that is, the county commissioners, in Kanahwa county, in which Charleston is located, are Democrats. It happens that the county relief administrator there — and Turner says he's "a damned good one" — is a Republican. For weeks they've been urging Turner to let him go and put in a typical politician, who happens to be a Democrat. Turner has refused. Last Thursday the board and the court got together and fired the Republican administrator and hired the Democrat.

"Now," said Turner, "I'm going back there and tell those birds that they've got to rescind that action or I'll withhold their funds. They'll give in, but my name will be mud in Democratic circles in Charleston from now on."

The political situation got so bad in Wheeling a few weeks ago that he arbitrarily, by threatening to withhold funds, took the control entirely away from the county court, named his own board, and put in his own people. The situation is a little better now, but there is constant friction. On August 26, for instance, there were no typewriters in the county relief headquarters. The county court, which pays the rent on them, simply had them moved out! Turner told me he thought he'd have to do in Mingo county what he's done in Ohio county, and of course he apparently is about to do it in Kanahwa county.

There are several bright spots in the relief situation in West Virginia.

For one thing, I heard relatively few complaints about the adequacy of the relief from the recipients, slim as it is. Nor about its administration. This is undoubtedly due in part — our own people say so — to the fact that many of those on the relief rolls have grown accustomed to getting on with even less. Some of the miners have not worked for eight years! . . .

The most serious complaints I heard were in Logan county, where two United Mine Workers' organizers had obtained affidavits from miners to the effect that they had been forced to work for their relief on private property, usually company property. There were complaints, too, that they had been required to work on the property of the road bosses, appointed by the politically minded county officials, and their friends. I heard some of this from other sources in Logan county, too. The union organizers told me this abuse had pretty much ceased during the last two months. They of course took the credit themselves. They

16

had taken the affidavits into Charleston, they said, and had shown them to Major Turner. In some cases — not very many, I judge — the companies have cooperated with the relief people and have given them a good deal of help, one way or another. . . .

Communism and the organizations of the unemployed are not as yet very prevalent in the state. Apparently the Communists haven't gone into Logan and Mingo counties at all — possibly because they feel the wretches down there are too far gone to bother with. Communist agitators have moved across the line from Pennsylvania and down into the center of the state as far south as Charleston. Apparently they are just getting started. Surprisingly, there seem to be none in Wheeling.

One reason there hasn't been more complaining about the inadequacy of the relief may be the prevalence of the gardens. There are only about three real cities in West Virginia, and the largest of these, Huntington, has a population of less than 100,000. The majority of the people live where it is possible to have gardens, even though under great difficulties. Most of the state is mountainous, with very narrow valleys. This is especially true in Logan and Mingo counties, and I've seen gardens down there on hillsides so steep that they must have had to shoot the seeds into the ground to make them stick! But gardens there are, right up to the tops of the hills — except where rains have washed them away.

The job of getting those gardens in was in many cases heartbreaking. They had no tools at all, except pitchforks and spades. First they had to clear the land in many cases. Then with pitchforks and spades they dug up that earth enough to get their seeds in. I remember one miner's family that had four acres of garden started that way. They say miners are lazy, but it seems to me you could hardly call a family lazy that would clear and dig up with a pitchfork and a spade four acres of land on a mountainside so steep that you could probably not drive a team of horses with a plow up there even if you had them. In Mingo county I heard of a man with heart trouble so severe that he had to sit on a box while working in his garden, but a garden he had, nevertheless. . . .

The agricultural extension division of the University of West Virginia has promoted the gardens and has done a grand job, especially up around Morgantown, where the university is located. Bushrod Grimes, of the agricultural extension department of the university, has had charge of the subsistence garden program in that county, and there families who are on the relief rolls — or who have been until recently — have 225 acres of land in gardens. In each mining camp Grimes organized the people into self-governing garden clubs, and it has done marvels for their morale. I visited one mining camp where the miners, through the garden club, had fixed their cabins all up, had

17

cleared land and made a park and a baseball diamond, and were planning to make a swimming pool and build a tennis court for themselves. They even had blueprints showing their plans. Most of those men have gone back to work in the mines — for how long it would be hard to say — but they say they are going to keep on with their plans. . . .

Canning is now going on all over the state. The great difficulty is to get sugar and jars. In some cases the people and the investigators have shown a lot of ingenuity in getting them. In Monongalia county (Morgantown), for instance, an investigator early in the summer had her women and children go out and pick wild berries, which she sold in Morgantown thereby raising enough money to buy 1,200 pounds of sugar for their canning! Because of the shortage of jars, they are teaching many of the women to dry their corn and beans.

Another bright spot in the West Virginia situation is the amount of work relief. In contrast to the procedure in Pennsylvania, where there is almost no work relief, the policy in West Virginia has been to provide work for all of the men on relief except those who were physically unable to work. And in spite of some abuses, the difference in the attitude of the people is amazing. Never once in West Virginia did I hear the complaint so frequent in Pennsylvania — "You're making paupers out of us." People on relief never talk about being on relief. They call it "working for the R.F.C."[1] and the kicks are always that some other fellow is getting more "R.F.C. work" than the complainant. I asked a miner up in Monongalia county how long he had been on relief, and he didn't know what I meant!

In West Virginia a few weeks ago they started paying all the men on work relief in cash. Major Turner said he did it because he found out that grocers were abusing the food order system. Now only emergency cases and families in which there is no one physically able to work for relief get food orders. . . .

Finding work for the people to do has taxed the resources of everybody. But they've managed to find it. For instance, in West Virginia there are hundreds of nurses out of jobs. They've been put to work all over the state, on relief checks, as public health nurses. And their work, in a state that hasn't any county hospitals with free beds, has been extremely valuable. In abandoned stores, in empty miners' cabins, in schoolhouses, they've set up little clinics. In a state where there were better facilities for taking care of the sick it might not seem like much — but in West Virginia it means a lot. In Monongalia county they even have uniforms, somewhat like Visiting Nurses' uniforms, supplied them by the American Friends.

In Mingo county they have a work relief project for the women — making up into garments the cloth sent down there by the Red

Cross. The director told me he now had on hand enough clothing to see them pretty well through the winter.

Monongalia county succeeded in getting $40,000 for materials and supervision out of the state board of control for cleaning up and beautifying the university campus. Men on work relief did the job, and enjoyed it. . . .

In West Virginia the rent situation does not seem to be particularly bothersome. There are no really large cities, and in the mining communities all the houses are owned by the companies. You have of course the picture of operators forcing their men to work in the mines for nothing or get out of their houses.

To solve the rent problem, wherever it does exist, Major Turner follows the policy of paying the landlord 6 percent of the assessed valuation of the property, plus insurance and taxes. It amounts, he says, to about $5 a month.

Another bright spot in the West Virginia picture has been the placing of nearly 4,000 undernourished children, from families on the relief rolls, in camps. The two National Guard camps in the state were used by the National Guard only 15 days this summer. Major Turner, himself a National Guard officer, borrowed the camps and their equipment from the National Guard and filled them with children for two week periods. They were taken to and from the camps from all over the state in school busses, local firms and private individuals donating the gasoline. Men and women on work relief have taken care of the camps — cooking, cleaning up, and so on. Counselors and directors volunteered their services. In a few cases he sent in members of his own staff to help. The only salaried persons in the camps were the doctors, one to each camp, paid $200 for a 30-day period. From the standpoint of sanitation and equipment generally, there are probably no better camps in the country than the National Guard camps.

He financed the undertaking in three ways. From the relief allotments of each county he took a little, he threw in some money from a small state fund for the care of "indigent children," and he collected from a Charleston bank $2,000 interest on relief funds deposited there. The camps were operated at very low cost. By careful buying and planning, the food cost per child per day ran about 30 cents! It was good food, too — and all they wanted. . . . I went out to one of the camps for supper. Nearly 1,000 boys, ranging from 8 to 14 years, had been in that camp a week. The people in charge said they were simply transformed. The average gain in weight per child for the two weeks' period has been five pounds. Supper, a good, filling meal, was served cafeteria style, and I saw some of the youngsters go back for three servings. Later in Logan county I visited the families of some of those boys, and the contrast between the homes they'd left and the camp where I had seen them was pitiful. The faces of their parents simply glowed when I described the camp to them. . . .

The most desperate need in West Virginia is for hospitals. There is not in the state a single city or county hospital with free clinics or free beds.

From long deprivation the health of the people is beginning to break down. Some of them have been starving for eight years. I was told there are children in West Virginia who never tasted milk! I visited one group of 45 blacklisted miners and their families, who had been living in tents two years.

I don't suppose anybody really knows how much tuberculosis there is in the state. Tuberculosis and asthma are common among miners, anyway. I heard of whole families having tuberculosis in some of the mining camps. There are the usual epidemics of typhoid — five babies have died of typhoid in Logan county recently, but the only wonder on the part of the relief workers was that more hadn't died. Dysentery is so common that nobody says much about it.

"We begin losing our babies with dysentery in September," one investigator remarked casually.

Diphtheria was beginning to break out in Logan and Mingo counties when I was there. Miss Sutherland, in Logan county, was deeply worried. In Logan county they have a little, makeshift detention home, where they take some of the children who are in the worst condition, to feed them up. The day I was there they had brought in from one of the mining camps a little girl desperately ill with diphtheria. In the afternoon they operated on her, putting a tube in her throat, and Miss Sutherland and I stopped by there to see how she was getting along. They had her isolated in a building back of the home, which is an old private house, and later it occurred to me that it must have been the garage!

The people handling relief in Logan and Mingo counties say there will undoubtedly be more illness there this next winter than ever before, because the resistance of the people is so low. And later, after I had left Logan county, I heard that there were so many deaths there last winter that they established as one of their work relief projects the making of coffins! All of the relief people, particularly Miss Sutherland and the American Friends' representative in the county, begged me to see if something could be done about starting a free hospital there.

The attitude of the privately owned hopsitals in the state is anything but cooperative. Undoubtedly they are in a bad way financially, but at any rate you have the spectacle of empty hospitals and people dying from lack of hospitalization. The practice generally is to refuse to admit a patient unless payment of the bill is guaranteed. Even when the bill is cut to the bone, it's considerable — operating room fee, anesthetist's fee, and so on. Now I know from personal experience, having several relatives in the profession, that doctors have been badly hit by the depression. Even our people in relief say that doctors and landlords have been the greatest sufferers outside the ranks of the unemployed. But nevertheless I don't think this sort of thing should happen:

Major Turner said that a week ago, on a Sunday, he was called at his home by someone from a neighboring county who wanted him to guarantee payment of a hospital bill for a woman, mother of eight children, who was about to die of acute appendicitis. He was told that she would live only a few hours unless she was immediately taken in for an operation. He explained that he was not permitted by the federal regulations to pay hospital bills, and that therefore he couldn't okay the bill. Whereupon, he said, he was told that he and the United States government would be responsible for that woman's death and for making those children orphans if he did not okay that bill! He stuck to his guns and didn't okay the bill — at the time, his funds were running out all over the state, anyway, and he didn't know what was going to happen in September. But the whole thing nearly drove him crazy. He said — and I agree with him — that any doctor who would refuse to take that woman into his private hospital, regardless of whether she could pay her bill or not, ought to be held criminally responsible if she died.

They seem to be having a good deal of trouble with doctors in West Virginia. Among our relief people, the profession has acquired most decidedly a black eye. In some cases the county pays $10 per confinement where care is given in the homes. An investigator told me of one doctor who made a practice of collecting his $10 from the county and then having the father, who didn't know that the county had paid anything, "work out" a bill for him! An investigator told me that one doctor admitted to her that he did not give his best services on relief cases.

Our relief people are highly incensed at the mining company doctors. Miners are assessed about $2 a month by the companies to pay the salaries of company doctors, some of whose salaries range from $500 to $1,000 a month when the mines are running. And then you have this sort of thing happening:

An investigator told me of going to see an old Negro miner who had collapsed while at work. He was carried home unconscious.

"A day or two later," the investigator said, "the company doctor, when he got good and ready, dropped in to see him. After he had looked him over, the company doctor said:

"'There isn't anything I can do for you. You're through — worn out.'

"And then he went off and left the old man there to die."

Another investigator told me she had never seen a company doctor.

"We don't even know who they are," she said. "They're never in evidence at all."

And this despite the fact that they are on salaries, paid out of the pitifully small wages of the men!

While I was in West Virginia Major Turner went into Wheeling to talk to the head of the state medical society and see if they could not get a little better cooperation from the profession. He told me later that the head of the society promised to put him in touch with the heads of the county medical societies to see what could be done.

One idea Major Turner had is turning some of the county poor farms, most of which were half empty, into hospitals. This could be done fairly easily, he and I both thought, with the installation of a little emergency operating room equipment. How much it would cost neither of us knew. He had also thought of appealing to the army medical corps for help.

The future in West Virginia, whatever happens under the NRA,[2] does not look particularly bright.

There has of course been a distinct drop in the case load these last few weeks. In the state, 40,000 families have been removed from the relief rolls since March. In Logan county alone, with the reopening of the mines, the case load was reduced from 6,000 to about 2,500. It has been greatly reduced in Wheeling, where the steel mills have opened up. In Monongalia county the load has dropped since May 1 from 5,665 to 3,885, but they don't expect it to drop below 3,000 before next summer.

Figures just now are apt to prove deceptive. The pickup in the mines, for instance, is undoubtedly due in part to labor troubles in Pennsylvania. Mines in West Virginia that haven't been running for years are operating now. But the chances are overwhelmingly, I am told, against their continuing to operate.

People on the operators' side to whom I talked, including the secretary of the state coal operators' association, told me that a great number of mines in West Virginia simply cannot be operated at a profit. Much of the coal is inferior. Freight rates are against them. And there's this sort of thing:

In Mingo county there are mines where the vein is only 30 inches deep. That means that a miner has to work on his knees and doubled up so that his back rubs against the top of the vein and gets calloused! I saw men down there with patches on their backs between their shoulder blades.

"That," an investigator explained, "is where their backs rub against the top of the vein."

Now, with the soft coal industry dying on its feet — or its knees — partly from over-production, it's obviously unprofitable and senseless to operate those mines. . . .

Thousands of men in the mining areas are barred because of age — men of 45 or so, with large, half grown families. A state field representative in Wheeling told of miners coming into her office one day, their eyes shining with happiness, and asking to be taken off the rolls because the mines were opening up, and they were going back to work.

"A day or two later they began drifting back," she said, "bewildered and frightened. They'd passed the age limit. There was no work for them. Some of them cried like children."

So far, while the case load has diminished, the cost of relief has not. I got the same reports in West Virginia that I got in Pennsylvania — that the cost of food has almost doubled. When the relief director bought her flour in Wheeling August 25 she said she found the price of flour had more than doubled since May. Clothing needs are increasing all the time, too. Most of the women you see in the camps are going about without shoes or stockings. I saw one woman obviously attired in only a slip and a dress — both in rags. She told me those were the only clothes she had in the world! It's fairly common to see children entirely naked. . . .

There isn't any use in counting on much help from private agencies in West Virginia next winter. For instance, in Monongalia county — probably the best county in the state, in that its people are "socially minded" and inclined to do all they can to help — only 45 percent of the $9,500 pledged to the Community Chest last year was collected. Two years ago the pledges totaled $25,000, and 80 percent of it was collected.

Even if things go along as they are now, therefore, West Virginia is apparently going to need just as much relief money next winter as it needed last winter. And the chances of things going along as they are now are pretty slim.

Whatever happens on the coal code, there is almost certain to be labor trouble, I am told. The operators will give "lip service" only, the relief people believe, and the miners, whether they get their union or not, are all set to make trouble.

In the last few months they have been joining the United Mine Workers by the hundreds. Obviously, if the code does not recognize the union, there will be trouble. And if it does, and the union begins to get a little power, there is every chance in the world that the miners — itching for reprisal — will run away from their leaders.

Right now the leaders are having trouble holding them in check. They want to strike on every sort of pretext. To understand why they feel that way one has to listen to only a few of the stories told by relief workers of how the operators have treated them. No Negro on a Southern plantation before the Civil War, our people say, was ever more enslaved than thousands of those miners have been. They're in the union now, and they want to strike — if for no other reason to "get back at" the operators. It is as understandable as it is regrettable.

Operators, afraid of the union, are making a last desperate stand against it. Miners are being discouraged, evicted from company houses, and blacklisted. They're on the relief rolls.

Next to the immediate and urgent need for hospitals, West Virginia's greatest need apparently is for rehabilitation. And it looks as though almost the whole state would need rehabilitating.

My visit to Wheeling, I was told, did not give me much of an idea of conditions in the steel mills. Most of the plants around there are owned by the Wheeling Steel Corporation, an independent outfit that has been more prosperous than U.S. Steel or some of the other companies. The Wheeling plants are now running practically full blast, and one of their people told me that, while their orders have fallen off a little in the last week or two, it is apparently a seasonal drop, and they are not worried. No estimate of the drop in the case load at Wheeling in the last month was available when I was there, although they expected to have it figured out in a few days. Apparently the decrease there will be permanent.

Among the Wheeling steel workers I ran into something I had been looking for ever since I first heard in Pennsylvania about the debt loads of the unemployed. Debtors in Wheeling have begun to attach the salaries of the men going back to work—in such numbers that the Wheeling Steel Corporation has protested. One of the worst offenders, I was told, was the retail credit man's association. I heard, too, of gas being turned off in homes where the man had just gone back to work. Banks and loan sharks—some of the latter charging 42 percent interest on loans—are pressing the people for payments. And the workmen and their families—desperately striving to get back to something like their normal living conditions—are complaining bitterly. Obviously some adjustment on those debt loads will have to be made.

"Since we started paying cash for work relief," one of the people in charge of the relief job told me, "it's happened, not once, but many times that a merchant would come into my office and ask if there was any way whereby he could attach work relief checks!"

1. Reconstruction Finance Corporation, created in 1932 during the administration of Herbert C. Hoover.
2. National Recovery Administration, established under the National Industrial Recovery Act of 1933.

To Harry L. Hopkins

REPORT   Field: Eastern Kentucky Coal Fields. August 31–
                                  September 3 [1933]   Inclusive

This is a story about what happens to the unemployed when relief is cut off.

I spent three days last week in the Eastern Kentucky mountains and mining camps. Owing to the Kentucky state government's delay in devising some way to meet the financial obligations of the Federal Emergency Relief Administration, there had been no distribution of relief there since August 12.

In ten of those mountain counties under the direction of Miss Caroline Boone, field supervisor with the Kentucky relief board, there are, she told me, about 28,000 families on the relief rolls. That means about 150,000 people — very likely more, because nobody ever heard of a family of five in those mountains. From ten on up would be more accurate. About 62 per cent of the people in those counties, I was told, are on relief, or were until the moratorium went into effect. The average for the whole state . . . is 22 per cent.

Pasted up on the doors of the relief offices to which those people until August 12 came for their work slips and food orders are typewritten notices stating that for the present there will be no more help for them.

Every morning little groups of people — those who still have enough strength to walk anywhere from one to ten miles — come straggling in and stand staring helplessly at those notices. Many of them cannot read.

"Every morning," the head of the relief staff in one of those towns told me, "I take the morning paper and go out on the steps and read aloud to them what's happened at the special session of the Legislature in Frankfort.

"Every morning what's happened is — nothing. They listen dumbly, and then they go away."

One morning Miss Boone at the relief headquarters in Pineville, county seat of notorious Bell county, looked them over, sent all the money she had in her purse over to the bank and had it changed into 50-cent pieces, and distributed it among them.

A word about these people. As everyone knows, they are for the most part of pure Anglo-Saxon stock. Some of them are descended from the finest families in American colonial history. They are passionately patriotic. In one of those ten counties there was no draft during the period of our participation in the World War. Man and boy, they enlisted, 100 per cent. . . .

They are a curiously appealing people. They all carry guns and shoot each other. And yet they desperately never think of robbing people. I cannot for the life of me understand why they don't go down and raid the Blue Grass country.

They are deeply religious. Whenever they do get worked up to the point of holding any sort of protest demonstration, they come straggling in to the meeting place — fathers, mothers, and children — the men with rifles slung across their shoulders, all singing spirituals. One of their favorites is "Were You There When They Crucified Our Lord?"

They shoot each other — and yet there is in them a great deal of gentleness. Toward their children, for instance. And you hear about them stories like this:

Relief in Kentucky having been none too adequate in the matter of clothing, most of them are scantily clad. An investigator visiting one of their villages back up in the mountains in Clay county a few weeks ago noticed that all the men and boys as they passed one cabin pulled their caps down over their eyes. When he asked why, they told him:

"Well, you see the women folks in that thar place hain't got no clothes at all. Even their rags is clean wore out and gone."

Some of these people live in mining camps down in the valleys — many of them in abandoned mining camps. The rest live in little communities, rather like Indian villages — and without any kind of sanitation whatever — back up at the headwaters of the creeks, in the mountains.

Their ancestors came in there as squatters. For years wild game supplied their food and money. As the game disappeared, they began cutting the timber on the mountains and selling it, and, as they cleared the land, they started little farms. These have always been subsistence farms, and each year's rains on those hillsides have left the soil a little "thinner." They've had some dry weather there this summer. Their patches of corn and their gardens are burned yellow. They are getting very little out of them.

About the time they got the timber pretty well cleared off the mountains coal mining started. They then augmented the living they were able to get out of their mountain farms by working in the mines. Some of them abandoned their cabins and moved into the mining camps and are still there. The young people, especially after the World War, began to drift away. Some of them even went as far north as Michigan and got work in the automobile plants. They've been driven back there by the depression, to live with "the old folks."

When relief was discontinued on August 12 these people were given grocery orders a little larger than usual and were told to make them last as long as they could — two weeks if possible. Three weeks had passed when I was there, and only the most thrifty among them had any cornmeal or lard or sugar or coffee left. You see the tendency, when you live on what is known as a "subsistence diet" — or "minimum subsistence diet" — is to have at least one or two good meals right after you get your grocery order.

When I was down there, the most cautious still had a little flour or cornmeal left. Said Mrs. Montgomery, wife of a crippled ex-miner in a camp in Harlan county, without a trace of resentment in her voice:

"I've still got flour enough for a couple more meals. My young ones think I'm stingy because I won't let 'em have but two meals a day, but, honey, in times like these you can't have more than two meals a day nohow."

Mrs. Montgomery is an exceptional woman. Her cabin was immaculate. Some of the less thrifty had been living for days on green corn and string beans—and precious little of that. And some had nothing at all, actually hadn't eaten for a couple of days. In Middlesborough Saturday night I heard of a miner's widow with six children who had had nothing at all to eat that day and had no prospects of getting anything the next day either. At the Continental hotel in Pineville I was told that five babies up one of those creeks had died of starvation in the last ten days.

"Well, probably they're just as well off," my informant, NOT a member of the relief staff, said complacently.

They're neighborly folk, down there in the Kentucky mountains and mining camps. Those who have share with those who haven't. Even, I was told, to the last string bean.

And when the corn and string beans have all been eaten, they start begging. The day I was in Middlesborough, the Episcopal clergyman had got in touch with the head of the relief staff and told him he would be glad to give the little boy who came to his door every morning a daily supply of food, if only he wouldn't come while he was at his prayers!

The attitude of her committees and the townspeople, including the grocers, Miss Boone told me, was anything but sympathetic. To them, all the people on the relief rolls are "poor white trash and Communists, anyway."

Somewhat distressed by being forced to watch human beings starve, Miss Boone, who said she felt like throwing up the job and getting out, but simply couldn't be a quitter if there was any chance at all of doing something for them, worked out a plan for helping some of the families whose condition was the worst. It consisted in persuading the grocers—partly by asking them if they wouldn't rather do this than have their stores raided—to make up packages that would last a family a week for 85 cents each, a little cornmeal, lard, sugar, and coffee, and to match with a free package every package purchased by the committees. Then the committees were to try to raise the money from private contributions. She agreed to contribute out of her own pocket $10 to each committee, to start them off. (I saw her myself give the head of the staff in Middlesborough $10 for that purpose.) Her committees, however, did not take kindly to the idea. They were tired of asking people for money, they said.

Actually the grocers apparently had little reason to worry about raids on their stores.

In Middlesborough Saturday afternoon some of the more energetic of the unemployed tried to organize a march on the stores, preceded by a meeting. Since they all carry guns, it looked as though it might be serious. The relief people were divided between a desire to see it happen, because it might have some effect on the Legislature, and a fear that many of the marchers would be killed if they began shooting.

27

Having kept in touch with the situation by telephone since Thursday night, Miss Boone and I heard in Harlan at noon Saturday that the meeting and march apparently were going to be staged. Across two counties we raced — I expecting that any moment her old automobile would fall to pieces — but when we arrived in Middlesborough it was all over.

I quote the head of the relief staff in Middlesborough:

"They came all right, but only about a hundred of them. They stood around a little while and listened to some speeches. A few of them formed an organization and elected me president! One of the speakers started getting a bit inflammatory, and I told him he'd better go back to Pineville where he came from. He went, without a protest. By the time the speaking was over, most of the crowd had drifted away — slowly, listlessly.

"Why, those people couldn't put on a riot! They were so starved that they didn't have the physical energy."

On Friday, September 1, I went with Earl Mayhew of the extension division of the College of Agriculture, University of Kentucky, back up to the heads of some of the creeks in the mountains in Knox county. Each trip made by an investigator into one or two of those communities takes about a day. You travel as far as you can over roads that only a Ford . . . in the hands of an expert could negotiate. Then you get out and walk.

On one of the trails we met an old woman. They called her "Aunt Cora." Half dead from pellagra, she stumbled along on her bare, gnarled old feet, clutching under her arm a paper bag containing a few scraggly string beans she'd begged off somebody.

I stopped and talked with her. As I started on, she reached out and laid her hand on my arm and said in a voice that was hardly more than a whisper:

"Don't forget me, honey! Don't forget me!"

To Harry L. Hopkins

REPORT   Field: New York State, outside the Metropolitan Area.
                                        September 12–19 [1933] Inclusive

. . . On a seven-day trip through the state, visiting Corning, considered fairly representative of the Southern Tier counties, Rochester and Syracuse, typical of the larger Up-State cities, and Watertown, Ogdensburg, Malone, and Plattsburgh, in the Upper Tier, I found relief administration and adequacy so far ahead of what I had seen in other states that there just isn't any basis for comparison at all.

New York State's Temporary Emergency Relief Administration [TERA] has just about achieved — particularly in cities like Corning, Rochester, and Syracuse — it seems to me, what the Federal Emergency Relief Administration is aiming at for the rest of the country.

The amount of relief given was, to one just out of Kentucky, a bit dazzling. They pay rent, up to $16 a month. Not only are medicine and medical care in the home provided, but also hospitalization, out of city or county funds. Clothing needs are met, on a scale far, far above that in Pennsylvania, for instance. In some cases families are even helped to keep up their insurance payments and payments on homes. Food allowances, compared with other states, are generous. And work projects are extensive, thoughtfully planned, and carried out with a good deal of imagination.

An attempt is made — particularly in Syracuse and in Rochester — to meet the needs of the individual families. As a result, a man with a large family may earn, on work relief, as much as $16 a week. All men on work relief are, of course, paid in cash.

Although local politics were boiling a bit when I was in the state — a primary election was held the day I left — I found much less political interference from Albany than I had found coming from other state capitals. In fact, there doesn't seem to be any at all. In communities that are largely Republican the recent appointment of Mr. [Alfred Hugo] Schoellkopf of Buffalo, a Republican, as head of TERA has done a lot to build up good feeling and confidence.

"I am a Republican, and I come from a Republican city," said Dr. Christopher G. Parnall, Commissioner of Public Welfare in Rochester, "but when I ask the State Board for anything, I feel that I am getting the same consideration I'd get if I were a Democrat, from a Democratic community." . . .

On the whole, however, I don't believe politics are interfering very seriously with relief administration in Up-State New York. If all the other efforts of the Federal government toward recovery met with as little political interference as the Relief Administration encounters, Up-State New York would be in grand shape. For instance, so far as I was able to find out — and I inquired in every place I visited — not a cent of Federal Home Loan money has been distributed in the state. Vincent Dailey has been appointed administrator for the state, and that's as far as it has gone. It looks very much to this humble observer (and again I hope this report is confidential) as though somebody were trying to find good Democrats to handle the Home Loan money in Republican towns. . . .

The same delays are encountered in trying to start public works projects. There was hardly a place I visited where they did not have a public works project — awaiting action in Albany and Washington. The delay seemed to be in Albany. An engineer, who must pass on projects before they go to Washington, had been appointed, I was told, only at the end of August. Some towns, perfectly able to raise their own share, had spent all summer trying to get some of that public works money from Washington. And one town had finally gone ahead with a water and sewer extension project, assuming that eventually it might get some reimbursement from Washington. Some federal highway money had got into the state, but — particularly in the Northern Tier — too late. In Clinton county, for instance, the man at the head of the Federal Re-employment Bureau had 834 men all ready to go to work on a highway job when the contractor announced that, owing to the approach of cold weather, the laying of the concrete top on the road would have to be postponed until next spring. It seems that, if the temperature is below 40 degrees above zero, they can't pour concrete without heating it by some complicated and expensive system.

To sum it all up, the efforts of the Federal government toward recovery, with the exception of the Relief Administration and NRA — which offers no possibilities for political patronage — simply aren't felt in the state. They somehow have failed to get down through to the people they are supposed to help. And the smaller the community, the less help from NRA. This sounds gloomy, but it reflects public opinion. In New York City, for instance, I heard of a clothing store that had put on two additional clerks and four additional tailors — and had enough business to warrant it. In Syracuse a department store man had increased his payrolls something like $30,000 a year and, so far at least, was breaking a little better than even. The Corning glass works recently took back about 500 men, with production up to the 1928 peak. But in little towns like Ogdensburg businessmen who are conscientiously trying to live up to the rules are having a tough time of it.

These last few paragraphs of course do not deal directly with our show. But the extent to which the whole recovery program works certainly has a bearing on relief.

I visited Corning first on my trip through the state, and there I got the impression that the relief people, with the machine functioning so smoothly, had begun to look about for new worlds to conquer and were, perhaps, "case-working" their people too much. There was, for instance, the "escrow system." The idea, I understand, emanates from up around Buffalo. It consists in letting a man work on a relief project a full week, holding back part of his money each week until enough has piled up for him to lay off a full week. . . .

The impression I received in Corning that things were running almost too smoothly was dissipated somewhat in Rochester and Syracuse, where I encountered some of the most interesting and, they seemed to me, most important problems I've run into so far. These same problems,

I was told, have begun to loom up in other cities, notably Buffalo and Schenectady. I found Ralph Drowne, TERA field representative, somewhat puzzled by them and a little worried because of what they might develop into.

First of all is the question whether relief is not so adequate that private industry cannot compete with it. It sounds funny, but it is beginning to be a real question, especially in Syracuse, where, I was told, relief was more adequate than anywhere else in the state. Under the individual family budget system there, a man with a large family, as I said before, may get as much as $16 a week on relief. The average minimum wage in private industry is $14. Under those conditions what incentive is there for a man to take a job, even if it is offered to him? And take the case of a man who is getting $10 or $12 a week on a part time relief job? Why should be he interested in going back to work on a full time job for $14?

Out of this apparently — and I heard it in other parts of the state, too — is growing a tendency on the part of the unemployed to be none too enthusiastic about going back to work. It isn't so very strong yet, but there apparently is a definite swing in that direction, and what is it going to lead to? I encountered a good deal more of it in the soft coal areas, but thought nothing of it, for there going back into the mines meant in many cases going back at starvation wages and into a system of virtual peonage. But this is different, and the question people like Drowne are asking is:

"Wouldn't it be a little better, perhaps, to make relief a little less adequate and therefore less attractive?"

An exaggerated case Drowne mentioned was that of a man who was getting $12 a week on relief and turned down a $25-a-week job, because, he explained, he got $35 before the depression and he'd be doggoned if he'd go back to work for less!

The other problem has to do with organizations of the unemployed. Now, as Drowne puts it:

"Can you give me one good earthly reason why they should organize in a place like Syracuse?"

And, except for that discontent that exists among all the unemployed, I can't. I spent an afternoon with a case worker in Syracuse. He didn't know I was from Washington until I told him after we had started off. He was picked just before we started, as an average case worker with an average load — neither the best nor the worst — and he didn't know anyone was going with him. Therefore there wasn't much chance of his having picked special families for me to see. He was just making his regular visits.

We went to half a dozen places. Two of the families were living in two-family houses, as comfortable and as well furnished as any home I ever lived in as a child. One family — a young couple with a baby — had a small house, which I would call extremely comfortable. Two women and a boy lived in a four-room apartment, not so well furnished as the other places, but not what I'd call uncomfortable at all. One large Italian family lived in a big, ramshackle, rather tumbled-down place, and an old man and his son lived in an abandoned stone quarry, in a shack they'd built. Even these last two places were away above the average I saw in Pennsylvania. The people were comparatively well dressed — the Italians a bit dirty. They didn't look undernourished. Whatever arguments there were were about whether the Italian should burn wood or coal in his heating stove, whether one family should move into a house where the rent was $18 a month, and whether the boy should have two pairs of trousers or one pair. His mother seemed to think he ought to have a suit, trousers and coat to match. This all gave me the impression that these people were far from being hungry or cold or really uncomfortable.

Of course, standards in Syracuse are higher than in any other city in the state, I was told. But they are almost as high in Rochester.

Yet in Rochester a couple of months ago 5,500 men engaged on work relief projects organized and went on a strike. And they are organizing in Syracuse. There has been considerable trouble, too, I was told in Buffalo and Schenectady.

The strikers in Rochester demanded 40 cents an hour, instead of 30, and got it. They are now asking 60.

"The thing that bothers me," said Dr. Parnall, the commissioner of public welfare, "is that they are forming a political minority — a grand field for small time politicians to work in."

The movement to organize in Syracuse began a few weeks ago with the arrival of two men, one of whom refused to give his name to the relief people. These two men began bringing cases to the attention of Leon H. Abbott, city commissioner of public welfare. At first most of their demands were reasonable, Mr. Abbott said, and he didn't have much trouble with them. As time went on, however, they began to ask more. . . .

Apparently playing along with the two outsiders in the organization of the unemployed in Syracuse was a junior at Syracuse University, an Italian lad, named [Charles] Rinaldo. Mr. Rinaldo is apparently a college boy who has been reading a little Tolstoy — and perhaps a little Trotsky — and my personal feeling about him is that he ought to be spanked and sent to bed without his supper. Rinaldo isn't even on relief himself! He apparently is just a young egoist out for glory. However, [Rolland B.] Marvin[1] has felt that citizens of Syracuse have a right to meet if they want to. So one night while I was in Syracuse he permitted Rinaldo to hold a meeting of the unemployed in the auditorium of Central high school. Drowne and I attended — inconspicuously.

Rinaldo, who because of his contact with Marvin has become a black sheep among the Communistically inclined, made a somewhat florid speech, in English first and then in Italian. He denounced the Communists, proceeded to give the crowd — about 350 — some misinformation, and presented a petition to be sent to Governor [Herbert] Lehman, asking that foremen on work relief jobs be prevented from "pushing" the men, that relief be made more adequate, and that something be done about the Lay Creek project, of which more later.

His misinformation consisted of a flat statement that all the men on work relief projects in Rochester got a 35-hour week at 40 cents an hour, whereas, as Drowne said, if one man with a large family was getting that much in Rochester, probably two were getting it in Syracuse.

The crowd was, for the most part, apathetic. But, as Drowne said, where is it leading to?

While in Syracuse I spent a forenoon with Crandall Melvin,[2] who took me along Lay Creek and also showed me his six miles of boulevard-park project out in the county. This is the most ambitious work project I've seen anywhere, and it's a dandy. It includes a public swimming pool, built at a fairly low cost and used by more than 100,000 people at the end of the summer, a reproduction of an old French fort, a salt museum — salt springs having furnished in the early days the principal industry of the people in Onondaga county — and an athletic field to be used by all the schools in the county. It provided for all sorts of skilled labor the kind of work they knew how to do. There were jobs for draughtsmen, stone masons — they've laid miles of some of the nicest dry stone walls I ever saw — carpenters, and so on. He said the men loved the work, and I believe him. Perhaps the only thing to be said against it was that it cost a great deal more than most communities could ever put into such a project. He said he's spent about $1,000,000 on it, including, of course, the work relief salaries of a large number of men. Included in the $1,000,000 was an item of $114,000 for taking a dredge up there from New York City. He said the dredge got him into difficulty because of the cost, and I shouldn't wonder if it were responsible for some of his other plans being balked.

We went over the Lay Creek project in detail! In fact, he drove me in his car almost to the headwaters of the creek. Had I been blind, my olfactory sense would have convinced me of the need of cleaning out that creek and putting in an underground sewage system. What it really amounts to is an open cesspool around one side of the city. It's a mess.

With the backing of the state board of health, which had been worrying about Lay Creek for 15 years, he said, Mr. Melvin managed to get shoved through the last session of the legislature a bill creating a commission to clean the place up. He has a very ambitious plan for building an underground sewer and a sewage disposal plant, cleaning out and straightening the creek, and building a boulevard.

The only trouble was that the appointment of the commission went into the hands of the political powers in Syracuse. Mr. Melvin, who obviously should have been a member, was left out, and now the commission is trying to get some public works money to build it, letting the job out to a contractor who is a brother of one of the commissioners. Melvin originally had planned it as a work relief project. The contractor, he says, will do the whole job with machinery, employing very few men, and will thereby defeat the whole purpose of the project, which whether it be done as a public works or as a work relief project, would be to provide work for as many men as possible.

"The only smart thing to do now," said Mr. Melvin, "would be for the Public Works department to turn it down, except for the sewage disposal plant, which would cost somewhere around $300,000 and would employ mostly skilled labor anyway, and throw the rest of it back as a work relief project."

I suggested that he get busy along those lines himself, but he appeared to be pretty thoroughly disgusted with the whole thing and ready to drop it.

The work relief project Mr. Melvin has accomplished and that which he had planned are, of course, pretty ambitious. But on a smaller scale some grand work relief projects have been carried out elsewhere in the state. In Fulton, for instance, under the direction of the local Episcopal clergymen, the outlet from a lake was cleaned up with a home made dredge, floated on empty oil drums, and, after the lake water had been thus purified, a grand little beach was made. In Corning, they dug up thousands of poplar trees that were winding their roots around the sewers and replaced them with other trees.

In the Northern Tier I ran into summer resorts, paper mills, and the milk problem. All in all, things looked pretty tough.

Some of the paper mills are running, apparently benefiting by the drop in the value of the American dollar, which formerly made it cheaper to buy the Canadian product, I was told. However, Lisle Burroughs, a TERA field representative, who has a number of them in his territory, can't see much future for paper mills just now.

The summer business up along the St. Lawrence was bad this year, so people who depended on that haven't any money.

The milk strike has been settled, but the farmers don't feel any too happy about it. A farmer up near Plattsburgh told me they are now getting out in Clinton county $1.40 per hundredweight for milk, and that, by the time it reaches the consumer in Plattsburgh only a few miles away, it costs $6.24. They had a drouth at the beginning of the summer, and it's a question how they're ever going to feed their stock this winter.

"Well, I know what we'll do," this farmer said. "Some of it's been done already. We'll have to shoot our cows."

When you consider the fact that it took years to build up those herds — some of the finest herds in the country — it does seem pretty tough. One after another, he told me, the milk farmers are losing their farms. Eighty-five per cent of the farms in Clinton county, he said, are mortgaged. Farmers who used to employ two or three men are doing all the work themselves now and letting their buildings and land go to pieces. There are public auctions all the time.

Generally in the North country . . . they approach the winter gloomily. Everybody seems to think that the relief load, especially in the rural districts, will be heavier than it was last winter.

Generally speaking, the cities and counties and townships in Up-State New York have held up their end of the relief load pretty well. The New York state set-up, with TERA reimbursing the communities on a basis of 40 per cent of the total cost of relief, has until now worked marvelously.

Some of the communities, however, may be getting near the end of the rope. I was told that Clinton county had a $63,000 load of unpaid taxes under the 1932 assessment. . . .

1. Mayor of Syracuse.
2. Chairman of the Onondaga County Emergency Work Bureau.

To Harry L. Hopkins

REPORT   Field: Maine, September 21–29 [1933]   Inclusive

. . . In discussing the Maine situation, I think one should first take into consideration the types of people one finds up there.

The majority of the people — and the ruling class — are of course typical "down East Yankees." Proud, reserved, independent. Shrewd, but honest. Endowed with all the good solid virtues on which this nation was founded. Pretty much untouched by the moral and intellectual by-products of the American "bigger and better" madness. Apt to be pretty intolerant of those who fail to live up to their standards. And, above all, thrifty.

On the other hand, the greater portion of the population now getting state and federal relief, up along the border, is French Canadian. Rather easy-going people, these. They've always lived, as far as I could find out, a rather hand-to-mouth existence. And the typical "Maine-ite" is apt to regard them pretty much as Southerners regard "poor white trash."

Outside of Portland, the rest of the so-called "foreign" population seems to consist only of a few Finns and Swedes, temperamentally a good deal like the "Maine-ites," only more apt to accept radical ideas.

35

A "Maine-ite," being the type of person he is, would almost starve rather than ask for help. In fact, his fellow citizens would expect it of him. It is considered a disgrace in Maine to be "on the town." At state headquarters in Augusta I was told that it was extremely difficult to get "white collar" people for work relief projects in Maine because there are practically no "white collar" people on relief. And the feeling in Augusta is that there must be thousands of people of this class in the state literally starving to death. But it is impossible to get at them. They won't ask for help, and it cannot very well be forced on them. And this attitude is quite general among the Yankee population.

This feeling of course is reflected in their attitude toward those who do ask for relief — especially the French Canadians. They still believe in Maine that "there must be something wrong with a fellow if he can't get a job." They really believe it, even as they tell you how desperate their plight is and how hopeless the employment situation looks for the future! A farmer who is a very great friend of mine and one of the finest men I know said, discussing our pork distribution plans:

"It just don't seem right for anybody to get something for nothing. It's pauperizing, that's all."

Too often this is the attitude of the people administering relief — head selectmen, for instance, and overseers of the poor. In their handling of the funds they are apt to be honest to the point of fanaticism, but this sort of thing is all too typical:

A man on the relief rolls told a case worker that he and his family were getting pretty tired of getting nothing to eat but vegetables — mostly beans.

"I can stand it," he said patiently, "but my wife's getting ugly."

When she reported this to the town official who made out the food orders, he said:

"Good! I'm glad to hear it!"

And yet that same town official, discussing the relief and employment situation with me from a purely academic viewpoint, was deeply concerned — and I think he was sincere — over the lack of prospects for work for the people.

All this, I believe, accounts for a good deal of the inadequacy and for some pretty bad administration. People on relief in Maine also have to stand for a good deal of discrimination based on purely conventional moral standards. You hear so much in Maine about "deserving cases." And to be a "deserving case" in Maine, a family has got to measure up to the most rigid Nineteenth Century standards of cleanliness, physical and moral. They just haven't any patience with people who don't. As a result, a woman who isn't a good housekeeper is apt to have a pretty tough time of it. And Heaven help the family in which there is any "moral problem!"

This same feeling that makes individuals go without rather than be "on the town" and that makes them so critical of those who finally do ask for help is reflected somewhat in community governments. Partly this and partly Yankee thrift.

State and federal relief monies are being distributed in only seven counties in Maine — and mostly in Northern Aroostook county, among the French Canadians. Along the coast there are only three communities getting any now, Portland — and there only because of a work relief project being carried out at the forts — St. George, and Eastport. Rockland has had some help and was about to ask for more when I was there.

The great majority of the communities simply will not ask for help. They prefer to "get along somehow." I actually encountered public officials in some of those towns who were firmly convinced that "all that money from Augusta and Washington is going to have to be paid back sometime!"

Probably typical of those towns is Calais. Conditions there, as described to me by Helen Hanson, a woman lawyer whose father, now dead, was for many years on the state supreme bench, were simply frightful. The town has never had any state or federal aid. It won't ask for it, even though in the last town meeting there was strong agitation for it. The people on relief in that town are subjected to treatment that is almost medieval in its stinginess and stupidity. But the mayor was actually proud of the fact that he had managed so far to pull through without asking for help. It had been a tough job, he said, and everybody had had to make sacrifices, including the teachers, whose pay had been cut until they barely had enough to eat. He was perfectly honest and sincere about it. He thought they'd done a pretty good job. I could see that he felt it would be a disgrace to ask for state or federal help. Incidentally, a member of Governor [Louis Jefferson] Brann's Council lives in Calais!

Inadequacy of relief in Maine I think may also be due, in addition to the town officials' lack of generosity and their inherent mistrust of anyone who can't get a job, to the fact that the family allotment there on account of the climate should, in the winter at least, be much higher than in many other localities to be adequate, and to the financial condition of the towns.

Obviously people along the Canadian border need more food in the winter than people farther south. They need more fuel and warmer houses. And, above all, they need warmer clothing. The Red Cross official who sent a lot of cotton goods up into Northern Maine last winter was a bright boy! They will need a lot of clothing up there this winter. Good, warm clothing. Wool. When I was up there nearly everybody was getting a little work — in the potato fields, for instance — but the indications were that it would all be over in a month or so. What they earned will undoubtedly help some to solve the clothing problem. "I've told them all that I'll feed them, but they must at least help to clothe themselves," said the head selectman in Van Buren, on the border. But their plight is much the same as that of the unemployed everywhere, on the clothing proposition. They just haven't anything to start with.

The financial condition of most of the communities I visited in Maine is pretty awful. The tax delinquencies are tremendous. In Rockland, for instance, the biggest industry used to be a lime quarry. The quarry is in the hands of receivers, and the company owes $76,000 in back taxes. In Presque Isle, in the heart of the potato country, I was told that delinquent taxes, running back as far as 1930, total $125,000, and the town is away over its debt limit. Houlton, also in the potato country, reported $58,000 in back taxes in addition to the $200,000 due this year. They hoped to get about $150,000 of this year's taxes and $10,000 of the back taxes, but said the town had $275,000 in bills to pay. I was told in Augusta that when Allagash, away up at the end of the road in the timber country, wrote down to the capital for help last winter it had to borrow a postage stamp . . . to send the letter! Incidentally, of the approximately 90 families living in the community, all but three were on relief — the game warden, the fire warden, and the ferryman — and he was paid in food orders.

Because of Maine's system of tax collection, the situation of the towns is sharply reflected in the state's financial condition. Taxes in Maine are collected by the towns, which in turn hand over a certain percentage to the counties and the state. When the towns cannot collect taxes, the state doesn't get any money, either. I was told in Augusta that the state's uncollected tax money, running back as far as 1930, amounted to more than $1,000,000. Obviously, there isn't much use in imposing additional property taxes when the towns can't collect any taxes as it is. A bond issue lost out last spring. The prospects of passing a general sales tax in a legislative session are not promising. The only general tax, collected by the state is a gasoline tax, five cents a gallon, supposed to be spent on road maintenance. Brann told me that the only way out he could see was to divert that money to relief, and that is what he is planning to do, the legislature last spring having vested in the governor and his council enough authority so that they can stretch a point and use the road money for relief.

Speaking of finances, I encountered in Northern Aroostook county this situation: The unemployed had been put to work on certain road jobs, to be built by the towns with a certain amount of state aid. The towns had no money, and state money would not be available until sometime in December. The result was that some of the men had as

38

much as $300 due them in back pay! In some towns the school teachers were actually on relief. Some of them hadn't received any money since last January. And before that their pay had been cut down to practically nothing. In one town they were going to close the schools, but the teachers, having no place to go and no way to earn a living, said they preferred to keep on working — for food orders. Their offer was accepted. . . .

Largely because it is handled by public officials, inexperienced and unsympathetic in their attitude, the relief administration in some places is awful. Weekly food orders are written out by men who apparently haven't the slightest idea of the food needs of a family. Nor its other needs. It has never occurred to some of them that people need soap, for instance.

One food order, turned over to me, contained the following items: 1 peck potatoes, .20; corn meal, .15; rolled oats, .25; two quarts beans, .20; pork, .25; two quarts of dried peas, .30; two cans of milk (and there were several children in the family), .13; 2 pounds of rice, .15; 1 quart of molasses, .20. Total, $1.83. No soap, practically no meat, no fish, no fruit of any kind, no fresh milk, no sugar. In fact, practically nothing except starch and a little fat and a little molasses! Pellagra, incidentally, has appeared up there. This order was supposed to last the family a week — and did. Across the bottom was written: "Mr. Higgins left this order for you, to be filled just as he gave it." . . .

Rockland and Van Buren had commissaries — Rockland's, probably, fairly good, and Van Buren's, where the head selectman administering relief happens to be a physician, excellent. He had set out to do what he could to build the people up physically, particularly children, and to combat diseases like pellagra. . . .

Eastport was one of the brighter spots. The town had bought some old shacks — a sort of "company town" that had once belonged to a factory — fixed them up, and moved some of their unemployed into them. They could hardly be called luxurious, but they looked fairly warm. Houlton had built some houses, out near the city dump, but an Indian woman living in one of them took me upstairs and showed me cracks, under the eaves, big enough to stick one's finger through. No plaster, of course. Although there were screens in the windows, the walls were black with flies that had come in through the cracks! . . .

With the exception of Rockland and St. George, nearly everybody in the communities I visited had gone back to work — for the time being, at any rate. In Aroostook county, of course, most of the work was picking potatoes, at 6 cents a barrel. And quite obviously it will all be over by the middle of October. But since a large percentage of the transient labor that always heads for Maine in potato-picking time had been

39

turned back at Bangor this year there was plenty of work temporarily for the natives.

I was in Aroostook county on my vacation last summer, and at that time the farmers were feeling optimistic, expecting eventually to get $4 a barrel for their potatoes. Last year they had got from 20 to 65 cents a barrel — and it cost anywhere from 85 cents to $1 a barrel to raise them. They dumped so many into the rivers and creeks that the authorities had to make them stop for they were blocking up the streams, I was told.

This time they were not quite so optimistic as they had been earlier in the season. The prices ranged from $1 to $1.75 a barrel this time. They were hoping that this was only the usual price slump that comes at picking time, but they were gloomy. Many of them couldn't afford to store their potatoes.

About 39,000,000 bushels of potatoes will be shipped out of Maine this year, I was told — 90 per cent of them from Aroostook county. But 75 per cent of the crop was under liens. In Presque Isle, for instance, the value of the crop surrounding the town was placed at about $3,000,000.

"But before $1 is spent here," the city manager told me, "$250,000 of that money will have to be paid back to the federal government for loans. Half a million more will have to be paid in other mortgages on the crop — for fertilizer and so on — before the farmers can even begin to pay up their debts to the banks. And they'll have to sell at a reduced price to get this $75,000 immediately. Those that they store won't begin to bring in a good price before early spring. And by that time they'll be needing capital to start another crop. It will take two good years at least to put these farmers back on their feet." . . .

Labor, in Aroostook county, has always been seasonal and rather casual. In the summer there was a certain amount of work on the potato farms. In the fall there was potato picking — a brief period of intensive activity, with whole families turning out into the fields and earning some money. And in the winter there was work in the woods.

During the depression, of course, summer work on the farms dropped away off. Farmers getting under $1 a barrel for potatoes costing $1 a barrel to raise obviously are not in a position to hire much help. Now about the only labor on the farms is potato picking in the fall. On the potato farms, as in many other places, improved machinery is taking the place of hand labor. For instance, the potato digger, that will do the work of 15 men. Another instance presented to me involved the shipping of potatoes in the winter. Much of the potato crop has always been shipped out of the state in January, February, and March. In the old days, to keep them from freezing, fires had to be kept burning in the cars, with one man to every five cars to keep them going. Nowadays the cars are automatically heated, and a potato train goes out with nobody aboard except the train crew. From all I heard, I should say that the need for manual labor on the potato farms will continue to decrease from now on, and that, in the future, the prospects for thousands of common laborers in Aroostook county for earning any living from that source are practically nil.

The winter work in the woods has of course been almost entirely eliminated. Whether it will ever come back nobody knows, but up there they feel decidedly gloomy about it.

Most of the cutting in recent years has of course been pulpwood. And American-cut pulpwood — largely, I was told, because of different labor conditions — cannot compete with Canadian and Russian pulp. It costs more to produce pulp in this country, therefore, why should the paper industry, able to buy Canadian or Russian pulp cheaper, since there is no protective tariff, bother with American pulp? The result is that practically no pulpwood is cut in Maine any more.

"Long timber" cut in the Canadian woods used to have two markets — the building industry and shipbuilding. The latter is out, of course, because nobody builds wooden ships any more. And, even when the building industry comes back, there will undoubtedly be less and less tendency to use wood in the construction of houses.

The result of all this is, of course, that in Aroostook county, Maine, there are thousands of unskilled laborers, depending on seasonal work, whose prospects of "getting back to normal" look pretty unfavorable.

When I was in there, however, there was more work, for the time being, than there had been in months. Temporarily, the relief rolls were cut away down. One thing that helped was a big contract for lumber for the Civilian Conservation Corps camps, and this was keeping a mill in Van Buren working day and night. But they had no contracts to keep them going after that one was filled.

In Eastport the principal industry has always been fishing and the processing of fish. Sardines and smoked herring. This, too, is a seasonal proposition somewhat, and they complain bitterly of Norwegian competition. Eastport will always have its ups and downs, I suppose. This happens to have been a bad year. The sardine canneries had contracts — someone said the return of beer was responsible — but the fishing had been bad. The fish had started to run about a week before I was up there, but by that time they were all so large that they had to be cut in two to make sardines, and naturally the canning people couldn't expect to get top prices for them. On top of everything else, the day I arrived five whales had come into the Bay of Fundy, and, as the mayor of Eastport put it, "What they haven't eaten they've scared away." The fishing season, too, was almost over. The canneries were running, but only in "a half-hearted sort of way." And the city officials expected that by the middle of November the relief rolls would be up where they were last winter, the only difference being that the people possibly would be a little better clothed than they were a year ago.

Rockland and St. George presented the gloomiest picture. Down there the chief industry has always been the quarrying of limestone and granite. St. George economically is dependent largely on New York City! They cut paving blocks. When New York City is doing lots of paving, St. George is prosperous. When New York City isn't doing any paving — and it hasn't in recent years — St. George is in the dumps. Rockland is worse off. The demand for limestone has always depended of course on the building industry. There just hasn't been any building industry since the depression, and, in addition, the use of substitutes for plaster has grown tremendously. Result: the lime quarry that used to support several hundred families is not running, is in the hands of receivers, and offers no encouraging prospects.

Another of Rockland's larger industries was a shipyard — building wooden ships. There hasn't been any activity to speak of there since the war, except for a little repair work. I went out to visit the plant and found it practically in ruins. Nobody builds wooden ships any more, and, in the coastwise trade, they aren't using ships, but barges with tugboats! "I might just as well burn up this junk," said the proprietor of the shipyard, and it certainly looked as though he were right.

The third ranking industry in Rockland used to be fishing and the canning of fish — again, a seasonal industry. It hasn't amounted to anything at all for some years. The canneries are all closed. The whole business has gone to seed. In Rockland I talked to a couple of fishermen who had gone out at 4 A.M. and, at 5 P.M., had just finished up for the day. They had used eight gallons of gasoline, at 19 cents a gallon, and 100 pounds of bait at 2 cents a pound, and [got] 200 pounds of hake, which brought them 1 cent a pound. After they got all through, they had 20 cents apiece for their day's work! In St. George, incidentally, the selectmen had bought a lot of rubber boots, and the unemployed were encouraged to go out digging clams — at 35 cents a bushel. Unless a man was experienced, I was told, he probably wouldn't get more than two bushels a day.

The businessmen in Rockland were deeply discouraged. Some of them, for instance a furniture man were almost hysterical.

"Our Main street is a mile and a half long, and on it there are thirty vacant stores," the furniture man said. "Not 15 per cent of the merchants are within six months of being paid up on their rent. Most of them are a year or a year and a half behind." . . .

Of course, not all parts of Maine are in such bad shape. Governor Brann told me that in the factory towns — such as Lewiston and Auburn — things had picked up considerably. Portland, which is really

42

only a trading center although it is the largest city in the state, was getting along only fairly well.

Among the businessmen in Maine I encountered a great deal of bitterness toward the bankers. With the Insull[1] interests controlling most of her large banks, Maine suffered terribly from bank failures. Many, many more were closed by the Federal government last spring because their assets weren't liquid enough. And now the bankers up there are all scared to death — afraid to lend money. They feel that the Government's policy is inconsistent, that, after closing them up last spring because their assets weren't liquid enough, although they considered themselves perfectly solvent, they are apt to get into trouble again even though the Government is asking them to loosen up. As a result many of the banks that have opened up have nothing but money, and they are afraid to lend it. . . .

The cautious attitude of the bankers naturally makes it hard for the small businessmen to borrow. One merchant told me that, having decided to pay up his bills, he offered at the bank $8,000 worth of bonds as collateral and was able to borrow only $3,000.

In Eastport, of course, there was a good deal of enthusiasm over the possibility — however remote — of the Cooper dam project going through. This $65,000,000 project, they said, would solve the entire unemployment situation for the state, they thought, and provide, if owned and operated by the Government, cheap electricity for all of New England, bringing in, probably, many new industries. They estimated that between 6,000 and 7,000 men would be given work for three years building the dam, and that thousands more would get work indirectly. Lumber from northern Maine could be used, for instance, and cement from the factory down near Rockland. And so on.

In Eastport they seemed to be exceedingly hopeful over the prospects of the project going through. (They neglected to tell me that Canada had declined to go in on it, and that there was a good deal of opposition to our Government going into it alone, confining the project to American territory, but I found that out later.) They assured me that nearly everybody in the state was enthusiastic about it and working for it. Elsewhere in the state I found that the project was regarded somewhat as "lost hope" — they were all for it, but didn't think they'd get it. . . .

In Maine, as elsewhere, my contacts with people outside of politics all revealed a decline — and possibly a very rapid decline — of the old major political parties. The story is the same:

"We're for the President. And if what he's trying to do doesn't work, people are going to be surprised, that's all!"

They never talk about being Republicans or Democrats. That is, the people outside of politics — the average citizens. . . .

The attitude of most of the unemployed is, I should say, almost tragically patient. Considering the treatment I could easily imagine they were getting, they were pitiful. Now and then I'd remember some wistfulness. Seldom any bitterness.

There were some exceptions, of course. In Bangor and in Portland, where the approach of cold weather and the red tape and delays had goaded them into a state of fury, there were semi-riots over fuel. Communism had got into a colony of Swedes and Finns who used to work in the granite and lime quarries at Rockland and St. George. Fifteen of them had organized a march on the relief office in St. George a few weeks ago. . . .

The Yankees had not yet shown much interest in Communistic ideas when I was there. The propaganda apparently hadn't spread up into the French-Canadian population at all.

Some of the things I have written about relief administration in the state may sound pretty harsh. I feel that I should add that the officials who are doing the job, however badly, are doing it as well as they can, according to their ideas. Their ideas simply do not fit in with ours, that's all. I believe there is very little graft in relief administration in Maine. And practically no political favoritism.

Sometimes they must work under great difficulties, too. For instance, when I was in Allagash, I heard of a couple of families living on relief away up at the headwaters of the Allagash river. Enough food and other supplies to last them the entire winter had to be taken from St. Francis, at the end of the railroad, twenty-four miles by truck to the rapids in the river.

Then the recipients were to come 16 miles down the river in canoes to get it!

1. Samuel J. Insull, Chicago financier and utility magnate whose financial collapse prompted a congressional investigation and helped discredit utility companies during the New Deal.

To Harry L. Hopkins

REPORT   Field: New York City, October 2–12, 1933   Inclusive

The City of New York, with the assistance of the State and Federal governments, is struggling today with the biggest community relief job on earth — the biggest job of its kind ever undertaken by any city since the world began.

The job consists of trying to feed, clothe, shelter and provide medical care for 1,250,000 men, women, and children wholly dependent on public funds for their subsistence.

Many thousands more of her citizens — I have been told that the number might run to 1,000,000 — should be getting relief and undoubtedly would be were the money available. These are skating along on thin ice, barely existing, undernourished, in rags, constantly threatened with eviction from their homes, utterly wretched and hopeless, their nerves taut, their morale breaking down.

The great majority of these people — those who are on relief rolls and those who should be there — are in this plight through no fault of their own. They are entering the third winter of their distress. . . .

New York City was wholly unprepared to take on this job. In that, she differed in no way from the rest of the country. She did not see it coming — any more than did the country at large. It has swept up with the dizzy, terrifying force and speed of a tornado.

Two years ago, in 1931 the entire load carried by official and semi-official agencies consisted of less than half a million persons, aided at a cost of a little more than $30,000,000. During the first six months of this year those agencies cared for — or attempted to care for — 1,417,675 human beings, at a cost of $50,524,309. And the amount they spent was many millions of dollars below what it should have been!

The magnitude of the relief job in New York City and its complexities are breath-taking. One city block will contain almost 200 families on the relief rolls. Those 1,250,000 human beings represent a complete cross-section of the population, the best and the worst — the most intelligent, the most highly educated and the most helpless and most ignorant. Among them are represented more than 30 nationalities. Thousands of them cannot speak a word of English. And among them are business and professional men whose incomes five years ago ran into many thousands of dollars.

There they are, all thrown together into a vast pit of human misery, from which a city, dazed, still only half awake to the situation, is trying to extricate them.

How successful New York City and the State and Federal governments are going to be at handling this job can only be judged by what eventually happens to these people. I have a feeling that the job is being done better than any one would have a right to expect, under the circumstances. But it is far from being good enough. It could be twice as good as it is now and still be a long way from being good enough.

There are bright spots in the picture of course. Undoubtedly some of the best relief work in the entire country had been done in New York City — for instance, among white collar people and along lines of adult education. The spirit of the group who have planned and, against overwhelming odds, have tried to carry out those plans has been right, but the measure of their success has been pitifully low.

Towering above all others, the problem in New York City, I feel, has been, still is, and will continue to be lack of money. Ninety percent of all the complaints one hears about relief administration in New York City go right to that source.

Under the new triangular system — with the Federal, State and City governments each furnishing a third of the money — this problem may be reduced somewhat. Under that system, which depends, as I understand it, on what happens to the state's relief bond issue, they are aiming at about $10,000,000 a month. There is not in the whole City of New York, however, a single person fully aware of the situation who will say that $10,000,000 is enough. It ought to be $15,000,000, they will tell you — and even that would be barely adequate.

The sum of $10,000,000 a month, however, will make it possible to do a better job than can be done on $6,330,981, which was the amount available in August. And $10,000,000 a month, if they can be sure of it, ought to wipe out one of the worst blots on the relief picture in New York City.

I speak of "foodless holidays." That's what the relief workers call them. "Foodless holidays" are periods of a week or more at the end of the month when thousands of families are temporarily removed from the relief rolls because the administration has run out of money. "Foodless holidays" mean, too, that thousands of men and women on work relief projects — including the investigators themselves — can never be sure from one month to the next whether they are going to be paid for their work. You have the pretty spectacle of an investigator, representing the Government of the United States as well as the State and the City of New York, inexperienced in his job, chosen because of his desperate need rather than because of his qualifications, often — and with reason — emotionally unstable, going into the homes of his fellow unfortunates, worried himself, filled with despair! . . .

I'll wager there isn't a person in New York City who knows anything about relief and who would disagree with me when I say that the practice of appropriating relief funds late in the month, this uncertainty as to whether there will be enough money to carry through the month, and the failure to plan ahead and prevent "foodless holidays" have done more to break down the morale of everybody — the people on relief and those administering it — than any other factor.

Anyone who starts asking questions will hear plenty in New York City about bad administration of relief. And most of these complaints — and I believe they are justified — can be traced directly to lack of funds. They simply have not had enough money to provide the proper housing and equipment for the Home and Work Relief Bureaus and to pay a decent salary to that most important person in the whole relief machinery — the interviewer or the investigator who actually contacts the people who are on relief.

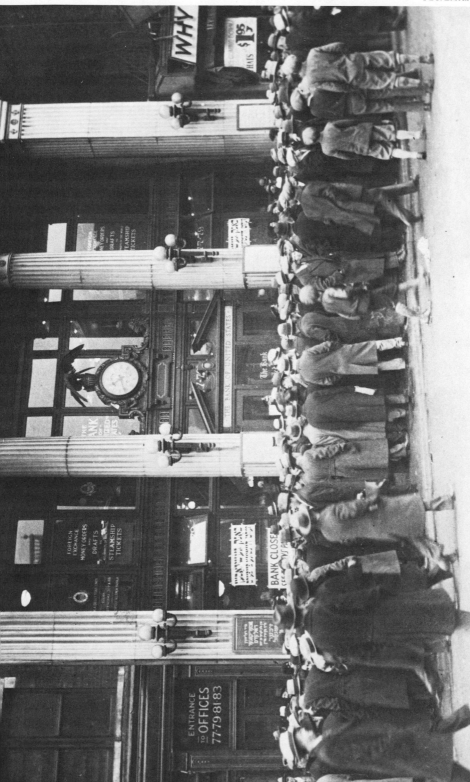

FDR closed the banks after his inauguration on March 4, 1933.

"Muffled figures, backs curved against the wind, selling apples on the street corners of New York. One's friends made jokes about 'unemployed apples.'"

The Volunteers of America staffed soup kitchens throughout the United States.

Jobs were scarce, and people devised ingenious ways to advertise their
willingness to work, as shown in this photograph from *The Detroit News*.

Breadlines seemed almost as universal as soup kitchens; this one was at Sixth Avenue and 42nd Street, New York City.

Makeshift shacks in which people lived were scathingly referred to as "Hoovervilles" — this one was on a vacant lot in New York City.

Let me try to tell you what happens when you apply for relief in New York City.

You go first to a schoolhouse in your neighborhood designated as a precinct Home Relief office. If you are the kind of person the government really should be interested in helping, you go there only as the last resort. You have used up all your resources and have strained the generosity of your relatives and your friends to the breaking point. Your credit is gone. You couldn't charge a nickel's worth at the grocery store. You owe several months' rent. The landlord has lost his patience and is threatening to throw you out. Maybe you've already gone through an eviction or two. I quote one of the case supervisors: "It does something to a family to go through a couple of evictions." The chances are you've been hungry for some time. And now there's no food in the house. You've simply got to do something.

If your children happen to attend the school where you must go to apply for relief, it just makes it that much tougher. It's true of course that you don't use the same entrance, that the chances are against your running into them or any of their playmates—but you don't know that.

There will be a policeman around—maybe several. A lot more would be there inside of three minutes if you caused any commotion. The Commissioner of Public Welfare feels that serious riots have been prevented by locating each Home Relief Station within a short distance of a police station. The policeman may be ever so courteous—and sometimes, I'm told, he isn't—but his presence there doesn't make you any happier. . . .

If you get by the policeman—and some people, I have been told, take one look at him, lose their courage, and turn around and go home—you have to tell some man at the door what you're there for. If you've got any pride, it hurts. And maybe he isn't any too patient. He's on relief himself, perhaps totally unqualified temperamentally for the job and worried about how he's going to make ends meet if he doesn't get his paycheck next week. . . .

You go into a room filled with people. Up at the front a line of makeshift desks, where interviewers are taking down the stories of relief applicants. You sit down on a bench in the back of the room. And there you wait, wondering if they're going to make you sell the radio, which wouldn't bring in enough to feed the family two days.

You're apt to wait a long time—and it doesn't improve your morale. Eventually you get your turn. Maybe the questions aren't so bad, but you hate answering them, just the same. If the person asking the questions were sympathetic and tactful, qualified by experience and temperament for the job, it might not be so bad. But the person asking those questions is just another victim of the depression like yourself. He's apt

47

to be without experience or training. Possibly he hates the job—and hates you because you're part of it. He, too, may be worried about the next week's pay check.

Finally you get out—and go home and wait. An investigator will call at your home—another "somebody on work relief," who got the job because he needed a job and not because he was qualified for it—and ask more questions.

The heads of the relief show in New York City and the trained supervisor, whom you never see unless there is some special problem in your case, intend that the investigator will get to your home quickly, with help. But:

"Crowded precinct offices, occasional hostile police guards, long waits for interviews, long delays in investigations tend to sap the courage and self-respect of clients," observes the TERA group in its most recent audit report.

And there you are.

Eventually, the idea is that you'll have some sort of work relief job. The Commissioner of Public Welfare, who is also head of the Work Relief Bureau, reports that there are now 75,000 heads of families on work relief jobs in New York City.

"Give me $9,000,000 or $10,000,000 a month for this relief job (instead of $6,500,000) and I'll take 50,000 more off the Home Relief rolls and put them to work," he says.

Well, if the present plans go through, and he gets his $10,000,000 a month, you may get a job of some sort. Here's hoping it will be one that you are reasonably well qualified to fill.

All this may sound exaggerated, but I don't believe it is. After all, I got my impressions largely from the people who are actually handling the relief job in New York City. . . .

Nobody pretends of course to believe that relief allotments in New York City are adequate. The most aggravating problem due to inadequacy was the rent situation. What groups in Philadelphia and in Pittsburgh were predicting a couple of months ago—that a time would come when landlords wouldn't take people on relief rolls—had actually come to pass in New York City. Because of lack of funds the system there was the same as in Philadelphia, Pittsburgh, and Washington: one month's rent for a cheaper apartment, AFTER a family has been evicted.

A communication on September 23 from the Coördinating Committee on Unemployment of the Welfare Council to the Board of Estimate and Apportionment of the City of New York contained the following statements:

"The highest monthly average relief given to a family in New York City was in the month of February and amounted to $39, while in August it had dropped to $23. This is barely enough to keep body and soul together. It leaves nothing for rent, with the inevitable result that evictions have increased at an alarming rate. The City Marshals reported that they had evicted 1,257 families in August as compared with 420 evictions in August a year ago. Of these, 675 *were on the rolls of the Home Relief Bureau.*

"With the low average of relief now being given there is little available for gas, electric light, or fuel, thus making the cooking of meals impossible for many families." . . .

I myself visited one woman with two small children and found her trying to heat their milk by burning newspapers under the pan! The gas was turned off, and, trying to use a borrowed electric grill, she had blown out all the electric light fuses in the place. The landlord had refused to have them replaced.

Quoting again from the Coordinating Committee's letter to the Board of Estimate:

"There is no margin for clothing or medical service in the present relief grants to most families, and, while the present law continues, no cash for carfare, medical supplies, and the other small, but indispensable, household necessities. The inadequacy of the present food allowance under Home Relief is emphasized by the fact that prices have risen markedly, so that the same quantity of food that could have been purchased last March for 96 cents nows costs $1.10, with a further rise in prices anticipated. The present plight of destitute families is bad enough in all conscience, but the unemployed man without a family receives almost no relief, and relatively few unemployed women without families are being assisted at the present time."

I was unable to get much dope on what was happening to these people — especially the women. Mary Simkhovitch, at Greenwich House,[1] seemed to know more about them — and to be more interested in them — than any one else.

"Single women? Why, they're just discards," she said. "I'll tell you how they live! Huddled together in small apartments, three or four of them living on the earnings of one, who may have a job. Half a dozen of them, sometimes, in one room. Sharing with each other. Just managing to keep alive.

"They've left the Y.W.C.A.'s and the settlement houses. They can't afford even to live in those places any more."

With what I've written so far I think people in the relief administration in New York City and the social workers generally would agree. Some of them are very bitter about it, their bitterness expressing itself in a variety of ways. Mary Simkhovitch, for instance, marched in a parade of the Unemployed Councils and other organizations of the sort to the City Hall one day while I was in New York. Some of the settlement houses have opened their doors to organizers of the more moderate un-

49

employed protest groups. Not so very long ago the wife of a professor at Columbia university was arrested for starting a riot in a Home Relief office. Said Frank Taylor, Commissioner of Public Welfare, after telling me that he had purposely kept to the precinct system — 89 small Home Relief offices, one in each precinct — because it made "mass action" more difficult.

"Sometimes I think maybe we've done this job too well — that it might be better if we had a few disturbances." . . .

I am certainly not so naive as to believe there is no political interference in the New York City relief picture. Outsiders, such as newspapermen, are of the opinion that Tammany is running the show completely. The World-Telegram a few weeks ago ran a series, making all sorts of charges and citing cases in which, they contended, clients were receiving relief when they weren't entitled to it. . . .

The World-Telegram's series described conditions arising from inadequacy much as I have in this report — almost word for word as they are described by the people who are doing the relief job. Their more dramatic charges, however, dealt with Tammany interference in the relief picture. . . .

I spent an afternoon visiting families with one of the investigators who had been working on this particular investigation. He told me that out of 235 families checked, including those mentioned by the World-Telegram, they had found five that were getting relief without justification. He said there were evidences, however, that a good many of the families in the group were there because of influence of one sort or another, not always Tammany.

I had a long talk with the man who wrote the series. He is considered one of the best reporters in New York, and I personally have a good deal of confidence in his sincerity, although I do think he might have gone wrong in this matter to some extent through ignorance and lack of understanding of the problems of administering relief.

He charged Commissioner Taylor with having placed Tammany men in key positions, where they could control the distribution of work relief jobs. The brother of a Tammany leader, for instance, is in charge of personnel for both the Home and Work Relief Bureaus. The inference is quite obvious. Commissioner Taylor's reply to that, when I asked him about it, was that the man in question also happened to have come from Catholic Charities and is an experienced social worker. He also said that all he had to do with personnel was the handling of records. Still — it WOULD seem, I should think, a rather unfortunate choice, to put the brother of a Tammany leader in such a job.

The World-Telegram man was vehement in his criticism of Mary Gibbons, head of the Home Relief Bureau, and of Taylor himself. He felt that Miss Gibbons, with the Cardinal [Patrick J. Hayes] behind her, could have kept politics out of the picture, but that she had failed to do so. . . .

It is true that other social workers, both in the picture and outside, praised both Taylor and Miss Gibbons very highly. They think he is away above the average political appointee in the job he has. Miss Gibbons, they feel, "may have to play a little politics now and then, but not where it really matters." . . .

There is no question in my mind that we have done and are doing terrible things to people on relief in New York City. For instance, we have let families be evicted three times in six months! We have starved them, failed to provide them with clothing or medical care, and have browbeaten them on top of all that.

Just how much more of it they can take nobody knows. There are the usual protest groups, running from the moderate crowds at the settlement houses — groups which have the sympathy, interest, and counsel of pepole like Mary Simkhovitch and Norman Thomas[2] — to the out-and-out Communists. Their demands are pretty much the same as those of the protest groups in places like Pittsburgh and Philadelphia — cash instead of food orders, clothing, medical care, more consideration at the hands of interviewers and case workers, and, above all, something more nearly approaching adequacy. . . .

1. A New York City settlement house.
2. Head of the Socialist party.

To Harry L. Hopkins

Enroute to Minneapolis, October 24th, 1933

Dear Mr. Hopkins:

I hate like the dickens to add another letter to the stack, but what I have to say cannot very well be said over the telephone when I call you from Chicago tomorrow.

Louis Howe[1] will probably see you tomorrow and will ask your permission for me to do some special work for him while I am in the Middlewest. I am putting the matter up to you myself, however, because I feel that I am directly responsible to you, as my boss, and to no one else. I shall not act in this matter until I hear from you. I explained to Colonel Howe my attitude, and he knows I am writing to you.

As he will undoubtedly tell you, he is interested in finding out what sort of treatment people are getting from government representatives who deal with them directly when they ask for help. This includes representatives of NRA, the Farm Credit Administration, Home Loan Board, and so on. He feels that it is a matter of great importance, and I certainly agree with him.

I am perfectly willing to give Colonel Howe anything I may hear on this subject — provided my doing so meets with your approval and provided I am NOT placed in the position of spying on other federal employees, in our department or in any other department. As I go about, I shall probably hear a good deal on the subject. I could very easily pass on to Colonel Howe on that matter the same information I would give you on the relief show — a general picture, without citing specific cases or individuals.

Henry Morgenthau[2] also asked me to pass on to him anything I might hear about the workings of his department out there. He explained that the Federal Emergency Relief Administration and his department have their offices together in many localities. He has also placed at my disposal a car to use while I am in that part of the country. The car belongs to his department, but he said that, as a federal employee, I was entitled to use it.

I am also of course perfectly willing to give Mr. Morgenthau anything I hear that might help him, but feel that in his case the proper procedure would be for you to turn over to him whatever you think may be useful to him from the material I send you.

Mr. Howe told me that whatever I sent him would be treated as confidential, but he understands, of course, that you must know about it. If you do approve, will you please wire me at the Leamington Hotel, Minneapolis, before Saturday morning?

I am heading first to Minneapolis because I know a lot of people there who will undoubtedly be able to give me the dope generally in that part of the country. I'm planning to leave Saturday morning for Nebraska, work my way from there up through the Dakotas and back into Minnesota, then down to Iowa, spending about a week in each state and perhaps a little more time in Minnesota because of the two larger cities there.

I am sorry to bother you with all this, but I feel sure you will understand how I feel about it.

1. Political mentor and secretary to Franklin D. Roosevelt.
2. Governor of the Farm Credit Administration.

To Harry L. Hopkins

TELEGRAM   Minneapolis   1933 Oct. 27   AM 7:04

Prolonged conversations today with head Minnesota Farm Bureau Federation and with city editors of two largest newspapers in northwest, also saw Leo Crowley Farm Credit Administration. [Governor]

Floyd [Olson] could not make it today but hope to get to him late tomorrow afternoon. Heard little on relief except it is and has got to continue to be a big job. In parts of Dakota and Minnesota no complaints on farm strike. Told little likelihood of violent disturbance, now chiefly work of professional agitators with opposition party certainly looking on with satisfaction if not secretly participating. Undoubtedly growing restlessness and bitterness among farmers. Personal prestige of big boss[1] at stake. Still feel generally he is sincere and acting in good faith but listening too much to theorists. Administration has lost good deal of ground. Feel Department of Agriculture rejected their suggestions and has not played quite fair. Appointment of old line bankers to pass on farm loans bitterly assailed. Good deal of suspicion about them. Farmers feel they haven't the right slant. Told farmers feel interest rate on government loans too high. They also feel too much needless red tape involved and that they should not be made to pay for appraisals. Favorite stunt in meetings is for agitator to shout quote how many of you men have gone out and borrowed ten dollars to pay for appraisal so you can apply for government loans unquote. Lots of hands go up. Agitator then asks quote how many of you have received any loans unquote. No hands go up. Demanding minimum prices on their products they say because otherwise processors will subtract process tax from them. Say corn loan announced today will actually mean only couple of cents to farmer instead of fifty cents. Say government purchase of hogs little actual help to farmer. Came too late and there was too much red tape. Was told some farmers managed with difficulty to pay freight on their hogs to processing points only to have them rejected. Charge huge slice of purchase price was allowed to go to commission men. Anti-NRA feeling probably diminished somewhat by release of towns up to twenty five hundred from code rule, but NRA by no means popular. You undoubtedly know Floyd quit as NRA head in Minnesota. Feeling is he was quote getting out from under unquote planning. To see Floyd, dairy and live stock men and relief crowd tomorrow and Saturday. Leaving for Fargo Sunday morning.

1. A reference to President Roosevelt.

To Harry L. Hopkins

Minneapolis, Minnesota, October 28, 1933

Dear Mr. Hopkins:

. . .Floyd Olson was very bitter about [C.T.] Jaffray's[1] appointment [to the RFC]. Jaffray has for years been a sort of overlord among the financial interests that have pretty much run the Northwest. He is exceedingly unpopular among the farmers. He undoubtedly is a competent banker, and undoubtedly a competent banker is needed for the job, but — if you heard Floyd Olson's remarks — I think you would agree with me that it was not a particularly fortunate appointment at this time.

I get nothing but gloom up here. Olson was the gloomiest of the lot. Generally, what they tell me is this:

The farmers, even the majority of those involved in the strike, still believe in the sincerity and good faith of the President. That is all that is keeping the situation from getting a lot tougher.

They feel, however, that he is getting a lot of silly advice from "theorists." They have a violent hatred of the so-called "brains trust."

Aside from the President himself, the Administration is "in wrong." That doesn't apply to the Relief Administration, but there the situation is the same as it seems to be generally. People generally don't know much about the Relief Administration, aren't interested, and idly remark: "Oh, that's allright. This fellow Hopkins seems to be doing a good job."

The feeling seems to be that the Public Works crowd, NRA, the Department of Agriculture, A.A.A.,[2] and so on — "are trying to do a lot of funny things, but aren't getting anywhere."

Governor Olson gives the President 30 days more. If there isn't a change within that period, the President's prestige will have crumbled, too, he predicts.

"And where do we go from there?" I asked.

He shook his head and replied: "Darned if I know."

He is hoping that the governors at their conference in Iowa next week may get together and draw up some concrete, workable plan to present to the President, but he's skeptical. He said he had thought of writing to the President himself, and that he may do so after the governors' conference.

If I tried to tell you all the complaints and theories and "isms" I've heard in my talks with people these last two days — I tried to get to people I felt would be "in the know" and would represent various agricultural groups — it would take all night. Here's one that's interesting, though:

Governor Olson talked earnestly and at length yesterday about a plan whereby all farmers and all purchasers of raw farm products would be licensed. Instead of trying to regulate the amount a farmer could *produce*, the government would regulate the amount he could *sell*, would fix a price, and, through licensing, would be in a position to penalize both farmers and their customers who did any "bootlegging."

This afternoon I found myself listening to the same line of talk from [William S.] Moscrip — a Republican dairy farmer.[3]

And I was told last night that this same plan has been advocated for some time by James Ford Bell, head of the Washburn-Crosby milling outfit and one of the outstanding capitalists of the Northwest![1]

You'll have to admit that's unanimity!

About our own show, as I said before, I haven't heard much. Had a talk yesterday with Frank Rarig, state administrator, who didn't seem to be particularly worried about how things are going. The Legislature, in this state, has apparently been fairly generous. . . .

And now, after all this grief, I think you should hear the latest farmer joke. Mr. Moscrip,[3] who told it to me this afternoon, said he had told it at a public dinner, in the presence of his wife, so I guess it's allright to pass it on to you.

It concerns a federal appraiser who went out to appraise some livestock. One by one, the farmer led out his cows and his horses and his porkers. Everything went along allright until the farmer came out leading a goat.

The appraiser hadn't any experience appraising goats. He called up Washington and asked for help.

"Well, what sort of looking animal is it?" inquired the official on the other end of the wire.

"Why, it's got a long, thin face, white whiskers, and a sad expression in its eyes," the appraiser said. "And it's all bare behind."

"Oh, hell," said the voice in Washington. "Why, you damned fool, you don't want to appraise him. That's the farmer himself!" . . .

1. Chairman of the board of the First National Bank of Minneapolis.
2. Agricultural Adjustment Administration.
3. Moscrip was also chairman of the board of the Regional Agricultural Credit Corporation and an official of the Twin Cities Milk Producers' Association.

To Harry L. Hopkins

Dickinson, N.D., October 30, 1933

Dear Mr. Hopkins:

I just wound up my first day's work in North Dakota. I must say there was nothing particularly joyous about it.

This afternoon, with a couple of Morton County Commissioners, from Mandan, I drove over a road so full of ruts that you couldn't tell it from ploughed fields up to a shabby little country church, standing bleakly alone in the center of a vast tawny prairie land.

Grouped about the entrance to the church were a dozen or more men in shabby denim, shivering in the biting wind that swept across the plain.

Farmers, these, "hailed out" last summer, their crops destroyed by two hail storms that came within three weeks of each other in June and July, now applying for relief.

Most of them a few years ago were considered well-to-do. They have land — lots of land. Most of them have 640 acres or so. You think of a farmer with 640 acres of land as being rich. These fellows are "land poor." A 640-acre farm at $10 an acre — which is about what land is worth hereabouts these days — means only $6,400 worth of land. Most of them have a lot of stock, 30 or 40 head of cattle, 12 or 16 horses, some sheep and hogs. Their stock, thin and rangy, is trying to find a few mouthsful of food on land so bare that the winds pick up the top soil and blow it about like sand. Their cows have gone dry for lack of food. Their hens are not laying. Much of their livestock will die this winter. And their livestock and their land are in most cases mortgaged up to the very limit. They are all away behind on their taxes, of course. Some of them five years!

After a succession of poor crops — this whole area apparently is in process of drying up and becoming a desert — these fellows had a good one last year. But wheat in North Dakota last year brought about 30 cents a bushel. It costs 77 cents a bushel to raise it.

This year they had no crop at all. I sat in with an investigator who was taking their stories. Again and again on the applications appeared the statement: "Hailed out. No crop at all." One man had sown — I believe, at that, they say "sowed" when they refer to planting of crops — 140 acres of wheat, 25 acres of oats, 20 acres of rye, 30 acres of corn, and 20 acres of barley. All he harvested was a little corn. He was lucky, at that. I drove past cornfields today that had never grown up at all. There lay the immature stalks on the ground as the hail had beaten them down — half-starved cattle rooting around among them. From 800 acres of land one old German had harvested this year 150 bushels of wheat and seven bushels of rye.

Of the men I saw this afternoon none had any income except a little here and there from cream checks. And this will soon be stopped, for their cows are going dry for lack of food.

For themselves and their families they need everything. Especially clothing. "How about clothes?" the investigator asked one of them. He shrugged. "Everything I own I have on my back," he said. He then explained that, having no underwear, he was wearing two pairs of overalls, and two, very ragged, denim jackets. His shoes were so far gone that I wondered how he kept them on his feet. With one or two exceptions none of the men hanging about the church had overcoats. Most of them were in denim — faded, shabby denim. Cotton denim doesn't keep out the wind very well. It was cold enough today so that I, in a woolen dress and warm coat, was by no means too warm when I stood out in the wind. When we came out to get into the car, we found it full of farmers, with all the windows closed. They apologized and said they had crawled in there to keep warm. . . . The women and children are even worse off than the men. Where there has been any money at all, it has gone for shoes for the children and work clothes for the men. The women can stay inside and keep warm, and the children can stay home from school.

I am quite sure that anything that could be done in the way of getting clothing out to these people IMMEDIATELY — shoes, overshoes, warm underwear, overcoats — would do quite a bit toward clearing up unrest among North Dakota farmers!

The plight of the livestock is pitiable. All these people have got to keep their stock alive this winter is roughage — and darned little of that. They've even harvested Russian thistle to feed to their horses and cattle. Russian thistle, for your information, is a thistle plant with shallow roots that dries up in the fall and is blown across the prairies like rolls of barbed wire. The effect on the digestive apparatus of an animal, if it were fed the dried plant, would be, I should imagine, much the same as though it had eaten barbed wire! However — "We tried to cut it while it was still green," one of the farmers said.

There is a good deal of complaint about the inflexibility of our rules governing the granting of livestock relief. The rules were made applicable, I was told, to farms in Wisconsin, for instance, smaller farms, with less stock. They point out to me here that they can't find a market for their stock — that, to conform to our rules for providing food for the stock, they will have to kill most of it. Or they'll cheat on us — pretend to sell it, but not actually do so. If they get rid of most of their stock, they say, they'll probably be on relief next winter, too, since they need the stock in normal times to get a living. It doesn't take much, they say, to keep this stock alive. One man said he lost seven milch cows last winter, and that $15 worth of feed would have kept them alive. I'm going to find out more about this Friday when, in Bismarck, I'm to see a man named Wilson, who, they tell me, knows all about it.

In the county I visited this afternoon the Federal Relief Administration, through the North Dakota State Relief Committee, is doing a 100 percent job. The county's financial resources are exhausted, and nobody will take their tax warrants. The job, as I wired you tonight, is shamefully inadequate.

I don't know exactly what is wrong. I'm going to try to find out when I return to Bismarck Friday. But what is actually happening, I was told, is this:

In the country there are now 1,000 families — a third of the population — on relief. Mostly farmers. To handle the job the County Commissioners are given $6,000 a month. That means $6 per family. And most of the families are huge — eight or ten children. The set-up in this county is different from that in most other counties in the state. The relief here is being handled by the County Commissioners. Bismarck apparently suspects them of using relief for political purposes. They are constantly after the commissioners, I was told, to cut down the load. Whether there's any politics in the show in that county I don't know. But this I do know—those people at that church applying for relief today certainly looked as though they needed relief.

The commissioners told me they had tried to work out a plan whereby the men could work on county roads this fall for more adequate relief—in order that they might get enough to buy clothing and fuel now, when they need it. To do this, the commissioners said, the families should be getting at least $15 a month for the next three months. That doesn't sound like much to me. They went ahead, on the advice of the state highway department, they said, and put the men to work. But today the State Relief committee told them to cease all road work and that they would get $6,000 a month for relief and no more. The commissioners say that, if they could have $15,000 a month these next three months—until the people get clothed and stocked with fuel—they might be able to get along, by half-starving them, on $6,000 a month the rest of the winter! . . . Well, anyway, it's our money that is being spent, and we're getting the blame. I'll try to get the other side of the story in Bismarck on Friday. But on the face of it, it looks as though somebody was responsible for a pretty rotten job.

I was told in Bismarck that in the county I visited this afternoon I would find a good deal of unrest—"farm holiday" spirit. I can't say that I did. They seemed almost too patient to me. I went to see one farmer who was supposed to be a chronic kicker. I found him doing the family washing! His wife died five years ago and left him with eight children, the eldest now 14. Somehow he has kept that family together—doing the washing and cooking himself, besides farming! With an expression of utter hopelessness on his face he was puttering around a dilapidated old washing machine. The rolls on the wringer were entirely worn away—right down to the iron bars. He said he had done some kicking. He wanted his boy (14) to substitute for him on road work. The boy was no good at housework, he explained, and, if he went out to work on the roads himself things went to pieces at home!

In Bismarck this morning I had a long talk with the chief justice of the North Dakota Supreme Court, who is also chairman of the state relief committee. He and the commissioners with whom I spent the afternoon, while not quite so bitter or so gloomy as Floyd Olson and some of the farm people in the Twin Cities, were not any too cheerful.

Chief Justice [Adolph Marcus] Christianson told me that "in most counties" no farm loans had been granted at all—that he had heard of cases where applications made last May had still received no action. He blamed it on red tape and inadequate personnel. I am trying to find out just what a farmer has to go through to get a federal loan, but didn't get much help from him. He said most of the applications had to be made in writing and sent to St. Paul, which would of course slow things up. The whole machinery is so complicated! I heard of organizations today that I didn't know existed. . . .

In the county I visited this afternoon farmers had received federal loans, but the impression was that the loans were granted to pay back the Twin City bankers. . . . When I pointed out that, even though the money did go to the banks, it probably saved their farms for them, someone remarked, "Well, the farms aren't worth saving now."

They are not at all impressed with Mr. [Henry A.] Wallace's[1] acreage reduction plan. This, they say is why:

Twenty-five years ago they used to get 21 bushels to the acre of wheat in this territory. If they get 10 bushels to the acre nowadays, it's a bumper crop. They insist that what they need is not reduction in production, but a decent price for what they do produce. Wheat was selling in North Dakota for 70 cents a bushel today. They say it costs 77 cents a bushel to raise it.

"In order to make a living," one farmer told me, "we've got to get 7 cents a pound for hogs, 9 cents a pound for beef, and $1 a bushel for wheat." . . .

1. Secretary of agriculture.

To Eleanor Roosevelt[1]

Bottineau, North Dakota, October 31, 1933

A pretty dreadful day. Not from the standpoint of weather. That has been perfect, though cold — deep blue, cloudless sky and sunlight that brings out all the gold and blues and reds and orchid shades in the prairie landscape. These plains are beautiful. But, oh, the terrible, crushing drabness of life here. And the suffering, for both people and animals. * * * I was talking this afternoon with a farmer, a Frenchman of the European type, not the French-Canadian type, a thrifty fellow who, in spite of four bad crop years, bank failures, and all, has managed to come through in fairly good shape. His farm looked neat and prosperous. He had a comfortable and attractive house. His barns were painted — if they ever started painting up here, there would be enough business to keep the paint factories running for years! Most of the farm buildings haven't been painted in God only knows how long! His stock — and even his dogs and cats — looked well fed. * * * "These people around here," he said, "don't know how to live, that's their trouble." They certainly do not know how to live. I wish you could see this hotel. There isn't — there can't be — any reason for a hotel to be so hopelessly uninviting as this one is. The odor alone is enough to knock you down. Stale soapsuds, old wet rags, some sort of disinfectant. Oh, gosh! Well, I'm getting out at 7 o'clock tomorrow morning. If I had to live here, I think I'd just quietly call it a day and commit suicide. * * * The people up here — farmers, people on relief, and those administering relief — are in a daze. A sort of nameless dread hangs over the place. Last Summer for the second year the grasshoppers — great big fellows, two or three inches long — came in clouds and ate up their crops. The farmers now say the soil is all full of grasshopper eggs. They feel utterly hopeless. The destitution in this county is said to be the worst in the state. What makes it so serious is the climate up here, only 12 miles from the Canadian border. One could survive with scant clothing and little bedding through a relatively mild Winter in Kentucky. But up here, dear lady, they have Winters! It was down to zero today. We drove up into the Turtle Mountains, which in the East might be called hills and in the Far West wouldn't be called anything at all — and had to turn back or run the risk of getting stuck in roads blocked with ice and snow. Down on the plains there wasn't any snow, but a bitter wind out of the Northwest. Last Winter the temperature went down to 40 degrees below zero and stayed there ten days, while a 60-mile wind howled across the plains. And entering that kind of a Winter we have between 4,000 and 5,000 human beings — men and women and children — without clothing or bedding, getting just enough food to keep them from starving. No fuel. Living in houses that a prosperous farmer wouldn't put his cattle in. There are probably many more than 4,000 or 5,000. They now have 850 families on relief, and applications are coming in at the rate of 15 or 20 a day. * * * I visited this afternoon one of the "better"homes of people on the relief rolls. Out on the wind-swept prairie it stood — what had once been a house. No repairs have been made in years. The kitchen floor was all patched up with pieces of tin — a wash boiler cover, ten can lids, some old automobile license plates. You could see daylight through the crack under the door. Great patches of plaster had fallen from the walls. Newspapers had been stuffed in the cracks about the windows. And in that house two small boys, one about Buzzie's[2] age, were running about without a stitch on save some ragged overalls. No shoes or stockings. Their feet were purple with cold. Their mother — bare-legged, too, although she had some ragged sneakers on her feet — is going to have another baby in January. And in that house! I simply couldn't bear it when she timidly sought from the relief investigator who was with me some assurance that the doctor would come out to see her through her confinement. The investigator asked her about her bed-

60

ding. She hesitated for a moment and then led us upstairs. One bed. A filthy, ragged mattress. Some dirty pillows. She said the last of her sheets and pillowcases gave out two years ago. On the bed two worn and dirty outing flannel blankets, just rags. That was all. "Do you and your husband and the children all sleep together?" the investigator asked. "We have to," she replied simply, "to keep warm." This, dear lady, is the stuff that farm strikes and agrarian revolutions are made of. Communist agitators are in here now, working among these people, I was told. What to do about it—I don't know. Certainly the amount of money the Government is putting in here now isn't taking care of it. "We just hardly know where to begin," the chairman of the relief committee told me. We started talking about bedding, figuring up what it would cost to get materials for making quilts to go round. I had an idea that perhaps someone like your friend Jimmy Gerard[3] would like to spend a little money up here. He figured up that, to meet the needs of the families now on relief, between 1,000 and 1,200 quilts and 2,000 blankets would be needed! To buy them retail would cost well up into thousands of dollars! One way would be for the Government to get them cheaply, on contract. But when you consider the fact that dozens of other counties in this state and elsewhere in the area are almost as badly off, well, it runs into money, doesn't it? * * * What we can do I'll be darned if I know. The need is so urgent. They should have these things right away. Well, all I can do is to impress the need upon the mind of Mr. Hopkins. That I am earnestly trying to do. * * * One thing that burns me up is a statement made to me today that the Red Cross is holding here, under lock and key, a quantity of sweaters, underwear, and blankets—for "an emergency." Good God, I wonder what constitutes an emergency in the eyes of the old ladies who run the Red Cross! Well, I'm meeting the head of the Red Cross committee tonight—along with the county commissioners and the members of the county relief committee. I'm going to try to find out.

1. The excerpts of this letter to Eleanor Roosevelt were done by Hickok.
2. Curtis Dall, Mrs. Roosevelt's grandson, nicknamed Buzzie.
3. James W. Gerard, a New York political figure and ambassador to Germany prior to World War I, defeated Roosevelt for the Democratic nomination for U.S. Senator in 1914.

To Harry L. Hopkins

Minot, North Dakota, November 1, 1933

I visited today another North Dakota county—Williams county—in which the Federal Relief Administration, through the North Dakota Relief Committee, is supposed to be doing a 100-per cent relief job.

Again, as in Morton county on Monday, I found indications of inadequacy and a most urgent need for clothing.

I wish I could find words adequately to express to you the immediate need for clothing in this area. All I can say is that these people have GOT to have clothing — RIGHT AWAY. It may be Indian Summer in Washington, but it's Winter up here. They've had their first snow. Snow is forecast for tomorrow. It's COLD.

Into the relief office in Williston, county seat of Williams county, came today a little middle-aged farmer — skin like leather, heavily calloused, grimy hands — incongruously attired in a worn light flannel suit of collegiate cut, flashy blue sweater, also worn, belted tan topcoat, and cap to match. These clothes, he explained, belonged to his eldest son.

"They're all we've got now," he said. "We take turns wearing 'em."

It was the first time he had asked for relief, he said, and he thought he could pull through the winter so far as food for his family and his livestock went, even though the grasshoppers did eat up most of his crop last summer.

But they needed clothes — badly and right away. They hadn't been able to buy any for three years. Even last winter his children had been unable to go to school for lack of clothing.

There were nine in his family — he had seven children.

They needed AT ONCE a suit of underwear apiece, overshoes, and stockings all around. He wasn't even mentioning shoes. Said they could get along if they had overshoes and socks to wear inside.

The secretary of the relief committee and I figured out what it would cost, at local retail prices, to provide these articles. It came to $40.50. Nine suits of underwear at $2 each, $18; nine pairs of overshoes at $2 each, $18; nine pairs of socks at 50 cents a pair, $4.50. Total, $40.50.

And that did not include things like jackets and sweaters.

"This is just a typical case," said the secretary of the relief committee. There was certainly nothing framed about it. The secretary did not know I was in town until I showed up in his office. And the man was just one of the "customers," who happened to wander in while I was there.

"What I'd like to know," the secretary of the relief committee added, "is where we're going to get the money to buy these things.

"In September we spent $8,000 on relief in this county. In October, Bismarck cut us down to $6,000. What we're going to get in November I don't know.

"It's all federal money. All this county has got is tax warrants, and the merchants won't take them.

"We've got 450 families on relief in this county now, and the number is increasing every day at the rate of about seven. Some days we have as high as 15 new cases. Six thousand dollars a month isn't anywhere nearly enough to feed them decently and buy fuel—let alone providing clothing."

So much for inadequacy. They told me in Bismarck Monday there were five counties in the state getting 100 percent federal relief. At this rate—$6,000 each for the two counties among the five I have visited so far—they're putting out $30,000 a month. Nobody up here seems to know what we're putting into the state per month. I mean to find out when I get back to Bismarck.

I get howls all the time about the administration of our livestock relief. They all insist that the limit on the amount of livestock a farmer can own and get relief is too low. That may or may not be true, but here's one that, on the face of it, is wrong:

It seems that in order to get livestock relief a farmer must first prove that he cannot get a feed loan. That means that he must apply to the Farm Credit outfit in St. Paul for a loan, pay a $10 appraisal fee, and get turned down before he is eligible for our relief! I quote a paragraph from a letter from the county agricultural agent in Williston, to whom applications for livestock relief are made, to a prospective client:

"You will see from this letter that there is considerable red tape involved in this whole deal, and it is very likely it would be a month before anything could be arranged, and then for a very limited amount of stock."

On the face of it, there is something wrong when letters like that are going out to people who are trying to get help from us.

I don't think the trouble was with the county agent, either. He showed me his instructions—which stated that a man must be able to show that he was unable to get help from any other source. . . .

All Summer I've been hearing, wherever I've gone, that there was going to be an urgent need for clothing this winter. As I write, I wonder, for instance, if any clothing has been distributed yet up in Northern Maine. It seems to have been a case of the relief people knowing all Summer that clothing was going to be needed this winter—but doing nothing about it. And now Winter is upon us. Up here in North Dakota, it has arrived. They must have clothing at once—NOW. . . .

The situation in North Dakota shapes up something like this:

A majority of the farmers—livestock breeders as well as wheat farmers—are actually bankrupt. I was told in Williston today that 95 percent of the farmers around there were bankrupt.

Those whose wheat crops were ruined by drouth or grasshoppers or hail—and there are a lot of them—are destitute.

Those who had a crop and the livestock men are not getting enough for their products to carry them through the winter.

Take the cattlemen. I enclose a check and a bill of sale I picked up to-day in Ray, about 100 miles West of here. If they don't tell a story, I don't know what would. Four cows, weighing a total of 4,000 pounds and raised at a minimum cost of $20 apiece, were sold on the Chicago market and netted the owner exactly $3.61! You never could convince that fellow that the price of farm products has gone up.

I now go through my notes.

The judge in Williston last night told me about a man who came into court to get an extension on a debt of some $1,800.

"He had thought that he might raise some of it by selling some of his stock," the judge said. "So he shipped 29 head of cattle to the St. Paul market. His net proceeds amounted to about $200."

In the closed bank at Ray today I spent an hour with two cattlemen, one of whom happens to be secretary of the Farmers' Loan Association.

One of them had sold to the other 30 head of cattle for $310. The buyer shipped 27 of them to the market, and, after deductions for freight and commissions, received a check for $178.54. I saw the entry in his books.

"They weren't prime," he said, "but good stuff. Better than canning grade. And at that I did fairly well. Some cattlemen around here have netted as low as 35 cents per animal!

"We figure everybody'd be better off if the government bought them up at a low price and slaughtered them here and distributed them to the starving farmers."

Both told me the cattle market right now is "worse than it has ever been before." They say prices were twice as high a year ago.

"A carload that you get $300 for now would have brought from $600 to $900 a year ago," one of them said.

Some of the stock, they admitted, was inferior, owing to short feeding. But they insisted that even the best beef is bringing this year half as much as it brought a year ago.

The wheat farmers' story is about the same, perhaps not quite so bad. Wheat in North Dakota today was selling for somewhere around 65 cents a bushel. They say it costs 77 cents a bushel to produce it. As much as they can, they're holding their wheat back, hoping to get better price this year than last, when it sold for as low as 25 cents a bushel, they admit, but it is still, they insist, selling below production cost. The judge in Williston said there are 5,500,000 bushels of wheat stored in North Dakota elevators today awaiting a better price.

Speaking of the crop reduction program, one of the farmers said:

"Hell, wheat production in North Dakota has been cut one third in the last three years anyway. We haven't been able to buy seed."

One man told me that most of his neighbors have moved away in the last five years. Just given up and pulled out. Incidentally, in St. Paul the other day I heard of an employee of the state highway department who had seen along the roads in Western Minnesota in a couple of days seven covered wagons. Farmers, he said, who had lost their farms, and were just roaming about the country, like gypsies.

The farm loan situation, they tell me, is beginning to look a little better since Henry Morgenthau's recent visit to St. Paul. Up until then, it was pretty bad.

The secretary of the Farmers' Loan Association in Williston today received his first loan check since the organization was set up, June 20! He has about 450 applications in, he said.

I leave it to you to imagine how a farmer would feel when he had applied for a loan back in June and by the First of November still didn't know whether he was going to get it or not! Especially when the money was available all the time.

Blame for the delay would seem to belong down in the Twin Cities. If you read my letter sent off last Saturday night, you can get a sort of idea of what might have happened! A farmer who is chairman of the Farmers' Loan Association in Williston told me he had to go all the way down to St. Paul, at his own expense, last summer to get appraisers sent up.

And when they arrived, they were, many of them, men who didn't understand the situation in North Dakota at all.

"They didn't understand and didn't try to understand," I was told. "Their attitude was apt to be wholly unsympathetic — the attitude of the money crowd down in the Twin Cities."

Having worked on the Minneapolis Tribune 10 years, I think I know the attitude of "the money crowd" in the Twin Cities . . . toward North Dakota farmers. Or any other farmers. They regard them as peasants — whatever fine speeches they may make to people from Washington these days.

There weren't enough appraisers, either, they tell me, and the office in St. Paul apparently was too small and all wound up in red tape.

Things have definitely changed for the better recently, however, they said. Local men, who understand the problems of the North Dakota farmer, are being sent out as appraisers. Applications are made to local men. Loans are beginning to come through.

"It's doing quite a bit, too," one of the farmers told me, "to change the attitude toward the Government around here. The Farm Holiday crowd and the Farmers' Union people have been laughing at us and telling us we'd never get any loans. But now, I guess, they really are starting to come through."

I heard today that at the recent Farmers' Union convention in Williston — in session four days and four nights, some 700 delegates, and crowds running as high as 1,500 — speakers stated that in the state so far the farmers had paid out $220,000 in appraisal fees and had received $191,000 in loans.

The more prosperous among the farmers — I actually talked today to one farmer who didn't owe a nickel! — are worried about the debts people are taking on.

A newspaperman in Dickinson yesterday remarked that when a farmer brings in his first load of wheat he has six or seven mortgages to pay off. Many of them had to sell immediately, whatever they had, to try to pay off some of their debts. The federal loan people, it seems, get first call. And in some cases, I'm told, that means everything. I heard of one disgruntled farmer who was carrying a check around in his pocket, refusing to cash it, on the grounds that he wasn't going to get any of it, anyway.

Some of the farmers, howling for the Frazier bill,[1] say these federal loans, along the present lines and at the present rate of interest, are the curse of the North Dakota farmers.

"Every time the Government makes us a loan we're a little worse off than we were before," one of them said today. "What we need is refinancing — and a decent price for the stuff we raise."

Into the office of the Farmers' Loan Association in Williston today there came a quiet, mild-mannered Scandinavian wheat farmer seeking a loan.

He'd been "hailed out again," he said. As a matter of fact, he hadn't had a really good year since 1916.

"Why do you stick at it?" I asked.

"No place to go," was his reply.

His assets were 30 head of cattle, 16 horses, some hogs, some farm machinery, a tractor, which he hadn't used for several years because he couldn't afford to, and 320 acres of land.

His liabilities were: Bank of North Dakota, mortgage on a quarter section of his land, $800; farm implement company, $400; blacksmith, $300; hardware company, for spare parts, tools, etc., $1,000; back taxes, $600; U.S. feed and seed loans, $500. A total of $3,600.

During the conversation the secretary of the Farmers' Loan Association, taking his application, asked:

"How are you fixed for the winter in food and clothes for your family?"

The man didn't answer. Instead, his eyes filled up with tears — which he wiped away with the back of his hand.

The question was not repeated. And for the second time since I've been on this job I found myself blinking to keep tears out of my own eyes.

---

1. Senator Lynn J. Frazier of North Dakota had called for a moratorium on federal farm loans.

To Harry L. Hopkins

[Bismarck, N.D.] Friday Night, November 3rd [1933]
Dear Mr. Hopkins:

I've been occupied these last two days entirely with our own show, and I'm pretty low in my mind.

I've seen nothing, heard nothing save the desperate need for things to keep people warm up here in this ghastly climate — bedding, fuel, clothing. And today, as if it wasn't bad enough already, there's been a blizzard.

Yesterday I spent in Bottineau, 12 miles or so from the Canadian border, one of the most badly hit counties in the state. Back in Bismarck today, I've been trying to find out why nothing was done to meet this emergency — although they MUST have seen it coming — until the emergency itself arrived.

Although Judge Christianson, chairman of the state relief committee, tells me that he has written asking for more money — $360,000 for November, he said — and that Governor [William] Langer was to see you about it in Washington today or tomorrow, I cannot understand why he didn't get busy about it before. And I get the impression that neither he nor John Williams, the executive director, nor any of the committee with the exception of Mrs. Minnie D. Craig — more about her later — know just how bad it is. I find them rather like the people in Maine, inclined still to think there is something wrong with a man who cannot make a living. They talk so much about "the undeserving" and "the bums." No doubt expert investigators could reduce the rolls here in North Dakota, but, damn it — people are suffering from cold in this state RIGHT NOW. Terribly. And I feel this is no time to be fussing about who should get relief and who shouldn't. They should have settled that a long time ago.

I find that they are now, at this late date, making an effort to get some clothing and bedding into the state. Miss [Pearl] Salsberry, their case supervisor — in charge of all the field staff and paid workers — is down in the Twin Cities now, trying to get some stuff from the Red Cross and the private agencies. She is also getting inventories of the surplus stocks of Montgomery Ward, J.C. Penney, and other similar outfits, hoping to be able to get a lot of stuff, cheap.

But so far, they haven't any money. The Associated Press carried a story that North Dakota was to get $116,000 for November. They haven't yet received the money. The Judge told me they have begun to draw against it, assuming they will get it eventually. My own impression is that they're damned slow about asking for their allotments, and that they do not ask for enough.

They say the Red Cross is holding back a lot of clothing throughout this area, and they are very bitter about it. The Red Cross people say they have to hang on to it, "to meet emergencies." Good God, I'd like to know what constitutes an emergency in the eyes of the old ladies who seem to be running the Red Cross! Up in Bottineau last night, the head of the Red Cross committee, who is also a member of the Emergency Relief committee, proudly showed me her storeroom, which she keeps padlocked. Yards and yards of outing flannel, cartons of quilts and blankets, piles of stockings, sweaters, underwear. True, as much as she has, it would only be a "drop in the bucket," but it would help. Miss Salsberry shipped a couple of hundred blankets in there yesterday that she had bought from Montgomery Ward for $1 apiece. They were almost afraid to start giving them out, lest it cause a riot! Miss Salsberry also has written Red Cross headquarters in St. Louis, asking them to release their stuff.

I'll try to give you an idea of what Bottineau is like. It is said to be the worst county in the state. They haven't had a decent crop there in something like four years. Last summer the grasshoppers ate up just about everything.

The most urgent and immediate needs are clothing, bedding, and fuel. Those people haven't been able to buy a thing for four years.

Their houses have gone to ruins. No repairs for years. Their furniture, dishes, cooking utensils—no replacements in years. No bed linen. And quilts and blankets all gone. A year ago their clothing was in rags. This year they hardly have rags.

Always the plea is the same—for bedding and clothes.

Yesterday I visited one of the "better-off" families on relief. In what was once a house I found two small boys, about two and four years old, running about without a stitch on save some ragged overalls. No stockings or shoes. Their feet were purple with cold.

You could see light under the door in that house. The kitchen floor was so patched up—with pieces of tin, can covers, a wash boiler cover, old automobile license plates—that you couldn't tell what it might have looked like originally. Plaster falling off the walls. Newspapers stuffed in the cracks around the windows.

The mother of those children—bare-legged, although she wore some sneakers on her feet—is going to have another baby in January. IN THAT HOUSE. When she diffidently asked the investigator who was with me for assurance that a doctor would be on hand to see her through her confinement, I could hardly bear it.

The investigator asked to see her bedding. She hesitated for a moment. Then led us upstairs. One iron bedstead. A filthy, ragged mattress, some dirty pillows—her bed linen, she said, all gave out more than a year ago—and a few old rags of blankets. Incidentally I heard yesterday of women having babies on beds with only coats thrown over them.

68

"Do you and your husband and the children all sleep in this bed?" the investigator asked.

"We have to," she replied simply, "to keep warm."

It was 5 degrees above zero in Bottineau county yesterday. Today they were having a blizzard up there. Last winter — and there was nothing unusual about it, I was told — the temperature went down to 40 degrees below zero and stayed there 10 days while a 60-mile wind howled down across the prairies from the Northwest.

In Bottineau I sat down with the relief committee last night, and we tried to figure out what their bedding, clothing, and fuel needs for the winter would be.

There are now in Bottineau county 800 families on relief. There are 50 more applications that have been passed on favorably, but those 50 families can't get any relief until they get some money. They had spent their last cent the day before I arrived and didn't know when they were going to get any more or how much. New applications are coming in there at the rate of from a dozen to 25 a day. The relief office in a little stone building on the wide, wind-swept Main street of the town was jammed all day yesterday.

Out of 196 families in one township, all are on the relief rolls save one. In another township there are only two families not on relief.

These are some of the things they need in Bottineau county right now:

Three thousand suits of overalls or play suits for children; 5,000 suits of underwear, for children and adults; 5,000 pairs of stockings and socks; 500 jackets or coats for children; 2,000 pairs of overshoes for adults and children; 5,000 shirts for men and boys; 20,000 yards of wash dress material — woolens would be better, but they haven't got the nerve to ask for them; 40,000 yards of flannelette for nightgowns, slips, and bloomers; 1,500 heavy quilts; 1,000 blankets. At the retail prices up there, it all amounts to about $35,000. The stuff could be bought much more cheaply, of course, on contract.

The fuel need in that county is desperate. They have very little wood to burn in this state, you know. It's all coal. It's mined right here in the state, but in Bottineau — because of freight rates and a rise in price attributed to NRA — it now costs $4 a ton. They say they're going to need 10,000 tons in that county this winter. They need flour, too — 84,000 pounds of it!

And all these things they need AT ONCE. Winter has arrived up there.

They're managing to skimp along some way on food. How adequately you can judge by the statement made by one man on relief to the case supervisor — "We haven't had a scrap of meat in our house for six months."

There. That just about describes Bottineau county, I guess. I'm sending along, for good measure, a sample or two of the letters the relief committees get on the clothes proposition. And some lists of clothing and bedding needs drawn up by the field supervisors.

In Bottineau I ran into Mrs. Minnie D. Craig—50, broad in the beam, bobbed hair—speaker of the House in the last session of the North Dakota Legislature. Familiarly known about the state as "Min." Mrs. Craig enjoys the peculiar position of being a member without pay of the state relief committee and, *with pay*, a field representative of the committee! As a member of the committee she is the boss of John Williams, the executive director. As a field representative of the committee, she recognizes Williams as her boss. Crazy? Until very recently she has been traveling all over the state. She now has a more limited territory. She seems to be a good soul, but I'm wondering how long it will be before she announces her candidacy for Governor, or United States Senator, or Congressman-at-large! However—with conditions as they are—that's nothing to bother about at present, it would seem to me. At that, she's been around enough so that she seems to realize, more than the other members of the committee, I imagine, just how bad things are. . . .

To Harry L. Hopkins

Ortonville, Minnesota, November 6, 1933

Dear Mr. Hopkins:

I shall now proceed to wind up the glad tidings from the great sovereign state of North Dakota, trying to give you a picture of it as it looks to me after a week's wanderings—something more than 2,000 miles—across its wide open spaces.

It's not a very pretty picture, on the whole, although the unrest there has not as yet taken the form of farm strikes or any sort of open rebellion. There is a good deal of trouble boiling just under the surface.

The rural population of the state—and, believe me, it's mostly rural—may be divided into two parts: those who had a crop this year and those who had none.

Those who had a crop will tell you they aren't much better off than those who had none. I found them a good deal more rebellious, on the whole.

Those who had none are our problem, and I have an idea that in many parts of the state their lot is a pretty miserable one.

On both crowds there are a lot of anti-administration forces at work. And I'm afraid they are finding a rather fertile field.

A. C. Townley[1] is back, going about with Governor Langer and Lynn Frazier, making speeches. I realize that at one time Townley had quite a reputation among the Liberals in the East. Being more or less a native of these parts, I never had much use for him. He is now, they tell me, indulging in some fairly eloquent oratory against the President. They say he manages to put quite an effective bit of sarcasm into his voice when he says, "the *Pres*-i-dent." Here is a bit of his lines, as it was handed on to me last night:

"So now the *Pres*-i-dent is going to lend money to Russia. Well, he'd better send some of it out here. They've always called us Bolsheviks!"

They say he's telling the farmers that the President and J.P. Morgan are thicker than thieves, that the government has "taken money away from the farmers to give it to the bankers and insurance companies," and is demanding that the government build factories — out here on the North Dakota prairies! — to put everybody to work.

So much for Mister Townley. Whether he's getting many farmers to "join up" at $16 a head, as he used to do in the old days, I cannot say.

The Governor does a lot of talking. He seems to be in wrong all around, however, with the Democrats, Republicans, and Non-Partisan Leaguers. He is said to have queered himself with the latter element by failing to consult the executive committee on appointments. At any rate, whatever he says, no one seems to be taking him very seriously. His wheat embargo is a joke, although, if the price goes up, he will undoubtedly take all the credit and say his embargo did it. The truth is that the farmers themselves are holding back every last bushel of wheat they can, hoping for higher prices.

In addition to what they get from Mister Townley and the noble Governor, the farmers are hearing a lot of talk from other "Reds" of various shades — Communists, the Farm Holiday crowd, Farmers' Union, and the like.

Meetings are going on, all over the state. The Farmers' Union had a four-day convention two or three weeks ago up in Williston. About 700 delegates, I was told, and crowds as large as 1,500.

Five or six hundred assembled in Bismarck the other day — Farm Holiday, mixed with the Council of the Unemployed — to raise Ned with the relief administration.

A couple of hundred last Thursday, reinforced by some agitators from South Dakota, went out and stopped a foreclosure sale at Oaks, N.D., and then marched into Ellendale to run a field representative[2] of the State Emergency Relief Committee out of town.

She had gone down there to try to find out why the county was some $2,000 overdrawn on its relief accounts. In addition to a nice little political mess — of which, more later — she found that a self-appointed committee of the "Reds" had set up committees in each township in the county, had had a thousand copies of the regular relief application blank run off on a mimeograph machine, and had distributed them all over the county!

They showed her a telegram purporting to be from Langer, authorizing them to do this, and she said she understood they kept the wires hot

71

to Bismarck and to Langer in Washington last Friday and Saturday. The state relief committee had heard of no such set-up. She was inclined to think the telegram was a forgery.

The field representative — a former policewoman in Grand Forks — talked to them a couple of hours, she said, and talked them down. She ended up by directing them to round up every last one of those applications and bring them in to her tomorrow. This, she said, they promised to do.

And so it goes.

So far, all this talk hasn't started any action. Whether it will — we'll just have to wait and see.

H. D. Paulson, editor of the Republican Fargo Forum, . . . thinks probably not.

"Things are looking a little better, I think," he said this morning. "There's no doubt about that, with wheat away down as it has been, there has been a great deal of bitterness. But the price of wheat is up a little now, although it's still below 77 cents (the estimated production cost per bushel). Farm and home loans are coming through at last. Pretty soon now about $9,000,000 in wheat allotment checks will be coming into the state.

"I don't expect to see North Dakota farmers 'blowing up bridges' this winter."

He referred, he said, to some of Governor Langer's remarks after the conference at the White House last Saturday.

Whether Mr. Paulson, being a good Republican, was trying to lull me to sleep in false security, I don't know. I hardly think so, however. He's a pretty good friend of mine. And he does know this state.

Incidentally, he says that my friend, "Min," Mrs. Minnie D. Craig, former speaker of the House, who now enjoys the unique distinction of being both a member of the State Relief Committee and a field representative in the employ of the Committee, will undoubtedly bob up as a candidate, Non-Partisan League, for governor. But he also added that she is a pretty good sort and, being the only member of the committee who gets out around the state, is undoubtedly valuable in trying, at least, to make the committee realize what it's all about.

Two other gentlemen I saw this morning — H. H. Perry, Democratic National committeeman, and F. W. McLean, Democratic state chairman — were not so cheerful.

You can put them down for disgruntled Democrats, if you like, but they are bitter, decidedly bitter.

It is generally conceded around the state that two things have stirred up bad feeling among the farmers, whether they have crops or not. One is low prices. The other is the way, up until a very short time ago, the whole business of farm loans has been handled.

Messrs. Perry and McLean just about pop whenever they think of the Federal Land Bank, the Farm Credit Administration, or Henry Morgenthau. The recent appointment of our friend, C. T. Jaffray, president of the First National bank of Minneapolis, to go through the paper in the closed banks, was, they said "like a slap in the face with a wet cloth" to the farmers of the district.

Mr. McLean startled me a bit by popping out with some of the very stuff about Jaffray and that crowd that I wrote you from Minneapolis a week ago last Saturday.

What's more, he said, when Henry Morgenthau was out in St. Paul recently Democrats gathered from all over the area — it's pretty generally known throughout the Northwest, according to Mr. McLean — to tell him about it, but never got a chance.

"Morgenthau saw only two Democrats while he was in the Twin Cities," McLean said, "and he saw them only for a few minutes. They were all primed to tell him about it in an open meeting, but he had to leave, to keep an appointment with the bankers. They hung around cooling their heels for a couple of days and then left, without ever having had a chance to talk to him." . . .

The dope given me by Mr. McLean is that the Twin City bankers began cashing in through the Regional Agricultural Credit Corporation soon after it was formed, a year ago.

He said the story is that the first $60,000 of loans granted by the Regional Agricultural Credit Corporation went right to the Twin City bankers, before any others were made at all. After they had cleaned up — "stolen millions of dollars," is the way he put it — making their big haul by getting back at their face value the Agricultural Credit Corporation paper they had brought from the Eastern banks, they began making good all their bad paper through the Regional Agriculture Credit Corporation, he said.

"And that," he said, "has been going on right up to the present."

He said Congressman Lemke[3] has in Washington an affidavit from one farmer who owed one of the banks $1,595, and obtained from the Regional Agricultural Credit Corporation a $1,500 loan, which he paid to the bank, *although the property on which he obtained the government loan was appraised at only $500 — "and probably wouldn't have brought more than $300 at a sale."*

Mr. Perry and Mr. McLean were both very bitter about the way the Federal Land Bank and the Regional Agricultural Credit Corporation — "both dominated," they said, "by the Hoover Republican Twin City banking crowd" — have run things.

"At the very time Mr. Morgenthau was in St. Paul," Mr. McLean said, "Hoover Republican lawyers were actually being appointed in every county in North Dakota to examine, for fees, abstracts in connec-

73

tion with farm loans. A year ago those fellows were out actively working for Hoover, against Roosevelt." . . .

All the appraisers sent up from St. Paul to go over farm property in North Dakota have been Hoover Republicans, according to Mr. Perry and Mr. McLean — "tough fellows, who realized that they were working not for the United States government, but for Mr. Jaffray and Mr. [Edward Williams] Decker."[4]

"Unless it was a loan by which the Twin City banking crowd would benefit," said Mr. McLean, "they got very tough and told the farmers that this was the best they could do — that it was a Democratic administration now, and economical!"

So much, for the time being, for Mr. Perry and Mr. McLean; I know I've done a lot of yelling these last few weeks about politics — trying to fit Democrats into Republican communities. I take it back, so far as this district is concerned. Nobody could ever convince me that Clive Jaffray or E. W. Decker or any of the rest of that crowd wouldn't do the President "dirt" if they got a chance. It simply isn't in the cards for them to do otherwise. I did newspaper work in Minneapolis for 10 years. I know what those boys are like. . . .

Neither Mr. Perry nor Mr. McLean can, of course, see any good in any of the personnel handling the loans out in North Dakota. I can't quite agree with them there. I talked to some and watched them at work and didn't see any reason for finding fault. I did not, of course, inquire as to their political beliefs. To be sure, knowing I was from Washington, they might, too, have put on a show for me. But I didn't hear any complaints from the farmers, although I talked to quite a few of them, day in and day out.

Well * * * the feeling generally about the state seems to be that nothing violent is going to happen, for the present. Just what effect the President's turning down the governors' program will have, I don't know. Mr. Paulson predicted "nothing." There was, I'm told, by no means any unanimity of public opinion behind the governors out here, even among the "Reds." And Langer, they say, is so unpopular in North Dakota that what he says won't make much difference.

Mr. Morgenthau is not very popular — too much identified with Jaffray and that crowd — and Mr. Wallace is even less popular than Mr. Morgenthau. They consider Mr. Wallace "just another crack-pot theorist."

The bitterness toward NRA is beginning to die down. Retail prices are pretty high, they say, but they won't mind that, if only — prices for wheat and livestock go up.

As a matter of fact, that apparently is about the only thing that is needed to clear the situation up — and very likely the only thing that will clear it up. But things like the wheat allotment checks and better and quicker service on loans should help.

They are by no means so bitter toward the President as they are toward some other members of the Administration, but, as Mr. Paulson put it, "They are beginning to doubt."

"They still have lots of faith in the President," said Mr. McLean, "but I don't know how long it will last."

And now to get on to our own show.

I get the impression that the Relief Administration is "in wrong" around the state. In fact, Mr. Paulson and Messrs. McLean and Perry, all three told me so today. I've got that impression, too, from little cracks made by businessmen, farmers, and so on.

This is undoubtedly due in part to the mess Langer made of it at the start. It was called at first, as you doubtless know, "The William Langer Relief Fund," or something like that, and I gather that politics got into it "something fierce."

How much part politics now play in the state administration I could hardly say, but the impression about the state is that they play quite a part. . . .

In Fargo a few months ago Mr. Paulson led the battle to take control of the relief show away from the county commissioners. As a result a good, strong committee was appointed, and, in Fargo, they seem to be doing a job more like the job in up-state New York than anywhere else in North Dakota. Of course, as T. A. Hendricks, the executive secretary, explained to me, the relief load around Fargo — in the Red River Valley, where they usually have good crops — is not so heavy, and the counties thereabouts have some money.

Hendricks was puzzled about one thing, though — and it's something I had never heard of before.

It seems there is a state rule here requiring the Relief committees to have a man sign a promissory note for his relief and then go out on the roads and work it out. And they say this is an order from Washington. I may be a bit out of touch with Washington, but I never heard of any such rule.

"The effect on the morale of the people," said Hendricks, "is bad, especially in the case of men who are crippled and cannot very well work it out."

He said the Fargo Relief Committee was about to cancel the rule last summer, when he received from R. A. Kinzer, then executive secretary of the state committee, a letter containing the following paragraph, which I copy from the letter itself:

"We also wish to notify you that, unless you make use of the notes by having them worked out by all those receiving relief, it may be that no more money will come to your county until this is done and completed. This is not idle talk, but a command from the Federal Administrator at Washington, D.C."

I enclose one of the notes and also a copy of a resolution publicly adopted by a Socialist group in Fargo last month condemning the practice. . . .

Since I have written you several times and at length of the clothing and bedding needs and their inadequacy, I won't go into that any more. It is true that I wrote from the worst spots in the state, and that the need everywhere is not so great. But in those places — and in several others, I am told — the need is very urgent. They should be supplied at once. Just how fully the state relief committee realizes this I don't know.

I found a good deal of interest in the Eastern part of the state in the transient program, but they haven't got going yet. No money.

And Miss Berg, being a former policewoman, is much interested in the problem of the single, unattached woman. At her suggestion, the University Women in Grand Forks established last week an office for registering unattached women without jobs. Forty-six registered the first day, she said. . . .

1. Founder (in 1915) and chief organizer of the Non-Partisan League, which became a dominant factor in North Dakota politics (and less so in neighboring states) during World War I by calling for state ownership of marketing facilities.
2. Mary Berg.
3. William Lemke was a Non-Partisan League congressman from North Dakota.
4. President of the Northwestern National Bank of Minneapolis.

To Harry L. Hopkins

Aberdeen, South Dakota, November 7, 1933

Dear Mr. Hopkins:

Cheer up. I'll be brief. It's been a long day, and I'm tired.

I am now in the farm strike area. Most of the creameries along the Yellowstone Trail between Aberdeen and the Minnesota border were closed today. Farm[er]s who had gone down to Watertown with loads of chickens and eggs had brought them back. Last night in Aberdeen Farm Holiday leaders met with some of the businessmen, who agreed to lend moral support to the strike. Tonight at Webster, about 50 miles east of Aberdeen, the Farm Holiday Association is meeting to declare a strike. I saw no pickets today, however, and no disorder. But plenty of talk, I heard.

I had a long talk today with the leader of that Webster group, a farmer named [Ralph] Hansmeier. There were other farmers present, and every now and then one of them would throw in a remark or two.

Hansmeier I found to be a rather reasonable chap, who doesn't really believe in this strike himself, but feels that it's their last resource. He doesn't believe in it, he says, because he doesn't think it will be really effective, but is willing to take a chance.

"Our feeling," he said, "is that down there in Washington they don't understand us right. We have asked for things, but they just ignore us. We have tried to help, but they won't even listen to us. They have ears only for the 'Brain Trust.'

" A lot of us don't want to strike, but we feel we've got to defend ourselves and somehow keep this part of the country going. We've done our part. Farmers have built up this country. We've built these churches and these schools. Somehow we've got to keep them going, too.

"All we ask is that we get what it costs to produce our crops. We don't even ask for a profit.

"I don't think myself that the strike will work. But — well, we've nothing to lose and everything to gain. We believe in our Government, but we think our Government should be made to fit us, as well as the people in the East.

"These other fellows (meaning, he explained, the Communists) want to make everybody as miserable as possible to get a revolution. They don't offer anything constructive. We don't feel that way. We think the way out is through cooperation between the Government and the farmers. We don't think we're getting any cooperation now, though.

"We feel that our Governors when they were down in Washington last week didn't get much of a hearing. We think the President and Mr. Wallace should have sat down with them and tried to work out some plan. The Governors' plan couldn't have been all wrong. Maybe it needed some changes, but, the way it looks to us, nobody would listen to them at all.

"Most of the farmers out here haven't any use for Mr. Wallace at all. I've been sticking up for him until he turned the Governors down without giving them any kind of a chance, it seemed to me. Now I'm not fighting his battle any more. And a good many farmers have had that same change of mind in the last few days.

"You see, those Governors live out here. They know what we're up against. As I said, maybe their plan needed changes, but we feel they should at least have been listened to — not just turned down cold. The President, it seemed, wouldn't listen to anybody but Wallace and the 'Brain Trust.' Well, Wallace and the 'Brain Trust' haven't done much for us."

Hansmeier admitted he had no particular confidence in [Milo] Reno,[1] but that, he said, made no difference.

"Don't you see," he said earnestly, "we have only one weapon left. We've exhausted our voices. All there is left for us is resistance.

"So far as Reno is concerned — he can't get any money out of us, even if he tried, because we haven't got it. All it costs to join the Association is 50 cents a head. That's all any of us could afford. I don't know what Reno gets out of it, but he can't get very much, at that rate."

It seems to me that somebody ought to come out here and explain a lot of things to these farmers. NOT General [Hugh] Johnson[2] or Mr. Wallace or Mr. [George] Peek[3] making speeches — which they don't read — in Chicago, the Twin Cities, or Des Moines. But a missionary. Someone who could travel about quietly, without a lot of puff and blow and newspaper publicity. Someone who knew all about it and who could talk to them, as man to man. I can't do it. I don't know enough about it. I get headaches trying to understand the whole damned complicated set-up. But there must be men who do understand it. And I wonder if such a man, traveling about unostentatiously, spending a week or more in each state, avoiding newspapers like the very devil, getting right down and talking with the farmers, couldn't do a lot of good. Believe me, the Communists are doing it! And the Farm Holiday and Farmers' Union people. Why shouldn't we? I don't mean that he should organize meetings and make speeches to them. But talk to them as individuals. He wouldn't have any trouble finding them. Go into any county seat and hang around relief headquarters an hour or so. Let him come out as an observer for the Department of Agriculture. Or the Farm Credit Administration. (MAYBE they wouldn't lynch him!) . . .

It's sad, but in our own livestock relief show I've heard at least half a dozen interpretations of the instructions since I came out here. Nobody seems to know what it's all about. In North Dakota, for instance, I ran into that county agent who was telling people it would take them at least a month to get any relief — because they had to prove that they couldn't get a loan first. In South Dakota, some counties, they have them apply for a loan and give them "emergency livestock relief" until the answer comes back. There's no uniformity.

And our show is simple, compared with that agricultural set-up.

At that, they are apparently handling it a lot more intelligently in South Dakota than they are in North Dakota.

I had dinner tonight with a chap named [H. M.] Cass, who is a sort of head of the field staff in the state[4] — another thing I can't keep straight is the title-business.

To handle the livestock proposition, he said, South Dakota increased its staff of state field supervisors from four to 16. They had all 16 down in Pierre, gave them all the instructions they could, and showed them how to fill out applications for barnyard loans. The field supervisors then went out and called in their county relief directors and gave them all the dope — including instruction on filling out applications for barnyard loans.

Result: the Regional Agricultural Credit Corporation outfit in Sioux City found itself with 6,000 applications for barnyard loans in South Dakota on its hands!

"Since they must first demonstrate that they cannot get a barnyard loan," said Cass, "we use this for the first screen to put 'em through. It may be tough on the Regional Agricultural Credit Corporation, but we're after results. We want to get that livestock relief out to the farmers who need it, as quickly as possible."

Cass said they had speeded the thing up so that, in some cases, they have been able to find out in five days whether or not a farmer could get a barnyard loan. Contact with holders of mortgages on stock are made as rapidly and as directly as possible — often by telephone.

Well — so much for that.

In Webster I also had a talk with Lewis W. Bicknell, county attorney — they call it "state's attorney" out here — who is a member of the state relief committee.

Bicknell is deeply worried about the Communist activity out here. He thinks Washington ought to send out some Department of Justice people. As a matter of fact, the propaganda isn't any different or any more widely spread, so far as I can find out, than it is in other parts of the country where I've been.

There's no doubt, however, that they are very, very busy. Getting right down among the farmers and working like beavers.

Bicknell and others out here seem to think the Communists are responsible for the more violent activities of the Farm Holiday crowd. Near Milbank the other day, for instance, the Farm Holiday gang gathered to stop a foreclosure sale. They began taking guns away from the sheriff's deputies and beating them up. One of the deputies let go with a tear gas bomb.

A fragment or something hit one of the farmers in the face and he was knocked down. As he fell, he shouted:

"They've got me, boys! Go after them!"

They ended up by tearing the sheriff's clothes off and beating him quite badly.

The other night a gang of them got up at 2 o'clock in the morning and tore off down to Watertown to stop a foreclosure sale.

All this sort of thing, Bicknell believes, may lead to a good deal of bloodshed and disorder before the winter is over.

As county attorney, he said, he has warned the Holiday crowd that he will tolerate no beatings or killings or destruction of property in this strike.

"Being in sympathy with them, however," he said, "I've tried to advise them how to do their picketing peacefully. I've told them that it doesn't do any good to haul a farmer out of his truck, let his steers loose, and beat him up. They only make an enemy that way. I've told them the way to do it is to go to his house, in a friendly spirit, and talk him around."

I'm wondering, though, myself, if that won't lead to some Ku Klux Klan tactics.

Oh, it's all such a mess.

I'm wondering, too, why there can't be a little more cooperation in this business — a little better strategy. Even if it means stretching a point sometimes.

Take Hansmeier, for instance. He farms in a large way — 3,000 acres. He owns his own elevator. Has a good deal of property. And until very recently has kept about 20 men at work, he said. I imagine he's a pretty good sort. Someone told me that he had carried along for years one of his tenants — paying his threshing bills, buying his seed and feed in bad years. For the last three years the tenant hasn't paid him a cent.

Well, some weeks ago Hansmeier applied for a $5,000 federal loan, he told me, offering as security 7,000 bushels of wheat, 3,000 bushels of seed barley, 20,000 pounds of sweet clover seed, and a half a section of land — all absolutely clear. He said he was turned down on the loan, on the ground that the warehouse receipt for the grain was unacceptable because the stuff was stored in an elevator he owned himself.

"So I've had to let 12 of my men go — and that meant they went on relief," he said, "and cut the other eight down to starvation wages. I couldn't carry them any longer."

Now of course Hansmeier may not have understood why he couldn't get a loan. Or he may not have told me the truth. And I realize how impossible it would be to investigate so thoroughly each application and each applicant.

But, gosh — $5,000 on what, apparently, was pretty good security, would have, according to his story, kept those 12 families off the relief rolls. That may not mean much in dollars and cents, but think of the effect on the morale of those 12 families. And, as it is — well, Hansmeier is head of the Holiday association, and the Holiday association met in Webster tonight to declare a strike.

I'm not trying to suggest wholesale loans to all who ask for them. But maybe there could be a little more consideration given some of these fellows — perhaps a little more careful investigation.

Oh, they're all confused and unhappy and broke. They need someone to talk to them, face to face, and explain things to them. I couldn't tell Hansmeier why he didn't get that loan. I have an idea that it might have been because in Minneapolis — he made his application there, for some reason or other — they thought he didn't need it. And maybe he didn't. I don't know.

That livestock relief business causes more bitterness! One farmer told me today he'd given away 19 head of cattle to comply with the rules. . . .

Up North of Webster there are a lot of Poles. The relief people have had a devil of a time explaining to them the difference between being "hard up" and "destitute." The Poles think that, because they haven't any money, they ought to have relief. They don't want to mortgage their property.

"It's like this," one of them said to me today, bitterly. "The deeper you are in debt, the more the Government will do for you. A man can work his head off all his life and go without everything to keep out of debt, and in the long run he's worse off than the fellow who's no good. The fellow who hasn't got anything — who never did have anything anyway — can get plenty of help, for nothing except doing some road work. The fellow who has kept out of debt must now get into debt to get any help from the Government."

There may be no justice in these statements. I'm just passing them along to you, for what they're worth, coming, as they do, from the people who are putting on a farm strike.

One of the finest farmers I talked with today was an old Norwegian — a grand looking old chap, with pure white hair and beard and clear blue eyes. He was well dressed and looked prosperous. They told me he was considered pretty well-to-do, although he has been hit pretty hard this year. There was drouth through here, and grasshoppers.

"Vell, I tink t'e President iss doing hiss best," he said in his broken English, "only maybe he lisstens to t'at faller Vallace too much."

He went on to say that apparently "other organizations" could get what they wanted from the Government because they were better organized, and that the farmers got little consideration because they were unorganized.

Now that man doesn't belong to the Farm Holiday Association nor to any of the other groups. He has no intention of joining. But that's the way he feels.

So far as our own show — with humans — goes, I feel encouraged. The reports I get are pretty good.

Judging by Bicknell, they have a good, active state committee. They know what they're doing. They have plenty of authority and backing from the Governor. Plenty of money, too. Marked contrast to that North Dakota gang. . . .

In the Eastern part of the state I ran into a rather urgent fuel need. Farmers were burning cow manure — they used to call it "buffalo chips" when I was a kid out here — and cutting rushes in the beds of dried up lakes for fuel. But the state is buying coal. It's just a little slow getting in, that's all. It was beginning to arrive today.

Well, that about winds up today's activities. Man, I'm tired!

I do feel that, while the destitution is much, much worse in this state than in North Dakota as a whole, the needs are being met much more intelligently, skillfully, and adequately. Of course, I may not feel this way a week from now, however. But that's my first impression. I didn't feel nearly so happy about North Dakota after my first day in the state. . . .

1. Leader of the Farm Holiday Association.
2. NRA administrator.
3. AAA administrator.
4. Director of field supervisors.

To Harry L. Hopkins

Pierre, South Dakota, November 9, 1933

Dear Mr. Hopkins:

I sat in, "incog," this afternoon in the Governor's reception room at the capitol while a bunch of malcontents from a county on the other side of the Missouri river — a couple of merchants, some Farm Holiday people, a state senator, members of the Rotary and Kiwanis clubs, and some farmers — told their troubles to the acting relief administrator for the state.

I submit herewith some of their statements, as I took them down, verbatim. Most of the grief centered around the "4-4-2" limit on our livestock relief. You know — four horses, four cows, two brood sows, and 20 chickens. They wanted the ante on cows raised to 10.

Here are some of the things they had to say:

"We believe that limit cannot be applied in our county, because we are not grain-growers, primarily, but stock breeders. Our families cannot get along with only four cows apiece." * * *

"We feel that the amount of stock you have allowed us is worse than nothing. If we're going to have livestock relief, let's make it adequate or have nothing at all." * * *

"We've already sold off 50 percent of our stock this fall — and for practically nothing." * * *

"Cattle are so cheap now that the man who has to sell down to four will lose so much — well, he can't do it, that's all." * * *

"If you make our farmers reduce to that limit, they'll be on relief for years to come. You'll be making paupers of them. You'll be forcing them into bankruptcy." * * *

"The only way we've managed to pull through all these tough years was by having our livestock to fall back on. Our livestock has been our only anchor in time of stress. We can't let that go, too." * * *

"We're only asking for existence. We're only asking to be allowed to keep 10 head of cattle instead of four, and, for us, ten head of cattle is less than half the normal herd." * * *

"Our situation is different from that of the laboring man in the city. We worked all summer for nothing. He didn't. * * * And we are now willing to go out and work on the roads to save some of our stock if you'll give us a chance." * * *

"If prosperity should return next summer, the city man gets a job and becomes self-supporting. But a farmer on that 4-4-2 basis can't be self-supporting." * * *

"When the Government confiscates the factory where the city man earns his living, we'll be satisfied to let the government sacrifice our stock." * * *

"There are 1,800 desperate farmers in our county. Seventy-five per cent of the population is dissatisfied. The relief committee has quit because the restrictions are so severe they can't carry them out." * * *

"We don't want any dole. All we want is a chance to carry ourselves through the winter so we'll be able to become self-supporting next year if we have half a chance."

And so it went. . . .

Frankly, it's rather hard to tell how the relief show is going in this state. I still have the opinion that it's going much better here than in North Dakota. But that wouldn't be saying so much.

The boys do a good bit of boasting. And the people on relief do some complaining. The whole human show is obscured a good deal, however, by the uproar over that livestock business.

They are just winding up the job of taking control away from the county commissioners. There is, of course, a good deal of yelling about that. Especially since the county commissioners are asked to pay the salaries of the county directors and investigators who are taking the show away from them. [E. J. B.] Longrie[1] tells me that in many counties, too, there simply aren't any funds for paying those salaries. Also the attorney general of the state has ruled that legally they are not obligated to do so, although he advised them, in this emergency, to do it. It's all causing a good deal of friction.

These next few days I'm going to try to spend less time listening to the relief crowd tell how good the job is and more time trying to find out from the people themselves what is actually happening. . . .

If the President ever becomes dictator, I've got a grand idea for him. He can label this country out here "Siberia" and send all his exiles here.

It is the "Siberia" of the United States. A more hopeless place I never saw.

Half of the people — the farmers particularly — are scared to death. I got that feeling this afternoon. They were terrified at letting go of that stock that had been their "anchor in time of stress." They were worrying about everything.

For instance, they begged Longrie to make sure that at all times an adequate supply of fuel was on hand in the various communities, pointing out that some of the families lived 30 miles from the railroads.

"If there should be another blizzard this winter like the blizzard of '88," said one old-timer, "and a lot of us starved and froze to death, whose hands would our blood be on?"

Theatrical, perhaps, but he really was scared.

The rest of the people are apathetic. "Oh, we're used to it," they say indifferently.

I ran into that in Mobridge last night. Mobridge used to be quite a town. It was founded while I was a youngster living out 50 miles west of Aberdeen, as a railroad terminal, when the Milwaukee railroad built a bridge across the Missouri river on its way to the Coast. It has a population of about 13,000, and things hummed there for years.

Some four or five years ago locomotives were developed that could make longer hauls. Now the terminal is away out in Montana some place, and 14 men — that's all — are employed in the Mobridge railroad shops. Most of the men who used to work in the shops have been out of work two or three years! They haven't even enough money to get out of Mobridge! And so there it sits — with the west wind howling down its wide, empty streets. Everybody just stays home and mopes.

You can get some idea of the desolation of this country from the hotels. Both in Aberdeen and in Mobridge I stayed in fairly new, modern hotels. Good buildings that had been fairly well equipped. They are simply going to seed. Practically empty most of the time — I don't believe there were half a dozen guests in the Mobridge hotel last night — they don't bring in even enough money so their furniture, plumbing, and so on can be properly kept up!

Such dreary little towns. Traveling across the Northern part of the state, I visited three towns where I lived as a child — Milbank, Summit, and Bowdle. They were all the same size as they were when I left Dakota, 25 years ago! Hardly a new house. On the main street of Bowdle there was a big gap where there were no buildings at all. Someone said they'd had a fire there 15 or 20 years ago. The buildings had never been replaced.

Real estate in those towns is nothing but a liability. You can't sell it — you couldn't give it away. One of the things bothering relief directors in those towns is what to do about people who should have relief but aren't strictly eligible because they own unencumbered real estate. Why, unmortgaged real estate in one of those towns isn't a resource — it's a liability. You couldn't raise five cents at a bank on any of it. All you do is pay taxes.

West of the Missouri — out where Tom Berry[2] used to be a cow-puncher — things are even worse. Somebody today made the remark that that country never should have been opened up. I think he was right.

Miles and miles and miles of flat brown country. Snowdrifts here and there. Russian thistles rolling across the roads. Unpainted buildings, all going to seed. Hardly a strawstack or a haystack for miles. Now and then a shabby little town spread out around two or three gaunt, ugly grain elevators. What a country — to keep out of! . . .

1. Acting FERA administrator for South Dakota.
2. Governor of South Dakota.

To Harry L. Hopkins

Winner, South Dakota   November 10, 1933

Dear Mr. Hopkins:

Dammit, I don't WANT to write to you again tonight. It's been a long, long day, and I'm tired.

But I think I ought to give you, promptly, the gist of a conversation I had this morning with Governor Tom Berry. And isn't he a nice little chap, by the way? Did you ever notice his walk? He walks as though he still had on chaps and high-heeled boots!

Most of our conversation revolved about that eternal livestock relief business which is raising such a rumpus out here. (Berry says: "I don't know a Hell of a lot about being Governor, but there ain't a damned thing I don't know about a cow!")

Berry himself feels that the 4-4-2 limit is too low on cows, although he doesn't go about the state saying so and doesn't feel that he ought to ask you to raise it. He is afraid you will think him ungrateful and honestly feels that you've done magnificently by South Dakota. He asked me several times to be sure not to give you the impression that he was kicking. Well, he certainly is NOT.

Berry told me confidentially that he agrees with the rest of the gang, although he doesn't admit that to them, and thinks the limit on cows should be raised to ten — and that that would be pretty low.

"The average farmer, especially west of the Missouri, where they depend so much for their little cash on their livestock and their cream and butter," he said, "can't get along with only four cows. That's true."

His idea is this:

The 4-4-2 limit, he said, made the farmers get out and hustle for feed a lot more than they would have otherwise. They've piled up stacks and stacks of Russian thistle — Berry says the cattle can eat Russian thistle for

85

roughage, although it makes their mouths sore at first. Every spear of hay, he said, has been cut out of the coulees. They've simply cleaned the country up. But there's no more to get now.

As a result of this activity, he said, the farmers have managed to get together enough roughage so that they will need quite a little less government feed than they thought last summer. He believes the limit on cows could be raised to ten, and that South Dakota could still stay within the amount of money allotted to the state for livestock relief. If they raised the cow-limit to ten, it would undoubtedly allay their discontent a whole lot. He agrees with Longrie that the 4-4-2 business has raised up such a howl that the effect of the livestock relief program is seriously discounted.

"That 4-4-2 limit was a good thing, though, for this reason," he said. "It made 'em get out and hustle. If we raised the limit on cows now, they'd all think it was grand, and I don't believe it would cost the Government any more. If we'd limited them to ten cows in the first place, of course, there'd be the same howl now — they'd want twenty. But, you see, if, after letting 'em think they'd be able to keep only four, we let 'em keep ten, they'd be happy.

"These farmers are nothing but children. You don't want to spoil a child, of course. But you don't want to starve him, either. If we cut 'em down to four cows, it really will mean that a lot of 'em will still be on relief a year from now." . . .

One reason why they get so little money out of the sale of their livestock is that the distributing cost — the business of getting it in to the markets — runs so high.

Berry told me that from his ranch out here West of the Missouri river — and that's where the big howl is coming from, not from big cattlemen, like Berry, but from farmers who go in for diversification, part grain and part livestock, with 40 or 50 head of cattle — it costs $5.70 a head, freight, to ship steers in to the Chicago market and $4.32 a head to Sioux City.

Piled on top of that, of course, are all sorts of charges — the commission man's fee, so much a head for inspection, so much a hundred pounds for the hay they eat in the stockyards before they are sold, so much a carload for insurance, and so on.

By the time the owner gets his check, at present prices, it simply doesn't amount to anything. There have actually been cases, Berry told me, where the owner at the end was in debt instead of getting a check!

And, as I said before, since the railroads are asking freight payment in advance, many of these fellows — most of them, I should say — actually cannot ship their stock to market. They'll simply have to shoot it.

Therefore, if they must get rid of it, they ought to feel a little less bitter if they had a chance to sell it for a little something — the market price, say, with some of the extras cut out.

There are processing plants right here in the state, Berry says, that could take care of it. . . .

I drove down through the Rosebud country today. It's tough down there—no doubt of that. But nowhere there did I see destitution that could be compared with what I ran into in Bottineau county, North Dakota.

They're clumsy here—the little people who are trying to run the show. They don't know much about relief. Right now they're having a hard time overcoming an impression—apparently spread by the highway department—that this is a government road project, not a relief project, that it's important to get the job done, and that a lot of men with teams should be hired for that purpose, without reference to needs. I think, incidentally, that that's what caused all that rumpus up in North Dakota—the highway department and the relief committee failed to get together on these special road projects designed to give farmers a chance to earn livestock relief!

But they're getting that situation cleaned up in South Dakota. And I have the impression that, at least, the people who need relief are being taken care of fairly adequately. They'll get their relief rolls cleaned up. They're hard at it. I wonder, sometimes, if they're not going to be a little too tough. . . .

P.S. I was today in what they call an "unorganized county." That means that they have no county government at all! They're sort of attached to the adjoining county. Half of the population is Indian, and tax free. You can imagine what a job it might be to get a good relief set-up in such a county! But they seem to be doing it.

I forgot to tell you what Berry said about the turn-down they got in Washington. Wait a minute—

Berry said he felt that they got a very fair hearing, and he thought the other four agreed with him, no matter what they may have said publicly.

"As a matter of fact," he said, "the only one who did much yelling was Bill Langer, and he's scared to death. The Communists got a big vote up in North Dakota last fall. And they've got a recall law up there, too. If Langer gets unpopular enough, they can kick him out. He knows he ain't going over so very big, and he's scared.

"He went down into Nebraska and made a couple of speeches after he got back, you know. He said Charley Bryan[1] invited him. He asked me if I wouldn't like to have him come into South Dakota and make a couple of speeches, but I told him, Hell, no—that I had troubles enough without having him shooting off his mouth all around the place.

"Poor old [Albert G.] Schmedemann[2] was afraid to go home. I told him he'd better come on out here with me, and I'd protect him. When he got off the train in Madison I told him he'd better walk in the center of the street because they might just accidentally blow up a cheese factory as he was going by. He just gave me a dirty look.

"The Administration isn't going to get much defending from Schmedemann or [Clyde L.] Herring.[3] They simply (I quote him verbatim) ain't got the guts.

"That fellow [Floyd] Olson's the real boy. He's smart, and he's sympathetic with the Administration at heart. But he ain't got no call to go around defending the Administration. It ain't his party. At that, he ain't said much against the Administration — nothing like the way Langer's been talking. He don't need to, I guess. He's a good smart politician."

Yesterday Berry met with a Farm Holiday crowd in Watertown.

"I gave it to 'em hot and heavy," he said, "talked to 'em like they was a bunch of children. I told 'em not to get the idea this bird Roosevelt wasn't for 'em or that he hadn't given us a fair hearing. Why, good Lord, we had one conference with him that lasted three hours and another that lasted an hour. And he told us any time we had an idea he wanted to know about it — to bring it down there and it would get a hearing. The whole crowd of 'em had that same attitude. They couldn't take ours — not that one — but that don't mean they didn't listen to us or won't listen to us again. I told that mob that in Watertown yesterday. I hope I convinced 'em.

"They seemed friendlier at the end, but every time I'd hear a noise outside, I'd say to myself: 'There goes another cheese factory!' "

And that's Governor Tom Berry's account of how the boys felt about it.

L. Governor of Nebraska.
2. Governor of Wisconsin.
3. Governor of Iowa.

To Eleanor Roosevelt[1]

Winner, S.D., November 10, 1933

. . . Most of the day was [spent] in what used to be the Rosebud Indian reservation.

It was being opened up for settlement when I was a child out here. It used to be grand grazing country, and it probably never should have been used for anything else. It's rather like Eastern Wyoming — rolling country, with buttes every now and then. Half the population is Indian. We stopped at three horrid little towns — Murdo and White River and

Mission, where there is an Indian school. Arrived in Winner, which is quite a nice little town with a fairly decent hotel, just before dark, after a magnificent sunset. It covered the whole sky, and the colors on the buttes were beautiful beyond description. * * * We stopped at one little country school because I thought I'd like to see how the children were dressed and so on. I found to my astonishment a ladylike little youth, with all the mannerisms of a "fairy," teaching a crowd of the dirtiest and toughest looking children you ever saw — mostly Indians. The place was terribly dirty and crowded, and the air was simply awful. The children were a miserable-looking lot, though fairly warmly dressed. Wandering about the schoolyard were six or eight shaggy cow ponies, and beside the door a pile of saddles. They ride to school. The funny little teacher said the children seemed to have enough clothes, and he'd noticed that they brought pretty good lunches to school — you know, we are doing a fairly adequate relief job in this state — but he thought some of them needed dental care pretty badly. Compared with the needs of children in some other places, "it ain't nothin' at all." * * * The relief director at Mission, a nice young woman, wept as she told me this story. Living there is a school teacher, a man, who was one of her teachers when she was a child. He has a wife and several children to support and gets paid in tax warrants which none of the merchants will cash. He hasn't received a cent of money for a couple of years, she said, and really ought to be on relief, but is too proud to take it. "Their house burned a year or so ago," the relief director said, "and they just haven't anything in the way of furniture or bedding. The other day I went there and found his wife piecing together parts of old comforters to make one quilt. I want so much to help them, but I don't even dare to suggest it. They have so few dishes that they can't all eat at the same time. And yet they not only won't ask for help — they won't even let you suggest it. Lord only knows how they manage to exist." * * * We stopped at a farm today — a fairly respectable looking place. The farmer told me his story, a pathetic tale. He is 61 years old now. Five or six years ago he sold his farm in the Eastern part of the state for $80,000, bought an apartment house in Sioux City, and retired. The depression came. The apartments could not be rented. Taxes were high. So finally, after using up most of his capital, he traded the apartment house for 1,400 acres of land where he now lives — nowhere nearly so good a farm as the one he sold, he said — and "got back into the harness." Day before yesterday he had to let his hired man go, and from now on, at 61, he's doing all the work himself. "It is pretty tough," he said. "You see, my wife and I had worked hard all our lives, ever since we were married, and we'd thought we'd have a nice, easy old age. But it seems that wasn't to be. But I guess there's people worse off than we are." * * * He apparently is a good farmer. I noticed he has several stacks of hay. "Left over from

89

last year," he explained. He had a barnyard loan coming, he said, to feed his stock this Winter—that is, to provide grain. "I think the Government is doing pretty well by us," he said. "I've always been a Republican, but I've got to hand it to this fellow Roosevelt. He's really trying to help us. I don't take much stock in that Farm Holiday crowd. Most of them never amounted to anything as farmers." * * * Oh, these poor, confused people, living their dreary little lives. Governor Berry says: "There's two crops out here that never fail— Russian thistles and kids." He's right. If you turn your back on a field for fifteen minutes out here, it's all grown up with Russian thistles. And—my God, what families! I went to see a woman today who has ten children and is about to have another. She had so many that she didn't call them by their names, but referred to them as "this little girl" and "that little boy." She had seven in school. And despite the fact that her husband was out of work and that they had no money and were terribly ragged, she seemed contented and happy enough. "This (White River) used to be quite a town," she said cheerfully, "but it's kinda gone down hill lately."

1. This letter was excerpted by Hickok before being added to her papers; we have edited the excerpted letter.

To Eleanor Roosevelt[1]

Huron, S.D., November 11 and 12, 1933

An interesting, but terribly depressing, day. All day I've been in the grasshopper area, the *real* grasshopper area, driving through miles and miles of fields that look as though they had just been plowed. They haven't been. What happened was that the grasshoppers simply cleaned them off—right down to the earth, even eating the roots. And there they lie, great black patches on the landscape, completely bare.

I was in farmyards today that looked as though there'd never been even a spear of prairie grass there. They were just black earth. Why, those grasshoppers even ate the bark off the few scraggly little trees that are in that country. People were afraid to hang their washings out. They even ate the clothes off the lines. * * *

I met an amazing and most fascinating person who is relief director in one of those counties. She is half-Indian and was brought up on a ranch in the Black Hills country, was sent East to school, and later lived for twelve years in Seattle, where she did social work.

She is about 40, tall, straight, slender, trimly dressed. Good looking, with grey hair and hazel eyes. She is fair-skinned—the only thing about her that would suggest Indian is a slight cast to her features, rather high cheek bones. She is, by the way, intensely proud of the fact that she is part Indian. You'd like her, I think. She has the same slant on life that you have.

Her marriage broke up in a divorce about a year ago, and she came back to get her mother and take her out to Seattle. Then this thing came along. So there she is — refined, sophisticated, a most urban sort of person — down there in those dreadful little Rosebud towns, working her heart out, not for her own people, but for the whites! The Indians are not under her supervision, since the Government takes care of them in other ways.

They tell me she knows livestock as well as any man, and in her battered Ford we drove across some range country today.

"That little heifer won't live through the Winter," she would say with a wave of her hand. "See that horse? The first snow that comes along will mean his death."

It was awful. Horses so listless that they didn't seem to care whether we ran into them or not. Mares, dull-eyed, every rib showing, their backs sagging, great hollows behind their shoulders, followed by scrawny colts. Sometimes they would come toward us with a sort of hopeful look, as if they thought we might be bringing them something to eat. The owners, without anything to feed them, have simply turned them loose to get along as best they can, hoping that a few of them will survive. It would be more merciful to shoot them.

In that whole county, she said, among the farmers eligible for relief road work, there probably are not half a dozen whose teams are fit to work.

"A farmer will show up in the morning and hitch his team to a road scraper," she said. "They'll work willingly and fairly well through the morning. By noon they are tired out. By night they are completely exhausted. They don't come back the next day.

"They die right in the barnyards, from starvation. There have been cases where half-starved horses have dropped in the harness, right on the road job. And that sort of thing has caused a great deal of bitterness among the farmers." * * *

One farmer today told me his horses were so weak that it took him a whole day to drive 11 miles into town and back. * * *

I thought I'd already seen about everything in the way of desolation, discomfort, and misery that could exist, right here in South Dakota. Well, it seems that I hadn't. Today's little treat was a dust storm. And I mean a dust storm!

It started to blow last night. All night the wind howled and screamed and sobbed around the windows.

When I got up, at 7:30 this morning, the sky seemed to be clear, but you couldn't see the sun! There was a queer brown haze — only right above was the sky clear. And the wind was blowing a gale. It kept on blowing, harder and harder. And the haze kept mounting in the sky. By the time we had finished breakfast and were ready to start out, about 9, the sun was only a lighter spot in the dust that filled the sky like a brown fog.

We drove only a few miles and had to turn back. It got worse and worse — rapidly. You couldn't see a foot ahead of the car by the time we got back, and we had a time getting back! It was like driving through a fog, only worse, for there was that damnable wind. It seemed as though the car would be blown right off the road any minute. When we stopped, we had to put on the emergency brake. The wind, behind us, actually moved the car. It was a truly terrifying experience. It was as though we had left the earth. We were being whirled off into space in a vast, impenetrable cloud of brown dust.

They had the street lights on when we finally groped our way back into town. They stayed on the rest of the day. By noon the sun wasn't even a light spot in the sky any more. You couldn't see it at all. It was so dark, and the dust was so thick that you couldn't see across the street. I was lying on the bed reading the paper and glanced up — the window looked black, just as it does at night. I was terrified, for a moment. It seemed like the end of the world.

It didn't stop blowing until sundown, and now the dust has begun to settle. If you look straight up, you can see some stars! . . .

1. Excerpted by Hickok.

To Harry L. Hopkins

Lincoln, Nebraska   November 18th, 1933

My dear Mr. Hopkins:

Three loud cheers for CWA![1] I may be wrong, but I think probably it's the smartest thing that has been tried since we went into the relief business. It is actually getting out some of that Public Works money I've been yowling about all these weeks. (In Lincoln today I actually saw, with my own eyes, my first public works project under way, with the exception of a few highway jobs. It's a sewer project.) You see what they apparently did back early in the summer was to ballyhoo that Public Works business too much, forgetting that those things take time. Result: a lot of people expected to get jobs before winter, didn't, and were sore.

CWA ought to take away a lot of the bad taste, and I believe it's going to. It has been greeted with enthusiasm out this way. The only dissenting voice I've heard so far was that of Governor Charles Bryan (Democrat, but, as you doubtless know, anti-Administration). He wanted to know what we're going to do with them after the Four Hundred Million runs out. I didn't tell him this, but my idea is that the time to start worrying about that is when the Four Hundred Million runs out. At any rate, it's going to ease a tough situation right now.

And now for the wind-up on South Dakota, delayed by my trip to Minneapolis.

I have an idea that the chief trouble with the people in South Dakota, the thing that is behind whatever unrest there is in the state, is sheer terror. Those people are afraid of the future. Some of them are almost hysterical.

I don't wonder at it. You've heard plenty about what the grasshoppers did. I could add a book, but I shan't. You're a busy man.

Well, those farmers — whose grain fields at the end of the summer looked as though they'd been newly plowed, the grasshoppers having eaten even the roots — are afraid of next year's grasshoppers. Whether there is any scientific basis for it or not, they're afraid the grasshoppers have laid eggs in the soil and will come back next year worse than ever.

Another thing that has them scared is the possibility of drouth. I think I'd be afraid, too, were I a South Dakota farmer. The whole darned state apparently is drying up and blowing away.

This fear is aggravated by the kind of thing that happened last Sunday. I spent last Saturday and Sunday nights in Huron, up toward the center of the state. All night Saturday night the wind blew, screaming and moaning around buildings. When I got up, about 7, Sunday morning, the sky right overhead was clear, but you couldn't see any sunrise. All around the horizon there was a thick, brown haze.

We started out about 8:30, intending to drive up into the Northern part of the country to see some farmers. By that time the whole sky was covered with the haze — the sun just a lighter spot in the brown curtain. I realized then what was happening. Dust storm. We used to have them when I was a child out there, but not quite that bad. If there had been snow on the ground to be blown about, this would have been a blizzard.

We'd gone less than ten miles when we had to turn back. It kept getting worse. You couldn't see a foot ahead of the car. It was a truly terrifying experience for me — and I don't have to live in the state. Like driving in a fog, only worse because of the wind, which, it seemed, would blow the car right off the road. When we stopped we had to put on the emergency brake because the wind, at our backs, actually started the car rolling. We wondered if we were ever going to get back to town. It was as though we were being picked up in a vast, impenetrable, brown cloud, which was whirling us right off the earth.

The street lamps were on when we got back to Huron. By noon it was as black as midnight. You couldn't see across the street. It kept it up until sundown, and all Monday morning we drove past drifts of — brown *sand*!

93

IT happened to be the worst dust storm they'd had within the memory of the oldest inhabitant, and the wind raised havoc generally over the Northwest. BUT — they've been having these dust storms, less intense, every two weeks or so this fall.

All this sort of thing makes for fear — and unrest. Some of the farmers I saw Monday looked like frightened children.

Another thing that scares them is their debt load. They're afraid to borrow any more money. Their land, their homes, their machinery, their livestock — all mortgaged. They owe for seed loans, and, since they didn't even get seed out of this year's crop, many of them, if they go on, must borrow money for seed again this spring — if they can get it.

They are afraid of losing their farms. They don't understand the federal loan set-up very well. They don't want to borrow any more money. If a man happens to have livestock that isn't mortgaged, he is afraid to mortgage it now.

Our livestock relief limit only makes them more afraid. You see, their cows have carried them through some bad years in the past. Now, for the first time, they cannot feed their cows. But they are afraid to let them go, to cut their herds ranging from 20 to 50 head, down to four. Especially since they can't get anything for them.

Therefore, they're turning them out to shift for themselves. During my trip down into Rosebud country and up around Huron, I saw livestock that would make you sick. But we can't feed all the livestock in South Dakota. So — that's that.

I'm hoping that CWA will take care of that situation somewhat. Give those fellows a chance to work and earn a little money, and they'll manage to save some of their livestock. And they'll feel a lot happier.

Whatever unrest there is in South Dakota is very largely due, I honestly believe, to fear. Agitators of one sort or another are going about among them trying to stir up anti-Administration sentiment. That they get anywhere at all may be attributed, I think, to the quality in man that makes him want to blame his misery and his apprehension on somebody. I think it was George Santyana who said that man invented God partly because he wanted someone to blame his misery on. Not very good grammar, as I express it, but you get the idea. And these fellows, afraid of the elements, pick on people like Mr. Wallace and Mr. Morgenthau. They blame their troubles on Mr. Hoover and Mr. Hyde.[2] They haven't started holding President Roosevelt responsible yet, but they find Wallace a good target. . . . If we're going to get to those farmers, I'm afraid we'll have to start boring in at the bottom, as the Communists and the other agitators do. Missionaries, who will get right down among them and speak their own language. Mr. Wallace spoke their language, but they wouldn't listen. It would help some, perhaps, if we had a friendlier press. But the papers are mostly Republican and, if they don't attack the Administration openly, they are friendly only in a negative sort of way.

Whether their resentment ever will lead to open revolt — and when, if ever — would be hard to say. It doesn't amount to much now, although the "Reds" are doing their darnedest to make it amount to something. Holding little meetings all the time. Going about from farm to farm.

Right now things are peaceful, on the surface at any rate. Nobody anticipates any real trouble this winter. Pretty soon there'll be lots of snow, I suppose, and they won't have much fight in them. And if things ever do blow up in that state, believe me, the cause will be 90 percent fear.

I came out of the state still feeling that our own show, so far as human needs are concerned, is being pretty well handled. God knows, it's clumsy, in places! You have to deal with so much ignorance. They're so well meaning, so many of those little country officials and relief committees — and know so little about relief. They probably don't understand more than about half of the instructions that are sent them. Some of them can barely read. But . . . I feel that the job is being fairly well done. It's certainly better than North Dakota. I saw some pretty thin, undernourished looking youngsters — one thing I did in South Dakota was to stop in at country schools and look them over — but I did NOT see any going about without shoes or stockings.

The two chief sources of irritation, so far as we are concerned, in South Dakota are livestock feeding and the eligibility rules. Maybe I'm expecting too much of CWA, but I'm hoping that it will be able to ease both considerably.

I've already told you how they feel about the four-four-two business. Another thing that bothers them is that farmers who are eligible for relief can't get it because their horses are too weak for the road work they must do to get relief. And there's no provision for feeding the horses.

I'm not just taking the disgruntled farmers' word for this. I saw some of those horses. And what I'm telling you was told me by our own people, handling the relief.

In one county the relief director told me there probably were not in the whole county four teams belonging to farmers eligible for relief that could be worked. The roads they work on are gravel. That means hauling gravel. It also means using scrapers, hauled by horses. There is relatively little work for men without teams. All the farmers have teams, but they are not fit to work.

One farmer told me his horses were so weak that, although he lived only 11 miles from town, it took him all day to get to town and back.

Relief people told me that a man will show up for work with a team of horses, that the horses will work pretty well during the forenoon, that

95

they'd begin to sag in the early afternoon, were completely exhausted by night, and didn't show up the next day. There have been cases where the horses actually dropped in the harness while at work on the roads. They've died. All that makes for a good deal of bitterness.

Well, I'm hoping CWA may take care of some of that. Some of these fellows, at any rate, will be placed in a position where they can buy food for the horses they must work on the roads.

The eligibility business is tough. You have thousands of people who technically are not eligible for relief, but need it — oh, HOW they need it. They are people with resources that aren't resources at all. Unencumbered real estate in small towns, for instance. They can't raise a nickel on it. Unmortgaged livestock, which they could manage to pull through the winter somehow, if they only had a little food for themselves. Horses too weak to work on the roads, which bars their owners, since in South Dakota there is no direct relief except that granted to men who are not able-bodied.

The plight of some of these people who certainly need relief, but, according to the letter of the law, aren't eligible, is pitiable. Up around Huron we drove by farm after farm with beautiful buildings on them — and inside those handsome houses hungry people. I talked to them.

I wrote you about how they were feeding Russian thistle to their cattle. Well, did you ever hear of Russian thistle soup? That's what some of those people are eating. They cut the thistles green and stack them up. Inside the stacks the stuff is still green — although perhaps rotted a little. They haul that out, stew it up with a little flour and water, and eat it!

I am most fervently hoping that some of these people may get in on CWA. They are unemployed allright and not on the relief rolls.

However, the people we ARE taking care of haven't any kick that I can see. And they are generally contented. They are getting coal. They are getting food. I talked to several women who had had some of our pork. They say it's good, too. And they are getting clothes. I saw the orders written out. And I saw the people — much, much more warmly clad than they were up in North Dakota. In Pierre I saw orders that had gone out to county directors, before your telegram came in, instructing them to see that clothing and bedding were provided.

I don't think we need be ashamed of the job in South Dakota, so far as we've been able to go with it.

I got into Lincoln this morning, having driven down to Omaha yesterday. Today I had talks with Rowland Haynes,[3] the chairman of the state relief committee,[4] Governor Bryan, and the managing editor of the Lincoln Star[5] (Roosevelt-Democrat). I move on to Fremont tomorrow night, after a talk tomorrow with a field supervisor who is coming in then from a swing through the northern part of Nebraska. I'll get a first letter on Nebraska off to you tomorrow or Monday night.

I gather that things aren't so tough in this state, although our show is really only getting started. As you know, they didn't have any federal money at all until August and it's taken until now to get Bryan swung around so they can handle him. He's a funny fellow. I spent an hour or more with him today. Most of the time he was yowling for inflation and making dire threats about what Congress is going to do to the President. He wound up by showing me, with all the naivete of a child, the furnishings of his office! Told me how much each thing cost and assured me that it was one of the most luxuriously furnished offices in the world! Gosh! . . .

1. Civil Works Administration.
2. Arthur Hyde, secretary of agriculture during the administration of Hoover.
3. FERA field representative.
4. W. H. Smith.
5. James E. Lawrence.

To Harry L. Hopkins

Omaha, Nebraska, November 20, 1933

Dear Mr. Hopkins:

Herewith a few observations after three days in Nebraska and Iowa.

I came back down to Omaha from Sioux City today to be here while the convention of the National Farmers' Union is on. In addition to the Union crowd, Milo Reno and the rest of the Farm Holiday leaders are to be here, and I understand they are meeting tomorrow to decide what to do about the strike.

Apparently about the smartest thing for them to do would be to call it off. It's not getting anywhere. At least not in this part of the country. There's no picketing and hasn't been for a couple of weeks. No picketing to speak of, at any rate. It just didn't go, that's all. Nobody seems to believe in it much.

Apparently one thing that is contributing largely to its failure is the arrival of wheat allotment checks. I have that from a chap named [Kenneth] McCandless, farm reporter for the Omaha World-Herald. I believe our CWA program will also do a lot to calm them down. Quite a few farmers will be getting jobs out of it. It will give them something to do and a little money.

McCandless sizes the whole farm "revolt" up something like this:

"Potentially, there's plenty of trouble for the Administration out here, but it isn't going to happen now.

"In the first place, they lack leadership. Nine out of ten farmers have no use for Milo Reno. He's just a racketeer. He got control of the Farmers' Union over in Iowa, took all its money, and wrecked it. The farmers all know that, and, especially here in Nebraska, where the Farmers' Union has a lot of influence, Reno hasn't any standing.

"[John] Simpson, head of the National Farmers' Union, is another leader of the Reno type, though perhaps not quite such a racketeer. He may tie in with Reno, but the leadership of the Farmers' Union in this state won't. And I doubt if they would in Iowa.

"The Farmers' Union convention will have about 100 delegates and probably 300 or 400 farmers attending. It's a cut and dried affair. They'll just get together and endorse Simpson's program. This outfit believes in lobbying, and they'll go to work on the congressmen.

"What the Farm Holiday crowd will do is hard to tell. Right now, they're licked, and they know it. Reno may think up some new ideas — if he stays sober. The last time they had a confab here, he passed out in the meeting, and they had to carry him out.

"Some of them were saying this morning that they thought they'd done too much talking. They were advocating an 'under-ground' campaign. But I don't know what that would get them."

I've had pretty much the same slant from other people I've seen. Jim Lawrence, managing editor of the Lincoln Star, said Saturday that he believed 60 percent of the farmers who engaged in the strike weren't farmers at all — but just kids, hoodlums.

I heard up in Minnesota of one farmer of some standing in the community who spent just one day on the picket line. Along in the afternoon it occurred to him that some of the boys whose cream they were going to dump might get tough. Someone might get hurt. There might be considerable property loss, too. He looked the pickets over and discovered that, in the whole crowd, he was the only one who had any money or any property. If anyone started out collecting damages, he'd be the only one who had anything to take. And that ended his stay in the picket line!

Governor Bryan takes unto himself credit for stopping it in Nebraska, by telling them the roads had to be kept open. I doubt if that had nearly so much to do with it, however, as wheat allotment checks.

Loans are coming through in pretty good shape down here — you don't hear nearly so much complaint against the Omaha farm credit outfit as you do against the Twin City crowd — and these, together with wheat allotment checks, the corn-hog program, corn loans, and so on are creating fairly good feeling toward Washington.

I had a chat with a farmer about 60 miles out of Sioux City, on the Iowa side, this morning. His county, he said, was the first in the United States to get its wheat allotment checks. About $15,000. It averaged about $60 per farmer. He said they were all going in for corn loans, too.

"If it weren't for that corn loan," he said, "these highways would be crowded right now with farmers taking their corn to market. Now they're holding it back, to help keep the price up, and the corn loan permits them to do it.

"We feel right in here that the government is doing a pretty good job. We're willing to play along and give 'em a chance. And if Milo Reno started making speeches in here right now, he'd probably get egged."

McCandless tells me that the Nebraska Farmers' Union is really a pretty conservative outfit. They've gone in for cooperative marketing in a big way. They even have their own wholesale house that sells supplies to the farmers. Their cooperative livestock market is making it tough for a lot of the commission men, he says. And they're much more interested in seeing this program go than they are in anything else. I have an appointment for an interview with [H.G.] Keeney, the president, tomorrow morning.

On the farm credit situation, Jim Lawrence offers a couple of ideas.

1. He thinks the appraisals are pretty low as a general thing. That, he believes, is due to the type of appraisers they send out. They're too cautious, he thinks, have too much the "big banker" point of view. He said he actually knew of cases where they had appraised at $50 or $60 an acre farm land that brought $75 and $80 at a forced sale. In addition, he says, they are apt to be tactless fellows, not very familiar with conditions in the areas to which they are sent.

2. He thinks a lot of money would be released and spent if something could be done to get farmers and their creditors together to settle up a lot of debts. They have a moratorium law in Nebraska. The result is, he said that about 48 percent of the state's farmers, who are mortgaged, are saving up what money they can get so they'll be ready to move in case they're evicted when the moratorium runs out. About half of the creditors, he says, are Nebraska people—the rest insurance companies and banks. The Nebraska people who hold mortgages on the farms are afraid to spend any money they may have because they don't know what is going to happen to their funds invested in those mortgages. He believes these creditors and the farmers should be brought together, that settlements could be reached in many cases, and that the effect would be to release a lot of money. * * * I don't know just how the Federal Government would figure in that picture, however.

The political picture in the state, Lawrence tells me, contains nothing particularly alarming. Bryan is whacking the Administration when he gets a chance. I got that in the talk I had with him. Lawrence, whose paper supported Roosevelt in the campaign, said they had practically to force Bryan to come out for Roosevelt about three weeks before election day, and that then he did it only because he realized he might take a beating if he didn't. Right now, Lawrence thinks Bryan is gambling on the possibility of the Roosevelt program failing. They say he has ambitions to run for the United States Senate in 1936. If Roosevelt has failed by then, Bryan can be the "voice that cried in the wilderness." Governor Bryan probably won't be running for the Senate, or anything else, in

1936, however. They say he really has one foot in the grave. Very bad heart trouble. He is just recovering from a long illness.

Up in Minnesota United States Senator Tom Schall is pulling the same stunt. A close friend of his backers told me so. Schall attacked the President in a speech at the University of Minnesota the other day and was hissed.

"But he should worry," my informant commented. "If Roosevelt fails, he can go around in 1936 and be the great prophet — the boy who told 'em when it took courage to tell 'em. All that kind of thing. If Roosevelt succeeds, everybody will be happy and will have forgotten all about Tom Schall's speeches back in 1933."

Maybe so. And maybe not. . . .

There isn't nearly so much anti-Wallace feeling hereabouts as there is up in the Dakotas. It may be due partly to the press.

In the Dakotas and Minnesota all the influential newspapers are Republican. Up until recently they haven't dared to attack the President. They are now, and getting a little bolder all the time. And when they're not attacking him, they certainly do not go out of their way to help him.

In Nebraska there are two strong Roosevelt-Democrat papers — the Lincoln Star and the Omaha World-Herald. Lawrence told me that probably 80,000 of the 117,000 farm homes in the state subscribed to one or the other. It isn't only their editorials that count. They play up in a favorable way the things Wallace and Morgenthau and Peek are doing. They do a lot of that "missionary work" that, it seems to me, is so badly needed in the Dakotas and Minnesota. On the front page of the World-Herald this morning I counted five stories, all of which would give the reader a very good impression of what the Administration is doing.

And now for our relief show.

It's just getting started in Nebraska. Rowland Haynes says the state is about 18 months behind other states in its relief set-up.

I guess I don't need to give you any background on the activities of the Governor and Mr. Smith, chairman of the relief committee. All that kept them from getting started.

Haynes said his first job was to get the Governor and Smith straightened around. He's got them working with him now, he thinks. At least they're doing what he wants them to do. I gather it's largely a matter of letting them think the ideas were their own.

One of his first achievements was persuading them to hire a first class supervisor. I met her Sunday and had a long talk with her. Was very favorably impressed. You can imagine how much of a victory it was for Haynes when I tell you that her father was a Republican judge! But she's won Bryan over now. She is a trained social worker, and, what is also a big help, she knows Nebraska and Nebraska people.

The big job now — or it was the big job, until CWA came along — is getting good county committees and good workers. They're beginning to make some progress, Haynes says.

One of the weaknesses just now is the fact that in Lincoln they know very little about conditions in the state, outside of the cities and the Northeastern section, where there has been drouth and some grasshoppers. There are counties in the Western part of the state with only two or three families on the relief rolls. That probably does not mean that the number shouldn't be much larger. It's going to be a job getting over them. The distances are so great. They have one county in Nebraska that covers 9,500 square miles!

One thing that is going to help them in this, however, is the work already done by the Public Works Board, a lively, aggressive outfit. This board, of which Lawrence is a member, went over the whole state last summer, county by county. They tried to map out a statewide public works program. They're mostly irrigation projects, ranging all the way from a few thousand dollars up to one for $42,000,000. Some of them have been approved, and the men are actually at work. Lawrence feels optimistic about most of them — even the one for $42,000,000.

In making their survey, the board members counted out ten counties in which there can be no public works project because the counties can't raise any money to hold up their end. The financial condition of some of the more prosperous counties, incidentally, was amazing. Lawrence said they found one county with a cash surplus of $85,000 in the treasury, and another county with $55,000! In those ten counties it happens the need for relief is pretty urgent. Lawrence had the dope on them. He turned it over to me, and I passed it along to Haynes. And he and Haynes are going to get together. Incidentally, Lawrence's boss,[1] the publisher of the Lincoln Star, is a member of the state relief committee. Haynes, as a matter of fact, was aware of conditions in about five of the counties, and things were going forward in those counties already.

Right now Haynes and everybody else down in Lincoln are working their heads off getting the CWA program going. Out of Omaha a hundred men went to work today, under CWA, on county roads. The whole Omaha relief crowd went to Lincoln this afternoon to try to sell Haynes and the relief committee the idea of taking on a big sewer project that never can go through as a PWA[2] project because Omaha can't raise its share of the money. They've also had the idea here of getting the government to build, out of public works money, a municipal university, which it would rent to the city. It impresses me as being rather quaint. I doubt if it gets anywhere. Lawrence didn't mention it in his list. . . .

1. Fred Seacrest.
2. Public Works Administration.

To Eleanor Roosevelt[1]

Omaha, November 21, 1933

An interesting, albeit at times irritating, day.

I spent part of it down at the shabby old Castle Hotel, a place of faded splendors, where the Farmers' Union is holding its convention.

A great big, smoky, dirty lobby, with worn, sagging leather sofas and chairs, paintings of naked ladies on the walls, cigar ashes all over the floor, untidy bellhops in worn, soiled uniforms.

The place filled with the delegates. Cowboys in high-heeled boots, overalls, and big hats wandering about, nervous and shy. "Dirt farmers," ill at ease in "store clothes" and unaccustomed white collars. Fresh haircuts, leaving strips of white above the leathery tan on the backs of necks. Farm wives in four- or five-year-old styles, staring curiously about. All through the scene a pathetic streak.

And mixing among them, slapping backs, shaking hands, the leaders. Town men. Perfectly at ease. Accustomed to being in cities and in hotels. Flattering them. "Bucking them up."

A radio loud speaker raucously blaring out a dance orchestra. And under the music the low, constant murmur of talk-talk-talk.

In this setting early this morning — I met him at 8! — I had a talk with a man named Keeney, president of the Nebraska Farmers' Union. A quiet, slow-spoken sort of man, Mr. Keeney, with that rough, red skin that farmers all seem to have, although he has been living in Omaha for several years.

"Well, I guess Reno and that crowd will seem to run this show," he said. "But you see that's because they make more noise than the rest of us. Farmers — real farmers — don't talk much. They're apt to do a lot more listening than talking.

"If you could ever get 'em started talking, you'd find a lot of these fellows don't hold with Reno and his outfit much. Nor with Simpson.

"Of course we ain't all very happy. Prices should be higher. The cattlemen are in a specially tight fix. A lot of us believe in price-fixing. And most generally we're for inflation, too. It seems as if there really ought to be more money out.

"But, whatever those fellows say, the average of us believes giving the President and the crowd down there in Washington [a chance]. We're from Missouri. We don't like Mr. Wallace much, but — we're willing to wait awhile and see what happens."

"There'll be a lot of noise here, I expect. Fellows like Simpson and Reno and Langer and Lemke are going to do a lot of talking. But that don't mean we all feel the way they talk." Incidentally, Keeney says,

102

"It's the newspapers and the magazine writers from the East who build up fellows like Reno."

And that's the substance of Mr. Keeney's observations. Of course the Nebraska Union represents the right wing of the outfit. They are much more interested in their cooperative marketing than they are in the ideas of some of the leaders. With as much enthusiasm as a man of his type ever shows, Keeney described their ventures—their cooperative livestock market, their creamery, their exchange through which members buy clothing, machinery, food staples, and so on, at wholesale prices.

He talked about relief for farmers, too, and predicted that out in the Western part of the state the applications will go up, now that CWA has come into the picture.

"Those fellows don't like to go on the county," he said. "They'll almost starve first. What they want is jobs."

He grinned when I asked him if Milo Reno had ever really been a farmer.

"Oh, I guess he worked in a dairy on somebody's estate once," he replied. "He used to be a preacher, too, you know."

He told me with some bitterness what I'd heard before, that Reno wrecked the Union's cooperative program in Iowa, by getting his fingers into the treasury.

"Well, do the farmers know that?" I asked.

"Yeah," he replied slowly, "but, you see, fellows like Reno have their followers who stick to 'em, thick or thin—"

"The crusading spirit," I ventured.

"Yeah, that's it, I guess," he said nodding.

This afternoon I went back and listened to some of the "noise," Keeney mentioned.

Incidentally, he clashed a bit with Reno on the floor of the convention this morning, I heard. Keeney, who, in addition to being president of the Nebraska Union, is vice-president of the national organization, was making his report and said something about the recent Chicago hog buyers' strike, which Hopkins broke up by going in and buying some 60,000—hogs or pounds, I don't remember which—and Reno pugnaciously interrrupted, implying that the Nebraska gang wasn't in sympathy. The idea, you see, is that the packing houses work in a sort of racket by buying directly from the farmer, each house taking an area so that there is no competition, and thereby getting the price down. The commission men at the markets may refuse to sell at that price, as they did in Chicago, but the packing houses, able to get all the pork they want, just thumb their noses at them. A similar strike is apt to occur here in Omaha, Keeney told me, and that was his answer to Reno today.

The meeting was both funny and pathetic. It had in it elements of a country church social, an old-fashioned camp meeting, and a "red rally" in Union Square, New York. It was held in the hotel ballroom, which was probably the last word in elegance west of the Missouri forty or fifty years ago.

They had songs — rather dreadful songs, with words made up to popular tunes, sung somewhat off-key by three corn-fed damsels from Western Nebraska. One of them was to the tune of "Happy Days Are Here Again." It failed to get a hand. Three children, ranging from six to eleven years old, performed. Tears smarted in my eyes — it reminded me so much of what I used to have to go through singing in public when I was a child and how bitterly I hated it. But these kids didn't, apparently. Their father, a funny little man with curly hair and glasses, marshalled them right down to the entrance after they were through, to make sure they were noticed and complimented. God, it was depressing! They had a "home talent" orchestra from some place in South Dakota, and a guy who sang a song he had composed himself — pretty bad — which he said was dedicated to "Henry Aloysius Dictator Wallace." I couldn't get the words. The Rudy Vallee crooning tradition had penetrated even into Nebraska!

Simpson is one of those evangelistic fellows. Calls everybody "Brother." God, how his type irritates me. "Brother Bryan" * * * "Brother Lemke" * * * "Brother Reno." Boy, I'd like to "brother" him!

Well, I listened to him and Governor Bryan — who talked nearly an hour, although he was down for less than 15 minutes — and Milo Reno.

Keeney had promised to introduce me to Reno, but I took one look at the guy, heard him talk for a few minutes, whispered to myself, "Oh, Hell!" Then I left. I couldn't bear it. I'd feel tempted to slap him in the face. He's just a cheap little organizer. Looks like a fat Judd Grey — remember the guy who was executed at Sing Sing with Ruth Snyder for the murder of the lady's husband? The corset salesman? No, you wouldn't, but I do.

Well, they had a pleasant afternoon abusing Henry Wallace. Lemke talked after I left, and the young man who drives for me[1] — his powers of endurance were greater than mine, and he stayed through — said Lemke was even more abusive than all the rest put together and also slipped in and socked a few at the President. Typical:

"The President drove the money-changers out of the Capitol on March 4th — and they were back again on March 9th."

Bryan made himself a political speech. So did Langer tonight. I listened to him over the radio.

The burden of Bryan's song was:

"Let the Government put out Three Billion Dollars in new currency and use it to pay cash for the Fourth Liberty bonds that are about to be refunded (or something like that) and to pay the soldiers' bonus."

He said a lot more. Speaking in a sort of weak, high voice, he repeated himself again and again, clumsily and ineffectively, until I want to groan audibly:

"Can this be the brother of the man who made the 'Cross of Gold' speech?"

He finally wound up with an account of how he had shipped a carload of pigs from his farm in compliance with Wallace's pig-destruction program — Boy, how they do love to rant about "them pigs!" — and held back another carload, waiting for the price to go up. It hadn't. And so he got a hand on that.

Incidentally, one gentleman I talked with today — John Latenser, PWA state engineer — characterized Bryan as "a thoroughly unscrupulous and by no means stupid politican." From which I gather that Hopkins isn't the only one who has had trouble with him out here.

Langer was more effective. He speaks rather well. He gave them an account of the five Governors' meeting with the President in Washington. If he was as inaccurate in that account as he was in some of the statements he made about conditions up in North Dakota — He had the nerve to assure them that nobody in North Dakota lacked food or clothing, because of his efforts! — I wouldn't bank on his story. Langer said also that there had been no foreclosure riots in his state. Hell, they had one while I was there!

"I guess I told him" was his theme song, "him" meaning the President. I'll bet he was actually meek as Moses in the conference! He didn't say exactly what he had "told him." I'd love to know! He kidded the "professors."

"Every time they wanted to know anything they'd push a button and in would pop another professor," he said. "It was like a football game — a substitution after every play. Olson finally wanted to know if there was a single dirt farmer in the set-up. There was — one. They brought him in and he agreed with us. So they took him out."

Oh, yes, he said that when they put the matter of a tariff on butterfat and oils up to the President, the President said it would take something like 70 days to find out what could be done about it, whereupon Olson called his "bluff" by pulling out a copy of the Recovery Act permitting the President to declare an embargo.

Lemke — there's a boy — gives the President 30 days to make good. After that — he doesn't say what's going to happen, but predicts it's going to be pretty bad. Incidentally, when I saw Olson in St. Paul, on October 27th, he, too, gave the President 30 days. HIS 30 days are nearly up.

Oh, hell, I don't know. I simply can't take them awfully seriously. I guess that fellow McCandless, on the World-Herald, has the idea, when he says:

"Potentially, there's plenty of trouble for the Adminstration out here. But it isn't going to happen now. They haven't got the leadership."

I believe the President said something of the sort the night the three of us had dinner in your sitting room. Remember?

Wallace IS unpopular out here—even among the gang that still believes in giving the Administration a chance. Young Dick Freeman, my driver, said tonight:

"I guess it was a shock to nearly everybody out here when he was appointed. They couldn't figure out why he should be Secretary of Agriculture." . . .

1. Excerpted by Hickok.
2. Richard (Dick) Freeman, who worked for the Federal Land Bank in St. Paul.

To Harry L. Hopkins

Sioux City, Iowa, November 23, 1933

Dear Mr. Hopkins:

. . . I spent most of the morning—starting at 7:30—out with a Federal Reemployment man, having a look at PWA and CWA projects.

His PWA men were working on some paving and grading jobs that will be finished pretty soon.

The CWA gangs, some 20 men, were putting in shoulders along an old and rather narrow paved road. It was a nasty morning. Cold. And sleet. But they looked cheerful. Thirty-hour week, 40 cents an hour—CASH, instead of grocery orders.

The Reemployment man, a big, husky Bohemian undertaker named Otto Kuk, is worried about two things:

1—On those Public Works jobs, that are let to contractors, he thinks it ought to be stipulated in the contract that a certain amount of hand labor be employed. * * * He took me out and showed me two road jobs to prove his point. On one, 40 men were at work with teams and shovels, building a road. On the other, the contractor had moved in $75,000 worth of road-building machinery that was doing the job twice as fast. EIGHT MEN WERE EMPLOYED. * * * "And I've had a hard time keeping them on," he said. "Have to keep fighting with the foreman all the time. They don't want to keep these men because they don't know so much about handling this machinery, and they are a little slow. They wanted to bring in their own gang." * * * The only difference between a "hand made" road and a "machine made" road, Mr. Kuk says, is that the latter may be a little firmer because of the heavy caterpillars running around over it, packing it down. And, of course, a "hand made" road takes longer. . . .

As you may know, this is a hotbed of the "reds." They've had a lot of trouble with them in Sioux City. Unemployed strikes, mass demonstrations, and so on. Last summer they threatened to kidnap the relief director of the county. They've quieted down there since a good, tough district attorney rounded up a lot of the Communist agitators and slapped them into jail. In South Sioux City they're still a nuisance. Only recently they called on the relief director there, about 30 of them, and demanded her resignation. They surrounded the home of her predecessor, a man, one night and threatened to lynch him. They've also threatened to "get" Kuk.

Of course there are only a few of them who are actually Communists. The rest are dissatisfied unemployed who follow along. . . .

Incidentally, the relief director in South Sioux City tells me she has seen evidence of . . . pamphlets, evidently put out by the Communist Party indicating that the organization of the unemployed is a national undertaking by the party. These pamphlets, she said, emanated from Kansas City and Omaha. They were regular political propaganda sheets, highly praising "good aggressive comrades" such as those in Sioux City, who had been raising Hell with the relief workers.

The Farmers' Union convention in Omaha didn't amount to so much. Everybody I talked to — farmers, businessmen, newspapermen — assured me it wouldn't. . . .

They abused Secretary Wallace, of course. One night, while I was listening to Governor Langer of North Dakota bemoan the fact that Simpson wasn't made Secretary of Agriculture, I growled into the radio: "Oh, HOW I wish you had been made Secretary of Agriculture, Brother Simpson!"

The whole truth is, I believe, that anyone — I don't care who — in the job of Secretary of Agriculture would be catching Hell right now. The young man from the Federal Land bank in St. Paul who is driving me about put it this way:

"Aw, farmers all love to sit around and hear somebody give somebody else hell. They eat it up."

I heard Bryan, Langer, Lemke, Simpson and Reno — all abusing Wallace. Once in awhile they'd slip in a dig at the President. For instance, this from Lemke:

"The President drove the money-changers out of the Capitol on March 4th — and they were all back on the 9th."

And this from Mr. Reno:

"We've forgotten all about Mr. Wallace. And we'll forget the man in the White House if he forgets us."

Bryan, in a weak, rather high voice, talked an hour, although he was down for 15 minutes. His cure-all is for the Government to put out $3,000,000,000 in new currency and use it to pay the soldier bonus and pay up in cash the Fourth Liberty loan. He kept repeating himself too much, and his delivery was so atrocious, that I wanted to stand up in meeting and say:

"Can this be the brother of the man who made the 'Cross of Gold' speech?"

Langer's theme song was, "I told him!" Meaning what he told the President when he was down in Washington with the other governors. I'd be willing to bet a month's salary he didn't "tell him" anything. He's an awful liar. He told them that — due of course to his efforts — "no one was cold or hungry or without clothing or bedding" in North Dakota. And that, after what I saw in Bottineau county. He also told them there were no foreclosure riots in North Dakota. They had one not more than 75 miles out of Bismarck while I was there!

The head of the Nebraska Farmers' Union — a conservative sort of chap, who told me there would be "lots of noise, but not much action" at the convention, offered to introduce me to Milo Reno. But after seeing Reno and listening to him for awhile, I said, "Aw, what the Hell?" and left. There wouldn't have been any point in my talking to him. He's just a cheap little racketeer. Do you remember Judd Grey, the little corset salesman who was executed in Sing Sing back in 1928 with Ruth Snyder for the murder of the lady's husband? Well, Milo Reno looks like a fat Judd Grey.

Incidentally, after Reno had bawled to the "vast audience" — it was a "vast audience" for the radio, although there weren't more than 300 at the session I attended, and a third of them were women and children — that nobody but God could stop the strike, the Farm Holidays leaders met the next day and called it off. What there was left of it.

An entertainment feature consisted of three corn-fed lassies from somewhere in Western Nebraska who sang, off-key, dreadful songs to the tunes of popular numbers. They had one, to the melody of "Happy Days Are Here Again." That didn't go over so well, but they had one dedicated to "Henry Aloysius Dictator Wallace" that got a hand.

Well, I guess it all boils itself down to what McCandless, the farm reporter on the World-Herald, said:

"Potentially, there's plenty of trouble for the Administration out here. But it won't happen now. They haven't got the leaders."

Incidentally, Bryan predicts plenty of trouble for the President when Congress meets in January.

As if THAT was news to anybody!

As I wrote you several days ago, it would be hard to tell much about relief administration in Nebraska because it's barely started.

But here is a story that will give you an idea of what they go through getting a relief set-up in a state. It is a bit exaggerated, perhaps — and one phase of it is of course not typical — but in its outlines, at least, it's been fairly general.

Ever since I've been on this job I've been compiling in the back of my mind, a list of "Unsung Heroes of the New Deal." Maybe some day, after I'm through working for the Government, I'll write a book about them.

Today I added to that list the name of Lowell Evans, emergency relief director of Thurston county, Nebraska.

Evans is a mild-mannered little chap, about 30. He wears horn-rimmed glasses and an old army service uniform, with the insignia removed, and his boots are heavily caked with good old Nebraska, Missouri river-bottom gumbo.

He draws from Thurston county the magnificent sum of $125 a month — in claims, which are what a county puts out when it cannot issue any more tax warrants. He cashes those claims at the bank, taking the discount, amounting to about $3, himself.

And for this he does — or valiantly tries to do — a job that you or I wouldn't want to tackle for a hundred times as much as he gets.

On October 5 he arrived in Walthill, a scrubby little town which is the county seat of Thurston county. Before he left Lincoln they said to him:

"Now you're the boss up there. Go on up and run the show."

And this is the situation into which little Evans — just one of those little guys who have to DO the job that the rest of us plan and observe — rode into on October 5 in his tired, wheezy Ford that could barely make some of the hills in the gumbo this afternoon:

It was up to the county commissioners to pay his salary and provide him with investigators and administration funds.

He was about as welcome to the county commissioners as a plague of grasshoppers.

1 — The county is broke. It can't even issue tax warrants any more!

2 — The county commissioners and the bankers, to whom practically everybody in the county owes money, were just itching to get their fingers into that money. Why, the very idea of having some young whippersnapper come in there and take it away from them? They'd soon fix THIS little bug!

One of the county commissioners dominates the rest of them — because they owe him money. In September Thurston county had

109

received its first allotment from Lincoln — $500. That was just dandy! The boss of the county commissioners had simply turned it over to his son-in-law to distribute!

They'd formed their own committee — the county commissioners and the bankers. The boss of the county commissioners is head of it. He still is, and it's still the same committee.

"Oh, we could probably move him off," said little Evans. "But what would be the use? He'd still have control because the county commissioners have to pay all the administrative expense."

And the miracle is that, in spite of everything, little Evans is probably doing a fairly good job. God knows he's trying. He wasn't complaining, either. He's a cheerful sort of fellow. When I suggested that perhaps if he went down to Lincoln he could get them to back him up and shake things up a bit, he replied: .

"I don't want to admit to them that I can't handle this situation. I CAN."

He was just a little wistful about his office expenses. It seems that he managed to get the office for nothing — all they have to pay is the electric light bill. And he's been as careful as he could be, he said, but the county commissioners won't okay a long distance call to Lincoln, and he has to pay for the stamps he uses out of his own pocket. They allow him $35 a month on that poor little wreck of a car of his — $35, minus a discount, because that, too, is paid in claims — and it just about buys the gas he uses. In three weeks he has had something more than $10 in repair bills on what used to be a Ford. He paid that himself.

"It's kind of trying," he admitted, "because all the other county officials drive county cars. They don't have to use their own.

"Oh, it's plenty tough, this job. It was still tougher at first. The boss of the county commissioners doesn't believe in relief, anyway. He has said to me more than once, 'Aw let the damned fools starve! They never will amount to anything anyway.' And every time I put any family on the rolls that he hasn't recommended — and most of those he recommends I have to take off after I've investigated them — he has a fit.

"But I'm beginning to get the bankers with me now, and that helps. They find that the grocers, since relief has come in, collect a little money and are able to pay a little on their notes."

One day, Evans said, one of the bankers came to him and wanted him to pay $15 for a couple of hogs that a half-starved farmer had killed to feed his family.

The banker held a mortgage on the hogs, and he said that, if Evans didn't pay for them, he was going to prosecute the farmer.

"I'll send him to jail," said the banker. "That will teach these birds not to slaughter mortgaged livestock."

Evans refused to pay the $15 and somehow talked the banker out of prosecuting the farmer.

I may have exceeded my authority, but I suggested to Evans that the next time any banker came to him with a threat like that, he tell him to go ahead and prosecute, but warn him that, if it ever got into the newspapers, the Farm Holiday crowd would probably lynch him.

Most of Thurston county is Indian reservation, and Evans has a lot of worry about the Indians. Indian relief, supplied by the state relief committee, is dispensed by the Indian agent. Evans says he has investigated every complaint against the agent's handling of the money, but has found that practically all of them were unjustified.

"I don't know why it is," he said, "but people will always take the word of 'a poor Red man' against that of a white man. So people come up here from Lincoln and get all sentimental over the Indians, swallowing whole everything the Indians tell them.

"They're a problem, those Indians. I really believe that in the beginning the white man ruined them. But now—they're the worst liars you ever saw. Half the population of the county is wearing mackinaws the Red Cross gave the Indians last winter. They sold 'em for whiskey. I had one Indian who went out and sold his wife's shoes for whiskey while she was sick.

"'Aw, she don't need shoes,' he said. 'She can't go out anyway.'

"They're a lawless bunch. And they get all hopped up on some kind of brew they make. White women don't go out after dark down here. Not very long ago—it's since I came down here—a big buck Indian tried to carry off the postmistress of a little village out here and rape her!

"Agitators have got in among them, too. They're dissatisfied. And they're beginning to dance about it. Last night I was driving up here in the hills when I heard a lot of yelling and drum-beating. Somebody told me the Indians were having a stump-dance. I'd never seen 'em dance, so I went over to have a look. And there they were, dancing around some stumps, beating drums, and yelling like mad.

"I asked an educated Indian what it was all about. He said:

'Oh, it's a kind of protest against the way relief is being handled here. They think if they dance long enough, they might get [an] idea on how to change it!'

"Believe me, I got out of there. I was a mile or more away when I got a flat tire and had to fix it. I could still hear their yells and the drums while I worked here in the dark. It kind of made the shivers run up and down my back."

I telephoned Evans this morning from South Sioux City, telling him I'd be down this afternoon. A few minutes later he called back and wanted to know if I would talk to the Chamber of Commerce at a noon meeting. Utterly horrified, I replied no, that I wasn't allowed to make any speeches—and I'm afraid I was none too gentle about it.

When I got down there and found out why he'd wanted me to make that speech, I was deeply ashamed of myself.

It seems that the poor little guy was trying to get some CWA work started. They were all opposing him, "just on general principles, I guess," he said. And there he was, fighting with his back to the wall. He'd thought that maybe, with the prestige of being from Washington, I could help him.

"Oh, it's allright," he said, after I had apologized and had explained just what my job was and why I couldn't go about making speeches. "I won out. I finally got desperate and, maybe I was bluffing where I had no right to bluff, but I said to them:

'Look here, I don't want this job. I'm perfectly willing to quit right now. But — if I go back to Lincoln, the relief money goes with me.'

"And the banker, who's been getting a little money on the notes he holds on the grocers, told 'em no, that that mustn't happen."

It may be silly and sentimental, but sometimes I feel damned ashamed for drawing down the salary I get for — just going around and observing!

To Harry L. Hopkins

Des Moines, Iowa, November 25, 1933

Dear Mr. Hopkins:

. . . Here's ONE spot in the United States where things are "looking up."

Today was the first CWA pay day in the state of Iowa. Something over 5,000 men, who went to work with picks and shovels and wheelbarrows last Monday morning, lined up and got paid — MONEY.

It was for only half a week's work. The payrolls were made up as of Thursday night, but for many, many of them it was the first money they'd seen in months. They took it with wide grins and made bee-lines for the grocery stores, NOT to shove a grocery order across the counter, but to go where they pleased and buy what they pleased, with cash. And along about a week from today these and many thousands more will be dropping into the drygoods stores, too, and the clothing stores.

I wonder if you have any idea of what CWA is doing for the morale of these people and the communities. Officials, like the mayor of Sioux City, tell me it's almost beyond belief. And they wouldn't need to tell me. I can see it for myself.

Here's the story of Iowa's first week under CWA:

F. H. Mullock, Iowa's state relief chairman, arrived in Des Moines from Washington at 7:30 A.M., a week ago yesterday morning.

At 11 o'clock Sunday morning 350 county supervisors, mayors, county relief committee members, and relief workers from the 16 most populous counties in the state assembled at the Capitol to get their instructions and get their projects okayed.

Meetings of representatives from other counties met on Monday, Tuesday, Wednesday, and Thursday.

At 7 o'clock Monday morning in those 16 most populous counties thousands of men went to work. They are the fellows who got their first pay checks today.

And did they want to work? In Sioux City they actually had fist fights over shovels!

Every day all week more men were put on — until today, according to Mr. Mullock's estimate, there were some 15,000 at work on $13,000,000 worth of projects, running from $175 up to $200,000, that had been approved since last Sunday. The projects okayed so far will take care of 23,000. Iowa was allotted 53,000 jobs. More men are being hired every day. . . .

I spent Friday morning going about with the city engineer in Sioux City seeing the men at work. Thousands of them, at work on roads, sewers, little odd jobs, big jobs, like making a public swimming pool in one of the parks and building a waterworks system in Stone park and moving a young mountain down to build a road across a valley.

You never saw shovels fly faster in your life. Said the city engineer:

"You just can't believe that these are the same men who were listlessly and unwillingly doing their time a week ago on work relief projects to get their grocery orders!"

Everywhere they greeted us with broad grins and a wave of the hand. And then there are people who say these unemployed don't want to work!

Away up on top of that hill in Stone park, from which you can look out into three states — Nebraska, South Dakota, and Iowa — a crew with shovels and wheelbarrows was leveling off the site of a water tower. It was a cool, raw morning, and the wind was almost strong enough to blow a man off the hill. I talked to an old fellow who was busy with a shovel.

"Does it seem good to be back at work?" I asked.

"Gosh, yes!" was his fervent reply.

And everywhere we went the attitude was the same. No more grocery orders for those fellows. . . .

So much for what the program is doing for Iowa right now. They tell me they are feeling better than they have in years, and that anyone who was through here a month ago wouldn't even recognize the state now! In the last two weeks especially there seems to have been a strong swing back to the Administration. Why, they're not even panning Mr. Wallace around here! They're still grouching a bit about the Federal Land bank and the credit situation, but apparently there is going to be a shakeup in Omaha that will ease that out. And the crowd in Omaha, they tell me, having heard there is going to be a shakeup, is breaking its necks now to get some of that money out into the hands of the farmers!

Now for a few warnings on our CWA show:

Apparently something has got to be done about the labor unions. I get this both from the state federal reemployment director and from Miss Ina Tyler, state relief director.

It seems that the Iowa Federation of Labor has been getting a bit cocky of late. One thing they've been doing — both the reemployment director and Miss Tyler say they have encountered it more than once — has been to send out paid organizers to organize the unemployed in unions with charters in the federation. They take the unemployed in for nothing, on their promise to pay their dues out of their first pay when they do go to work. . . .

In Ottumwa — I'm going down there tomorrow — the relief workers and the chairman of the relief committee reported that men on the relief rolls are being coerced into joining the unions — are being told that they cannot get CWA jobs unless they belong to the union.

I don't know what the attitude will be in Washington, but this makes me boiling mad. . . .

I've encountered this cocky attitude on the part of the American Federation of Labor before, you know. In Kentucky and West Virginia, for instance, where their organizers were going about telling miners they wouldn't be under the code unless they joined the United Mine Workers of America.

I know what I'm talking about. I've met some of their organizers. Fellows who were going around telling West Virginia miners that every soft coal mine in the state would be running full blast as soon as the code, recognizing the United Mine Workers of America, went into effect.

I don't think they're playing fair with us. And if any organization in the country ought to play fair with this Administration, the American Federation of Labor ought to! . . .

If possible, something ought to be done, too, to protect these people from the installment houses and the loan sharks who got them into trouble before. They're getting busy — right on the job. I don't see how anything could be done about this, however, But, gosh — if the average American citizen only had more brains!

Another thing to watch out for — I'm getting this, you realize, from people who are actually on the scene, putting this thing over — is that PWA is ready to go when CWA stops. (Or shall we take all three billion away from Mr. [Harold L.] Ickes[1]?) They simply MUST be ready.

And again yesterday and today I heard a lot about that business of machine versus hand labor.

They built a beautiful new post office in Sioux City a year or so ago. The day the contractor started excavation — using just as much machinery and just as little labor as he could get away with — the unemployed went down there and threatened to wreck the machines, staging one of the nicest demonstrations you ever saw.

Thursday the reemployment director in South Sioux City, Nebraska, took me out and showed me two road jobs — one, using 40 men with teams and shovels, the other, using $75,000 worth of road machinery and eight men.

Friday in Sioux City the city engineer urged that it be stipulated in all PWA contracts that a certain amount of hand labor be used.

And tonight in Des Moines, the state federal reemployment director told me a long tale of his troubles with the contractors on hiring men.

They all agree that the contractors will NOT live up to the spirit of the PWA program unless they are forced to do so. There is in the PWA act a clause that they are to use hand labor wherever it may be feasible and won't add too heavily to the expense — or something like that. . . .

And that about winds up tonight's tale, except for a bit I got yesterday from Max Duckworth, County attorney in Sioux City.

Sioux City, as you probably know, has been the seat of all kinds of trouble — unemployed organizations, Farm Holiday, United Workers, and all the rest of them. They got so they'd put on a demonstration about once a week. It was a mess.

One night a few weeks ago Duckworth sent some sheriff's deputies out to a private house, where it was known that the Communists congregated, with liquor search warrants, and raided the place. They brought in the whole flock — Communist organizers and their local followers — and clapped them into jail. The little local fellows he let go, after a couple of days in jail. Four of the Communists he had indicted on some sort of syndicalism charge.

In a mass of Communist literature and correspondence which he seized — I went through some of it with him yesterday — he found indications that the Communists actually were behind the nationwide organization of the unemployed. He read me a letter from a Communist organizer in Minneapolis to one of the four he arrested in Sioux City. It stated that in a recent election a Communist, who was also head of the unemployed organization in the ward, had come within a thousand votes of being elected alderman of the Sixth ward. The letter contained this comment:

"This just goes to show what leading the struggles of the unemployed will do for us."

Duckworth also found in the correspondence and literature — there were pamphlets on "How to Lead and Organize an Unemployed Demonstration" — evidence that this was a nationwide movement and on the part of the Comintern, about which Mr. [Maxim] Litvinoff[2] was so virtuous. It was mentioned repeatedly. He had one letter, written from a Communist worker in New York City to one of the brethren in Sioux City, telling how they organized unemployed demonstrations there. . . .

Duckworth also found documentary evidence that the Communists were mixing in the Farm Holiday group.

"I hesitated to try for an indictment against the four Communists," Duckworth said. "I realize that they love to make martyrs of themselves, and that it helps their cause.

"But I finally did it to throw a scare into some of these local people. And I think I succeeded. I let 'em go, and we haven't heard a yip out of them since. They weren't really Communists, just following along, but making us plenty of trouble. A couple of days in jail did those boys a lot of good.

"I called in some of the Farm Holiday leaders, too, and showed them what I had on them. I think I threw a scare into them, too. They protested most earnestly that they didn't want the Communists in, realized that the Communists had been playing them for suckers, and went out of here in a chastened mood."

Duckworth said it was his belief that much of the violence around Sioux City during the recent farm strike — including the burning of a couple of railroad bridges — wasn't the work of Farm Holiday members at all, but a few Sioux City "reds," missed in the raid and therefore not quite so scared, "who got drunk and went out there to do some damage realizing that they probably never would be caught, and that the farmers would be blamed for it."

Governor Herring told me today that he'd been promised there was going to be a shakeup in the farm credit gang in Omaha, and in that connection he remarked that Floyd Olson, while the five of them were in Washington, had a private talk with the President about the Minneapolis situation. . . .

1. Secretary of interior.
2. The first ambassador from the Union of Soviet Socialists Republic.

To Eleanor Roosevelt

Ottumwa, Iowa Sunday, November 26th [1933]

My dear:

. . . The day has been simply beautiful, and my window gives a view toward the West, off across the rolling Iowa countryside into the afterglow of a lovely sunset.

Well, no matter how they may be pounding the President in the East, Iowa and Nebraska, for the time being at any rate, seem quiet and contented enough. I mean people generally. And, although I've been moving so rapidly that I haven't been aware of it as I might have been had I remained in one locality — Sioux City, for instance — I believe that in the month since I came out here there has been a remarkably swift and strong change in the current of public opinion in the "Farm Belt" — sweeping back toward the Administration. They never were really against the President. And now Wallace and Henry Morgenthau seem to be getting back. NRA is not at all popular, to be sure. Well, how *could* it be? Their prices *did* go up faster than their incomes. And businessmen in smaller cities — just above 2,500 for instance — that are trading centers wholly dependent on agriculture, and as a matter of fact practically every city and town in Iowa, from Des Moines down, is almost wholly dependent on agriculture, must have been having a tough time if they tried to live up to NRA. The truth is — they haven't. Hotels, for instance. You see the same crew on all day and far into the night. Clerks — some hotels apparently have only one. Waitresses. Dick and I had dinner at 8 o'clock in the coffee shop at the Warrior in Sioux City one night last week, and at breakfast at 6:30 the next morning the same waitress served us. I doubt if the Warrior *could* take on any more help and remain solvent. There couldn't have been more than a dozen guests in the place while we were there, and it's practically new, not over 3 years old, and a very good hotel. The day we had lunch with the bunch of city officials, one of them, who has an interest in the Warrior, although it's under chain management, told Dick that it had never paid a cent to its stockholders and that they'd had to shell out more than once, some of them, to keep it open. Which would indicate that it really *is* bankrupt, although it hasn't actually been placed in receivership. Walk up to the desk in any of these hotels and look over the mail boxes. Certainly 80 percent of them will be empty, with the keys lying in them. Many of them — the Warrior, for instance — keep only one elevator running. Take situations like that, combined with — let us say the rather brusque — tactics of General Johnson, and NRA isn't going to be very popular. You know a lot of these small businessmen really are *for* the President. Among them there seems to be no organized attack as there is in so-called "Big Business." I think most of them, perhaps, would like to comply. But they can't and stay in business. They might be able to if the incomes of their customers had kept pace with prices. But they didn't. And they haven't caught up yet, although things are beginning to look a little better.

Sioux Falls, South Dakota, interested me. Its population, in figures, hasn't changed since the depression — which is 10 or 12 years old out here, remember. But in the *character* of its population there has been a change most disastrous from an economic standpoint. It's the largest

117

city in the state. It's always been purely a trading center, and many, many traveling salesmen working out through the Dakotas, Montana, Wyoming, and Iowa into western Nebraska, made their homes there. There are darned few traveling salesmen on the road out there any-more — and, if you could have overheard, as I did the other day, an oil-burner salesman trying to sell an oil burner to a small town restaurant proprietor, you'd understand why. Only the man selling the absolute necessities of life can get by even. Take a commodity like paint, for ex-ample. Why, there obviously hasn't been a paint brush on those farm buildings in years. And that's true of Iowa, too. What chance has a paint salesman had out here? And the condition is the same this year — what with closed banks, low prices and crop failures.

Well, the result, they tell me, has been that most of those traveling men and their families — good, solid, paying customers — have left Sioux Falls or have been forced on to the relief rolls, and their places have been taken by farmers and their families who lost their farms and moved to town, hoping they'd be able to get work there.

Now what chance have merchants in a town like that to take on more help and raise wages? And can't you imagine how they resent being called "chiselers?" That of course is *not* what General Johnson had in mind when he used the term. But they all took it to themselves. I hon-estly think it would have been better had he stayed in Washington and kept still. I don't believe any of these fellows put on anymore help as the result of his visit out here. He only made them and the farmers sore. Why not leave them alone and apply the pressure in the Eastern Indus-trial sections where NRA has a chance and is working — or at least it ap-peared to be working when I was last there.

You see, a Blue Eagle doesn't mean much when it's unpopular both with the retailer *and* the consumer. Why, half the stores out here don't even display them, and most of those you do see are all faded and curled up and covered with dust.

And yet, despite NRA and some of the rather inept remarks of Gen-eral Johnson, things are beginning to look up — in Iowa and Nebraska, at any rate. Wheat allotments have come in, corn loans are arriving, the corn-hog program is getting underway, Henry Morgenthau is appar-ently going to kick some of the "Tories" out of the credit picture, and the farm strike died on its feet.

I think I shall have to quit reading the Chicago Tribune. Their latest was to run — today — two weeks after it was all over — pages of farm strike pictures battles! They looked to me as though they'd been posed, by the scrub football teams of Northwestern and Chicago universities! They *do* make me so *damned* mad!

I must go and eat. . . .

Gotta hand it to those Republican papers in Des Moines, though. They *did* give the corn loan payment a good play.

A coal miner's children (*top*) and another coal miner and part of his family in the back of his home on Bertha Hill (*bottom*), Scott's Run, West Virginia.

Marion Post Wolcott, FSA

"Out on the wind-swept prairie it stood — what had once been a house." Williams County, North Dakota.

The child of a farmer in North Dakota.

"Horses so listless that they didn't seem to care whether we ran into them [with our car] or not. Mares, dull-eyed, every rib showing, their backs sagging, great hollows behind their shoulders." Near Dickinson, North Dakota.

One part of the aftermath of the drought: a dead Longhorn in Sioux County, Nebraska.

Arthur Rothstein, FSA

"What happened was that the grasshoppers simply cleaned [the fields] off — right down to the earth. . . . People were afraid to hang their washings out. [The grasshoppers] even ate the clothes off the lines." Grant County, North Dakota.

"Today's little treat was a dust storm. . . . It was as though we were being picked up in a vast impenetrable, brown cloud, which was whirling us right off the earth."

Christmas dinner at a home near Smithfield, Iowa.

Meal time at the Homeless Men's Bureau, Sioux City, Iowa.

To Harry L. Hopkins

Sioux City, Iowa   December 4, 1933

Dear Mr. Hopkins:

Two weeks' ago today men went to work for the first time under the new CWA set-up. Everything I've heard indicates that the plan is certainly fulfilling — and possibly exceeding — your hopes for it. . . .

Everywhere I've gone in the last week the story has been the same. They are all most enthusiastic about CWA. I've talked to the men at work. I have visited their homes and talked with their wives. I have talked with businessmen and professional men. The day before Thanksgiving, in Charles City, Ia., I visited some grocery stores.

I went to Charles City because it was supposed to be one of the toughest spots in Iowa. Last summer they kidnapped the county relief director there and ran her out of the county. Last Wednesday morning I visited with her successor [at] the home of the ring leader in that demonstration. He was back at work, and his wife was getting ready for Thanksgiving, in a most cheerful frame of mind.

"The first thing I did was to go out and buy a dozen oranges," the wife of one of the other men told me. "I hadn't tasted any for so long that I had forgotten what they were like!"

"They got their first checks last Saturday night, and they came in here and ordered steaks. I have talked with people on relief who said they hadn't tasted meat in six months!" a meat dealer in Charles City told me. "And, although they'd got pay for only part of a week, quite a few of them made small payments on the bills they had accumulated before they went on relief."

"Every Saturday there's a big crowd around here," a coal dealer in Fairmont, in Southern Minnesota, said today. "They've been a pretty gloomy crowd these last two or three years, but — say, you should have seen 'em last Saturday! Laughing and joking — why, I hadn't had so much fun in years! They all had a little money in their pockets. They were all going to have something in the house to eat for Christmas. You wouldn't have known them!"

In Charles City I visited the home of a man who had once earned $15 a day in the tractor plant there.

"This $15 a week looks bigger than $15 a day ever did," his wife told me.

And so it goes.

I spent yesterday and last night in Fairmont, Minnesota, at the home of a district judge, who is a friend of mine. I went down to see him because he has a wide acquaintance with Southern Minnesota and Northern Iowa. Along back in August, he was writing very gloomy letters about conditions there to his son in New York. Fairmont is not many miles from Le Mars, Iowa, where they tried to hang a judge early last summer, I believe. They had riots on the courthouse lawn in Fairmont and last summer my friend, the judge, was bitterly complaining that loans were not coming through and was predicting a very bad winter. Conditions have entirely changed now for the better, he said, and he attributed the change to quicker action on loan applications, wheat allotment checks, corn loans, which are beginning to come through, and to CWA.

"If any one had told me a month ago that things were going to improve as much as they have in the last three or four weeks, I'd have said they were crazy," the judge told me. "It's almost unbelievable.

"The pick-up started after Henry Morgenthau came out to St. Paul. I don't know what he did, but, anyway, we began to get action on those loans. They've been coming through in fine shape since — and the first loan that came through started the change in sentiment. All that was helping, and then CWA came along and turned the trick. Up until a month ago, everybody around here lived under a sort of cloud of apprehension. With the feeling that existed among the farmers and among the unemployed — well, you didn't know what was going to happen next. But we aren't worrying now."

The judge said he had hesitated to leave Fairmont, even when court was recessed, because no one knew what might happen next, and he might be needed. He is now planning to go to California for Christmas!

You get a feeling of optimism all through the area. All the little towns have got out Christmas tree decorations. They've strung evergreens above Main street. I did a little shopping Saturday in Minneapolis. The department stores were jammed — as crowded as they used to be when I lived here, back in the "boom days." I don't know what it was like out here a year ago, but they tell me it wasn't anything like this. Even last summer, when things started booming in the East, and the stock market was going up, there was very little optimism out here, they say. But this, you see, is a matter of a lot of people — thousands and thousands of them — having a little money to spend, CWA wages, wheat money, corn money, after several years of being broke. I hope I'm not unduly optimistic, but it does look darned good.

Now for what kicks and fears there are left.

Of course, you hear some complaint about how much it's costing and who's going to have to pay, but not as much as you might expect. Your natives of Iowa are inclined to be a contentious people. (Begging your pardon.) They seem to love to argue. Now and then, against my will, I get drawn into an argument. I have personally so much more enthusiasm for this CWA program than I ever had for the relief business that I always want to defend it. The other day a county supervisor in Tipton, Iowa — undoubtedly a bit irritated because he couldn't get his fingers into the pocketbook — was yelling like thunder about taxes and all that sort of thing.

"Who's going to pay for all this?" he demanded over and over.

Finally, I couldn't stand it any longer, and I said to him:

"You read in the papers about what happened in Princess Anne, Maryland, didn't you? And you read about what happened the other night in St. Jose, California. Well, how would you like it if a mob of unemployed ran amuck and strung up a few county supervisors?"

He laughed at that and cheered up a little and said that, well, maybe we were right.

It wasn't such a joking matter, at that, judging by what happened in Le Mars — only, of course, they were farmers irritated by foreclosure sales — and taking in the Charles City kidnapping episode, and the state of mind my friend, the judge, said existed in Southern Minnesota and Northern Iowa up until a month ago.

But, as I said before, you don't hear much kicking about the cost.

From the Federal Reemployment people, however, I get a worry that should be given more serious consideration. That is the fear that PWA won't be ready to pick up where CWA leaves off and never will, for various reasons, do the job. . . .

Another bothersome thing is this business of contractors on PWA projects using as little hand labor as they can get away with. I have written you previously at some length on that. Everywhere among the Federal Reemployment men I hear the same story. They all feel that something should be done about it — that there should be some stipulation in the contracts about the use of hand labor and that there should be some means of enforcing it.

Another thing to consider is that PWA won't operate nearly so widely as CWA. A lot of counties, for instance, haven't applied for PWA money. Some of them are so broke that they couldn't raise any money for a PWA project. Others don't want to on account of the wage scale — they feel they could get the work done more cheaply in their own good time. Of course they are willing to accept CWA because the Federal Government is paying the wages and all they have to dig up is money for materials, equipment, and so on. That's probably very wrong of them, but — the men in those counties are going back to work, under CWA, and what are we going to do with them when CWA runs out?

Another kick is that it doesn't put everybody back to work. That's a bit foolish, I'll admit — but it doesn't seem so foolish to a Federal Reemployment man who has 392 jobs and 1,100 men who ought to have them. They are constantly tempted to change crews after each project, although I haven't heard of any of them doing it so far.

The Union Labor business is perhaps not quite so serious as the Iowa Reemployment director thought it was. I went down to Ottumwa, where he said he had heard the unions were telling men they couldn't get jobs unless they belonged to the union, and talked to a union leader.

He denied it, but I only half believed him. I talked to some of the relief committee there about it, but they were businessmen, and there has been a good deal of friction between the unions and the businessmen in Ottumwa. The businessmen can't talk sanely or reasonably about union labor there, so you can't believe them, either.

I also went to Burlington, where the Hod Carriers' and Common Laborers' Union had supposedly gone before the city council, reminded them that they had an agreement whereby common labor working for the city was to get $20 a week, and demanded that men working on CWA projects be paid $20 a week, although the 30-hour week at 50 cents an hour pays $15.

The Mayor of Burlington told me they had done something of the sort. What they wanted was a 50-cent hour — and more hours, to bring it up to $20 a week. And this in spite of the fact that they were furnishing to private industry in Burlington men at a lower wage scale and more hours that paid $16 a week! I do get a kick out of the attitude of the American people toward their government. Just a big sucker — that's all Uncle Sam is to them.

Well, they didn't get anywhere with it, and the Mayor said that, since it was only one local, and the demand hadn't even been considered by the Trades and Labor Assembly, he wasn't expecting any trouble. . . .

And now that they've got CWA going, they're all starting to find jobs for unattached women. Mrs. [Blanche] La Du[1] in St. Paul told me she had lined up, in Minneapolis alone, 800 CWA jobs for women. Out in the smaller cities and towns it's harder to get them interested, though. Your average businessmen just won't believe there are any women who are absolutely self-supporting!

I'll write you in a day or so how things look in Sioux City, Iowa, after a couple of weeks of CWA.

PS — Incidentally, if the Labor Unions are trying to chisel in on CWA, they probably aren't alone in it. I've heard repeatedly that the American Legion, under the soldier preference law, is trying to use CWA to build up its membership — i.e., telling the boys they have to belong to the American Legion to get CWA jobs. . . .

1. Chairman, Minnesota State Board of Control, which is responsible for public welfare.

To Harry L. Hopkins

Fergus Falls, Minnesota December 5, 1933

My dear Mr. Hopkins:

Well, I went back to Sioux City, Iowa, today to see how things were going after two weeks of CWA.

When I was there about ten days ago they had great hopes of what CWA was going to accomplish. Today they were positively ecstatic. . . .

I went first to South Sioux City, across the river, in Nebraska, and saw Otto Kuk, the tough Bohemian undertaker who is Federal Reemployment man there.

Otto reported his entire quota, 299 men, at work. Of the slightly more than 900 unemployed who registered with him, 800 now have jobs, he said, either in private industry, on a PWA river job, or under CWA. Of the hundred or so left, most of them are women, many of whom will be placed under CWA, or men who are unable to work. Not so bad, eh?

Otto was in a terrible stew, however, because, owing to the fact that the man who was appointed disbursing officer refused to take the job, his CWA men hadn't been paid. They are a tough crowd in South Sioux City, and they've been after him pretty hard. I got in touch with the chairman of the relief committee. He said Lincoln was sending the checks up today, he thought, and that a new disbursing officer was about to be appointed. . . .

In Sioux City I saw the relief administrator, the chairman of the relief committee, the reemployment man and a field man from the state reemployment office in Des Moines, the Mayor, the City Engineer, and several other city officials.

In spite of some difficulty over their records, the relief and reemployment people were feeling pretty good. I was surprised myself that there wasn't more difficulty. Out of some 3,000 men now working on CWA projects in the county and city, there were some 75 or so whose records were not straight. They seemed quite distressed over it, but I didn't think it was so bad. Putting a thing over as fast as CWA was put over is bound to result in some tangling up of records. They expected to be all straightened out in a couple of days.

The field man from Des Moines, a fussy little chap, was worried about politics. He said he detected some in transfers of men from common labor to better jobs. He wanted to know what to do. I told him it was not my party, but that, if I were in his place, I'd watch it, report it to Des Moines when I saw it, and quit worrying. There's bound to be some politics mixed up in it. You simply can't get entirely away from it. But I don't think it's so very serious in Sioux City — not nearly so bad as in some counties here in Minnesota where, because there is no relief set-up (less than half the counties in Minnesota had applied for federal relief money when this came along) and it's turned over for the time being to the county commissioners. Mayor [W.D.] Hayes told me that he had promised to keep politics out of it and that he was doing everything he could to keep politics out. If he is living up to his promise 90 per cent, that's not so bad.

The mayor nearly threw his arms around my neck when I walked in this morning. . . .

"Why, our people here in Sioux City are now saying that in another 20 days we'll be out of the depression!" yelled that Irishman, banging his fist on his desk. And he's the fellow who, a month ago, was asking the Governor to send National Guard troops to Sioux City because the Farm Holiday strikers and the unemployed were getting so tough!

"Two things have done it," he said. "CWA and the corn loans. They've accomplished more than all the other efforts of the Government combined."

The Mayor is, of course, a rather vociferous fellow, but from other, more temperate citizens I got pretty much the same picture.

They said the department stores in Sioux City last Friday and Saturday were more crowded than they had been since 1921. The street cars every morning are jammed with men going to work. The packing plants are beginning to take back the men they let out during the Farm Holiday strike. And everybody in town is going around wearing grins that extend from ear to ear.

I heard similar reports from other towns. The reemployment field man was in Fort Dodge last Friday. He said businessmen told him they did more business there that day than they had done in years.

Enroute North I stopped for lunch at a little town in Southwestern Minnesota, just south of the drouth area, Luverne.

"Oh, things have picked up a lot around here in the last two or three weeks," said the proprietress of the restaurant. I went to the post office, to buy some money orders.

"Yes, business around here is a lot better, with all these men going to work on those projects," said the postmaster.

And it all ties in with what the Judge told me in Fairmont Sunday.

I have been out in this area since October 25. In that time, I am inclined to think, I have witnessed close up—so close up, in fact, that I was hardly conscious of it at first—one of the swiftest and most complete changes in the public opinion that this part of the country has ever seen.

And that despite a press that, for the most part, is distinctly hostile toward the Administration! . . .

To Harry L. Hopkins

Brainerd, Minnesota   December 7, 1933

Dear Mr. Hopkins:

I wound up tonight a three-day trip through Western and North Central Minnesota—through the drouth area and up into the cut-over timber country.

My observations certainly convinced me of one thing—i.e., that CWA is going over a whole lot better where there is a good relief set-up than where there is none or a very poor one.

This is partly due to the fact that a good relief set-up comes as close to being entirely out of local politics as it is possible for any government agency to be. Also, where there is a good relief set-up, the administrator knows his peole and, cooperating with the federal reemployment man, has been able to start the CWA show off with a bang. Where there isn't a good relief set-up, you have a perfect mess—politics and confusion.

I must say that, so far, I've got a pretty poor impression of the relief show in Minnesota. I suspect Governor Olson of having his finger too much in the pie. Frank Rarig, who, as secretary of the state board of control, is the relief administrator for the state, seems to be just a kid—I don't know how old he is, but he certainly looks and acts young and in-experienced—who doesn't know what it's all about. About the only reason I can see for having a man as weak as that for state relief adminis-trator would be that the governor wanted to run the show himself. And where the governor runs the show himself—even if he is not directly us-ing it for political purposes—it's apt to be badly run because he hasn't time to do it properly.

Here's something I've noticed. Of the five states through which I've been traveling these last six weeks, Iowa and South Dakota seem to have the best relief shows. And in those states, apparently, there is no inter-ference from the governors. Berry and Herring both back the relief out-fit to the limit, I'm told, but keep their fingers out. That's true in Up-State New York, too, and Up-State New York has the best relief show I've seen anywhere. And neither Roosevelt nor Lehman apparently has tried to meddle with it.

Bryan and Langer have certainly messed things up in Nebraska and North Dakota, and, as I say, I suspect my friend Olson in Minnesota. He's a politician, this fellow Olson. He has this state sewed up tight as a drum, and I think it would be too much to expect that he would keep his fingers out of the relief show.

It may be, of course, that I'm doing both Olson and Rarig an in-justice. I can tell better, I expect, after my trip through the Iron Range, where, I'm told, the relief show is older and functioning better, and after a few days of looking it over in the Twin Cities. Rarig may be bet-ter than I think. I've seen him only a couple of times—but both times he seemed to be in a complete muddle and didn't appear to know what he was doing.

Yesterday and today I sized the show up fairly thoroughly in three towns—Fergus Falls and a little town called Perham, in the Western drouth area, and Bemidji, up in the timber country.

Fergus Falls and Perham are both in Otter Tail county, where the relief show is brand new. And while I was poking around in Fergus Falls the young man from the Federal Land bank, in St. Paul, who is driving around with me, went to Morris, in an adjoining county, to look over the farm credit set-up and brought back some dope on the CWA business.

As I said, the relief set-up in Otter Tail county is new — only three weeks old. That, obviously, isn't Olson's fault or Rarig's. The county had not asked for help previously. As a matter of fact, less than half the counties in Minnesota are getting federal aid now, on relief, and consequently have no set-ups. Until a short time ago only about 20 counties in the state, out of some 80, were getting federal relief money.

The relief committee in Otter Tail county had its first meeting a week ago last Saturday. They hadn't even got going when, last Saturday, they met to go over CWA projects. One thing that slowed them up was that relief in the county is handled on a township basis, and they have 84 units of government to deal with.

Be that as it may, they are obviously darned slow about getting the CWA show started. Neither in Perham nor in Bemidji, a much larger town, had a single man gone to work under CWA yet! Their projects were not sent to St. Paul to be okayed until this week. And that's a pathetic showing compared with the weakest county in Iowa. . . .

Bemidji, in Beltrami county, has been the scene of a good deal of Communist agitation and resultant disorder. They had a near-riot there last Saturday, out in front of the relief office. Beltrami county has been getting federal money for something over a year, but the whole thing has been badly handled. The new administrator, who arrived there about three weeks ago, said that was why he was sent up. He found a mess. No records worth mentioning. Apparently cases hadn't been investigated at all. A huge case load. The policy had apparently been to try to buy off the agitators by giving them plenty of relief. One of them had $65 worth of grocery orders, clothing, medicine — everything you could think of — in the month of July. . . .

All through here, too, the reemployment offices are simply swamped with registrations. Everybody wants to go to work, of course, and, with no very good relief set-up, it's going to be pretty hard to pick out the first 50 percent, off the relief rolls, let alone deciding who of the second 50 percent really need jobs and should have them.

Beltrami county, for instance, was allotted something like 300 jobs. There are 900 heads of families on the relief roll alone — although proper investigations would undoubtedly cut that down a good deal. And 3,000 men in the county have registered for jobs!

One thing that will help them a good deal is a forestry project about to be started in the Chippewa National forest. That means 600 jobs for men from three adjacent counties in addition to their allotments, and the Minnesota Forestry Experimental station is taking on 100 more from the area. Once they get out of their muddle and know where they're at a little better, they should be in fair shape up there.

So far as destitution is concerned, I can't see that there is any comparison between what I've seen in Western Minnesota and what I saw in the Dakotas. If Floyd Olson ever gave you the idea that the need in his drouth area could even touch that in the Dakotas, he was either crazy or a liar.

So far as I could find out — and I talked to plenty of people, including an auctioneer who travels constantly through North Dakota and Western and Northern Minnesota — the drouth here was spotty and hasn't been a matter of a farmer not having a crop for several years, as is the case pretty generally in South Dakota and, for instance, in Bottineau county, North Dakota.

In Perham I saw a member of the Otter Tail county relief committee. Perham is supposed to be in the center of one of the worst drouth areas.

"No, they're a bit shabby, but they're warmly dressed," was his reply when I asked about the clothing situation.

"What our people need mostly is a little money to carry their livestock through the winter," he explained. "This is dairy country. There's been no feed. And they haven't any money to buy any. The result is that the farmers are selling off their good milk cows at $5 or $6 a head to be butchered. And they won't have any stock left when spring comes." . . .

There are, of course, isolated cases of destitution. I heard of one family that had been living in a tent, and an investigator found two of the children with frozen feet. I was assured that the family had been taken care of, and I was told that the father was a drunkard, and that that particular family was usually on the relief rolls in the winter.

One thing that has complicated the situation a bit in Western and Northern Minnesota is the fact that droves of families and transients have moved in from the burnt-up areas in Dakota. In Bemidji for instance a large number of men who normally would be working in the woods are out of jobs because the Dakotans got in early and grabbed them.

So far as I could learn, there hasn't been any such general and widespread drouth in this state as there has been for years in South Dakota. It's spotty. In some cases, I was told, one farmer would have a good crop, and his neighbor would have nothing.

There was no crop around Perham, but less than a hundred miles north of Perham the auctioneer told me he had sold two carloads of furniture to farmers this fall, and three carloads of horses.

Here's an interesting thing. The auctioneer also dabbles — and quite successfully — in horse trading. He buys them in Montana, mostly colts out of the wild herds, he says, and sells them to farmers in North Dakota and Northern Minnesota. In the last year he has sold something more than 3,000 head of horses. Which partly explains why that tractor plant in Charles City, Iowa, isn't running.

"It doesn't pay for a farmer to buy gas for a tractor when grain is selling at present prices," was his explanation.

Driving through the country I've seen more than once tractors abandoned in the fields — apparently right where they ran out of gas!

Generally, the auctioneer told me, conditions in North Dakota and Northern and Western Minnesota are nowhere nearly so bad as Langer, Olson, Townley, and so on would have you believe.

"The great squawk, of course, is over beef prices," he said. "Get them a better price for their beef and maybe a little better price for their butterfat, and those boys would be allright."

He wondered why something couldn't be done for the livestock and dairy people along the lines of the corn loan, in Iowa and Nebraska.

For the information of Mr. Morgenthau, there seems to have been considerable improvement in the farm credit situation since his visit out here in October, although some communities are still kicking. Generally speaking, loans are coming through much faster, and people feel better.

From reemployment men all over the area I get the same complaint about PWA, and here's a honey that I picked up in Bemidji this morning. It was passed on to me by a reemployment man who has several counties under his supervision.

Near Baudette, in Lake o' the Woods county, up on the Canadian border, there is a 28-mile road graveling job now under way, a PWA project.

They knew it was coming up there for months before it was started, and everybody had his hopes up, including Northern Minnesota contractors and farmers with teams and trucks.

Right off the bat, the contract went to a big Twin City firm, and the reemployment man told me that this firm's bid was $5,000 higher than the low bid, which was made by a Northern Minnesota firm.

The contractor who got the job next awarded a contract to another Twin City contractor to do the gravel hauling. Right away this firm came in with 48 big trucks — some of them with Mississippi and Missouri licenses on them.

"They didn't even bother to take off the Mississippi and Missouri licenses," the reemployment man said, "until they got to Baudette, and there in the Main Street men with smaller, but perfectly good trucks, who had expected to get some of that work, stood around and watched them take 'em off and put on Minnesota plates.

"I got so mad that I wired down to St. Paul about it. In most of the contracts in this state it is specified that they use as far as possible trucks from the community and no out-of-state trucks.

128

"I got an answer that the state highway department had granted this company special permission to use outside trucks."

Now, if his story is true, somebody is getting a cut out of that deal, or I'll eat my hat. And, since the state highway department is involved, the finger would point toward Governor Olson.

Incidentally, the reemployment man said he'd been asked to furnish 38 men for the job, where he had expected to furnish 150 or 200.

"If they get away with that kind of thing," he said gloomily, "the National Reemployment Service might just as well shut up shop. And the people up in Baudette are feeling just about as agreeable as a crowd of snarling dogs."

And that's about all the news I've got tonight on FERA and CWA and PWA.

I heard the President's speech over the radio last night in the hotel lobby in Bemidji. The lobby was half full—men in work shirts and sweaters and coats and trousers that didn't match. One of them listened so hard that he didn't realize he was leaning on the cigar lighter, which burned a hole in his coat!

Before the speech, I was writing some letters at a desk in the lobby, and I overheard a group of them talking. One of them was willing to bet that the President would be reelected in 1936.

"Well, I dunno," another said. "A lot of things can happen in three years."

"Aw, Hell," put in another, "he's got more friends right now than he had when he went in."

And they all agreed on that. . . .

To Eleanor Roosevelt

Hibbing, Minnesota   December 8, 1933

My dear:

. . . Hibbing! It's a sort of story-book town. It used to be called the richest village in the world. The mines pay about 98% of the taxes, and Hibbing right now—the village, township, and school district—has an income of $2,500,000 a year. The chief of the Fire Department drives about in a Cord car half a block long. They have a $5,000,000 high school. And—the other day the town went "red" and elected a lineotype operator in the local newspaper office mayor! In boom times, Hibbing's total tax income from the mines used to run around $4,000,000 a year. Back about 1920 one of the mining companies simply picked up the town and moved it three or four miles west, so they could get at the ore under the town-site. They paid millions for it—you should see Hibbing's public buildings! I get a kick out of all this because U.S. Steel really pays the bills, since it controls the Iron Range.

You ought to see that high school! They've got a clinic in it that would do credit to the most perfectly equipped metropolitan hospital. They have a doctor, dentist, and a staff of nurses there—all on fulltime salaries. Why, the Hibbing Board of Education has a million dollars a year to spend—and they have a hard time finding ways to spend it, legally. Crazy stuff.

Well, anyway, there's darned little destitution up here—compared with the Dakotas, for instance. The relief director *thinks* there is. He took me out to see some of his most destitute families. Then *I* told *him* about Bottineau county, North Dakota. I hope he felt better.

There is, to be sure, an unemployment problem here that will never be cured, probably. In the last three years the open pit mines—the largest open pit mine in the world is at Hibbing—have gone in for western machinery. They've bought electric shovels, for instance, and one man, with an electric shovel, can do the work of eight men on a steam shovel. Well—among other things we really *have* an industrial revolution on our hands, haven't we? . . .

To Harry L. Hopkins

Minneapolis, Minnesota, December 10 [1933]

My dear Mr. Hopkins:

I have completed my trip over the Iron Range and I am still obliged to confess—with some chagrin, since this is my home state—that I have not a particularly favorable impression of Minnesota's Relief and CWA shows.

The Iron Range, as you may know, is located in St. Louis county, which they tell me is larger than the states of Massachusetts, Connecticut, and Rhode Island combined. It has an area of 6,611 square miles and is 114 miles long and 60 miles wide!

I found a lot of confusion up there and a good deal of strife. Everybody seemed to be suspicious of everybody else, charges of political favoritism of one sort or another were being bandied about, and there had apparently been a lot of delay in getting the CWA men working.

Three thousand, four hundred and five men were paid off in the county last night. The county was allotted jobs for 7,301 men, including 1,800 who are to go to work this week, I understand, on a federal project in the Superior National Forest. That makes a little more than 3,000 men working out of 5,478 who were supposed to get jobs on local projects. A large number of men, to be sure—they couldn't tell me exactly how many—are supposed to go to work tomorrow morning on local projects.

The majority of the men paid yesterday — some of them received their second checks — were residents of Duluth, where 928 men went to work on November 21, on projects that had been okayed over the telephone from St. Paul. I could find very few men actually at work outside of Duluth. Generally much less than half the quota.

When I was in Hibbing Friday, not a single project there had been okayed yet, and 114 men, all relief cases, who had been put to work two weeks ago on a state conservation project that was later cut off had received no pay! I understand half a dozen Hibbing projects were okayed by wire yesterday.

The principal trouble in St. Louis county, as in other parts of the state I visited, seemed to be delay over getting projects approved by the State Board of Control, which functions — rather badly, I judge — as the state Relief and CWA committee. Apparently they have been swamped, although I judge they have done better by the Twin Cities than by the rest of the state. The morning paper today stated that $160,000 was paid out in CWA wages in Minneapolis yesterday.

In any criticism I make of the State Board of Control I'll try to be as fair and as impersonal as I can. I have heard the charge of course that they are playing politics, and the relief director in Virginia, on the Iron Range, suspected Governor Olson of being the real cause. . . . Most of the people who made the charges, however, were themselves apparently mixed up in local politics, too. So what they say should be taken with a grain of salt, I think.

The State Board of Control, consisting of three members, is appointed by the Governor. Being a member of the board is a life job. A member can be removed only for cause. The chairmanship is assigned to the senior member. It is supposed to be non-political. Its present membership consists of one Farmer-Laborite (new), one Democrat, and one Republican. The Republican, Mrs. La Du, is chairman.

Heretofore, the duties of the board have consisted in administering the various state institutions. And I think that may be one reason why it is not more efficient in the CWA show. It is an institutional organization, not a relief organization.

Right from the start, apparently, outside the Twin Cities, there has been delay and confusion in getting the CWA show going.

This might be partly due, in a large part of the state, to the fact that there were no county FERA organizations, and I can understand that it would be difficult to get going without a set-up.

I picked St. Louis county, however, for a fairly careful study because they have had a relief set-up there for a year or more. No reason for delay on account of lack of organization there.

W. A. Newman of Duluth, chairman of the St. Louis County Relief and CWA committee, said that on November 18, at the end of the week when you had all the governors, mayors, and so on in Washington, Mrs. La Du called him, long distance, and told him he must put men to work Monday morning.

He got his committee together the next day, Sunday, November 19, he said. They drew up 21 projects — all in Duluth — and these Mrs. La Du gave blanket, verbal approval, over the telephone. The next day, Monday, November 20, was spent selecting the men, notifying them and so on. On Tuesday, November 21, men went to work. . . .

From what I could learn — nobody seems to KNOW anything, and that's one trouble with the Minnesota set-up — only the men in Duluth have been getting their money, because their projects were okayed over the telephone. . . .

To complicate matters more, there is all kinds of friction going on in St. Louis county — and always has been going on — between the Iron Range and Duluth. It's a matter of taxes. No need of going into it here, except to state that most of the tax money from the mining companies, and indirectly from U.S. Steel Corporation, goes into the towns on the Range. In Hibbing, for instance, "the richest village in the world," the chief of the fire department rides around in a Cord automobile half a block long, they have a $5,000,000 high school and $1,000,000 a year to spend on it, and the town recorder gets a salary bigger than that of the governor of the state! Incidentally, the village of Hibbing has been spending something like $64,000 a month on labor, trying to keep the unemployed at work. But they're out of funds now.

All this jealousy, however, may have something to do with delay in getting projects started on the Range. Believe me, last night, after two days of it, I felt like taking a bunch of the leading citizens of St. Louis county across my knee, one after the other, and spanking them. . . .

It looks to me, though, as though the whole set-up in this state was — pardon the vulgarity — lousy with politics. If it were any other state, we could get tough with them. Put somebody in here to straighten it out, I imagine. But here you've got Olson. Believe me, he's got control of Minnesota! And, on the surface at least, he's been friendly toward the present Administration in Washington. And running the Democratic show, you've got Joe Wolfe, who has managed to make practically every Democrat in the state sore as Hell. No harmony or organization there, that I can see. And you've got a state in which most of the money and the press are Republican and hostile. I know politics are not supposed to get mixed up in this show, but they ARE. And, after all, we're part of an Administration, and that Administration needs friends, in this state.

And that's about all I know except that:

1 — On the Iron Range, where they have underground mines, things are looking up — 300 men went back to work, part time, for about $20 a week, in the vicinity of Ely and Tower within the last 10 days.

2 — On the Iron Range, where they have open-pit mines, there's a bad unemployment situation and there isn't much hope. The open-pit mines have installed a lot of machinery in the last three years. Electric shovels that can be operated by one man, instead of six or eight needed on a steam shovel. Electric cranes that, in moving track about, can enable three or four men to do the work that used to require 40 or 50.

3 — There are more open-pit mines on the Range than there are underground mines.

4 — They're anxious to get their transient camps started up there. Living in shack communities — still called "Hooverville" and "Hoover City" — around Hibbing and Virginia are 400 or 500 transient laborers. Mostly Finns. Mostly aliens. And mostly, I gather, Communists. They'd like to see them deported. Anyway, they want to get something done with them. For one thing, there are no sort of sanitary equipment or facilities in those camps, and the townspeople are afraid of epidemics. And, remembering an epidemic of good old black smallpox, with a very high mortality rate, that started up there in the woods several years ago and swept through Duluth and down into the Twin Cities, I don't blame them for being afraid.

5 — Farmers suggest that CWA work in purely farming communities, where there will be, say, only four or five jobs for the whole outfit, ought to be split up more — that there is hardly ever a farmer who can't get along if he has a little help — $25 or so — but that there are many who need that much. This agricultural relief business IS a problem, isn't it?

6 — I visited families on the range that were supposed to be in terrible shape. They weren't — not if compared with what I saw in the Dakotas. I spent part of the afternoon in Hibbing talking with teachers, the school superintendent, and nurses and the doctor in the clinic in the $5,000,000 high school. That clinic, incidentally, would do credit to an up-to-the-minute metropolitian hospital! The children are warmly clothed, they told me, and there is very little evidence of destitution. The doctor, who is on a full-time salary and examines every child in the school district, said he hadn't seen a single badly undernourished child this year.

Generally on the Iron Range, barring relief people who were crabbing about CWA, I encountered among the people, including the unemployed, a spirit of optimism I have seen nowhere else outside of Sioux City! They shipped a lot more ore out of there this year than they have for several years past, and, although in the open-pit areas that didn't mean that a lot of men went back to work, it somehow made people feel good. . . .

PS Reading this over, I find it sounds confused. Well, *I'm* confused. I'm only passing on to you what I hear. Much as I suspect Floyd Olson of politics in the relief show, I'm inclined to think that if — as was indicated to me — he is planning to force control away from Mrs. La Du and her crowd and run it himself, there'll be at least a more efficient administration. He's the strongest man in the state — right now. And, once he gets hold of it, it would be to his advantage politically, I should think, to stop all this wrangling and delay and make it a good show. But it will be a "political" show, if Olson runs it. However — it's apparently something of a "political" show right now. And, for all I know, he may be actually running it now, too. Everywhere I've gone in this state, it seems to me, I've heard nothing but politics. Of course — CWA, with *cash* involved and lots of it, *would* be more attractive to politicians than the relief show.

To Harry L. Hopkins

Minneapolis, Minnesota   December 12, 1933

Dear Mr. Hopkins:

Well — I arrived over in St. Paul yesterday just as Floyd Olson was taking CWA away from the State Board of Control. The board was in session when I got there, and late in the afternoon Olson told me what he had done, although I didn't get the details and didn't ask for them. Believe me, I want to keep out of the row if I can!

I dropped in to see Frank Rarig in the morning. He asked me what I had found in my trip through the state, and I told him. Whereupon he proceeded to open up and tell me all his troubles.

He said he realized that CWA had got away to a very slow start — and blamed it on Olson. He said the Governor and Mrs. La Du, chairman of the Board of Control, were at loggerheads and always had been, and that the Governor refused to cooperate with the Board. Olson, he said, refused to give them any help whatever in getting CWA started, and the facilities of the Board for handling the job were entirely inadequate. He charged that Olson wanted control himself and had always wanted control of the relief organization, for purposes of political patronage and so on, and that he simply would not play ball unless he did have it. He had heard that you had authorized Olson to take the show over and was awaiting a call into the board meeting to be demoted or fired. I don't know what happened yet. Olson didn't tell me, and I tried to keep away from personalities as much as possible in my talk with Olson. Rarig said he didn't care what happened, that he had done all he could — that he had finally taken over a bunch of the projects and had them gone over and okayed by his staff because the board was so slow getting at them. He was called into the meeting while I was there, and that was the last I saw of him.

I had my talk with Olson in the late afternoon, having written for an appointment from the Northern part of the state last week. . . .

He said that some time last week — Saturday, I believe — you called him, long distance, told him the CWA show was moving too slowly in Minnesota, and wanted to know why. He said he told you he didn't know much about it, but that he suspected where the trouble lay. He said you asked him for suggestions, and that he told you he'd take it over and run it himself, but that he must have full authority, and that you told him to go ahead.

"And so," he said, "I took CWA away from the State Board of Control this morning. I'm going to turn it over to the State Highway department, and we'll get these men back to work."

He told me that he had made engineers from the state highway department available to help the Board in going over projects. I did not tell him what Rarig had said.

The Governor said he had had no trouble with Mrs. La Du until CWA came up. He said he had kept his fingers out of the relief business entirely. On the Sunday after the sessions in Washington, however, he said he attended a meeting at which Mrs. La Du explained CWA. He said he was responsible for the order to put men to work on that conservation project on the Iron Range, that the St. Louis county committee called off. . . .

Governor Olson and the State Highway department are going to run the CWA show in Minnesota, although it hasn't been publicly announced as yet. At least it wasn't in this morning's papers.

Well, it will undoubtedly mean a more efficient handling of the show. There will be politics in it — but, gosh, there was plenty of that in Mrs. La Du's set-up, apparently. And very little efficiency. Whose fault it was doesn't really matter, although I am inclined to believe Rarig's statement that Olson would not cooperate with the board. But the trouble is that Rarig never should have had the job he had. He's too young, too inexperienced. . . .

Floyd Olson really is a remarkable man. I wish I had more faith in his sincerity. Oh, I don't mean that he is a crook or anything like that. And sometimes when I'm talking with him, under the spell of his personality, I feel like a dirty dog for ever doubting him. The truth is that he is really an expert politician — a darned smart one. He's terribly ambitious, and — "Floyd is for Floyd." And that's that. He'll be your friend, anybody's friend, as long as it serves his purpose. He climbed on the Roosevelt bandwagon in the early spring of 1932. That was smart. As it turned out, Roosevelt undoubtedly helped his campaign — although at National Democratic headquarters they seemed to think Floyd was going to help Roosevelt. On Election Day in Minnesota, Roosevelt led Olson by some 50,000 votes, I've been told. And in the meantime, a split had developed in the Democratic party in Minnesota. The Administration Democrats won't admit this, but the "Rumpers" swear that they pulled out, not so much out of loyalty to Al Smith, as because they felt that Roosevelt was selling them out to Olson and the Farmer-Labor party. And there's no use kidding ourselves. The "Rumpers" were the better element in the party in this state. Now you've got the National Committeeman, Joe Wolfe, and his family holding down $20,000 worth of federal jobs, and Mrs. [Stanley U.] Hodge, the National Committeewoman, holding one of the best paid federal jobs in the state, and all the rest of the Democrats in the state, including their own crowd, sore as Hell. The Republicans of course took such a licking that they're completely disorganized, for the time being at any rate. Why, in 1934 Olson ought to be elected without even making a campaign! I understand he's going to run for the Senate.

All of which, I suppose, really has nothing to do with our relief show, except that he will undoubtedly use it to build himself up. Well, suppose he does go to the Senate. He ought to be a rather valuable ally for a liberal administration — if it serves his purpose. But I wonder sometimes if Floyd is looking ahead to 1936 when, if the Roosevelt program flops, a "Red" ought to have a darned good chance of being elected President. And believe me, this boy Olson is, in my opinion, about the smartest "Red" in this country. . . . I guess the reason I've told you all this is to justify, in my own eyes, my suspicion of him. I've known him for a long time and liked him. He's a very close friend of some of my best friends. And until the last year or so, I just looked on and grinned. It never would have occurred to me to be critical. I never believed it was possible to have any idealism in government. The trouble with me, I guess, is that I've gone idealistic. I was happier, at that, I'm afraid, when I didn't believe there was an honest or sincere politician or government official in the country.

But Olson — he's so darned likeable. He has so much personality. And he's so much more intelligent, darn it, than the average governor. When he went to Washington with the other four, he must have stood out like a peach in a basket of rutabagas! And — he came back and boasted quietly, but not so quietly that it didn't come to me through mutual friends, that the Administration was playing ball with him, that he could get what HE wanted. Unfortunately the mutual friends he told it to were not Farmer-Laborites. They are Republicans, and they threw it up to me. Incidentally, don't you ever think I haven't had to stand a lot of razzing out here in Minneapolis where most of the people one knows are Republicans! Olson's confidences came out in an argument when I was being kidded about my so-called "idealism." . . .

In the Twin Cities just now everybody is all stirred up over an upholsterers' strike. The strike in itself doesn't amount to so much, I gather. But both sides seem to be making an issue out of it. From three sources — Olson, one of my Republican friends, and a good Democrat, who is not active in politics, but is just a business man (miller) — I get the story that the businessmen are organizing and preparing for a showdown with Labor. It's got so bad that people can't even talk calmly and impersonally about the Administration any more. You find old friends ready to fly at each other's throats — all that sort of thing. Generally, the younger businessmen are inclined to support the President. The older men suspect him of going Socialist — and they are afraid. You've no idea how passionately worked up they get over this thing! I had all I could do to control myself and keep from getting into a bitter quarrel with one of the oldest and best friends I have in the world the other night. His voice was actually trembling with anger!

My Democratic friend tells me the Citizens' Alliance is getting into the show. The Citizens' Alliance, made up of Twin City businessmen, was organized back during or immediately after the war, to break strikes. You remember, there was a lot of trouble then. They got along fairly well until along came a printers' strike, and they imported some thugs from Chicago to beat up the head of the Typographical Union and intimidate him. They went out to his home, in a St. Paul duplex apartment, early one morning to get him as he was leaving for work. But they got the wrong man — a high school principal, who lived in the other half of the house — and nearly beat him to death. The thugs were arrested and "told," and, since then, the Citizens' Alliance has been pretty much out of the picture. But my Democrat told me last night they are really behind this organization of the business men for a showdown.

Olson has heard that the businessmen are making up a fund to buy firearms — which I doubt. But anyway he said:

"You go back to Washington and tell 'em that Olson is taking recruits for the Minnesota National Guard, and he isn't taking anybody who doesn't carry a Red card."

Ho-hum! . . .

Here's some more cheerful news. I had a talk with the transient man yesterday in St. Paul. They're actually getting going! Their first camp, to care for 150 men, opens at International Falls today. And I gather it was badly needed. The transient man . . . told me that when he went up there he found men sleeping in the basements of speakeasies — so packed in that you couldn't walk without stepping on them. Nine more camps are practically ready for their occupants, he said. In all, they will take care of 3,000 men. And in shelters in the Twin Cities and Duluth, he said, about 1,500 men were cared for out of our money in November.

This is a long letter. Well, it's the last one I'll be writing you before my return. I'll be back in Washington sometime around the end of the week.

From Aubrey W. Williams[1]

[Washington, D.C.]   December 28, 1933

Dear Miss Hickok:

You are authorized and directed to perform such travel as may be necessary in your capacity as Chief Investigator of the Federal Emergency Relief Administration during the period from January 1, 1934 to December 31, 1934, within the limitations prescribed by law for civil employees in the Federal service.

Your actual and necessary travel expenses will be paid by the Federal Emergency Relief Administration and you will be allowed $5.00 per diem in lieu of subsistence while away from your official headquarters, Washington, D.C.

You are further authorized to use your personal automobile in lieu of railroad transportation, and for this service you will be paid $.05 per mile in lieu of actual expense on your automobile.

1. Assistant administrator, FERA.

To Harry L. Hopkins

Washington [D.C.], December 29, 1933

Memo on "The State of the Nation"
in the Great City of New York

Not that this will be news to anyone, but of course there is a great deal of confusion in New York City at present. There would be a lot of confusion there anyway — the show is so immense, with 135,000 human beings going to work in so short a space of time. The CWA and CWS[1] offices in New York City occupy three and a half acres of floor space — 135,000 square feet — in the Port Authority building, and there are 1,500 men and women working there. Never before in my life had I seen so many stenographers assembled in one place. . . .

The most encouraging news I heard was about the Home Relief situation. It apparently has improved vastly since I was there about October 1. The relief now is much more adequate. Budgets have been increased to meet the higher prices, gas and electric bills are being paid, and — best of all — rents are being paid. Back in October the rent situation was worrying everyone. Thousands of people were being evicted, it had become exceedingly difficult to find landlords who would accept relief clients as tenants, the "reds" were using evictions as a trouble-starter, and altogether the situation was very bad. A scale of rents has now been worked out, rents are being paid, and the evictions have ceased. . . . In fact, excepting clothes — they still haven't enough money, they say, to take care of that situation adequately — the people on direct relief in New York City right now are in fairly good shape.

This improvement is due, according to Miss Mary Gibbons, Home Relief director, to CWA, which took over most of the Work Relief cases. She now has $4,000,000 a month to spend on Home Relief — and the assurance that she is going to have it. One thing that was driving them all crazy last October was the uncertainty. They never knew where they were going to get their money, or when, or how much.

New applications for relief are mounting — in some districts quite rapidly, although, taking the city as a whole, Miss Gibbons sees no cause for alarm. For the five boroughs, they jumped at the rate of 500 a day in September, 1,000 a day in October, 2,000 a day in November. During December they dropped back to 1,300 a day. . . .

So much for the relief show — in the hasty glance I was able to give it I found a good deal of encouragement. Everyone seemed to think so, from Mary Gibbons down to a little Irish investigator with whom I spent an hour in an East Side cafeteria.

In New York City the effect of CWA seems to have been felt less than elsewhere. During the month of December the sum of $7,000,000 was paid out in New York City in CWA and CWS wages. But you don't hear very much about it! One can only guess why, but there are a couple of factors that might be responsible.

First, it may be that because of the size of New York City, a $7,000,000 monthly payroll would not be felt there — that it would be just a drop in the bucket. I was told that stores like Macy's, Gimbel's, and Bloomingdale's were jammed just before Christmas, but it was pointed out also that those stores always were crowded at Christmas time. And that is true. When figures on department store business for December are available, they may show something. I tried some of the little merchants, but got very little out of them.

Secondly, the people who went off work relief on to CWA were already getting cash. In many cases they remained right on the same projects, only getting more money. In fact, they refer to CWA as "that raise we got." In places like Sioux City, Ia., the people who went off relief to CWA had been getting grocery orders — and not very fat grocery orders, either. The change was bound to be much more noticeable.

It may be, too, that the effect of CWA in New York City was reduced because of delay in getting out the pay checks. There was considerable delay, at the start, and all sorts of grief. Getting the checks out at the start was an awful job, as a matter of fact. For instance, work relief checks had been made out to "Bearer." CWA checks have to be made out to the individual. And the whole thing had to be done with a force of stenographers of whom some had not worked for two years or longer. They had forgotten how to use the typewriter. It takes most of them several days, I was told, to "find the keys" again. And when you consider the fact that a check can have no erasures — well, it IS a job. Travis Whitney, Civil Works Administrator for New York City, told me that last Saturday (December 24) everybody was paid up to December 14. He expected to have everybody paid up to date at the end of this week.

In discussions of CWA and CWS, you hear a lot about wage rates. Much more than I heard in the West. It's the usual complaint — that the rate is too high and that private industry cannot compete with it. I was told that private industry in some fields had practically stopped in Up-State New York. Mr. Whitney quoted one building contractor as having said: "I'll wait until this thing peters out — then I'll get busy. I can't compete with that wage rate." Whitney said that, whereas he is paying a minimum of 56 cents per hour, the rate, he said, that is paid at the Brooklyn Navy Yard for common labor, the actual prevailing wage rate for that kind of work in New York City is 40 cents per hour.

Miss Inez Ross, state CWA director, was having difficulty, too, over the difference in wage rates on federal CWS projects and those she was administering. She complained that federal projects pay too high a rate as compared with CWS wage rates she has established in conformity with local wage rates, and as an example cited the artists. The artists, she said, on a federal project were getting $34 a week, whereas the musicians, on projects under her direction, were getting $25. Naturally, all the musicians want to be taken over by the federal government.

"We'd have much less trouble," she said, "if Washington would not set arbitrary wage rates on federal projects without consulting local people."

She was somewhat appalled, too, by the jump in size of some of the CWS projects. On her desk the day I saw her, awaiting her okay, was a project entitled: "Extra Clerical, Supervisor, Professional, and Miscellaneous Help in the Public Welfare Department, Including Public Welfare Offices in Eighteen Towns in Westchester County!" Originally the project had called for $5,000. It had suddenly jumped to $34,000. She felt that there "must be something funny somewhere," and that she couldn't approve it without careful investigation. It was terribly clumsy anyway. But, as she pointed out, the careful investigation slows things up, too, delays getting people to work.

In the women's program, Miss Ross said, suggestions are badly needed. She cited a district in Up-State New York — along the Canadian border — where a great majority of the women out of work are factory workers, wholly untrained to do anything else. She would like to know what to do with them.

The stage relief program is apparently at a standstill, awaiting some action from Washington. I saw Antoinette Perry[2], who came down here with Brock Pemberton[3] a few weeks ago. A plan for some sort of national project, with a traveling stock company in each state, had been talked over, she said, with two outlines, one by the New York crowd and one out of Washington. Then they were told, she said, about some idea of using some Hartford, Conn., Little Theater group, and that was the last they'd heard. Incidentally — to a professional actor, producer, or director the very words "Little Theater" are anathema. Too much amateur. . . .

But Miss Perry says: . . .

"All we ask is that you don't do anything that will cost the theater its future audiences (I gather that they think Little Theater productions are so bad that they would do that) and that you don't do anything that will make conditions worse than they are."

She said that the Little Theater crowd do not compete fairly with the so-called "professional" theater because of their use of amateur actors and because they are not bound by the union rules that bind the professional theater back stage. Stage hands, electricians, and so on. The professional theater is a closed shop. The Little Theater, she said, is not.

Now that he has something more than 100,000 people at work, Mr. Whitney is going into the business of providing projects for white collar and professional people. Some of them sound interesting.

Physicians, for instance.

His interest in doctors started with his concern over the possibility of compensation liability suits. He has a feeling that there may be a good deal of that sort of thing — that thousands of men went to work on hard, outdoor physical labor who were unfit for it, and that before we get through we may find ourselves in all sorts of trouble. His idea is to have them all undergo physical examinations and throw out or transfer those who can't pass.

He began looking about for doctors. He talked to the heads of the medical societies in the Five Boroughs. The head of the Kings County Medical society told him that 30 percent of the doctors in Brooklyn had had their telephones taken out — which meant that they had been forced out of business. The percentage in Manhattan, he was told, is even higher!

Mr. Whitney has in mind a project for doctors, examining these people. It would do two things, he points out, prevent a lot of liability suits, by making it possible to weed out a lot of people who shouldn't be doing the kind of work they are doing, and provide a most interesting survey on the health of the unemployed, both on the relief rolls and off.

One thing that happened in New York, he said, was that thousands of men who had never done any heavy, outdoor work in their lives before registered as "common laborers" because they thought they would get jobs more quickly that way. In that connection, an investigator told me about one of her clients who had been a private chauffeur for 18 years and who, after he got a "pick-and-shovel" job on a playground-building project at Hunter college, went over and stood around for several hours the day before he was to report for work, watching the men to see how they handled shovels so that he wouldn't look so awkward when he started!

In picking his professional men, Mr. Whitney and the Reemployment people are working with their own professional organizations — the medical societies, engineers' club, the newspapermen's guild. Incidentally, he has several projects for unemployed newspaper reporters, one of which is "trouble shooting."

"When I hear that something is going wrong on a project," he said, "I'll send one of those boys out there to find out what's wrong — and he'll find out."

He said he had a note recently from someone who suggested that there were a lot of old wooden ship hulls rotting to pieces around New York, and that they ought to be cut up and given to the unemployed to burn.

"I sent one of my newspaper men out to look into it," he said. "Within 24 hours he was back with a report, showing just where they all were, just what could be done about them and so on. In less than a week they were being cut up into fuel for the unemployed. If I'd sent one of my engineers out on that one, it would have taken him a week to find out about it."

Incidentally, Mr. Whitney has 50 engineers at work and is quite proud of them. He took me over where some of them were working and pointed out one grey-haired man who, he said, had in his day handled subway contracts involving millions of dollars.

Mr. Whitney has been having some difficulty, he said, with borough governments which, announcing they are reducing their budgets, are trying to let out civil service employees and persuade him to hire them to work on CWA projects. Manhattan tried to slip over 250 of them he said, and Queens 500. It's caused all sorts of a fuss, but he is sticking to his guns, apparently, and refusing to take them on.

He reported he had uncovered evidence of a good deal of politics in the work relief bureau and elsewhere. . . . I asked him to give me the accompanying slips which he said are evidence of that part that politics have played in distribution of pork and other food at the surplus commodity stores. He is using, he told me, some unemployed newspapermen who last summer worked on the World-Telegram series charging politics in the relief show to conduct these investigations.

While the whole thing is big and clumsy and a bit slow at times, and while you don't hear so much rapturous comment in New York City as you hear in smaller places, there is one group of people that certainly does appreciate CWA, there as elsewhere. . . .

142

1. Civil Works Service differed from CWA in that its funding came from FERA monies. CWA had its own allocation.
2. Stage director and actress.
3. Theatrical producer.

To Harry L. Hopkins

Athens, Georgia, January 11, 1934

Dear Mr. Hopkins:

. . . Generally speaking, I have encountered down here a good deal of gloom about the economic future of the South. . . . On the other hand, some newspaper people I dined with in Atlanta last night said it was a lot of bosh, that, with 10-cent cotton, the farmers down here are better off than they've been in years, and that there was nothing to be gloomy about. Today I talked to a couple of cotton growers and three or four small town merchants — the kind who sell supplies to farmers and farm laborers — and they also were very cheerful. . . .

CWA seems to be very popular, despite some worry over the wage rate. Especially in Georgia. I've been begged repeatedly not to take Governor [Eugene] Talmadge seriously. I'm a little afraid, though, that some of these peole down here do not realize that the CWA business can't go on forever! One cotton grower today, however, was counting on its tapering off before planting time, which, in Northern Georgia, begins about the end of March.

They've done things a little differently in Georgia, as you doubtless know. Instead of hiring 50 percent of the men off the relief rolls and 50 percent from the Federal Reemployment rolls, they simply transferred all the men from work relief projects to CWA, and that took up practically all of the jobs. One of the results has been a big jump in their applications for relief — 890 in Atlanta, for instance, during the first week in January.

A lot of these are white collar cases. I spent yesterday morning in Atlanta going about with an investigator who in one day had had 16 new cases, all white collar people, living in a very good residential section of the city. At the Atlanta relief office they feel that the majority of these white collar people are not applying for relief now only to get CWA jobs, but that it just happens that right now a lot of them have reached the end of their resources.

Atlanta has always been, I'm told, a "white collar" town. Nearly every big firm in the country has maintained branch offices there, with junior executives and clerical forces. Thousands of traveling salesmen have made their headquarters there, too. Mostly they've been people who have made pretty good money and have had good credit.

143

The plight of some of them is pitiable. For instance, a man in his late fifties, a salesman all his life. He paid cash for his home, now mortgaged, sent his two sons through college, and believed, when he lost his job something over a year ago, that he had enough to live on the rest of his life. His investments went bad, however. One of his sons is studying to be a priest in Washington and [he] cannot help him financially. The other boy, a graduate of Georgia Tech, is out of work and has been for a long time. Out of the money he borrowed on his home, the old man had supported himself, his wife, his son, and the latter's wife and two children until day before yesterday. At first he asked only for a little coal, saying he thought he could still get credit at the grocery store — always hoping that his son, at least, would get a job. Night before last, however, he called up the investigator and told her the grocery had cut him off. The investigator told me that on her first visit, when she was getting the family background, this man's wife suddenly burst into tears and left the room.

"I told him," the investigator said, "that they mustn't feel that way — that they must try to regard me as they would the family physician. But you can see how they felt, can't you? It's awfully hard.

"A couple of times lately I've found myself in a most embarrassing predicament. I discovered that I was being sent to investigate people I'd known all my life — one man whose son I had once been engaged to!"

"As far as it's gone," the feeling around Atlanta is that CWA is a grand business. They all yell for more jobs, of course. It was in Atlanta that I encountered mostly that apparent lack of realization that CWA might not go on forever. It's brought a $1,000,000-a-month payroll into Atlanta, and that seems to be all they're thinking about — that and wanting more. Merchants are of course delighted. I was told that the credit manager of Rich's, the largest department store, said that, whereas the store's Christmas business a year ago had been 40 percent cash and 60 percent credit, this year it had been reversed, 60 percent cash and 40 percent credit.

I was told about a furniture store in a South Carolina town that about a year ago ordered 50 mattresses, thinking that would be all they could possibly sell in a year. Recently they put in their sixth order of 50 mattresses each. Ten-cent cotton got credit for that pickup, however.

And now to return to "the state of the nation" in the South. The gloom is mostly about the agricultural future of this section of the country — and, despite the growth of the cotton mills, they still regard themselves as predominantly agricultural states. . . .

Generally the feeling seems to be that these states are just about through as cotton producing states — that they can't compete with states like Texas, where more cotton can be produced per acre at lower cost. The problem, as it is described by some people, seems to be pretty much the same as that in some of the wheat producing states — worn out soil — although I was told today that they'd never been able to grow cotton in this part of Georgia without using fertilizer, which is the largest item of expense in its production.

Mr. [Malcolm J.] Miller[1] told me about one county in South Carolina in which before the Civil War all wealth was based on rice and indigo. Rice could be raised more cheaply in Louisiana and Texas, he said, and coal tar dyes ruined the indigo business, so that now not a bit of rice or indigo is raised in that county, which is in dreadful shape. And he sees cotton going the same way.

With cotton gone, the only basic "money crop" left would be tobacco, he said, and tobacco is expensive to raise, requiring lots of fertilizer and being exceedingly susceptible to weather conditions.

"We also raise fruit, garden truck, and pecans," he said. "For garden truck we have too much competition in the principal market, New York. Fruit the same way. And pecans are regarded as a 'luxury food' — not included in staple diets."

Mr. Miller believes in our wage rate on CWA, even though, he says, it is going to work hardship on the farmers. Common labor on farms in his area gets $3 a week or less. For common labor on CWA projects we're paying $9. He insists the farmers can't afford to compete with us.

"However, it may be a blessing in disguise," he said. "It may cut production by forcing farmers, who can't compete with us in the labor market, to plant less. I'm strong for the federal wage scale. For sixty-five years the South has been the sweatshop of the nation. That's because we were afraid of the Negro. We wanted to keep him down — and did. But we dragged ourselves down, too."

Mr. Miller thinks the only hope for the agricultural South may lie in diversification, reforestation — which already has been started in South Carolina, he said, on a fairly large scale, but which won't produce any money for some years — and government control of production.

"The government will just have to come down here and tell each farmer what to plant and how much," he said. "And make him do it." . . .

Before quitting — here's a bit. I had lunch day before yesterday with the director of women's projects for the state of Georgia. She's having the usual difficulty, wangling jobs for women, but the interesting thing about her grief is that her two most difficult groups are:

1 — Southern gentlewomen, last survivors of the old aristocracy.

2 — Negresses.

She had an idea for a project that would consist in having the gentlewomen train the Negresses for domestic service.

"The only trouble," she said, "is that the Negresses won't go in for it. They don't want to learn how to be servants." . . .

1. South Carolina FERA administrator.

To Harry L. Hopkins

Augusta, Georgia, January 14, 1934

Dear Mr. Hopkins:

Well, here's what I've heard about the alleged controversy between Southern farmers and CWA over farm labor, so far.

I have yet to talk to a farmer who seems to be worried about a possible labor shortage. And I have gone into the matter at some length with about a dozen of them, ranging from little fellows who farm 200 acres or less to one big fellow who "operates between 150 and 200 plows," which means that he has several thousand acres under cultivation. All were cotton and peach producers. I take it back — one banker, who raises peaches, but not, I was told, on a particularly large scale, was pretty sour about our wage rate.

The overwhelming majority of the farmers I've seen so far appeared not even to be worried about the possibility of our wage rate forcing up very much the wages they pay. Most of them, however, do not pay wages, but have tenants farming on a share basis. In either case they were not worried, they said, and pointed out that the difference between what we are paying under CWA — $9 to $12 a week and what they pay in wages — around $3 a week — was not really so great as it might seem at first glance. Theoretically, at least, a man on CWA has to provide his own housing and fuel and all his food out of his wages. Tenant farmers and farm laborers are provided with houses, however poor, fuel, and garden plots. Right now of course in the rural areas many CWA workers are living rent free in tenant houses on the farms, but, if CWA should continue beyond the time when farm labor will be in demand, and if those men refuse to quit CWA and go to work for the farmer on whose property they are living, I suppose there's nothing to prevent his moving them off to make room for men who haven't CWA jobs and want work.

They are not worried about a shortage of farm labor, they say, for two reasons.

CWA has by no means wiped out unemployment in the farm districts. It's really only a drop in the bucket, if one may mix figures of speech. They estimate, for instance, that there are in Jackson county 1,500 unemployed farm workers in addition to the 278 who are working on CWA projects. Said the Federal Reemployment director for the county, himself a farmer:

"We could put a thousand more men to work on CWA and keep them there right straight through the summer and all next winter, and there'd still be no shortage of farm labor in this country."

The big fellow, who raised several thousand acres of cotton, voiced the second reason. He said we must not forget that the acreage reduction also means an employment reduction. He estimates this year's reduction in farm employment at about 25 percent.

"I've got men living on my place right now," he said, "for whom I'm not going to have any work this year. And if it weren't for CWA, I'd be having to support all of them, too."

Generally, the farmers seemed to be most enthusiastic about CWA. They felt that it had helped them, by reducing the number of tenants and laborers they would otherwise have had to support. There have been many cases, relief people tell me, of farmers asking that some of their men be put on CWA.

Incidentally, the feeling among the farmers down here seems to be much better than it was among the farmers in the Middlewest when I was there. All those I've seen say that 10-cent cotton has been a big improvement — they got only 5 cents a pound in 1932 — and they appear to be cooperating willingly and with intelligence in Secretary Wallace's program. They are strong for the President and are unanimously critical of Governor Talmadge's attitude on CWA — which is interesting, because his following is supposed to be entirely agricultural. With the illiterate tenant farmers and farm laborers, who have CWA jobs or who hope to have them, his remarks may be said to have been even less successful than with the land owners.

"Talmadge was just hollerin' because he couldn't run the show hisself," one little farmer remarked. "I reckon he has a big followin' allright, but he won't be holdin' it, 'less he'll hush up."

The farmers I've seen were all in the Northern part of the state, where planting doesn't begin until about April 1. Down here, about 150 miles South and East, they are already beginning to do a little plowing, and the county CWA administrator tells me several farmers have called her up and said they couldn't get their men, on CWA, to come back. I may hear more of that as I get to talking with farmers in the Southern part of the state. . . .

One thing I can't help thinking is that these Southerners are being darned good sports about on the whole is the fact that we are paying such high wages to Negroes under CWA — much, much more money than Negroes have ever received, of course. I guess it's the first time in the South that Negroes have ever received the same pay as white men for the same work. And I haven't heard a word of complaint — that is, outright complaint. Some of them just smile when the subject is mentioned. That they are as tolerant as they are about it is surprising, I think, for, believe me, the race problem IS a problem down here.

For instance, I was thoroughly — albeit politely — lectured for driving alone late at night out in the country. Got caught in bad weather and on bad roads Friday and didn't get into Augusta until 11:30 P.M.

The county relief director, a woman, began it by telling me that no woman in the South ever drives in the country after dark without a gun on the seat beside her. I laughed and remarked that I would be more afraid of the gun than of anyone who might molest me. Whereupon she assured me that it wasn't any joking matter, pointing out that the roads down here are lonely and pretty much deserted at night. . . .

I was inclined to regard what she had said as a Southern hangover from "carpet bag" days — and most of the people I've talked to tell me the South is suffering, economically and socially, not from the Civil war, but from the Reconstruction period — until I was talking later with a man, a Northerner, who has lived down here 20 years.

"I came down here thinking all men were equal, Niggers and whites," he said. "I've been forced to change my mind. There are good Niggers and there are bad Niggers, and I'm sorry to say that almost any Nigger is apt to turn bad Nigger if he catches a white woman alone on a country road at night."

Some of the Negroes down here are rather terrifying, at that, in appearance. They seem so much bigger and blacker than the Negroes up North, and many of them look more like apes than like men.

I had a talk yesterday with the pastor of the First Baptist church — and, believe me, in Georgia, the pastor of the First Baptist church is an influential citizen. They tell me he is a typical Southerner. He indicated that he understood Negroes and loved them — as one loves horses or dogs. He also indicated, although he didn't come right out and say so, that he still believed in slavery! He assured me that under the slave system the Negroes were much better off, economically and socially, than they are now.

Well, that's a long digression, but I do think, with that attitude taken into consideration, it is rather remarkable we haven't heard more complaints about the CWA wages paid to Negroes. As a matter of fact, my somewhat limited experience so far would indicate that the whites are more generous — or tolerant — than the Negroes themselves. A Negro preacher yesterday assured me there had been a marked increase in consumption of "white lightnin' " among Negroes since CWA came in! White merchants have told me that the Negroes for the most part are spending their money on clothing and food — and second-hand cars, which are becoming something of a menace on the highways.

Augusta is an industrial town. Big cotton mills. And here I had my first encounter with industry in the South.

I had a long talk yesterday with a labor leader and found him most despondent. His complaint is that the mill operators are not living up to the spirit — the "intention," as he put it — of NRA and the code.

They have raised the hourly wage — or lowered it, in the case of skilled labor — to the minimum, he said, but they have seen to it that no man earned any more per week than he was earning before by cutting down the number of hours the mill operates. Which means that the mills operate on a 40-hour week, too. He says the payrolls have not increased at all — either in the number of men employed or in the weekly wages per man. They've shortened hours, but haven't taken on any more men because they've also shortened the number of hours the mills operate. They had a big strike here in the fall over the "stretch-out" system. The mills, he said, were letting men out and, on the plea that they were paying higher wages now, making one man do part of the work of two men. The strike was settled by arbitration, and the mills are running now, part time. . . .

The Negro preacher complained that colored labor is being discriminated against, especially skilled labor. Under PWA they are building some schools in Augusta, both white and colored. He thought Negro skilled labor should be given a chance on schools for Negro children. The relief director for the county tells me that contractors won't take Negroes for skilled labor, but for common labor they prefer Negroes to whites.

The Negro preacher told me this story to indicate what was happening to his people under NRA. He said that one of his parishioners had been employed at Western Union for five years at $6.25 a week. Under the code, for the work he is doing, he should be getting $13. He (the preacher) took the matter up with the compliance board, and Western Union promised to pay the Negro the code wage. Sometime later, he told me, the parishioner told him they'd raise his wage to $10 a week, $3 under the code rate, and told him not to tell the preacher or they'd fire him.

"I could make an issue of this case, perhaps," the preacher said, "but I know that, if I did, sooner or later the boy would be fired. So we're not doing anything about it."

There are Negro plasterers' and painters' unions in Augusta, the white labor leader told me, and the Negro mill hands in one mill are organized. He didn't seem to be particularly interested in seeing to it that the white unions took the Negro unions under their wing to see to it that Negroes got the same wages as whites, although I suggested that, so long as employers could get Negro labor at wages below the white man's minimum, the white man's wages might stay down, too. The Negro problem IS a problem in Augusta. About half the population is colored.

My friend, Fred McDonald[1] in Atlanta, and another engineer I met here last night observe that the Negro is going to "get it in the neck" anyway. Wherever the higher wage scale is adhered to, they say, the tendency is to throw out Negroes and hire whites. Negro workmen are uniformly lazy and shiftless, they say — and judging by the color of the bathtubs in some of these Southern hotels I'll say they are — but heretofore have been tolerated because they were cheap. Now that they are having to pay higher wages — when they do — employers are going to hire whites, who do the work better. Negroes, they say, are being replaced by whites in filling stations, for instance, and even as bell boys in hotels. I noticed that the hotel where I stayed in Atlanta had white bellhops, and I've seen white waiters in a number of restaurants. I've seen darned few Negro attendants at filling stations down here.

I wonder, though, assuming that we are going to have to support a portion of the population, if it wouldn't be just as well to let the more efficient people have work and support the less efficient. But I can't help feeling that, so long as there are in fact different wage scales for whites and Negroes, many employers will hire the cheaper Negroes, and that will force the white man's wages down.

Despite all these problems, "the state of the nation" in the South is, I should say, darned good. There is generally a feeling of optimism down here. Merchants, particularly the little fellows, are most enthusiastic about improved business, and they don't attribute it entirely to CWA either. Every merchant I've seen has told me that his business is a whole lot better than it was a year ago. One little fellow, running a store at a country cross roads, said it was more than twice as good as it was a year ago.

What with the farmers having more cash and with CWA in operation, the stores in all these little country towns were simply jammed at Christmas time, they said. One merchant said:

"My store has always been crowded at Christmas time, but the difference this year was that people were buying, instead of standing around looking at the things they'd like to buy if they had some money."

That same merchant, in a rural community, told me that the CWA workers were using a lot more sense spending their money than they were usually given credit for.

"These farm hands and farm tenants don't expect CWA is going on forever," he said. "The first thing they do is to outfit the whole family, from the skin out. And after that they start laying in supplies — buying flour by the barrel, for instance — so they'll have something ahead when the work stops."

The white Baptist preacher who is one of the leading citizens of Augusta told me yesterday that before CWA came in, anywhere from two to 15 beggars used to come into his study every day seeking help. He said the number had dropped down almost to zero in the last month.

"I believe the situation is steadily growing better," he said. "You know, one of the most sensitive barometers of business conditions that exists is church financing. If times are bad, the churches are the first to feel it. My church isn't in debt, but my salary during the depression has been cut $1,840 a year.

"My church, with a so-called wealthy congregation, hasn't begun to feel the uplift yet, but the other day in another Baptist church down in the milling district they voted to raise the preacher's salary. That means those mill hands have more money than they had a year ago!"

A doctor in the little town of Commerce, up in Jackson county, told me that he was actually beginning to collect a little on back bills.

And in the Augusta Chronicle this morning I read that Augusta bank deposits in 1933 were $2,000,000 more than in 1932.

1. A consulting engineer.

To Harry L. Hopkins

Jesup, Georgia, January 16, 1934

Dear Mr. Hopkins:

Here's all about Savannah, the loveliest city I've ever seen, next to San Francisco.

Savannah's nice, but, oh, Mister, what an "argufyin' " bunch of people! I heard more kicking and griping in Savannah than I've heard anywhere else in the country, it seems to me now. Apparently the only people in Savannah who are happy about CWA are the merchants — and retail merchants everywhere like CWA — and the people who have CWA jobs, particularly the Negroes. And this despite the fact that Savannah is said to have had more liberal treatment in the matter of CWA jobs than any other city in Georgia and possibly more than any other city in the South. Savannah got slightly more than 10 percent of the state's allocation of jobs, they tell me.

The Negroes on CWA naturally are happy. The more illiterate and emotionally religious among them, I'm told, actually believe the "second coming of Christ" has occurred. They go about saying, "De Messiah hab come!" Meaning the President. I'm also sorry to report that one or two employers of Negro labor told me the Negroes call CWA "guv'ment easy money."

Dissatisfaction in Savannah, I believe, may be traced to five sources: (1) racial prejudice; (2) a popular belief that thousands of Negroes are moving in from the countryside to get CWA jobs, thereby creating for Savannah a difficult social problem when CWA ceases to function; (3) poor investigation back before CWA took over the men on work relief projects, resulting in the charge that a lot of people are on CWA who really don't need the work; (4) fear of a labor shortage; (5) politics.

If you compare it with the feeling down in Savannah, racial prejudice simply doesn't exist in Northern Georgia at all. Although they would never admit it, I imagine, the whites in places like Savannah must be a little afraid of the Negroes. More than half the population of the city is Negro — and SUCH Negroes! Even their lips are black, and the whites of their eyes! They're almost as inarticulate as animals. They ARE animals. Many of them look and talk and act like creatures barely removed from the Ape. Some of them I talked with yesterday seemed to me hardly more intelligent than my police dog. Only a little more articulate, that's all. At that, I could barely understand them.

For these people to be getting $12 a week — at least twice as much as common labor has ever been paid down there before — is an awfully bitter pill for Savannah people to swallow, even the most kindly disposed and tolerant of them. I don't say the "most enlightened of them" because — Northerner that I am, raised in the sentimental tradition that all men are created equal — I'm not so sure these Southerners aren't right. What makes it tougher for the Savannians, as they call themselves, is that while these illiterate creatures, whom they regard as animals, are getting more money than they ever had in their lives before, hundreds of white workingmen are unable to get CWA jobs, and their families are hungry.

I don't know who was responsible for permitting Georgia to disregard the regulation requiring a division of jobs on a fifty-fifty basis between people on the relief rolls and unemployed who were not on the rolls, but I seriously question the wisdom of it. You hardly ever find a Negro who didn't grab at the chance to get on the relief rolls. But in this state, as elsewhere, there were thousands of white workmen who held off, using up their credit, making heavy sacrifices, living off their relatives, doing everything they could to keep off the relief rolls. By recruiting their CWA workers almost entirely from the relief lists, they simply barred these worthy white people from getting CWA jobs down here. Our own relief people in Savannah say this is true. And now, excepting a few hundred jobs that have been held open for skilled white labor on building projects that haven't started yet, Savannah's allocation of jobs has been used up. It was practically used up November 16, as a matter of fact, when all men on work relief projects were simply transferred to CWA.

Although investigation has shown that this is not entirely true, there is a popular belief in Savannah that thousands of Negroes are moving in there from all about the eastern part of the state — and even from South Carolina — hoping to get CWA jobs. A lot of people think they've got them, too. Major Will Artley, CWA administrator, says they haven't — that they couldn't have, because there haven't been any CWA jobs for Negroes since November 16.

Major Artley says he turned over to the Mayor, for investigation by city detectives, a list of something over 100 Negroes who had applied for relief since November 16 — that doesn't by any means represent the total number of Negroes who have applied for relief in Savannah since November 16, but was just one group. These cases had not yet been investigated by his people and were not on relief yet. City detectives looked them all up, he said, and found that only 6 out of the bunch were nonresident. This was some weeks ago, however.

In spite of this, however, the Mayor of Savannah is convinced that there are thousands of non-resident Negroes in Savannah, either working on CWA or hoping to get CWA jobs. He figures it out this way: the population of Savannah is about 83,000; there are nearly 8,000 people working for CWA; there are some 5,000 registered as unemployed with the Federal Reemployment service; that would make the total of unemployed in Savannah 13,000; multiply that by four, and you have more than 50,000 out of 83,000 people in Savannah on the unemployed side. He says that's impossible. Major Artley replies that the Mayor's figures are incorrect — that several thousand people registered for reemployment are single persons. And so on.

In Savannah, too, they don't like our transient system. They say Savannah is already too attractive to transients, and that we're only encouraging more of them to settle there. They don't want them. And they insist that too many of these transients are going to be Negroes from out around the country.

I suspect that underneath all this is a sort of unconscious fear of Negroes. They don't want their Negro population increased.

They are worried, too, about what's going to happen when CWA is taken away — especially if, as they believe, CWA has brought thousands more Negroes into Savannah. You see, there are already more blacks than whites in Savannah.

"I'm afraid we're going to have a lot of trouble," the Mayor told me. "And at any rate it's going to mean a big burden for Savannah, because we'll have them on our hands to support."

Apparently case investigations in Atlanta before CWA came in were not particularly thorough. As Miss Rose Marie Smith, a Chicago trained social worker who has been sent down there. . . to survey the situation, puts it, "They didn't know their people." There were no trained investigators to speak of, politics played a big part in the selection of workers — politics and social prestige, apparently, for Miss Smith tells me the relief staff is "full of Junior League members" — and the whole thing was done badly.

Everybody except Major Artley says this is true. The Mayor is simply howling for investigators now — although I suspect them all of having fought like the devil against trained investigators at the start. The Mayor wants to put his city detectives to work investigating! And the only argument against it that I could find that seemed even to make a dent in him was that, while Savannah Negroes might not resent it, it simply wouldn't go in the North at all, and that, if the federal administration let Savannah do it, they couldn't turn down any Northern mayor who might want to do the same thing. Gosh, imagine what would happen if he were permitted to turn city detective loose investigating relief cases! . . .

Even people in our own show down here seem to think we are paying the Negroes too much. The Federal Reemployment director observed yesterday:

"Any Nigger who gets over $8 a week is a spoiled Nigger, that's all."

Major Artley—who, incidentally, was cited by General [John] Pershing as one of the most efficient officers in the A.E.F. —has always been in the contracting business, on a large scale.

"The thing that's happening is this," he said. "The Negroes are getting a distorted idea of the future. CWA can't go on forever, of course, but the Negroes don't see it that way. They regard the President as the Messiah, and they think that, if only they can get on CWA jobs, they'll all be getting $12 a week for the rest of their lives." . . .

Artley, at that, thinks the Negro wage scale should be higher than it has been, but perhaps not so high as we've made it — partly because Southern employers can't keep up with it.

They give you all sorts of arguments, of course, as to why Negroes should not get the same pay as whites. They tell you the Negro diet is different, that their needs are simpler, that everything Negroes buy costs less money than the whites pay. And, even on CWA as they were, they say, the Negroes come around at Christmas time to get their customary hand-outs from their white former employers! Well, it's all something of a problem, isn't it? I'm wondering a little if perhaps we'd not better do a lot of educational work among the Negroes before we assume that, given the same amount of income, they will adopt the white man's standard of living. I talked to a police captain in Savannah, who told me that the amount of drinking among the blacks had increased enormously since CWA came in. It may have increased among the whites, too, though.

They're so damned irresponsible, those Negroes! I've heard again and again of cases where a Negro, getting a CWA job, has simply walked out on his family responsibilities, whatever they were. Maybe not all of these are true, but they were told me, most of them, by relief workers.

Labor shortage, however, is largely, I gather fear, rather than fact, so far. I haven't met anyone yet who said he'd had trouble getting labor. There's a popular belief in Savannah that all the Negro servants have gone to work on CWA, but Major Artley says when you try to run those rumors down, you don't get anywhere, and that, anyway, people in Savannah pay shamefully low wages to their servants. On the other hand, though, if you hire a cook down here, that means you take on the job of feeding, not only the cook, but her whole family. They clean out your ice box every night. The housewife actually does her marketing with that in mind! It's considered just as regular as tipping a waitress . . . in New York.

There's another side to the labor question down here, too. I got this from a businessman — a very sound, level-headed sort of businessman, who was very anxious that his name be kept out of this.

"The other evening," he said, "a couple of white girls who work in a burlap bag factory came out to my house to see if I could help them. (He is a rather prominent citizen of Savannah.) They told me they had gone to work in the factory as learners, on learners' wages, $8.93 a week. After six weeks they were supposed to go into the skilled class, getting $12 a week.

"The number of bags they were supposed to turn out in a day had been increased, until just before they were to go into the $12-a-week class, they were required to turn out 1,800, each girl, a day.

" 'And now,' one of them said, 'they tell us that, beginning next week, we've got to turn out 2,500 a day. Mister, I've tried it. I've worked just as fast as I could all day, never taking my eyes off that machine, and the best I could do was 2,050.'

"Then they told me that this was what the company does. It hires learners, keeps them on six weeks at the learners' wage, and then, when they have qualified for the higher rate, they put the requirements so high that nobody could fulfill them, let them out, and — hire more learners."

He said he had reported the matter to the NRA compliance board.

This same man told me that he believed the real trouble with CWA and the relief show in Savannah had always been politics. . . .

To Harry L. Hopkins

Moultrie, Georgia, January 23, 1934

Dear Mr. Hopkins:

First of all, I imagine, you'll be interested in any dope I may have on how the cut in CWA hours was received. I haven't much yet. It's still a little early. But so far I've heard surprisingly little grumbling. I just left the CWA administrator of this county. She said her people, some 450 of them, took it this way:

"It's a whole lot better than being laid off. I'd rather work for $3. a week than be laid off."

It meant cutting most of them from $9 to $7.20 and $4.50 a week and from $12 to $9.60 or $6, depending on whether they lived in Moultrie or out in the country and on the kind of work they were doing.

The reduced income is still larger than most of these people have had for years, if ever, and they are still getting surplus commodities. That's because the CWA workers in the South — in Georgia, rather — are your relief cases. One of the big complaints I've heard has been that people on CWA were getting not only such high wages, but surplus commodities as well! Mrs. [Charles J.] Knapp, the administrator here, did point out one thing on this wage rate, though, that has been generally over-looked, I think. Those high wages did give people a chance to get caught up — to buy things they'd been needing for years. And she agrees with merchants I've talked with that they did it, the majority of them.

"Merchants in Moultrie told me," she said, "that they'd sold shoes that they'd had in stock, covered with dust, for years."

Since I last wrote you, all about Savannah . . . I've spent a day in the turpentine belt, had talks with some small farmers in one of the most benighted agricultural areas I ever saw, and have had some long con-versations with some more of the thoughtful people, notably Lincoln McConnell, in Macon, state reemployment director, and Miss [Gay] Shepperson[1] herself, who is a grand human, I think, and one of the most interesting women I ever met in my whole life. A boy, Wright Bryan, who works on the Atlanta Journal, and whose father is head of the state agricultural extension set-up in South Carolina — I intend to see him when I get up there — also gave me some food for thought.

The things that are worrying them chiefly are: a huge surplus of labor that has been mounting for the last ten years or so, with the chances of its absorption by private industry, no matter how well the New Deal goes, looking pretty slim; an overwhelming ignorance and backward-ness among the people comprising that surplus, the situation being ag-gravated by terrible health and social problems; an unpromising agricultural future, with high taxes on farmland and cotton, which can be raised much more profitably elsewhere, still the big "money crop."

Miss Shepperson says — and I get the same impression, too — that, out-side of the relatively few industrial centers, this unemployment isn't an emergency matter in Georgia. The same condition is probably true in the Carolinas, too.

Take Lincoln McConnell's figures, for instance. When I talked to him, last Thursday, he had registered for employment in Georgia — and this list had been "weeded out," too, he said — 206,647 men and women. And not a job for any of them. In addition to those, he had been able to place — through CWA, PWA, and in private industry, including men hired for farm labor — 18,012, and private industry had taken less than 8,000 of those.

A day or two before my visit, he had had to go to Carnesville, in Northeast Georgia, where 1,800 persons, mostly white, who had registered for employment, but had been unable to get jobs, were threatening to riot and burn trucks and sack the CWA office.

And most of that sort of thing is in the rural areas, where people have been out of work for years. . . .

"A few months ago," he said, "there were a lot of kicks about relief, before CWA came in — that relief was taking men out of private industry, away from the farms. I sent out hundreds of letters, with stamped, self-addressed postcards enclosed, offering to supply labor to any farmer or employer who had been a victim of this situation. I never got a single reply."

And that's what all the farmers I've talked with say. There's NOT any shortage of labor in the vast rural areas of Georgia — there's not a Chinaman's chance of there being any shortage, no matter how many men are on relief or on CWA. What there is is a darned serious SURPLUS of farm labor in this state. And that's why the farmers get labor for almost nothing.

"Why, there are thousands and thousands of Niggers in this state living in slavery just as real as it ever was before the Civil War," said Mr. McConnell. (Remember, if you please, I assured him that whatever he told me would be passed on only to a few, responsible people, and that it would NOT get out in connection with him in any way. Mr. McConnell is a rather prominent citizen of Georgia, and, as he said, "It's a tough break down here to be named 'Lincoln.'")

"A farmer considers every Nigger living in a house — or the worst kind of shack you ever saw — on his place employed, whether he is paying him anything or not. For a few weeks each year, perhaps, he actually will pay the head of the family 30 or 40 cents a day. BUT — he works the whole family all year, and *he won't take a nigger who hasn't got a big family.*"

I've heard other stories along that line, too.

One day last week one of the biggest turpentine producers in this county took me out to a camp to call on another producer, who, I had already been told, has a very hot temper. I wish I could make you see the place — away off in the woods, miles from everywhere, years away from civilization itself. A few unpainted, tumbledown shacks. A turpentine still. All hidden away in the pines, cut off from all the world by trees and swamp.

In the course of the conversation, our host, who was complaining that his Negroes were dissatisfied because other Negroes, working for CWA, were getting $9 and $12 a week, remarked most of his men were "good Niggers" but that he occasionally had some trouble. And, with a grin, he held out his fist. There were several bruises on it, painted with mercurochrome. (Or however you spell it!) As we drove away, the man who took me out there, said:

"You have seen Simon Legree. That fellow has killed a couple of Niggers in his camps."

"What do you mean?" I asked.

157

I got no answer.

The CWA administrator and the federal reemployment director in this county were telling me this afternoon about farmers in this section, and this is away above the average rural community in Georgia, who take advantage of the fact that their share-croppers cannot read or write, with the result that in many cases, at the end of the season, the share-cropper doesn't get a thing, and there isn't anything he can do about it. He just works for a shell of a house, a few sticks of wood to burn, a few grits and a little pork, that's all.

Now all this, they point out, is due largely to one thing only—a surplus of labor in these rural areas. Blacks and Whites, who are hardly more than beasts.

Miss Shepperson feels—and from my much less extended observation I agree with her—that the $7,000,000 a month we've been spending in Georgia has been largely wasted, outside the cities, where an emergency DOES exist. Wasted, in that outside the cities it ISN'T an emergency, and relief and CWA don't do anything to remedy the situation, permanently.

By some means or other, these people have got to be removed from the labor market in Georgia. Then—and only then, they say—will farm labor get any sort of a break in this state. Then—and only then—will the situation where half-starved Whites and Blacks struggle in competition for less to eat than my dog gets at home, for the privilege of living in huts that are infinitely less comfortable than his kennel. . . .

It seems fairly obvious that the only way out is to remove from the labor market enough poor Whites and Blacks so that members of both races who are left will have some sort of chance. . . .

From all I've seen and heard of them, these people would be perfectly suited to a subsistence farming program. They wouldn't need much in material aid—anything would be better than what they have. But they would need a lot of supervision—leading. They are admirably suited for it. One kick I've heard in the North against subsistence farming is that, under government supervision, it doesn't permit "a man to get anywhere." They say, "You can get a living out of it, all right, but how are you ever going to get anywhere?" That wouldn't enter in with the present generation of poor whites and Negroes down here, I gather. The climate isn't conducive to it, and they're so messed up with pellagra, and tuberculosis, and one thing and another that they simply haven't any morale to ruin at all. God, they're a wretched lot! . . .

They're lazy—I guess you'd be lazy, too, if you'd lived the way they have always, the way their fathers and their grandfathers lived before them—but they're docile. Everybody seems to think they could be taught.

Teach the parents how to live decently and give the children better health and better schooling. At least it would make this a better state to live in.

158

The school system down here seems to be in a mess — I'm talking now about the rural areas, not the cities. In Jesup, in the turpentine belt, I met a girl who, with a college degree, got a job four years ago as principal of the village school — AT $45 PER MONTH. She finally quit after three years, she said, because never in all that time did she get one month's full pay. She was succeeded by a girl who had not finished high school.

If there is a compulsory school system in the state, it simply isn't functioning. It can't. The children just can't go to school, hundreds of them, because they haven't the clothes. The illiterate parents of hundreds of others don't send them. As a result you've got the picture of hundreds of boys and girls in their teens down here in some of these rural areas who can't read or write. I'm not exaggerating. I've been told that again and again. Why, some of them can barely talk!

I just can't describe to you some of the things I've seen and heard down here these last few days. I shall never forget them — never as long as I live.

One thing, of course, that may be said to have contributed to the collapse of the public school system — if there ever was anything to collapse — is the terrific tax burden on farm lands down here. In many rural areas, I'm told, farmers actually pay higher taxes than people pay in the cities, with all their improvements. . . .

A man who owns 5,000 acres of turpentine timber near Jesup has lost his home and several thousand acres more. He is trying to save the rest, I was told, by paying up his taxes at the rate of $100 a month!

The turpentine business is all shot, of course. Substitutes of one sort and another have robbed them of their market. There's a surplus of turpentine. . . .

There's a more cheerful side — at least, it may make you feel good to know that people are appreciative.

The other afternoon I drove into the square of a dusty little town called ODUM. All turpentine operators and small farmers around there. It's in a part of the state, separated from Savannah by miles of swampland, where there actually were no slaves before the Civil war. It was settled by poor whites, who couldn't afford to own slaves. Except for a paved road through and a couple of filling stations, it probably looks much as it did before 1861. Unpainted buildings. Not a spear of grass in the place. Just dust — grey dust — and tall pines. And in spite of the unpainted building and the dust, curiously attractive.

Half a dozen men wandered out into the square to talk to me — the village doctor (who looked more like the "horse doctor," who was a familiar figure around the farms of my childhood), the village postmaster, who told me that the sale of stamps had gone up 30 percent since the middle of December, a turpentine man, a couple of little merchants, and a couple of farmers.

It was a funny, drawling sort of "pep meeting" over CWA. (This was before the cut was announced.) And one of the little storekeepers said:

"Ma'am my business was increased 200 percent — and I mean 200 percent — this last month. If it hadn't been for CWA, I reckon both us fellows woulda gone clean under. We didn't have no stock, as it was, when business began to come in."

As I drove out of Odum, I saw a man with a blacksnake whip in his hands going into a dooryard. I've been wondering ever since what he was going to do with it. . . .

1. Georgia FERA administrator.

To Harry L. Hopkins

Tallahassee, Florida   January 24, 1934

Dear Mr. Hopkins:

Here's my last gasp on the great state of Georgia.

I spent a couple of hours this afternoon in conference with a group of "leading citizens" of Moultrie, Georgia.

Moultrie, in South Central Georgia, a few miles from the Florida line, is the county seat of Colquitt county and is the center of what is generally regarded around the state as Georgia's most progressive and prosperous agricultural community. It's younger than most of the towns I've visited. Younger and more progressive. For some years the farmers thereabouts have gone in for diversification and crop rotation. The Moultrie National bank has followed a policy of financing farmers who diversify, on the ground, one of its officers told me today, that "it's safer for a bank to gamble on a farmer who has three or four chances to come through than on a farmer who raises only one crop, such as cotton." The result is that, where they used to plant 90,000 acres of cotton in Colquitt county every year, they now plant about 45,000 acres. I should add, however, that they now raise on 45,000 acres, because of more expert farming, as much cotton as they used to raise on 90,000 acres! At any rate, the farmers in Colquitt county are a progressive crowd, willing to experiment. They've gone in for livestock. Just now that isn't helping them much, they tell me. The local Swift packing plant buys most of their cattle — at 2 cents a pound, or less. They've increased their tobacco acreage. They've gone in for watermelons in a great big way, and cabbages and other truck.

At the conference today were a banker, a railroad official, a turpentine producer, the head of the local cotton mill, the newspaper editor, the mayor of Moultrie, who is also a farmer, several big farmers — farmers down here as a rule live in town, not on their farms, which are

160

run by share-croppers and hired hands—the reemployment director, and the county relief and CWA administrator.

They turned out to be incorrigible optimists. They approved of everything the Administration has done—even NRA codes and our CWA wage scale! Not one of them had lost a single employee because of CWA. They thought it was an excellent idea to "pour money in at the bottom," as CWA had done. Business had picked up. They got 10 cents a pound for their cotton and a fairly good price for their watermelons last season. The mercantile businesss was humming. Bank deposits had increased. Even the building trades had picked up, several handsome new homes in Moultrie having gone up within the last year! They seemed to be sitting right on top of the world, that crowd.

"A year ago," one of them said, "I couldn't see how we were going to make out, here in Moultrie. But, I tell you, right now this whole country is a lot better off than it was a year ago." . . .

There are at work on CWA and CWS projects in Colquitt county about 470 persons, mostly common labor working on drainage jobs. The great majority of these people were on relief when CWA came in. In addition to those 470, who may be described as "unemployed," since they are at work on CWA, there are registered with the reemployment office 1,376, who haven't any jobs at all. That makes a labor surplus for the county of almost 2,000 persons. About half of them, I am told, could be described as farm laborers. The rest are semi-skilled—former mill hands, men who used to work in the packing plant, men left behind by road contractors who did a lot of paving in the county a couple of years ago, young men who had gone North to work before the depression and have now drifted back to live with their families, who can't support them.

At present that really IS a labor surplus. The mill operator said there wasn't much prospect of his absorbing many of them for some time. There isn't much chance in the packing plant. Suppose, however, all save the farm hands are absorbed—you've still got about 1,000 of those on your hands.

Farm work is under way, full swing, in Colquitt county. The only increase will be during the comparatively brief cotton picking season, when everybody, men, women, and children, goes into the fields. Except for that period, the farmers in Colquitt county have got all the labor hired that they're going to need this year. That includes both share-croppers and laborers. And there are still, according to their estimate, about 1,000 farm hands in the county who can't get work.

One big farmer told me that at least 100 men had been in to see him since January 1, begging work—at any price. The others were having pretty much the same experience. So was the reemployment man.

Optimistic as they were, they admitted that this surplus of labor had been growing for several years.

"I guess it began," one of them said, "when we began cutting down our cotton acreage. You don't need so many hands to raise livestock or watermelons or cabbages."

Assuring them that I had no official knowledge whatever and that I was neither qualified nor authorized to interpret the Administration policies, I pointed out that nevertheless CWA could hardly be expected to go on forever and that even federal relief might conceivably stop sometime, and asked them for ideas as to what to do with those people.

They came back with — subsistence farming.

I found that several of them had been watching the West Virginia colonization project with interest. A similar project has been authorized for Georgia, to be carried out under the direction of the University regents. They were inclined to be critical, to think that that sort of colonization was too expensive — that "they're doing too much for them" — although they pointed out that the climate in West Virginia and in North Central Georgia, where Georgia's colony is to be placed, is more severe than in Colquitt county.

They were interested, however, in the possibility of something being done along that line, only less elaborately, in South Georgia. . . .

They finally decided, at the suggestion of the mill operator, to go over the list of their unemployed, get their work histories, and analyze them, to see what could be done with them. And they promised to send me a copy of their analysis.

"We may be all wrong in our figures," one of the farmers pointed out, "both as to the percentage of our unemployed who would qualify as farm laborers and as to our figures on how much it would cost to establish them on subsistence farms. But it could easily be worked out, I should think." . . .

I spent the morning visiting some of the tenant farmers around Moultrie. Conditions were not so bad as I had expected to find them. The relief workers who took me out thought they were terrible, but — I had seen much, much worse in the Kentucky mountains, in the West Virginia mining camps, away up in Maine, in Bottineau county, North Dakota, and in squatters' camps on the Missouri river bottoms in Nebraska. And I told them so. But I'm inclined to think that the condition of tenant farmers in Colquitt county is immeasurably above that of tenant farmers in most other Georgia counties. I saw Negro cabins around Warm Springs, for instance, that looked much worse than anything I saw today.

It's true of course that these people WILL buy shotgun shells and snuff instead of shoes for their children — but somehow it doesn't seem so terrible for children to run about with bare feet [on] days like today. Camellias were blooming in Moultrie dooryards today. . . .

To Harry L. Hopkins

Miami, Florida, January 28,1934

Dear Mr. Hopkins,

. . . So far as CWA and relief are concerned, this state seems to be chock full of politics and petty graft. It seems to be worst in Tampa, which, I am told, could teach even New York City something about political control. But I'm told it's pretty bad all over the state. . . .

The Governor[1] has a bad reputation around the state, and it's getting worse. He and Talmadge, in Georgia, are in about the same fix that way, I gather. It's generally assumed on the part of the public apparently that he is playing politics with CWA. For instance, this is what E. R. Bentley of Lakeland, county CWA administrator, secretary of the State Bar Association, district governor for Florida of Rotary International, and former state commander of the American Legion, said of him:

"I voted for that — blankety blank — but I'm ashamed of it now." . . .

For instance, Florida followed the procedure used by Georgia in putting men to work on CWA — transferring everybody off the relief rolls and giving what was left over to the self-sustaining unemployed. And from all I've heard, the state committee just went ahead and did it, without saying anything to anyone. It's caused all sorts of grief down here, as it did in Georgia. It's done more than anything else I know of to give CWA and the Administration a black eye. Same thing happened here as in Georgia. Putting it charitably, we'll say the "weaker brethren," from an economic and industrial standpoint, were the first on the relief rolls. That meant a good share of the low grade white and Negro populations. When CWA came along, they got the jobs at $12 a week, and the people who had managed to stay off the relief rolls by using up their credit and living on their relatives and friends — and that includes most of the white collar class apparently — got nothing. . . . I found that even Bentley, as prominent as he is in the state, didn't even know that the policy in Washington had been to give out the jobs on a fifty-fifty basis. . . . The impression around the state seems to be that the Federal Government came down here and put all the bums to work at more money than labor had ever been paid down here before. It hasn't gone down so well. They think the wage rate is pretty high, anyway, and feel that, if such wages are going to be paid anyone, honest, self-respecting people ought to have some of it at least. You know and I know and all the CWA and relief people know, of course, that not all the people on relief were bums. But I think we must also admit that the people on relief — well, let's put it this way: the LAST people to come on relief are the best, because they've made one damned no-

163

ble effort to keep off. Now they tell me—the social workers—that the relief rolls everywhere are growing in this state, and many, many of the people coming on are those who have heretofore managed to stay off and might never have had to come on relief at all if they had been able to get CWA jobs. This statement is made with due consideration of the many people [who] are now applying for relief solely because they think that is the only way to get CWA jobs. . . .

It seems to me that I've seen more greed in this state than anywhere else I've been. The whole attitude, both of communities and individuals, seems to be:

"It's Government money! Come on, let's get our share!" . . .

Saturday I went to the Orange Festival, a sort of county fair, in Winter Haven. CWA had fixed up the grounds for them, even building the stands. But they also wanted CWA to pay the guards during the fair! And, by golly, they'd actually got away with it one week! But it had been stopped. I was told that payment of the guards had been submitted as part of the project and okayed in Tallahassee!

They're having a big fair in Tampa this week or next. They tried to get CWA to pay their ticket takers. . . .

Among individuals the greed manifests itself in all sorts of petty graft and fighting for jobs in the skilled labor group. Automobile trucks! . . .

[J.C.] Huskinson[2] said he had heard repeatedly that owners of truck fleets in Tampa were getting around the order that owners of single trucks must be given first consideration. He said he had in his office statements signed by men who said they had endorsed checks made out to them, but had received none of the money, which went to owners of fleets of trucks. . . .

At Fort Myers I heard of a Baptist preacher who bought a truck, got it in on CWA work by having it listed as belonging to the driver!

Bentley said his works director had actually been approached by a group of businessmen in Lakeland who wanted to form a corporation, buy a fleet of trucks, and put them on CWA. They offered the works director something like $100 a week if he would let them in! . . .

1. David Scholtz.
2. Federal Reemployment director in Tampa.

To Harry L. Hopkins

Miami, Florida, January 29, 1934

Dear Mr. Hopkins:

. . . Now I'll tell you right off the bat for being mean-spirited, selfish, and irresponsible, I think Forida citrus growers have got the world licked.

This winter they're taking a terrific beating on prices, getting as low as 50 cents a box for oranges that cost $6 a box retail in New York. But there isn't a thoughtful man among them, apparently, who won't tell you that it's absolutely their own fault. They simply will not pull together. Therefore they lay themselves open to exploitation by the jobber.

"I've attended meetings of them," one grower told me, "again and again, where we'd agree to get together on some sort of marketing plan for our fruit. We'd agree not to ship out any fruit for a certain length of time. The meeting wouldn't be over before they'd begin to slip out, one by one, and over to the telegraph office, where they'd wire their people: 'Go ahead and ship. Nobody else is going to.'" . . .

They don't like CWA and, as you know, they raised such a howl about CWA taking all their labor that recently there was a meeting in Orlando at which we agreed to pull off CWA and return to them any of their men they couldn't get back. I made a point of asking administrators in the citrus belt what happened — how many men they had pulled out and sent back to the groves on those requests.

The administrator in Orlando told me he had had only four requests. Bentley, in Lakeland, had had ONE. Bentley said he made every employer who wanted men back put it in writing and promise that they would be given employment at once and fairly steady employment. He got one request. [W.H.] Green[1] did the same thing with the tomato and bean growers down this way. He never got any requests — although they'd been howling that all their men had gone on CWA — and when he made an appointment with some of them to go around on CWA projects and pick out their Negroes, they failed to keep the appointment.

It seems to me that the citrus grower in Florida is about as irresponsible an employer as you could imagine. Even the turpentine men, the Georgia and North Florida farmers, and the tomato and bean growers PRETEND at least to take care of their people during the long summer months when there is no work for them, although Green says that, if the labor department were to send investigators down here, they'd find plenty of evidence of peonage. They provide houses, of a sort — some of them very bad — and give them credit at their commissaries, even though they do manage to keep their laborers owing them money all the time. But the citrus growers simply turn them off whenever they feel like it, with no thought at all of what's going to become of them in the meantime — and after paying them so little that they couldn't possibly get along on it until they get work again. And that's how a lot of workers in the citrus belt got on relief and, I expect, into CWA.

Do you know what happened just before Christmas this year? Two weeks before Christmas the whole citrus industry just closed down for the holidays and turned everybody loose — without money or jobs. No wonder there's an "outlaw union" in the citrus belt and a strike.

I can't find it in my heart to sympathize very deeply with the Florida citrus growers. They say they can't pay their labor decent wages because they're getting such low prices for their fruit — and at the same time they tell you that it's their own fault that they're getting such low prices.

They all howl about this business of shipping bulk fruit out in trucks — and yet, they admit themselves, that every man jack of 'em does it. Now you tell me what you're going to do with a gang like that.

They are neither fair nor honest in their criticism of CWA. For instance, one of the biggest growers in the gang said to me Saturday:

"Well, we can't compete with CWA. All our men are quitting and going over on CWA."

When I finally pinned him down — and it took a long time, for I had to be as tactful and as patient as I could be — he admitted he had actually heard of ONE citrus worker leaving his job to get a job with CWA. He didn't know whether the man had actually got a CWA job or not. And he'd only HEARD of that case. He didn't KNOW that it had happened.

As a matter of fact, I don't believe there is a Chinaman's chance of any labor shortage in the citrus belt or anywhere else in this state.

Here are some figures.

Everything right now is going full speed in Florida — tourists, truck gardening, citrus. There certainly is as much employment now as there is going to be this winter and more than there has been for several winters, in the resort business.

Take two counties in the citrus belt. In the county in which Orlando is located, right now there are 2,000 men on CWA and 4,203 unemployed registered with the Federal Reemployment service. I'm not counting in those on direct relief, because it is assumed that all of the able bodied among them are registered at the Reemployment office. That makes that county's surplus of labor, right now at the height of the work season, 6,203 men, considering that a man working on CWA is really on relief.

Bentley, in Lakeland, told me that on the day of that meeting in Orlando, where the citrus growers all howled that they couldn't get labor, there were in his county 3,997 on CWA and 5,600 registered at the Reemployment office, making the surplus something over 9,000.

Both of those counties are in the citrus belt. In Hillsborough county, where Tampa is located — outside the citrus belt, but I'll give you the figures anyway — there are 11,000 on CWA and 15,000 registered for employment.

In this county, with the tourist and truck gardening season in full swing, there are 6,800 on CWA and 10,000 registered for reemployment.

And yet they talk about not being able to get labor! . . .

To complicate matters a bit, there's a drouth down here this winter in most of the truck garden areas, except in irrigated places and in the Everglades. It's so dry that there are lots of forest fires — a kind of swamp fire, that doesn't burn the tops off the trees, as forest fires do in the North, but just burns along on the ground. All along the highways in some parts of the state you see signs, "Beware of Fog and Smoke."

I drove in the rain Thursday from Tallahassee to Lake City. The road was full of cattle, and I noticed that they seemed to be licking up water from depressions in the pavement. I asked about it and was told:

"They're thirsty. All the water holes are dried up."

I could go on and on. But I'm tired, and I daresay you are.

1. Dade County CWA and relief administrator and a retired naval officer.

To Harry L. Hopkins

Daytona Beach, Florida, January 31, 1934

Dear Mr. Hopkins:

I am not fond of Miami. Principally because I do not like tourists. But Miami likes them. And, by all accounts, Miami should!

The streets of Miami are a mess, what with hundreds of out-of-state automobiles, whose drivers are either smart alecks trying to pass everything on the road or timid old gentlemen who never signal you what they're going to do because they don't know themselves, and what with tourists from New York in white flannel pants — and why must tourists, especially tourists from New York City be so damned arrogant? — walking all over you.

You get several accounts of just how good the season is. The newspapers rave. "Best Tourist Season Miami Has Ever Seen" and all that sort of stuff. The merchants and hotel men and real estate men are not quite so enthusiastic, but they do believe it is "going to be" a good year. In the meantime, I heard about one woman spending the winter there, who had to go to eight stores before she could buy a beach umbrella and was unable to get any beach sandals at all — they were all sold out. I imagine it's a little early to tell just how good a season it is going to be, as a matter of fact. The heavy months are supposed to be February and March.

The hotels, I should say, are not crammed, but just comfortably filled. There were no single rooms with baths left by 7 o'clock last night at the Alcazar — medium price, Biscayne boulevard — where I was staying. But it's still possible, hotel men told me, to get a single room with bath, in the $5 and $6 class, almost any night in Miami without making a reservation in advance and without having to wander about much. An elevator boy at the Alcazar told me that, while there frequently are no cheaper rooms left, "you can always get one of the $14 suites here — they aren't occupied." That tallied with what I heard about other hotels. They say the $150-a-day suites at the Miami Biltmore, for instance, aren't selling any too well.

One thing has happened. The tourist homes — private houses where they take 'em in — the automobile camps, and apartments renting at $50 or $60 a month ARE full. Real estate men differ in their opinions as to the value of this business. The general feeling seems to be that it's better for Miami that these places should be filled up than for the big winter hotels to be doing a capacity business, because this means that the money will stay in Miami, even though there isn't so much of it, whereas if the big hotels got it, it would go North — just now to mortgage holders. . . .

Miami undoubtedly leads in the number of tourists. I've heard that around the state, and, judging by the crowds on the streets, I should say it was true. Other cities say they are doing "just a good business" this year. Tourists tell you rents are extremely high — 35 or 40 per cent higher than they were last year. Real estate men say they aren't more than 10 per cent higher than they were last year, and that apartments that used to bring in between $200 and $300 a month before the depression are still renting at $50 and $60. Restaurant prices, outside the big hotels, are low. Even in Miami you can get a pretty fair dinner for half a dollar. Tea rooms. Traveling men tell me that hotels generally in the South have raised their rates about 50 cents a night. They all say it's because of the code, but there is little evidence of their having put on much help, outside of Miami. You're apt to have the same waitress in a hotel coffee shop at 7 A.M. and 9 P.M.

"We're supposed to be under the code," a girl in one coffee shop observed, "but I can't see as it's much different."

I get complaints about department stores — that they haven't taken on any more help, and that they are beating the minimum wage. . . .

Green in Miami seemed to think the stores and hotels there had been more cooperative. He estimated that between 1,000 and 1,500 Miami unemployed had been put to work in the hotels, although many of the larger hotels bring most of their help down from the North, and that the stores had taken on at least 500. Just now, with the season not yet at its height, stores and hotels are hiring about 150 a week.

One businessman, NOT a merchant, who asked that his name be withheld, thought NRA ought to send someone down to investigate the department stores. In one store, he said, one of the biggest stores in Miami, the management had made most of the clerks "junior executives," so that they could work them just as many hours as they liked.

"I KNOW this is true," he told me.

"One thing that CWA started and that a good tourist year is continuing," a merchant told me, "is a great improvement in the morale of Miami businessmen and people generally."

He said that at the cosmetics counter in his store more high priced perfume had been sold this year than in several years. A prominent lawyer in Fort Myers, incidentally, complained that people on CWA at Christmas time bought perfume and lip rouge!

At the moment, this would seem to be the "state of the nation" in Florida.

CITRUS: Low prices. Much haggling about cooperation. I see by the papers they succeeded in getting that decision they wanted, declaring AAA control unconstitutional. One fairly prominent citrus man told me that the man who started it, on the ground that he had a lot of third grade fruit to ship out, and that he would be ruined if he couldn't ship it out, was out buying fruit the day after the temporary injunction was granted! Wages low. Employment uncertain. Probably much less than normal employment in the groves during the summer, when they ordinarily do some cultivating, pruning, and so on.

TRUCK GARDENING: Low prices. Plenty of work for a few weeks, but at low wages. Little likelihood of farmers being able to carry their employees through the summer as they would normally do. Fairly generally over the state a "short crop," due in some sections to drouth and in others to too much rain. Around Miami it's been so wet that where they usually get three crops during the winter they are getting only one this year.

CIGAR MANUFACTURING: Bad. Little demand except for cheap cigars. Machinery taking place of hand work. Lots of unemployment in Tampa, cigar headquarters, and little prospect of its being much decreased.

TOURIST: Promising year, especially in Miami and nearby resorts. February and March will tell the story. Tourist business very little help with summer unemployment problem. . . .

Miami has a funny unemployment problem. Mostly in the South, the labor surplus seems to be agricultural. But 40 per cent of the unemployed in Miami are workers in the building trades. And a huge percentage of the rest are old people, retired, unable to work.

The carpenters and bricklayers and so on came down, of course, during the boom. For two or three years they made lots of money. Many of them bought — and paid for — homes. Now there's no building going on down there, and they're stranded.

"The old people constitute a more serious problem, though," said Commander Green, the CWA and relief administrator. "Most of them came down here with a little nest egg — enough to have kept them comfortably for the rest of their lives, if it hadn't been for the boom and the depression. They lost their money, and here they are, too old to work and no work for them, even if they could do it.

"You can't put them out. The great majority have lived here long enough to qualify as bona fide residents of Miami. And there would be no place for them to go if you did put them out. They'll just be on relief, of some sort, the rest of their lives."

His suggestion is a centralization of all charitable organizations and funds, together with whatever money the city and county can furnish, with Federal Government aid, on some matching basis, and under federal direction. It would be a temporary thing, of course—the great majority of them won't live more than 10 years longer. . . .

One thing pointed out to me in Miami was this:

While it's true that picking and packing in the tomato and bean gardens is going full tilt down around there now, the labor is largely migratory, for the reason that much of it is really highly skilled work. Grading and packing tomatoes, for instance, is a delicate job. They have to be handled with great skill and care, or they will get bruised. So with picking. It's all work that requires a lot of experience. Many times it's handed down from father to son. There are in the area what are known as "tomato families." Tomato growers and packers won't hire inexperienced men. They can't afford to. These highly skilled workers follow the tomatoes, they say, from the tip of Florida up to New Jersey! Another name for them commonly used is "tomato buzzards." So, even a good tomato season doesn't help out Miami's unemployment situation much.

Got a little more dope on the citrus situation yesterday. It seems that fruit stealing is one of the biggest rackets in Florida. They go in and clean out whole groves, take the fruit out in trucks, and sell it all over the South, and as far North as Washington and Baltimore, at prices away below what the grocers would have to charge for Florida fruit. I talked to a woman who said that her five-acre grove was completely cleaned out in one night last winter.

All this stolen fruit goes out in trucks—and yet the growers won't get together and stop truck shipments. They won't even back up the AAA in an effort to keep low grade fruit from being shipped out by truck. . . .

To Harry L. Hopkins

Columbia, S.C., February 5, 1934

Dear Mr. Hopkins:

. . . It is apparent that the tourist season in Florida, outside of Miami, is "nothing to write home about." The newspapers carry enthusiastic reports, but they aren't very well borne out by facts. Daytona Beach, according to the newspapers, is enjoying "a mild boom." It must be very mild indeed, judging by the appearance of the mail boxes in the hotel where I stopped. I was the only person in the diningroom for breakfast, and the head waiter told me the hotel was "starving to death." The CWA administrator in Daytona Beach only laughed when I mentioned "mild boom." In St. Augustine Negro bellhops stand out on the curbs and all but hit you over the head and knock you out to drag you into the hotels. The second largest winter resort hotel in St. Augustine is closed, as it has been for the last two winters. The largest — a very elaborate and huge Flagler hotel — offers a room, dinner, and breakfast for $5, American plan. I didn't try it, but I was told that the price was about half what it would be in normal times for the very cheapest accommodations in that place.

The feeling seems to be generally that Florida is going to be in a bad way this coming summer — worse off than last summer, perhaps — and, Lord only knows what will happen if we try to pull out of there too suddenly.

"Gosh, I don't know what we'll do if you pull CWA out all of a sudden this spring," said the secretary of the Chamber of Commerce in Jacksonville. Incidentally, he thinks that the CWA rate was "the best thing that ever happened to Florida."

"You can't build a state on the wages labor has been receiving down here," was his observation.

Apparently that same fear that we may cease our relief activities too soon and too abruptly exists in South Carolina, too, although for the last week I've found that people are beginning to try to figure out what will be done — what can be done — after CWA. In Jacksonville on February 20 the largest women's club is going to have a forum discussion on "After CWA, What?" The Rotary club here in Columbia had a discussion along the same line last week. Which is encouraging, I think. At least they're getting it through their heads that CWA may not go on FOREVER.

There's a lot of interest in subsistence farming. I had a talk today with the Protestant Episcopal Bishop Kirkland G. Finlay, generally considered one of the finest and most socially minded citizens of South Carolina, that lasted nearly two hours — practically all about subsistence farming — and I believe he would have gone on for another hour if I hadn't had to leave to keep another appointment. You get them started on that subject, and they never want to stop. Some of them, like Bishop Finlay, have been interested in it for a number of years. Others are just beginning to read up on it. There is a great deal of enthusiasm. . . .

Well — CWA came, fulfilled its purposes, and, I believe, should go. We made mistakes. They were bound to be made. No doubt there's been graft. No doubt there's been politics. No doubt there's been misuse of CWA. All that money constituted too much of a temptation for many American politicians, businessmen, and small fry in the office personnel to withstand. And yet — I think you will find that most people will agree that it did more good than harm. It just pulled us through what might have been one very nasty winter. People all tell me that. And right now many who have seen and recognize its faults keep warning me that there will be serious trouble if it is pulled out too abruptly, although they realize that it must go and think it should go. Something, however, must be found to take its place.

From all I hear we are by no means through with this relief job in the South. Everywhere I hear the same thing. A tremendous labor surplus that is not an emergency surplus, but CHRONIC. A labor surplus in the rural areas among illiterate Negroes and poor whites. Already there is evident a tendency for them to crowd into the industrial centers, competing with labor already there. I don't think the Mayor of Savannah, in his fear that thousands of Negroes are moving into Savannah looking for CWA jobs, is ALTOGETHER groundless. . . .

Everybody I talk to has ideas of his, or her, own about subsistence farming. They certainly are all thinking about it. Generally, here in the South, they are agreed on some things.

First, that there should be a minimum amount of money spent on equipment and a maximum amount of money spent on supervision — these people need leading and teaching. With the mild climate down here, there doesn't need to be so much money put into equipment.

Secondly, that it be substituted for an emergency relief program — done as a relief measure, possibly with the present relief setup in charge.

Thirdly, that there be some sort of compulsory education system for adults connected with it, NOT to teach these people to read and write, but HOW TO LIVE. To put it badly, one doctor said, "What these people need to be taught is how to build toilets."

They all impress upon me the fact that the equipment can be of the simplest. Let them do as much as possible of it themselves, possibly on a work relief basis. LET THEM clear the land, build their own cabins, with a lot of supervision of course, do the work themselves. The big item would be supervision — people to teach them how to raise vegetables and care for chickens and a cow and SEE THAT THEY DO IT. Dieticians, nurses, doctors to clean out the hookworm and pellagra. They tell me you would just have to stand right over them and MAKE them do things. It all sounds very paternalistic, but, from what I've heard, they would lend themselves to it as Northerners never would. And it's a grand chance to get hold of this situation and clean it up.

It probably wouldn't have to be permanent. Clean out the hookworm and pellagra and raise the standards of education, and the next generation might be better able to look after itself. But this generation—it looks as though, having started it, we'll have to go on. As Bishop Finlay put it, "The good Lord only knows what would happen if you pulled out now." It looks as though we may have this generation on our hands for some time.

An illustration of what might be accomplished was given me this afternoon by Verde Peterson, who has charge of rural education for the state board of education. Under CWA he had 400 teachers turned over to him. He ruled that they could NOT duplicate the work of the teachers of children in the public schools and put them to work educating adults—going right out among them, working with them, teaching them how to repair their houses, delouse their chickens, build toilets, raise gardens. The results, he said, are exceeding his fondest expectations.

"As you drive around the state," he said, "watch for new boards nailed onto the cabins. Where you see those you'll know those teachers have been." . . .

Before I close, here are a few observations and complaints:

I visited a number of women's work rooms in Daytona and Jacksonville. The kick you hear on the sewing projects is that they are creating a surplus of clothing for the unemployed. They are, locally, but I wonder if they are nationally. I am thinking of Bottineau county, North Dakota, where the people are so isolated that I imagine it would be practically impossible to have a sewing room. Why not handle the output of these sewing rooms as we do surplus commodities? Send them where they are needed.

I don't think you have any idea of what they have done to the women themselves. The results are marvelous. They came in, sullen, dejected, half starved. Working in pleasant surroundings, having some money and food have done wonders to restore their health and their morale. They are like different people.

One observation I have to make is that possibly many women got jobs who shouldn't have had them. Widows, for instance, who should have been taken care of by the communities. No doubt plenty of "Nigger washwomen," as exasperated citizens insist. Not enough unattached, "white collar" women. I thought the women's show was set up principally to take care of unattached women. Perhaps if the rolls were cleaned up, and some of the women taken off and put where they belong, the surplus of the sewing rooms could be reduced. I gather, from what the South Carolina director of women's projects told me today, that there is now under way a survey of women's projects, possibly designed to weed out some projects.

There is some criticism of our distribution of surplus commodities.

For instance, Malcolm Miller, South Carolina administrator, said today he had been informed that a couple of million pounds of oranges are to be sent to South Carolina as surplus commodities. He pointed out that you can buy oranges at 5 cents a dozen in South Carolina. Couldn't they be shipped somewhere else, where oranges are more expensive?

Some people think we're shipping too much pork down here, where the tendency is to eat too much pork. "We are simply swamped with pork," said the head of the social service department at Daytona Beach. It's rather discouraging to people who are trying to get their clients to eat less pork and get rid of pellagra for the government to keep sending pork down here. And a lot of it, they tell me, is spoiling, for lack of proper storage facilities.

Another kick is on wheat, shipped in for livestock food. There's plenty of pasturage for livestock here in the South. They don't know what to do with the wheat. The chances are that they really don't need it.

The suggestion is made that surplus commodities be distributed with an eye to local needs and conditions.

There is also a criticism of our mosquito control ditching, by Dr. [Henry] Hanson of the State Board of Health in Florida, one of the best known malaria experts in the South.

He makes the suggestion that no more ditching be done without the approval of state geologists and sanitary engineers. He bases the suggestion on the fact that much of the ditching may do more harm than good, by draining in such a way that sub-surface water levels are lowered too much, and that some of it is done wrong.

"You see nice, pretty ditches," he said, "dug square, with flat bottoms. That's worse than no ditching at all. Mosquitoes don't breed in deep water — they breed in shallow water, such as collects in the bottoms of those ditches."

He ought to know what he is talking about. He was assistant health officer in charge of malaria control in the Panama Canal Zone during the World War and later spent several years studying tropical diseases on the West Coast of Africa. And he doesn't recommend that the mosquito control program be abandoned — only that it be carried on a little more carefully.

"People seem to have an erroneous idea," he said, "that drainage will stop mosquitoes. What they might better do is to treat the edges of the swamps and water holes, where the mosquitoes breed."

Incidentally, he told me there are between 80,000 and 90,000 cases of malaria in Florida right now and some 250,000 cases of hookworm infestation. Hookworm reduces a person's efficiency 66⅔ percent — which may account for a lot of your "poor white problem" down here. And it's a comparatively easy thing to clean up, with proper sanitation. . . .

To Harry L. Hopkins

Greenville, S.C., February 7, 1934

Dear Mr. Hopkins:

If you want to take the word of some South Carolinians for it, you can pull CWA out of this state by May 1 without much difficulty, if you don't try to do it too abruptly, reduce your relief expenditures along all lines by half by the middle of the summer, and be out of here entirely before the end of the year.

I have this from Dr. W. W. Long, head of the department of agriculture at Clemson Engineering and Agricultural college, which corresponds to the colleges of agriculture attached to the state universities in other states, and from B. E. Geer, president of Furman college, former head of one of the largest cotton mills in the state, and chairman of the textile code authority. I also have it, not quite so enthusiastically given, perhaps, from two smaller fry, actual farmers, whom I went out to see today.

I must add that our social workers down here do not concur. Miss Leila Johnson, professor of sociology at the University of South Carolina, on leave for a year to act as assistant state relief administrator in charge of social work, believes we can take CWA out of the rural areas by early summer, but that we cannot take it out of the industrial centers that soon, and that we shan't be able to cut our relief along other lines, either in the rural or urban areas, for some time. She strongly urges that, before we make any decision, the relief set-ups in this and in other Southern states survey this whole unemployment situation — "take stock," so to speak. . . .

Incidentally, Miss Johnson and the field supervisors say that Dr. Long doesn't know anything about it, although he should. They say he and the county agricultural agents, who are under his direction, have been decidedly non-cooperative in the relief program, and that they consistently refuse to have anything to do with the small fellows and the tenant farmers, but devote all their time to the big, successful farmers, with whom they can "get results." . . .

Mr. Geer I am inclined to take more seriously. He should know a lot about the textile industry, and everybody concedes that he is probably the best informed man in the state along that line. He also has the reputation of having the well known "broad-social-viewpoint."

He says that there has been a most remarkable — an almost unbelievable — change in the attitude of the mill owners. That they are cooperative with NRA away beyond his expectations.

At the same time, he says, the textile business has vastly improved. He says they are running above normal here in the Piedmont section — I notice they are running night shifts — that they have taken on between 156,000 and 160,000 employees, and that, if cotton goes up to 20 cents a pound, the mills "will be begging for labor." . . .

Right after we left him, Miss Johnson and Mrs. B. S. Hill, one of the field supervisors, took me for a drive down through the mill villages. They showed me blocks and blocks of shabby, tumbledown little houses in between the neat, if monotonous, mill villages.

"There," they said dramatically, "is our case load. In those houses live what is known as 'spare help.' They've never had steady employment in the mills — just a little, now and then. They never will have steady employment. Right now they are not getting any. They are the people we are looking after now, on CWA or direct relief. What are we going to do with them? They are surplus labor."

There are two classes of labor employed in textile mills, they tell me. The best of the workmen live in the mill villages, on company property. The mills feel a sense of responsibility toward them. They are the last to be laid off. And if the mills really want a workman, on full time, they will make room for him in the mill villages.

The second class is part time labor — "spare help." A lot of it lives in those miserable houses on the edges of the mill villages. More lives on farms, working part time in the mills.

Now the social workers — especially Mrs. Hill, who organized the somewhat famous Abbeville farm colony, has lived around here all her life, and has been in the relief show here since away back before there was even any RFC — think that the colony the Subsistence Farms crowd are planning to set up down here near Greenville is a serious mistake.

As they understand it, the plan is to build up a colony right near Greenville and put on those little farms, about three acres apiece, some of these part time workers. She says it won't work because there can never be any assurance that these people will actually get part time work in the mills. She says mill owners have told her this. She says furthermore that they'll never get people who live farther out on farms to come and live in the colony, because they know there is no assurance of regular part time employment in the mills, and they prefer to stay where they are, with freedom to raise and sell some cotton to see them through if they don't get any work in the mills. That colonization plan is not very popular down here, partly because they feel that the people who are to be colonized are not the people who really need to be colonized. Of course it's hard to convince them that putting people on the land, without letting them sell any of their produce, is going to work. They do concede that, as an experiment in teaching people who work short hours how to spend their leisure time, it may be allright, but they seem to think it's a pretty expensive experiment. I am inclined to think they are a bit jumbled in their thinking at times. And possibly they don't understand the plan very well.

Yesterday with Mrs. Hill I visited the colony at Abbeville. It is certainly one of the best arguments for the back-to-the-land movement I ever saw. And I wonder if we couldn't learn a good deal from it. You are probably familiar with it — I understand it has had a good deal of publicity — but briefly I'll tell you the story as Mrs. Hill told it to me. Incidentally, I think she is one of the best social workers I ever saw, and I agree with the statement you made after your trip through the South last summer, that, by and large, the best staff of social workers in the country was located in the South. Taken as a whole, I've certainly found them away above the average. There just isn't any basis for comparison between the people who have been handling the relief show down here and those in Maine, for instance, or North Dakota.

Back in the fall of 1930, the Red Cross and the Family Service outfit had combined their resources — planned to take care of a case load of 250 families, where they had 600 to take care of — to handle the relief problem. Robert W. Hudgens, a stock broker — who is now on the board handling that colonization proposition, and who confided to me this morning that he'd had to sell the idea to himself — was chairman, Miss Margaret Laing, now a field supervisor, whom I am to meet in Charleston Friday, was executive secretary, and Mrs. Hill was one of the case workers.

"Many of the people we were working with had been through two bitter years of unemployment already," Mrs. Hill said, "and we noticed that they kept saying they'd like to go back to the country and have farms. Finally we decided it might be worth while to try to put some of them back on the farms.

"We selected a group of families, basing our selection on their farm experience, on their eagerness to go, on their work histories, and on their intelligence and adaptability. . . .

"I'd been raised on a farm. So Mr. Hudgens and Miss Laing told me to go out and see what farm land might be available. I found 32 farms here in Greenville county that were about to be abandoned. They were in pretty good shape and could be rented. Over in Abbeville county I found a thousand acres that had fallen into the hands of the First Carolinas Joint Stock Land bank. It was all overgrown, and the buildings on it were terrible. The bank said they'd rent it for $25 per family per year, the first year's rent to be paid in advance, and they said they'd use the first year's rent to clean the wells and fix up the houses some.

"Mr. Hudgens kept going to Washington, and finally the American Red Cross said they'd let us have $5,000, provided we didn't tell where we got it and provided the county would match it. Well, the county couldn't match it. We begged and we pleaded, so finally the Red Cross gave us $5,000 anyway, with the understanding that we were to put not less than 40 families out on the land.

177

"I went to work and bought their equipment, just figuring out the best I could what they'd actually need. Thirty-two families I put on the individual farms. They didn't need so much. Most of them had something. But the ten who went into the colony were taken right out of Greenville, and they had to be started from scratch.

"For each family in the colony I bought one mule. I gave the Red Cross a mortgage on all the mules so the people couldn't sell 'em. That was all the livestock I bought.

"The equipment I bought second hand from farmers who were hard up, and I got it cheap: two wagons for the colony, one for each five families, one plow and harrow for every three families, smaller tools—such as hoes, rakes, shovels, and so on—for each family. I spent about $308 per family in the colony.

"We moved them out to the colony in April, 1931, and they started cleaning up the land. In the meantime, I had supervision over the 32 families we'd put on farms in Greenville county and an additional case load of 175 families scattered all over Greenville county, which is 65 miles long and 45 miles wide. So I didn't get out to Abbeville very often.

"On the Fourth of June, however, I went out there and discovered that that colony wasn't doing so well. They were just standing around wringing their hands. Some had their gardens in, a little cotton had been planted, but there wasn't a bit of corn or any other food for the stock in the ground. I realized then that what they needed was supervision. So I just put on a sun hat and went out into the field and said, 'You do this' and 'You do that.'

"By the end of July, about a month late, we finally got the crop all in. Each family had six or eight acres of cotton, ten acres of corn, and seven acres of garden, peavine hay, potatoes, and sugar cane.

"Then I stood over them the rest of the summer. I'd manage to spend two days a week out there, usually the weekends. They were the most helpless people you ever saw. They wouldn't even have their mules shod without advice!

"To complicate things, our Red Cross money ran out in July. The colony had to have food. So I went to the merchants in Greenville and arranged credit. Every week I sent a truckload of food out there. By the end of the summer we owed the merchants $900.

"Then in September our organization here in Greenville ran out of money and folded up. Here I was, with ten families out there in that colony and $900 in debt.

"I stuck along, on a volunteer basis, and set out to get that $900. I went out there and superintended the harvesting of the crop. It was a pretty good crop. I took the home demonstration agent out there, and we set up a makeshift cannery. When we got through each family had about 30 quarts of canned vegetables and fruit, we had a good supply of dried beans and peas, 800 bushels of sweet potatoes, and 950 gallons of

178

syrup. Our cotton was good, long staple stuff. I borrowed a couple of trucks from my husband and took it to the gins and marketed it myself, selling it at a premium. After it was sold, and I'd paid the $900 to the merchants, there was $840 left to be divided up among the families.

"They got through that winter in good shape. Next spring I got them seed loans. They've had seed loans each spring, and each year they've grown more independent. They're arranging their own seed loans now. They've always paid them back. They don't owe a cent, any of them."

There are four families left in the colony now. Only one of the six families who have moved off has gone back to the city. Five have moved onto better farms.

I visited all of the four families yesterday. It was most inspiring, I assure you. You ought to see those children — red-cheeked, healthy youngsters, all of them. They've all acquired stock. One family, so low grade mentally that Mrs. Hill said they "just had sense enough to do what they were told to do," had, in addition to the mule, a cow, three calves, two pigs, and 50 chickens. They had slaughtered two hogs and had enough meat to last them a year. "And I don't owe a cent on any of this," the man said contentedly.

They were a cheerful, contented lot — very proud of what they had accomplished, very hopeful about the future. Every one of the four men assured me that nothing could ever get him back to town.

They haven't much. Their clothing is shabby — some of them are getting some CWA work now. Their houses — every one of them, except that of the family that is so low grade mentally, spotless — are pretty bad. By no means weather proof. But they have enough to eat and a little money to spend, and they are healthy and contented. Incidentally one of the women when they went out there had a bad case of pellagra. They say she's completely cured. And they're going it on their own. Mrs. Hill hadn't been near the place for a couple of months when we went out there yesterday.

I must tell you about their schools. And about another of my "unsung heroes of the depression." Only this time it is a heroine.

In the autumn of 1931 Mrs. Hill suddenly awakened to the fact that there must be a school. There were 26 children, of various ages. The town was six miles away, and there was no bus. Also, she thought the children would not be very happy going to that school because they couldn't have the clothes that the town children had.

She appealed to the county and state superintendents of schools. She was told that if she could raise the first month's salary, $60, a teacher would be provided. She earned most of that money herself, baking cakes, which she sold in Greenville at $1 apiece.

"Finally I got so tired of baking cakes every night — you see I was still trying to carry my case load here in Greenville county — that I just couldn't stand it any longer," she said, "so I put in some cash myself and some businessmen here in Greenville gave me small contributions."

The bank fixed up an old house for the school. Mrs. Hill made the blackboards herself, out of beaver board. She got the Junior Red Cross in Atlanta to adopt the school, and they furnished books and crayons.

They hired Miss Elizabeth Wilson to teach in the school. Miss Wilson and her mother, a widow, are members of one of those impoverished aristocratic Southern families. They live about two miles from the colony, Mrs. Hill told me, in a terribly run down old Southern mansion, so heavily mortgaged that they are constantly in fear of losing it. Most of their land they've lost.

Mrs. Wilson has a college degree. Her daughter has had two years of college. There are a younger daughter and son, who are now working their way through college. Last year the daughter had to quit. She was cooking her own meals in her room, "and just didn't have enough to eat," as Mrs. Hill put it, so she broke down. But she's back there this year.

Miss Wilson was not at the school yesterday, but her mother was. And what a woman! She's almost 70 — little, frail, refined. And that woman walks five miles every day, carrying education to the people in that colony!

She has always assisted her daughter in the school, without pay until recently. . . . This has been going on since the fall of 1931. She spends her mornings helping her daughter with the children. And in the afternoons she goes about from house to house teaching the adults. Most of them can neither read nor write, except what she's taught them.

"I have one woman," she told me proudly, "who can read quite well. She is now reading Lamb's Tales from Shakespeare."

She has taught them other things, too. Cooking, for instance. And she has tried to organize some sort of community life, around the school. You should have heard her tell about the little chicken pie supper they had, each of the women contributing what she could! She and her daughter come over every Sunday and conduct a Sunday school there in the school.

And all this she has done, until very recently, without pay, when, as Mrs. Hill says, "at times she probably wasn't getting any too much to eat herself." . . .

To Harry L. Hopkins

Charleston, S.C., February 8, 1934

Dear Mr. Hopkins:

. . . Well, I met with those 15 farmers Dr. Long got together in Columbia today — 15 farmers, Dr. Long, a couple of agricultural extension agents, Malcolm Miller, Miss Leila Johnson, and, of all people, Julia Peterkin.[1] . . .

The gentlemen did not have what you would call a social viewpoint. They were quite frank in their statements that they wanted to keep the price of labor down. I think they really believe they can't continue to farm if the price of labor goes up much. And all of them except the cotton and tobacco men would have pretty tough sledding right now, I guess if they had to raise wages very much.

They told me quite frankly, too, that they used a lot of women — more women than men in the asparagus business, for instance — because they were cheaper then men. They said they used them, too, because they are more skillful at handling delicate, perishable things, like asparagus and tomatoes. One man told me he paid men and women the same wages. The normal rate, they said, in all agricultural labor was about 75 cents a day. The truck men admitted they are paying now as low as 40 cents a day — because, with the price of truck as low as it is, they can't pay any more.

A fruit grower calmly told me that he used the Negro "urchins" to help gather peaches, those that had fallen off the trees, because they could get around under the trees better than grownups. I could hear Leila Johnson, who has worked for years for a child labor law in this state, grinding her teeth, clear across the room! . . .

The truck men say they are actually suffering now from a shortage of labor. The rest of them haven't so far, but they've got the jitters. Oh, yes, one peach grower told me that he had had to use women to prune his trees this winter and that last Monday not a single one of the Negro hands who live on his place showed up to do some spraying they were supposed to do. He said he had more than 300 Negro families living on his place, and he felt very resentful about their all "going to work under CWA" because in the last two or three years he had spent between $35,000 and $40,000 to keep them fed. And now, he felt, they were deserting him.

Mostly they charge that CWA has created dissatisfaction among their Negroes. They all want to be on CWA, working for 30 and 40 cents an hour. Their hearts are no longer in the work on the farms. They are very anxious that this cause of dissatisfaction be removed before farm work really gets under way.

They say that, if we keep it up in the towns, all their Negroes will be moving into town, hoping to get CWA jobs, unless we make those jobs less attractive by working them longer hours for the same weekly pay. As a matter of fact, the social workers tell me there has developed a marked tendency among farm labor to move into towns like Greenville and Anderson and Spartanburg, the textile centers, but they say it is because there has been no work for the people on the farms. They said they had reports from real estate men that there was a shortage of small houses in Greenville and Spartanburg. . . .

The first man to speak his piece was a representative of the trucking interests down here around Charleston. Their season, he said, runs from about September 1 until June 1. It is on, full swing, now. He said there actually existed in this area a shortage of labor, that he had managed allright himself, but some of his neighbors were seriously handicapped, because of CWA. According to his story, those Negroes must have been on relief — they had to be on relief in November to get CWA jobs, and there've been darned few CWA jobs given to common labor in this state since then — during the trucking season. My own hunch is that a lot of those fellows were darned glad to have their Negroes on relief because they didn't have to feed them and that they deliberately let them off, part time, to work on relief projects. Well, anyway, they are squawking now.

They use all black labor — day labor — in the truck gardens, but in many cases have them live on their plantations. A Negro man now gets around 60 cents a day, and a Negro woman, working in the fields, 40 cents a day. The normal rate, he said, would be 75 cents a day for a man, and 50 cents a day for a woman. He thinks we ought to pull all CWA out by May 1, starting in right now. That seemed a little inconsistent, because their slack season begins June 1 and extends to September 1.

"What will the hands do during your slack season?" I inquired.

"Oh, they can fish," he said. "We could use CWA in the summer, but I don't think it's necessary."

The next to present his case was a representative of 500 asparagus growers. The asparagus is raised in a sandy belt that runs through the center of the state. Asparagus raising down here is a highly seasonal business. It extends from about March 1 to May 15, and during those weeks, he said, those 500 asparagus growers use about 6,000 laborers, including a large number of women and children. During the rest of the year they get some work in the corn and cotton fields, he said. There is a period of about three months, extending from November 1 to February 1, when there is very little work for them. They get, when working, about 75 cents a day.

There is no shortage of labor in the asparagus belt now — the season hasn't started yet — but it is this gentleman's opinion that, if CWA continues, "certain asparagus growers will be seriously handicapped." He thinks we ought to begin to pull it out right away.

Next was the peach grower who said he had had to use women to prune his trees. Incidentally, one of the kicks they made was that the Negro women wouldn't work in the fields as long as their husbands had CWA jobs! Julia Peterkin explained this attitude later, in private, by saying, sarcastically, "You must understand, Miss Hickok, that down here Negroes are not people." Which was rather interesting, because she is a descendant of a long line of Southerners and told me that her grand-mother told her when she was a child that Abraham Lincoln was an il-legitimate son of John Calhoun and that that was why he freed the slaves, because he resented Calhoun's treatment of his mother!

"I'm three weeks behind in my work right now because of CWA," the peach grower said. "I could have got along if they'd taken half my hands to work on CWA, but I can't get along with ALL of them working on CWA."

He, too, recommended that we begin pulling it out right away — and get it out as fast as possible.

The next gentleman was a tobacco grower. Their slack season runs from November 1 to March 1, he said. The rest of the year there is a great deal of work. He was more moderate than the others.

"I feel," he said, "that this talk about a prospective scarcity of labor may be mostly hearsay. We've certainly got more than we need right now. But many of us are afraid the high wage rate on CWA is going to cause dissatisfaction among our hands, and we're afraid to put in a big tobacco crop with the chance of having to use dissatisfied labor."

He recommended that we pull it all out by the middle of March. He was also strong for increasing the number of hours, thereby auto-matically lowering the hourly wage rate.

The cotton growers aren't having any trouble yet, because their work isn't in full swing, they say, but, said one of them:

"This CWA wage is buzzing in our Niggers' heads."

They are afraid of dissatisfied labor. The reduction of acreage, under AAA, will run to about 100,000 acres in this state, they said, but they in-sisted that the reduction in acreage would NOT mean a reduction in employment. They pointed out that part of their agreement was not to lay off their men and swore by all that was holy that they were living up to it. The Georgia cotton growers were more frank and said that the cot-ton acreage reduction would mean probably a 25 percent reduction in employment this year. . . .

1. Author of the Pulitzer Prize novel, *Scarlet Sister Mary* (Indianapolis, Ind., 1928), and other novels about the South.

To Harry L. Hopkins

Charleston, S.C., February 10, 1934

Dear Mr. Hopkins:

. . . They are having here today the worst ice and sleet storm since "befoah de Wah." Somebody said it was the first snow since 1915. The children love it, but their elders are wringing their hands. Just how much damage it's going to do I don't know, but obviously it's not very good for the truck business. Nor for the famous gardens that attract their big tourist crowd here in March and April. The palms are sheathed in ice. Icicles hang from the eaves. The pavements are as slippery as skating rinks. I had intended to drive on toward Raleigh this afternoon, but the Automobile Club told me it was worse north of Charleston, and still having a cold and being unwilling to match what driving skill I have against the inexperience of these South Carolinians who don't know how to drive on sleety pavements, I decided to wait over until tomorrow. It does look as though the truck gardeners — or farmers — already complaining about the low prices they are getting for their stuff, are going to be hit pretty hard.

Since coming to Charleston, I've been hearing the other side of the story—"other" from that told me by the 15 farmers in Columbia Thursday. The Mayor of Charleston,[1] the county CWA and relief administrator,[2] and the social workers, the county home demonstration agent[3] — all have earnestly warned me not to accept unreservedly the statements of those farmers. They insist there is no farm labor shortage, or wouldn't be, if the farmers were willing to pay a living wage, and that there is very likely to be a surplus of labor. They think we should be able to pull CWA out of the rural areas down here along the coast and possibly out of Charleston, but they insist there must be some kind of relief.

These people say the farmers who are doing the kicking are Bourbons — or Tories, as the President might call them — and that they want as big a surplus of labor as possible, so they can keep wages down. The more unemployed there are hanging around begging for work, the lower wages can be.

The farmers, on the other hand, would no doubt point out that mayors like to have "Guv'ment easy money" pouring into their cities, and that CWA and relief administrators and social workers are afraid that, if we pull out, they'll lose their jobs.

Mrs. Alsop, the county home demonstration agent, who comes from a family of planters and has been a planter herself, was gentle, but firm.

"The trouble with them is," she said, "that they haven't progressed beyond the slave labor idea. They still think of farming as riding around over their plantations on horseback, superintending their slaves.

"That idea is what has kept the South down where it is. . . . But that kind of farming isn't paying any more.

"Those people are through — all through — whether they realize it or not. I'll wager there aren't more than five of those big planters in the county right now who are solvent. Why, even the seed salesmen have stopped coming down here from the North! They quit a couple of years ago. They know these fellows are through. One of them told me so." . . .

The farmers, as nearly as I can figure them out, want everything pulled out except during their slack season, and each year they want it pulled out far enough ahead of the beginning of their work "so these Niggers will be good and hungry." In effect, they want us to take over the load they say they used to carry — that of keeping their peons alive during the slack seasons on pork and meal — and have everything nice and lovely so they can go on getting all the cheap labor they want when they want it, without any responsibility toward that labor. They'd be perfectly happy, I think, if we'd give their Negroes during the slack seasons a little extra, for clothes, so they could hire them for even less when they want them — say, 20 cents a day, instead of 40! Remember, I'm quoting their own figures on present wages — 40 cents a day for a Negro woman, 50 cents a day for a Negro man, and they employ about 75 percent women, they tell me. They certainly are a fine lot of gentlemen, aren't they?

Mayor Maybank is inclined to boil over whenever he gets started on the subject. He points out the millions the Government has spent down here in the South trying to help the farmers, pumping up the price of cotton, giving them seed loans, helping them to hang onto their farms, and — well, he just boils. He is an interesting chap, the Mayor. He is about 40, I should say, and belongs to one of the state's best-known families. He told me his grandfather ran for President of the Confederate States against Jefferson Davis. He is related to most of the aristocracy in Charleston. His family has always been in the cotton business. He is himself in the cotton exporting business — which is certainly on the bum now. Any Government program that effectively reduces cotton acreage and raises the price is going to ruin him permanently, he told me.

"But I reckon some of us have got to fall by the wayside," he added calmly.

He is almost fiercely loyal to the President and the Administration generally. You see, he and several other prominent Southerners I've met feel that Mr. Roosevelt is the first President since the "War between the States" who has recognized the South as a part of the Union. Really, that's the way some of them feel. I've had it said to me over and over again:

"He's the first President who has even tried to help us, down here. He's the first President who has made us feel that we really are a part of the United States." . . .

Another thing that burns Mr. Grice and the Mayor up is that "these farmers beg us to take their Niggers off relief and CWA and turn right

185

around and try to get us to put their own sons on as foremen at a dollar an hour." They both feel that, if CWA should be continued much longer, some of the higher wage rates should be materially lowered.

"That's what's causing us most of our trouble," Mr. Grice said. "The white people keep exerting pressure to grab off those good jobs. And it's bad for the Negroes, too, because they keep hoping that they'll be promoted."

They very earnestly begged me to try to give you the mental makeup of these farmers.

"They are all gamblers," the Mayor assured me. "They think only in terms of big money — $100,000 a year. They're not interested in any ordinary, even income. (They are talking, of course, of the truck farmers, not Southern farmers generally.) And the kind of gambling they do doesn't make for any stable employment. They're up today and down tomorrow. And what they want is plenty of cheap labor, to grab on a moment's notice, whenever they happen to want it." . . .

1. Burnet P. Maybank, later governor and U.S. Senator.
2. Edmund P. Grice, Jr.
3. Caroline S. Alston was the county home demonstration agent for Charleston from 1933 through 1937 and possibly longer. Hickok referred to her, undoubtedly erroneously, later in the letter as "Mrs. Alsop."

To Harry L. Hopkins

Raleigh, N.C., February 14, 1934

Dear Mr. Hopkins:

. . . The truth is that the rural South never has progressed beyond slave labor. Their whole system has been built up on labor that could be obtained for nothing or for next to nothing. When their slaves were taken away, they proceeded to establish a system of peonage that was as close to slavery as it possibly could be and included Whites as well as Blacks. That's all a tenant farmer is — or has been, up to the present time — a slave. You know how the system has worked. The tenant lived on the landlord's farm, in a house owned by the landlord. During the slack season, when there was no work, the farmer took care of him — "furnished" him, as they call it down here — either by buying his food and giving it to him, or by giving him credit at a store he owned. The tenant never had any money — never could "buy himself out." The property owner was his lord and master, could impose any terms he liked.

186

In addition to the share-cropping tenants, there has always been plenty of day labor, mostly black, that just managed to exist somehow when work was slack, and that was hungry enough, when there was any work, to go into the fields for whatever the farmer wanted to pay. Say, 25 cents a day.

During the depression, the paternalistic landlord was hard put to it to "furnish" his tenants. He was darned glad to have us take over the job. But now, finding that CWA has taken up some of this labor surplus — both day labor and those tenants without farms, of whom there was always just a convenient number enough to aid the landlord in imposing his own terms on the tenants on his property — he is panicky, realizes that he may have to make better terms with his tenants and pay his day labor more, and is raising a terrific howl against CWA.

Whatever we do down here that may take up that rural labor surplus is going to make these farmers yell. Right now they are, for the most part, inclined to overlook the fact that whatever improvement there is in their condition — raising of cotton and tobacco prices — is directly due to government aid. They won't "play ball." They are like the department store proprietors I heard about in Tampa, who joyfully pocketed all the money brought in by a big Christmas business on CWA — government — money, without cooperating with the government by taking on any extra help. . . .

My feeling is that CWA should be stopped, and as quickly as possible without causing too much disturbance. Especially in the small towns and rural areas. But we may as well face the fact that there'll have to be something else. And the gap between CWA and this "something else" should not be too great. CWA was an emergency measure, I think, and should be treated as such. If we continue it too long, I'm afraid the harm it will have done will outweigh its good effects.

In this I do not agree with people like Dean [Howard W.] Odum,[1] Mr. [Jonathan] Daniels,[2] Mr. [J. S.] Steed,[3] Mr. [Charles H.] Robinson,[4] and many of the administrators. They all want it continued, but with some changes. The change most universally requested is that the hours and wage rates be made more nearly to conform with the hours and wage rates of the codes in the different communities. It DOES seem a little tough to impose hours and wage rates on industry and then go into the labor market and compete with them offering even shorter hours and higher wages. Even if we limit our operations so that we don't take their people away from them, how can you expect a man working 40 hours a week in a cotton mill for whatever their code limit is — somewhere around $13 or $14 a week — to be satisfied when his neighbor, too often of the "unemployable," indigent type, is working 30 hours or even 24 hours for $12 or $13 a week or $10 or $11 a week? Here's your man in the mill working five eight-hour days each week.

187

And here's another man working perhaps three days a week and getting almost as much for it. It gets everybody all sort of mixed up and dissatisfied. Besides, what impresses the men is NOT the WEEKLY income, but the HOURLY rate. Thirty, 40, 45 cents an hour is big money down here and generally, I'm told, considerably above the code rates. . . .

With regard to the people who are actually at work on CWA wages, the story seems to be pretty much the same everywhere. I get it from engineers, administrators, social workers. When CWA came in, the men were "tickled to death." Their morale jumped up about a hundred points. They went to work with a will. Now they are beginning to be bitten by the urge to get even more. They want to get 65 cents an hour instead of 40. They want to be foremen, at $1.10, and they suspect every foreman of having got his job through political pull. I guess it's true that, the more you do for people, the more they demand. . . .

Here in Raleigh I ran bang into a lot more enthusiasm about some sort of large scale subsistence farming program in the rural areas. They've done more than think about it. They are actually at work on a survey of the rural surplus labor problem — as represented by tenant farmers who haven't any "farms" — and have worked out a plan. It's the same old plan — subsistence farming on an extensive scale, with a minimum of equipment, but a maximum amount of supervision, and confined largely to people who are now actually on the land, as squatters, or who have been recently forced to move to town because there wasn't any land for them to squat on. . . .

The survey so far indicates that in Eastern North Carolina, practically all farming country, there are 10,000 of these displaced farm tenants — families whose whole work background is farming, but who now have no way of making a living because they have no place to farm. Share-croppers with no opportunity to raise a crop. The number has been increasing for some years, owing to a reduction in acreage forced by the depression. Some of these families haven't been able to get a place to raise a crop for five or six years. They are our relief load. Hundreds of them have moved to town, where they don't belong and where they are increasing the number of unemployed we expect the mills to take on. And as their number increases, due to the PRACTICAL results of AAA acreage reduction — I don't care HOW much the farmers talk about that agreement not to lay off hands — they are moving to town faster. . . .

As they move to town, they apply for direct relief. The intake office in Wilson today was so crowded you could hardly get into the place. Every house, every abandoned shack, is filled with them. They even break the locks off empty houses and move in.

Members of the relief committee, two clergymen, the administrator, and the case work supervisor in Wilson today told me that 300 of these displaced tenants and their families have moved into Wilson — a town of about 13,000 population — in the last three years, and of that 300 families, 200 have moved in this winter. The case work supervisor told there were AT LEAST FIFTY CASES in which the landlord, to get rid of them, had moved them in himself and had paid their first week's rent!

Seventy-five percent of these families that have moved into Wilson, they told me, are Negroes. Most of them are illiterate. They are afflicted with tuberculosis and the social diseases. Of the white families many have pellagra and hookworm, although hookworm isn't so common up here as it is farther South. They are a dead weight on the community, both from the social and from the economic standpoints. They don't even want to live in town. The administrator and the case work supervisor both said that there is a constant stream of them in and out of their offices, begging for a chance to "git a place on some farm."

They're NOT all bums, either. They HAVEN'T come to town to get work in the mills or on CWA. They've come because there's no place for them to live in the country. Every abandoned shack in the countryside is filled up.

I drove out into the country today near Wilson to look over some of those "squatters." A dozen or more of their shacks — miserable hovels — were pointed out to me. We stopped and visited three families.

One family was obviously very low grade mentally. Probably that man never would be able to make a living, farming or any other way, unless someone stood right over him and told him what to do. The house, in which he and his family were permitted to "exist" on a farm, without being allowed to plant anything, was about as weather proof as an old-fashioned Western corn crib. Last week, when it was so cold and snowy down here, someone went out there from the relief office and tacked some tin sheeting up against one side of the place to keep out the snow, which was blowing in through cracks an inch wide! Sooner or later the farmer is going to get tired of having those people around. They'll be in Wilson.

The next family was of better grade mentally. The house — hardly more than a shed — was about as clean as it could be under the circumstances. There were eight children. They were well clothed — the father has been working on CWA all winter — but that place, even with the sun shining outside, and a fire in the stove inside, was COLD. It's just a few old boards hanging together, that's all. Some day the owner is going to tear it down — if it doesn't collapse — and THAT family will be in Wilson, too. At present the landlord is letting them stay on, charging 75 cents a week rent.

"He's walked this country over," the wife said, referring to her husband. "He can't git no place to crop."

The third family was living in a tobacco barn, which the owner has announced he is going to move away in a few weeks. A tobacco barn has no windows, you know. In order to get any air, except what blows in through the cracks, they have to keep the door open.

This family was distinctly high grade. The man has an excellent reputation. He farmed as a share-cropper until 1927, when he moved onto his father's place. His father lost his farm a couple of years ago. For two years he and his brother doubled up, share-cropping on the farm where they are now living. This year a new landlord took the place over. He brought in his own tenants. This family has been allowed to stay on in the tobacco barn for a few weeks while hunting another place. There is no other place, apparently. And they've got to move out shortly.

The mother in this family is an invalid, and, when they moved into the tobacco barn, her brother took her into his home. Two daughters, one about 18 and one 16 were left in charge of the household.

The place is so clean that I'd have been willing to sit down and eat with them. And this despite the fact that every drop of water they used had to be carried a good half mile. The children, all with bad colds, were neat and clean. I talked with the 16-year-old girl. She was terribly worried.

"Seems like we just keep goin' lower and lower," she said. "He can't git no crop. (Referring to her father.) He's been everywhere. All of us has had colds ever since we moved into this place. And pretty soon we ain't even goin' to have this place any more."

When I told her I didn't see how she managed to keep the place so clean, she replied dejectedly:

"Oh, this ain't clean. I can't seem to keep it as clean as when we lived in a better place."

Rather slight, with fair hair and the kind of blue eyes that look right into your own, this girl wore over her thin dress a pair of overalls, worn but recently washed.

And pinned on her bosom, as one wears a brooch, was a campaign button of 1932 — a profile of the President.

1. Professor of sociology at the University of North Carolina and chairman of the state CWA and Emergency Relief Committee.
2. Editor of the *Raleigh News and Observer*.
3. Chairman of the National Emergency Council in North Carolina.
4. Collector for the Internal Revenue Service for North Carolina.

To Kathryn S. Godwin[1]

Greensboro, N.C.   February 18th [1934]
Dear Mrs. Godwin:

You ought to see my car. It looks as though it had been through the Argonne! Three traffic accidents in one week. And that, after being in the South nearly six weeks and driving it 5,000 miles without a scratch!

Number One happened in Fayetteville, N.C., last Monday. A big milk truck, backing out diagonally, without being able to see where it was going, crumpled up my right rear fender like a piece of cardboard. I think the owner's insurance company is going to pay for a new fender.

Number Two happened in Chapel Hill Thursday night. My fault entirely. Scraped the left front fender on a retaining wall driving into the rather narrow, curved entrance to the hotel.

Number Three happened in Durham Friday morning. Got caught in a traffic jam behind a bus. Had sat for about a minute, when suddenly the bus started backing. I couldn't back because they were crowded in behind me. I honked as loudly as I could — and, having two horns, I can honk fairly loudly — but he kept right on coming and didn't stop until he had put a nice big dent in my left front fender, broken one of my horns, and bent my bumper. "Oh, excuse me," he said, "I thought that horn was a truck." I don't think I'll collect on this one, although it certainly was the bus driver's fault. An official of the company, looking over the damage, observed that crumpled rear fender, and I think you'd have a hard time convincing him [it was] the driver's fault. He has undoubtedly put me down as a careless driver, who has lots of accidents.

These, together with my cold — I really thought I was going to have to go to a hospital last Monday — and that damned article in Time magazine, have made something of a wreck out of me, although I feel much better today.

The way I ran into the Time article was funny.

When I got to Charlotte Friday night, half dead from fatigue and worry about the car, I found awaiting me a delegation from a little town up on the Blue Ridge, known as Old Fort. Their only factory, a tannery, burned down, and nobody has any work, and they are quite desperate. They had come down to see if I wouldn't try to get some help for them out of Washington — I don't see how I can, but I'll talk to the Boss about them if I get a chance — and had waited two hours, poor things.

As I came in, they handed me, with beaming smiles, a copy of Time. I read the thing and wanted to curse until the air was blue.

I don't suppose I ought to kick. It's friendly, and fair, on the whole, to the Boss and the administration. Only—why the Hell CAN'T they leave me alone? After South Carolina, I'm so fed up with publicity I want to kick every reporter I see. Which is a bad state for me to get into, since I'll probably be back in the business myself after I get through with this.

I suppose I am "a rotund lady with a husky voice" and "baggy clothes," but I honestly don't believe my manner is "peremptory." And I bitterly resent the implication that I got this job solely because I was a friend of Mrs. Roosevelt. I love Mrs. Roosevelt dearly—she is the best friend I have in the world—but sometimes I do wish, for my own sake, that she were Mrs. Joe Doaks of Oelwein, Iowa! I'm a bit sick, too, because it got out that I'm going to Puerto Rico with her. I had hoped it wouldn't—that I could sort of slide in, as part of the background, that she would get all the publicity, and that I could go fairly quietly about my business. Oh, well—I'll do my best. And, even with all the publicity, she will be a help. She's a wonder at that sort of thing, you know. She could handle my job a thousand times better than I can.

Unless I get wrecked altogether, I'll be back in Washington Tuesday afternoon sometime and shall report in Wednesday morning.

It's nice and warm here today—the fifth warm, sunny day I've experienced in nearly six weeks in the South!

1. Secretary to Hopkins.

To Harry L. Hopkins

Greensboro, N.C., February 18th [1934]

Dear Mr. Hopkins:

. . . Someone—I've talked to so many people this week that I can't remember who it was—remarked the other day that "it is those white collar people, when they get desperate, and not common labor, who start revolutions." . . .

It is quite apparent that the majority of those now coming on relief rolls have exhausted every possible resource. They don't take to relief with much pleasure. As a matter of fact, I know personally people in the white collar group—and you probably do, too—who have been eligible for relief for months, who were certainly eligible for CWA or CWS jobs, but who wouldn't apply for them. They don't want "that kind of job." They are pretty bitter, too, some of them, and when they are finally forced to apply for "that kind of job"—and don't get it—they are dangerous. . . .

Aside from this white collar group, Charles H. Gilmore, the administrator in Charlotte, believes CWA should be pulled out for the same reason, apart from its cost, that I think it should — that attitude of the public, particularly that portion of it which is now benefitting by CWA, the people on the payroll.

"Last year at this time," he said, "we were paying 50 cents a day on relief. Now we are paying 45 cents an hour. I admit that 50 cents a day was too little, but, paying 45 cents an hour, we are now having more trouble, more discontent than we had while paying 50 cents a day."

I quote a paragraph from a report sent on to me here by Miss Leila Johnson, Assistant State Administrator for South Carolina, in charge of social work. The report was written by her director in Aiken, S.C.

"It is quite discouraging indeed, Miss Johnson, to see how the people, in order to get what they term 'adequate' relief, have learned to threaten us and say that, if we do not give them what they want, they will write to headquarters about it.

"I notice the great majority of the complaints have no justifiable grounds and are greatly exaggerated, while others are requests for work which we cannot give them, as they did not apply at this office until after November 15th.

"It is a sad sight to see the attitude of people asking for direct relief changing from one that used to be a modest request for help temporarily, until they could get on their feet again, to the present attitude of demanding their share of what the Government has to give.

"Some of them can do without Government relief, but they do not seem to be able to stand the sight of a less fortunate neighbor receiving help from us.

"This attitude is becoming more predominant as the months roll by, and makes it difficult to think of the time if and when the Government withdraws emergency relief from the people of the county."

So much for that. * * *

I have given a good deal of time the last few days to talking with Negroes. Until I came to North Carolina I had not had much contact with Negro leaders. There are several Negro colleges in this state, however, and in Durham is a gentlemen named [Charles Clinton] Spaulding, head of a big Negro life insurance company,[1] that does business all over the South, president of a big Negro bank, and said to be the largest Negro employer in the South.

I spent all of Friday morning in his office in Durham, talking with him and with Negro businessmen and teachers. And on Thursday I attended sessions of the Interracial Commission in Raleigh and talked with several of the leaders.

I haven't learned much of any value, I'm afraid.

193

I have met some very fine Colored people—intelligent, well educated, cultured. Little by little, they are probably getting somewhere, but it's awfully slow. Spaulding is himself a wonder, I think. You can imagine the force of character, the "stuff" it would take to rise to his position. He is a remarkable man.

The trouble is that the white people, even those who belong to the Interracial Commission and might therefore be said to be sympathetic toward the Negro's efforts to raise himself, socially and economically, are really indifferent.

That was apparent in the attendance at the Commission's meetings. Its membership actually numbers two white persons to every Negro, which, Professor Roy M. Brown (department of Sociology, University of North Carolina, assistant state relief and CWA administrator) says, is about right for the proportion of Whites and Blacks in the state's population. But at the meeting, there were about three Negroes to every white man.

They listened to some reports, passed some resolutions—one against lynching—and that was about all. During my twenty years in the newspaper business I covered too many meetings to have much faith in resolutions! About the only practical thing the commission has ever accomplished in North Carolina, Professor Brown said, was to get for Negroes permission to ride in busses after busses had forced many streetcar companies out of business and had also forced the railroads to discontinue many of their short runs.

The conference in Mr. Spaulding's office didn't amount to much—it was largely a matter of trying not to step on each others' toes!

I tried to get from them some idea of just what is happening to the Negro under the New Deal—if he is getting his job back in private industry, how he fares under the code, how great are the chances of his being forced back onto direct relief with CWA out, and so on. I didn't get much except charges—expressed as politely as their bitterness would permit—of white discrimination against the Blacks. A good deal of this is no doubt true. But I have a feeling that their bitterness—I'm not saying I'd not be bitter, too, were I in their place—colors everything they have to say.

They expressed a belief that the great majority of the permanently unemployed will be Negroes. They noted a tendency on the part of employers to discharge Negroes and hire white people in their places. They said that about the only field of employment still left entirely to Negroes in the South is domestic service. They expressed a fear that, with a demand for higher wages all around, white people would invade that field, too.

One charge they made was that an organization of white women in Atlanta—they couldn't remember its name—actually and openly fostered a movement to fire Negroes and hire white people. I don't doubt it's true. I've heard something of the same thing from white people themselves down here. The attitude, quite naturally, I suppose, is that if two men are hungry, a white man and a black man, and one of them must go on being hungry, it must be the black man, of course. And if the black man has a job, and the white man hasn't why, the black man must give it up to the white man, of course, if he wants it. Sometimes I think the white people in the South would be perfectly happy if we'd take over the job of feeding all the Negroes just enough to keep them from starving in droves and cluttering up the streets and alleys with their dead bodies! . . .

The cashier of Mr. Spaulding's Negro bank was very bitter about white prejudice.

"Why, they won't even let us keep our jobs as truck drivers, let alone anything higher," he said. "White men are taking our places on the trucks. White waitresses are taking our places in the restaurants. White people threaten employers if they don't let Negroes go and hire white help. Occasionally even the white labor unions do it. The Depression and now the New Deal, with its higher wages, is just forcing us Negroes out of our jobs, that's all."

One of the most interesting things that Mr. Spaulding and his associates had to say was that they thought the CWA wage rate had been too high. Since their people have benefitted by that high wage rate more than the white people, and since we've been so sharply criticized for it because it was applied to Negroes, I thought their reaction was exceedingly interesting.

"The code wages are fair," Mr. Spaulding said. "We agree that CWA shouldn't have paid wages higher than the codes."

In spite of their assertions that the Negroes, because of racial discrimination, are not getting a fair break under the New Deal, statistics from Spaulding's life insurance company indicate that in the last few months — and before CWA came in — their income had increased. His company, the North Carolina Mutual Life, does business only with Negroes, in the Carolinas, Virginia, Maryland, District of Columbia, Alabama, Tennessee, and Georgia.

During the month of August, 1933, the company received 9,137 applications for life insurance, as compared with 6,839 applications in the corresponding month in 1932 — an increase of 28 percent.

During the week of December 1, 1933, it received 3,015 applications, as compared with 1,337 during the corresponding week in 1932 — an increase of 56 percent. This, of course, was after CWA came into the picture.

During the month of January, 1934, there were 9,705 applications, against 5,078 in January, 1933 — an increase of 48 percent.

The company attributes 90 percent of this increase in business to CWA.

From a Negro case work supervisor came the suggestion that Negro women working in the sewing rooms be given an opportunity to enroll in classes under teachers who would train them as house servants. I wasn't particularly enthusiastic, but she put it this way:

"It's the only way to get their wages up. Train them. Make better servants out of them. Right now in the South a trained Negro maid will draw $6 a week, against $2 paid the average."

Many of them, they told me, are working for nothing at all now, save their board. And Professor Brown quoted (indignantly) a white woman, a friend of his family, who, he said, announced with satisfaction the other day:

"At last I've found a woman who will come in and clean up my house for her dinner!"

I suggested a course of training for housewives employing labor. They loved it!

Well, we didn't get anywhere much — except to a feeling, on both sides, that the Negro's treatment under the New Deal ought to be watched pretty carefully. I have a feeling that Negro labor, by accepting lower wages, can break the whole thing down here in the South. . . .

1. North Carolina Mutual Life Insurance Company.

To Harry L. Hopkins

[Washington, D.C.]   March 20, 1934

Dear Mr. Hopkins:

Here are some observations and conclusions drawn out of what I saw and out of a great mass of material that was hurled at me during my recent trip to Puerto Rico.

First of all, it doesn't look to me as though Puerto Rico were our job. ("Our" meaning the Federal Emergency Relief Administration.) They may be eligible for relief, but not "emergency relief." There's no emergency about it. It's a situation that has been developing for years. The so-called "depression" has very little to do with it — if anything. It's a case of over-population and lack of means for the population to support itself. The population has doubled in 30 years. The island, 100 miles long and 35 miles wide, now has 1,600,000 inhabitants, or nearly 460 to the square mile (Rex Tugwell[1] says there are six Puerto Ricans behind every bush), and a good many of those square miles are mountainous and not much good for producing anything to eat. As the population has grown, the chances for earning a living on the island have decreased. One of their major industries — it used to be their leading industry in the days of the Spaniards — has been coffee. It was ruined by a series of hurricanes beginning in 1928, after a 30-year lapse. Economically, they now have all their eggs in one basket, sugar. And that is a seasonal industry which, under the present system, pays the workers barely enough to live on during the season and leaves them nothing to live on during the five or six months they are idle. I was told that, out of the 1,600,000 people on the island, not more than 100,000 earned enough to live on. (And I gather that a goodly portion of them work for the government — i.e., the insular government.) Other industries are: needlework, which is pretty much of a mess and doesn't provide very many families with anything like a living; tobacco, which is pretty hopeless because they raise cigar tobacco, for which there isn't much market any more; citrus fruits, also badly damaged by hurricanes and, probably more or less permanently, without any market to speak of; and a little truck gardening, in which they cannot successfully compete with Florida, Georgia, and the Carolinas. The total income of the island this year, from all its agriculture and industries, will run, I was told, to about $75,000,000 and between $40,000,000 and $50,000,000 of it will be sugar money, most of which leaves the island.

So there you have them — 1,600,000 humans, with only about 100,000 of them able to support themselves. It's a chronic condition, not an emergency.

Secondly, I don't see how the Federal Emergency Relief Administration could handle it as a relief proposition, adequately. When I was there, the case load consisted of 175,000 families. The average family in Puerto Rico consists of six persons. According to that figure, we had at that time 1,050,000 of the 1,600,000 inhabitants of Puerto Rico on relief! The number has been cut down about half, however. James R. Bourne, the administrator, cut off 25 per cent of his direct relief cases while I was there and was planning to cut off 25 per cent more when I left, this action being necessitated, he said, by the cut in his funds. Mr. Bourne told me that he could do "a fairly decent job" with $1,000,000 a month, cutting his case load down to 100,000 families, making them work for their relief on projects that required no materials — filling up holes in the roads, for instance, grading, and ditching. This would mean minimum subsistence relief. When I was there, the average was $1 a week for a family of six. He is now getting $500,000 a month.

So far as I could see, however, we could spend any amount of money we liked down there for relief — millions and millions of dollars. There's no "middle class" on the island. Just a few wealthy or well-to-do people. All the rest on the same level, a level that is pretty low. No matter how many people you carried on relief — unless you took practically the entire population — there would always be thousands who were just as needy and weren't getting any. Obviously, we can't do it. Especially since it would be a permanent job unless other Governmental departments took a hand and tried to straighten out the economic situation down there.

If other departments in the Government were to spend some money down there — doing some housing, for instance, starting a reforestation program, starting some industries, perhaps — I believe we could get out of the relief business pretty quickly. At least, the population wouldn't be any worse off than it is now. Jobs provided by those undertakings would take care of the situation just as well as our relief does now. Probably better, since a job would bring in more money per family. A Puerto Rican who has a job, I'm told, usually supports several people besides his own immediate family.

If other departments in the Government do not spend any money down there — i.e., if they make no attempt to remedy the economic situation, but leave it as it is — we could still pull out relief. That would mean that, with an increasing population and with no increase in opportunities for self-support, the people would be back where they were before we stepped in. The situation would be getting worse all the time — but it's been getting worse for years and years. It's not any "emergency." . . .

On the whole, although $1 a week for a family of six seems pretty low, and, as Mr. Bourne and the social workers say, by no means adequate, I think we've done a fairly good job down there. People outside the picture tell me that the population as a whole is in better shape, since we've been in there, than it's been in for years. I drew my own conclusions somewhat from the appearance of the children of families on relief. True, I saw individual cases of malnutrition that were much worse than any I'd ever seen before, but, by and large, the urchins looked healthier and better nourished than children in some of the mining camps in West Virginia, for instance, or in the Kentucky mountains, or in some places in the South.

For the very poor Puerto Rico has one great blessing to offer. Climate. Sunshine. Rickets, for instance, are practically unknown down there. Doctors say there is a quality in the sunshine that makes up for dietary deficiencies.

Because of the climate, relief needs can be reduced to a minimum, too. No one is going to freeze in Puerto Rico, no matter how few clothes he has or how open to the weather his shack may be. Relief can be cut right down to a feeding program and nothing else. As a matter of fact, that's all we're doing now.

Unless the transportation costs are too high, we might be able to cut down on the cost of relief in Puerto Rico by sending down less cash and more surplus commodities. There's one place where they would be glad to get anything we want to send. I heard only two kicks on surplus commodities while I was in Puerto Rico. One — from the Commissioner of Agriculture, himself a coffee planter, was that we were sending cocoa instead of buying Puerto Rican coffee, which, he insisted, drunk with hot milk, as the Puerto Ricans drink coffee, was just as nourishing as cocoa. The other kick was against the possibility of our sending oranges down there where they already had a surplus of citrus fruits. On the whole, however, they seem glad to get surplus commodities. I notice that in the last month or so you have authorized purchase of two allotments of foodstuffs, all of 1,811,000 pounds each, for the island. This should help somewhat to offset the cut in funds. Doctors told me that what they needed most were protein and calcium. Their greatest need is for milk. Because of the great difficulty in raising cattle — there is a kind of tick down there that gives cattle spotted fever — the milk supply on the island is pitifully inadequate. Incidentally, powdered milk seems to go pretty well down there, and it might be lighter and therefore less expensive to ship than condensed milk. The suggestion was made that we buy up the milk surplus in dairy states, such as New York, powder it, and send it to Puerto Rico. They also need meat and cheese. Meat is expensive because of the difficulty in raising livestock. They are now experimenting with rabbits as a possible meat supply, but there are many parts of the island, I'm told, where even rabbits won't thrive. The island is apparently alive with parasites that kill chickens and cattle. Even dogs, except those that are born down there and eventually have some sort of immunity, have a hard time in Puerto Rico. Army officers told me that dogs brought in from the outside usually die.

In making the suggestion that we substitute food for cash, I am going on the assumption, of course, that we have to buy surplus commodities anyway. If we do, Puerto Rico would be a grand place to distribute them, it seems to me.

If we continue relief in Puerto Rico, everyone agrees, I think, that it should be given in exchange for work. At present they call it "exchange relief." A man works a day for $1 in relief — that is, a man with a family of six works one day each week for $1 in relief. It's not the most efficient labor in the world, but they do accomplish quite a bit.

The most serious drawback is a lack of money for materials and equipment. Against the $600,000 we sent down there last summer for relief, the insular and municipal governments put up $300,000 worth of materials and equipment. When you consider that the island's total income from taxation is only about $11,000,000 a year, I think they did fairly well. Mr. Bourne tells me, however, that they are now at the end of their rope, and we can't expect much this year. At present "exchange relief" is pretty much limited to work on roads.

The biggest job in Puerto Rico — next to getting some industries started so that the people will have a chance to support themselves — is in public health. And undoubtedly the first thing that should be done along that line is to eliminate over-crowding and extremely bad housing in the urban slums. There are two sources from which these slums have grown up — the rapid growth in population and the hurricanes, which have destroyed the homes of people living in the country and have driven them into the towns.

No one could give you an adequate description of those slums. You'd have to see them, that's all. Photographs won't do it, either. They don't give you the odors. Imagine a swamp, with stagnant, scum-covered, muddy water everywhere, in open ditches, pools, backed up around and under the houses. Flies swarming everywhere. Mosquitoes. Rats. Miserable, scrawny, sick cats and dogs and goats, crawling about. Pack into this area, over those pools and ditches as many shacks as you can, so close together that there is barely room to pass between them. Ramshackle, makeshift affairs, made of bits of board and rusty tin, picked up here and there. Into each *room* put a family, ranging from three or four persons to eighteen or twenty. Put in some malaria and hookworm, and in about every other house someone with tuberculosis, coughing and spitting around, probably occupying the family's only bed. And remember, not a latrine in the place. No room for them. No place to dispose of garbage, either. Everything dumped right out into the mud and stagnant water. And pour down into that mess good, hot sun — that may be good for rickets, but certainly [it] doesn't help your stomach any as you plod through the mud followed by swarms of flies and animals and half-naked, sick, perspiring humans. All this may give you just an idea of what those slums are like.

There's one in every town on the island. Half the people, for instance, in Ponce, the second largest city on the island, live under those conditions. Ponce has a population of about 87,000. In Humacao (25,000 pop.) it is down on the bank of a shallow, stagnant river. The river is nothing but a sewer, in which the water hardly moves at all. People bathe in that river. Children play in it. I saw women washing clothes in it. In Mayaguez (58,000 pop.) there is a slum in which there aren't any streets at all. One family to every room. In one of those rooms, with children swarming about her, a woman lay sick in bed. "Smallpox," the native case worker said. I think I must have jumped about a foot. Then Mr. Bourne explained that he meant chicken pox — the two words being very similar in Spanish.

In San Juan, the largest city on the island (114,000 pop.), where the water is so impure that you can't even brush your teeth except with boiled water, there are five of those slums. Open ditches and sewers. Swamp water. No sanitation whatever. Between 40 or 50 per cent of the population living in them. And in San Juan, the U.S. Health officer told me, they have lots of rats and the kind of fleas that carry bubonic plague. Plenty of breeding places for mosquitoes, too, carrying malaria. And always the possibility that a few live mosquitoes will sneak in on an airplane from Pera.[2] They haven't any yellow fever in Pera at present, but they're having it elsewhere in Brazil.

The most serious health problem on the island is tuberculosis, with a very high death rate. It's constantly spreading through those slums. Dr. Garedo Morales, insular commissioner of health, told me there were 25,000 "open" cases that he knew about. It's so bad that all he can hope to do is to isolate as many of the "open" cases as he can, without trying to cure them. But it seemed to me perfectly ridiculous to try to do anything until they clean up the condition that is causing it.

I think that anyone who has ever gone to Puerto Rico must have been impressed with the necessity of cleaning up that housing situation as soon as possible. Well informed people on the island certainly are aware of it. Many of the municipalities — Humacao, for instance — have land available onto which to move the people. But they are helpless because they have no money. There are dozens of plans for getting rid of them — subsistence farms, for instance, moving them into little colonies up in the mountains — but there is no money to do it with.

And it will take a lot of money. It costs money to build houses in Puerto Rico. Wood is expensive, the Spaniards having stripped the mountains of timber years and years ago. Even the simplest sort of wooden house, with plumbing and electric lights, will cost a couple of thousand dollars in San Juan. They can be built more cheaply away from the city, of course, and they could manufacture on the island concrete, which is the best material for building a hurricane-proof house. But even if you got the cost per house down to $400 or less, the job is going to cost a lot because so many houses will have to be built.

In the meantime, Governor Blanton Winship is doing what he can to clean up those slums a little. After one visit around the slums in San Juan, he ordered that lime be taken down there and put all around. And he told the municipal authorities they must clean up those streets and alleyways — at least remove the garbage. And he has ordered them to clean up the water supply, too, so that it will at least be safe to brush one's teeth in it. I think he realizes, though, as everyone else does, that the only way really to clean them up is to move most of the people out. A good, clean fire would be a grand thing for those slums!

Clean up those slums, and you will have gone a long way, I believe, toward solving the health problem in Puerto Rico.

The insular government has a four-point health program, in which it has been using CWA labor and money for materials. It consists in building tuberculosis hospitals, which are really nothing more than isolation houses since they haven't the money to give the patients the sort of diet and care that would cure them, building latrines and providing treatment to clean up the hookworm in the rural areas, a malaria control project, and a child hygiene program, through public health units.

The hospitals are nearing completion in various parts of the island, at a very low cost — $125 per bed. If they are finished, they will have facilities for some 1,000 patients. Dr. Garedo Morales has before the insular legislature an appropriation to take care of them if the hospitals are finished. He is confident it will go through. The municipalities in which they are located have agreed to equip them. Mr. Bourne estimated that they were about 65 per cent finished.

With CWA funds and labor they started to build 30,000 latrines, at between $4 and $6 each, to clean up the hookworm situation in the rural areas. They have built 10,000, so far. With $2,000,000, they told me, they could cover the island with latrines, treat all the victims, and rid the island of hookworm.

The malaria control project involves 24 municipalities. They have been working in eight. The job is mostly ditching, with 90 per cent of the money going for labor. As far as I can see, it can go on and on until eventually they get the job done. I don't see why they can't use unskilled, relief labor on this, as well as on the latrine and hospital building projects, although they assured me they couldn't. However, I think they will if no other labor is available. The chief objection to relief labor, I fancy, really comes from the engineers in charge of the work, because it is slow and inefficient. . . .

All this brings me to a complaint from Mr. Bourne, which, on the face of it, certainly seems justifiable. That is a lack of communication with Washington. It is perhaps best illustrated by what happened on CWA.

Mr. Bourne said he received no notification back in November about CWA. It only takes two days to get to Washington from San Juan by air. If he had been notified, as the governors and mayors were notified here in the States, he could have got up to Washington for the meeting.

He said he never even heard of CWA until sometime in December, when he read a story about it in the New York Times. . . . His instructions finally arrived on December 26.

The projects were started January 15, with the idea that they were to be completed by May 1. While I was there he received a cablegram from Washington indicating that CWA was to stop by March 31. And his funds had been cut to $500,000 a month. . . .

I'm not going to burden you with a lot of detail on the economic situation. I fancy you'll hear plenty about it in the next few weeks. . . .

The ideal plan, of course, would be for the Government to put some money down there to remedy the housing situation and get some industries going, the Relief Administration to carry on as economically as possible until the program is under way, using relief labor to work on some of those public health projects. And I do think Bourne ought to come up to Washington and get straightened out. . . .

1. Rexford G. Tugwell, undersecretary of agriculture.
2. A possible reference to the Brazilian province of Pará, of which Belém is the chief city.

To Harry L. Hopkins

Birmingham, Ala., Sunday, April 1, 1934

Dear Mr. Hopkins:

. . . During the last few days I have directed my inquiries principally along two lines: employment prospects, both on public works and in private industry, and an effort to find out what this white collar business is all about.

I haven't been able to find anyone who feels that the employment prospects are very bright, although the newspapers keep carrying stories that things are looking up. The Birmingham paper this morning, for instance, carried a story that 300 workers had been called back to the department stores here, because of increased business, but I didn't hear anything about it yesterday in all my talks with industrialists and our relief people. Some employees have been called back to the railroad shops here, both shop and clerical workers, but that, I was told, is due to the fact that the L & N shops in Louisville, Ky., burned, so things are picking up here. And for every man who has gone back to work here, I daresay we have two coming back on relief in Louisville.

Thad Holt[1] tells me he now has on relief in Alabama between 72,00 and 73,000 families. He expects that in April this figure will mount to 90,000. He is assuming that most of those who were on CWA are either back on the rolls now or will be coming back within the next few weeks. . . .

Miss Roberta Morgan, relief director here, tells me that reemployment in the big steel and iron and coke plants in Birmingham will not be felt very soon by us, for the reason that they take back first their own people, thousands of whom have not been on relief and are not now on relief. In thousands of cases the industries have been carrying on their own relief work — on a loan basis, of course, so far as the employee is concerned. Others, running part time or on greatly reduced output, have managed to spread work enough to keep their people off the relief rolls. All these people will of course be taken back on full time before there are any jobs for people on relief. . . .

Anyway you look at it, the PWA prospects in Alabama are not particularly bright.

They've got plenty of projects—little projects, involving $30,000 or $40,000 each. They've got 22 actually approved in Washington, including seven that were left over from the old RFC. But all but three, they tell me, are being held up in a tangle of legal technicalities involving bond procedure.

A flock of their projects, many of them approved, are for building little waterworks plants. They are all being held up on the question whether revenue bonds, sold by the community to finance its end of the project, constitute a debt on the community or are to be charged only to the revenue produced by the project. The Alabama Supreme court gave a ruling that they were to be charged only to the revenue produced by the project. This is the only condition under which the bonds could be sold, because most of the communities are bonded up to the limit. The Supreme court ruling was by one vote, however, so now, I'm told, Washington is insisting on a test case being fought through the courts. . . . I should say, "Goodbye waterworks projects." . . .

Birmingham's principal industries are coal, coke, iron, steel, and cement. All these are materials that go directly or indirectly into a big public works program.

One of their biggest industries is the making of cast iron pipe, the kind that is used in waterworks and drainage. As a matter of fact, they tell me they make most of the cast iron pipe used for the purpose. They've got one pipe plant that, in normal times, employs between 1,000 and 1,200 men. . . .

Very few of the mines, coke plants, steel mills, or pipe plants around Birmingham are actually idle, but they are mostly running on a greatly reduced schedule. . . . And there isn't much prospect for their going back on full schedule very soon unless the PWA program actually gets going.

That business in Birmingham and generally over Alabama is better than it was a year ago. . . . But it's not enough better—and there's no prospect of it becoming enough better very soon to make a dent in that 90,000 relief roll—unless PWA gets going. . . .

1. Alabama CWA director.

To Harry L. Hopkins

Birmingham, Alabama, April 2, 1934

Dear Mr. Hopkins:

A few words on white collar people. Probably quite a few words.

I have had talks in the last few days with 15 white collar people. I have talked with them individually and in small groups in the relief offices, here and in Montgomery. I have talked with them in their homes. I have talked with white collar people who have been on CWA, but not on relief. I have talked with some who have been on relief and on CWA, with some who have been on relief but never on CWA, with some who hadn't minded being on relief once they made the jump — largely because they got interested in the work relief projects they were engaged on — with some who were not so happy in the work relief jobs, with some who had not been engaged on work relief jobs, but who had merely received relief. The list includes a certified public accountant, an insurance man, a pharmacist, a couple of engineers, an architect, a man who had his own lumber business before the depression broke him, a musician, a pawnshop clerk, and a masseur, who extends his income a little by peddling in a basket around Montgomery the whole wheat bread his wife makes at home.

I tried to pick just average white collar people. The group you saw in Washington a week ago last Saturday could hardly be called average. At least, they were worked up to the point of making a pilgrimage to Washington. The people I've seen are not that articulate — or indignant. As a matter of fact, they were very mild. Had few kicks to make. Generally I'd say they were dumb with misery. I asked them for suggestions on how we could best take care of white collar people, taking our program and our resources into account. I got very few suggestions. . . .

Yet they weren't demanding — any of them — that we continue CWA. Not a single one of them even asked me if we could. They quietly accepted the fact that CWA was out. All they seemed to be hoping for was that they might be permitted to work for whatever relief they received — to save their self-respect.

The only real complaints I heard from any of them were about inadequacy and, in a couple of cases, about what seemed to me very stupid procedure on the part of some investigators. Their complaints on adequacy I got only indirectly by going into details on how they were getting along.

"For a few weeks it isn't so bad for a man and his wife and a baby to get along on $4.80 a week, paying $3 of it out for rent," one of the younger men said. "But when it runs into months — and you can't see anything better ahead — you get damned discouraged."

About the most nagging problem in connection with white collar relief, as I see it, is that of inadequacy. They want to cling to some semblance at least of their normal standards of living. And we can't give them enough relief to make that possible. We can't pay rents to any great extent. We can provide overalls, but not tailored business suits. We can't keep those white collars laundered.

Take the matter of rents. To white collar people it's damned important to live in a decent house or apartment, in a decent neighborhood. I honestly believe that, if we force them to give that up, we shall, in many, many instances, either break their morale completely or make Communist leaders out of them. They've somehow managed — God knows how — to keep up that much of their standards of living before they came onto relief. And they'll do it after they're on relief, even if they starve.

Take your little man who was getting $4.80 a week for relief and paying $3 of it out in rent.

"I do everything I can to pick up a little money to pay that rent," he said. "I've washed windows. I've even gone out and competed with Niggers to get jobs mowing lawns. But some weeks I don't make it. I seldom can make the whole $3.

"We've pawned everything we have — my wife's engagement ring and all her other trinkets, all our silver, all my instruments (he is a musician), my watch and other jewelry, most of my clothes. We've cut down expenses every way we could. We have a seven months' old baby. Until recently I've washed all the diapers myself. My wife wasn't able to do it, and we couldn't afford to send them out or have a Nigger come in and do them.

"Most of the time we honestly don't have enough to eat. Take a week when I haven't been able to earn any of the rent. We have exactly $1.80 cents for food. We buy all the flour and bacon we can — what we call "white meat" down here, cheaper than the bacon you'd ordinarily eat — and a few green vegetables. The first night we have a pretty good dinner, the next night not quite so good, and so on down until the last two nights we're eating nothing but bread and flour gravy.

"My wife is losing all her teeth. I got a relief order for her to go to a doctor. He said it was due to bad and insufficient diet. Well, she's still nursing the baby, for one thing. Because we can't afford to buy enough milk for the baby."

Well, I suppose another family — not a white collar family — might have broken down, let themselves be evicted, moved into cheaper quarters. But these people won't. Apparently they won't even let themselves be starved to it.

And I don't see what we can do about it. We can hardly increase their allotments. Hardly, with the unions howling bloody murder for an increase both in hourly rate and number of hours per week for skilled labor. BUT — mark my words — if you let the unions get away with it, if you accede to that demand and fail to increase the allotments of the white collar people, too, you're going to have trouble.

The second difficulty is in getting white collar people to register at all. God, how they hate it.

"I simply had to murder my pride," one of the engineers told me.

"We'd lived on bread and water three weeks before I could make myself do it," said the insurance man.

"It took me a month," said the lumberman. "I used to go down there every day or so and walk past the place again and again. I just couldn't make myself go in."

In Birmingham it was made easier for them. Long before FERA came in they had set up here what they called "A Placement Bureau for Professional People." They let "professional" cover the whole white collar group. The bureau was NOT located in the relief office. At first there was no home visiting at all. The applicants simply gave references, and these were contacted by telephone. Later — because, I regret to say, they found that some of the white collar people, only a few of them to be sure, had cheated on them — home visiting had to be put in, but it was very limited, and the visitors were picked with extreme care. They are now planning to set up the bureau again.

This method of introducing white collar people to relief is about as painless as any could be, I guess. The white collar people here in Birmingham tell me it took a lot of the horror out of it for them. But if we should adopt it as a national policy, I can see plenty of trouble ahead. From Union Labor. Ever let them get wind of the fact that we are granting to the white collar group any sort of privilege that we deny their skilled labor, and listen to the howl. And let skilled labor in, and then you'll get demands on behalf of unskilled labor. Well — we can't take EVERYBODY out of the intake.

A couple of the white collar men told me of a practice that I think is about as stupid as any I ever heard of. They were asked to give the names of some NEIGHBORS as references.

"Good God," one of them said, "can't they realize that the very last people in the world we want to know we are on relief is any of the neighbors?"

At least, it seems to me, we can spare these white collar people THAT sort of thing.

In some cases, too, they were a little critical of some of our investigators. They resent "pretty young girls, just out of college." The most acceptable investigator, if an investigator must come into their homes, they say, is a middle-aged man.

"He's less conspicuous," one of them said. "At least, we can kid ourselves into thinking the neighbors think he's a salesman of some sort.

"It's our wives who resent the pretty young girls. Suppose you were my wife — and I'll bet you're thanking your lucky stars you're not — run down, without any decent clothes, looking ten years older than you ought to look. How would you like it if some smooth-faced — not a wrinkle anywhere — young girl, nicely dressed, all made up, came into your house, sat down on the edge of a chair and began to ask you a lot of personal questions. You'd want to throw something at her, wouldn't you? The contrast is just too painful, that's all."

From these remarks I think we might take a few hints on how to deal with white collar people — and perhaps some other people, too.

Once on relief, they don't seem to mind so much — at least they are apathetic. They want to work, of course — all of them. And they are not fussy about the kind of work they get, just so it's work. . . .

Several of them said they'd rather work because it kept their minds off their troubles.

Here in Birmingham the white collar people apparently have been handled most successfully on relief. For instance, they set up a sort of council of white collar people on relief — engineers, architects, teachers, former businessmen, and so on — who helped plan work relief projects. The administration treated them NOT as "people on relief, poor devils," but as EQUALS, professional people, whose knowledge and training were worth something. Out of this council, Miss Roberta Morgan, director, told me came some of the best ideas for work relief projects — and here in Birmingham they had some dandies. In most cases these people gave all their time to the work — even though all they were receiving was a small relief check.

"Sometimes," one of the engineers told me, "we'd get so busy and so interested that we'd actually forget we were on relief at all!"

Out of this council, I understand, came the idea, started in Birmingham long before we ever thought of it, of repairing houses in lieu of rent. Architects and engineers, ON RELIEF, took charge of it. I saw some of the houses. I talked with real estate men for whom houses had been repaired. The plan has WORKED. One real estate group, to be sure, would rather we paid taxes, water-rent, and insurance on their houses, instead of giving them repair jobs, in lieu of rent. But their spokesman agreed that the plan had been satisfactory. It was just a matter of their wanting cash.

For our plan of having their professional societies deal with us for them the white collar people with whom I talked had nothing but approval — but, they say, it doesn't cover enough of them. As a matter of fact, of all those I talked to, only the two engineers and one architect belonged to any professional society. The certified public accountant said he belonged to an association of CPA's but that it had headquarters only in Washington. . . .

And now, before I quit, here's a story that has nothing to do with white collar people, but which is, I think damned interesting.

I had a talk tonight with the head of one of the largest industrial concerns in the South — an outfit that employs thousands of men. Before he'd talk with me at all, he made me promise not to use his name, even in a confidential report to Washington.

Business in this man's concern has picked up a good deal, and they've taken back a lot of people.

The wife and children of a sharecropper in rural Arkansas.

Migrant workers converted their cars into homes. Winterhaven, Florida.

A tenant family before their home in Davie County, North Carolina.

This family in Iredell County, North Carolina, reported that their principal food was hickory nuts.

A man and his wife in rural Arkansas.

A sharecropper's family in Walker County, Alabama.

A one-room schoolhouse in Alabama.

"Our accident rate since we opened up has been very high," he said. "The other night I tried to figure out why. One reason, of course, may be that the men have grown clumsy. They've forgotten how to handle themselves in there with all that machinery.

"But there's another reason, I decided. I think they're worried — about finances.

"During the depression we've carried most of our people on extended credit. As they come back to work, they owe us about $200 apiece. We've made the terms pretty easy, I think. We pay every two weeks, and we have made a ruling that, first of all, $25 of that check, no matter how large or how small, goes untouched to the man. Of the balance, if there is any, we take only 20 percent.

"Those terms seem pretty fair to us, and most of the men seem to think they are. But I figured out on paper the other night that in many cases, on those terms, it will take them from eight to seventeen years to pay us back.

"And I think a lot of the accidents we're having can be traced to that. They're worried — and absent-minded."

The gentleman did not suggest — it had apparently never occurred to him — that the company, a very rich concern with powerful financial backing might wipe those debts off the slate. . . .

To Harry L. Hopkins

New Orleans (The One and Only), April 7, 1934

Dear Mr. Hopkins:

I spent my last two or three days in Alabama on the rural rehabilitation program, going out into the small towns and plantations to get the reaction of the people generally.

Wednesday I went to a couple of counties west of Montgomery, where there is a mixture of white and black farmers and farm tenants. I talked with business men in the small towns, a county agent, members of a "cotton committee" who are going to be directly in charge of the people we are going to try to rehabilitate, a doctor, a couple of judges, some large landowners — nearly everybody I talked to owned land, as a matter of fact — one woman who is running a plantation, a most interesting farmer who is trying out on his own the idea of decentralizing industry, and some Negro tenants.

Thursday, enroute to Mobile, Thad Holt and I went to see his wife's cousin, who has a plantation of several thousand acres, about the largest in the vicinity of Montgomery. Down in the "Black Belt" — called that both because of the Negro population, about 80 per cent, and because the soil is black — we had lunch with a county agent.

Earlier in the week, up in Walker county — the Bankheads'[1] home county — where they are having mine labor troubles, I also contacted some farmers.

To our own relief workers the rural rehabilitation program offers more hope than anything else these days. I might say, in many cases, it's the only thing that cheers them up. By and large, they are not feeling particularly happy these days, especially in the cities, although in New Orleans they seemed today to be feeling more cheerful than those I saw in Birmingham and Montgomery and Mobile. I'll go into all that in another report, winding up Alabama, which I shall write tomorrow. Anyway, our own crowd are absolutely sold on the rehabilitation program. . . .

It is still a little early, I find, to get much of a public reaction. Right now, I should say, the public — I'm speaking of rural and small town public — favors the principle, but is inclined to be critical of our procedure. Largely through ignorance.

One of the first objections you hear is:

"Well, it might go, but you're gettin' started too late. They ain't goin' to make no crop this year nohow. They oughtta be plantin' right now. They're never goin' to get no crop startin' so late."

This is mostly from landowners who live in town. Actual farmers — men who work on the land — tell me that even in Southern Alabama a crop can be planted until May 15. . . .

Another subject of debate in the country stores is: mules vs. oxen, which they call steers in Alabama. You should have heard some of the oratory I've heard on THAT subject these last few days.

A good mule in Alabama costs from $100 to $150, and I'm told they're scarce at that price. A good work ox can be bought for anywhere from $15 to $30. Therefore, it's going to be oxen, so far as the Alabama Relief Administration is concerned. One of their worries right now, incidentally is over the money they've got to put out right at the start and where they're going to get it. There's been some publicity to the effect that they're going to buy oxen instead of mules. And so:

"Hell! This ain't no New Deal if we-all got to go back plowin' steers!" one gentleman remarked with some heat.

The funny part of it is, though, that, although he is a landowner, he doesn't work the land himself, but lives in town. And I don't believe he actually knows much about "steers," as he calls them.

For instance, he gloomily told me that it was almost impossible to break a steer to a plow unless you had had a lot of experience handling them.

"'Nother thing," he said, "they won't work in the heat. Let it get to be noon, and they jest lay right down — or wander off to the swamp, draggin' the Nigger with 'em, if he ain't leadin' 'em."

When I got out into the country, where they were working with steers, I found they were little animals, hardly larger than Shetland ponies. And I doubt if they could drag anybody around very much. They seemed mild and patient and willing to work.

Two of the other chief objectors to steers were a doctor and a county agent. I didn't think the doctor knew what he was talking about. And county agents, I have observed, are apt to think in terms of model farms. I'll expand on that subject a little later.

Anyway, I solved the problem in my own mind by going out and talking with Negroes who were working with steers and watching them work. They hadn't had any trouble breaking them in, they said. One man told me he'd broken his steer to the plow in two days. He called him "Hustler," incidentally. . . .

I think the steer-mule argument is rather typical of the public's attitude toward "guv'ment easy money." If it's Government money that is being spent, why take the cost of things into consideration? The opposition to steers can be worn down fairly easily, however, by telling them that we simply can't afford mules and that, anyway, we want to give these people a chance to show us that they mean business before we start spending a lot on expensive stock and equipment.

I think the public rather doubts our ever getting anywhere with our "victims." It is to them rather humorous that we should take all that trouble for "jest pore white trash an' Niggers." The more thoughtful businessmen and big landowners . . . think we have a chance of actually rehabilitating perhaps fifty percent or a little better if we give them plenty of supervision.

"You jest gotta stand right over 'em," the landowners will tell you.

Our relief people have a higher opinion of them. It's mostly a matter, they think, of their never having had in all their lives any sort of a chance. They think lots of supervision will be needed, too, and they expect results.

One thing we've got to do is to change the viewpoint of the county agents and home demonstration people. In Alabama the relief people — field supervisors, county directors, and so on — have very little use for the county and home demonstration agents. In the past, they say, they've never been able to get any sort of help or cooperation from them at all. They're skeptical now.

My own observations lead me to agree with our relief people. During the weeks I've been in the South — over in Georgia and the Carolinas, as well as in Alabama — I've met darned few of that crowd who had any interest in people on relief. The agents are inclined to be too silo-minded. They're interested only in better farming—more intensive cultivation. They like working with big, successful farmers. And the home demonstration agents—well, they seem to spend most of their time fooling around with girls' clubs. They've got a kind of Chautauqua slant on life. They shudder at the idea of walking into a tenant farmer's shack and teaching the wife how to clean the place up. Of course that isn't true of all of them, but I've seen traces of it alright. . . .

There is also a feeling among the social workers that the people in the Agricultural Extension Service are quite a bit more "political-minded" than we are. I don't know whether that is true or not. But I do believe that, if it comes to a choice between a man with superior technical qualifications, but neither any understanding of these people nor any real desire to help them, or a man who is just a practical individual with a lot of common sense and understanding and sympathy—well, give me the latter, as supervisor. . . .

Pretty generally, I should say from talking with them, the large land-owners are going to be willing to cooperate with us, both by letting tenants use their land that is out of production—production of cotton, that is—and by waiving debts. I think they'll have to be watched, though, about the time our people begin to get ahead a little. As a matter of fact, I'm told, hardly any tenants ever got any of the cotton reduction money. The landlords always could present bills for the entire amount, and the tenants, being illiterate and never knowing exactly what they did owe the landlords, were just out of luck. It looks to me as though we shall have to protect these people as well as teach them. . . .

In one county up in Northeastern Alabama you've evidently got a stranded population of several thousand people. As a matter of fact, the population of the county is 12,000, and there are 10,000 people on relief! They're in the mountains, trying to farm. Can't make a go of it. No industries of any kind. Three doctors in the county—one of them the health officer, one practising without a license, and the third an old man about to die.

Not very long ago the county relief director up there got a call out into the country one night. They said a woman was very sick. As escort the county NRS[2] director went with her.

When they got out there, they delivered a baby—using the headlights on their car for light!

In another county up in that vicinity there are 300 displaced tenant farmers. Every now and then one of them will come in and beg the relief director:

"Please buy us a tent, ma'am. We can't find no house.". . .

1. U.S. Senator John H. Bankhead and his brother, U.S. Representative William B. Bankhead.
2. National Reemployment Service.

To Harry L. Hopkins

New Orleans, April 8, 1934

Dear Mr. Hopkins:

And now to wind up on Alabama.

In my communication last night I wrote you that our relief workers seem to be pretty much discouraged. I should add that, the higher up you go among them, the more discouraged you find them. In Alabama, for instance, Thad Holt was the most discouraged of the whole lot — although naturally he isn't saying so publicly nor among his subordinates. He told me that he didn't like to burden Washington with his troubles, either, feeling very strongly that the state administrations should go ahead and carry out your program and do the best they can without bothering you. . . .

This union labor situation is a honey.

Those boys are just out for all they can get — whether from private industry or the Federal Government.

Their attitude toward the Federal Government — I speak now of the organizers who are out in the field — is funny. They seem to think the A.F. of L. [American Federation of Labor] IS the Federal Government. Their attitude toward me, for instance, is apt to be one of ordering. "I want you to do this and see that." . . . My assumption is that they are NOT running the Federal Government — at least not YET — and I have a hard time to keep from getting a bit hot under the collar at their attitude. They are certainly "feeling their oats."

This same crowd were down in Montgomery at the conference . . . drawing up plans on Union participation in the relief program. In discussing the thing with me, their attitude seemed to be one of bargaining — bargaining with the Federal Government, with an Administration that has put the A.F. of L. ahead 50 or 100 years! I can't help having the feeling that their attitude is one of getting all they can — out of the Federal Government, as well as private industry — for the Unions, rather than wanting to help put this program over. And I also can't help feeling that it is the UNION they're interested in — the UNION, with its dues and its potential political power — rather than the men themselves. These are the professional labor organizers, the people from outside, who are representing the A.F. of L. . . .

213

They were so damned eager to take advantage of your telegram from Washington of March 28 — "No person shall be employed in work divisions less than 54 hours a month for unskilled labor or 30 hours a month for OTHER labor" and so on. With that they combined another Washington regulation that skilled labor was to be paid "the prevailing wage rate," set up $1 an hour as the prevailing wage rate for "skilled labor" in Alabama, and were all set for their people to get $30 a month instead of $16.50, overlooking of course the fact that the relief director had the right to investigate a man's need and certify him for work for that amount, and that, if he didn't need $30 a month, he wouldn't be certified for work if that was the minimum we were permitted to pay him. Well, they were talked around into waiving that business. But now:

"We've got representation on the committee that is going to handle adjustments on the work program," one of them said to me the other day, "but what control are we going to have over what is done to our people on direct relief?"

Their idea seems to be that a union representative ought to sit right in with the relief director all the time and tell her what to do!

Up in Walker county, the Bankheads' home territory, there had been a strike in the coal mines. Three hundred men were still out when I was up there last Monday. Although the United Mine Workers representative — driving around in a large and very handsome new Studebaker — complimented our people on the way they had handled the relief end of it, the "higher-ups" down in Birmingham were critical. The thing that makes them sore is, of course, that they have to accept our certification, with our investigations, rather than our accepting theirs. They have all sorts of little, petty complaints. Their most serious complaint is that all the local governments and the relief people in those coal counties are under the control of the operators. Well, the local governments may be, but I can't help feeling that our own people have done a pretty darned good job, in a difficult situation, carrying out our policy.

In some cases, I can't help suspecting the organizers of taking advantage of our strike relief policy. You have this sort of thing:

In one county, East of Birmingham, there is a struggle on — or has been until very recently — between a coal operator, who is something of a despot, he'd probably like to be called a "benevolent despot," and organizers for the United Mine Workers. His ideas are paternalistic and all wrong. And he has been firing everybody who joined the Union. . . . From a field supervisor in charge of that territory, I got the following:

"They come into our offices and say President Roosevelt wanted them to join the union, that they must join the United Mine Workers to come under his plan, and that he has said the Federal Government will take care of them if they lose their jobs.

"They are not satisfied of course with the amount of relief we can give them.

" 'That ain't enough,' they'll say. 'There's plenty of money up there in Washington for us. We know it's there. President Roosevelt's got it there, to take care of us.'"

To be perfectly fair, I should add that . . . they may have acquired these ideas from listening not too intelligently to some of the President's radio talks, as to the kind of talk they are getting from the United Mine Workers' organizers.

It's funny, but people down here all seem to think they know the President personally! It comes in part, I imagine, from their having heard him speak — so much more than any other President — over the radio, and in such a friendly, man-to-man fashion. They feel he is talking to each one of them, personally! And of course they don't always understand exactly what he means, are inclined to read into what he says what they themselves WANT him to mean. Another funny thing is the number of letters you see around over the President's and Mrs. Roosevelt's signatures. They are seldom anything more than the briefest and most formal acknowledgment of a letter — usually a letter of complaint or an appeal for help. But I doubt if any other President — or his wife — has ever been so punctilious about acknowledging letters. And these people take them all very seriously, as establishing a personal relation. In one way, it's a darned good thing. It's made them both very strong with the people. A lot of these people who used to look up that way to their paternalistic landlords and employers have now switched to the President and Mrs. Roosevelt! They just expect them to take care of them! . . .

A little more on business conditions and PWA, and then I'll quit.

In Birmingham the other night I had a talk with a steel man, whose name I promised not to reveal. He's a pretty important man in the Birmingham area. You're probably fairly good at guessing. This is, in substance what he said:

His own business had improved 300 percent the first quarter of this year over the first quarter of last year. They were putting out three times the tonnage they were putting out a year ago.

BUT —

Ninety percent of it, he said, was directly due to "Government priming." Seventy-five percent of it was due to Government loans to railroads to buy rails and track accessories.

"Withdraw this Government aid," he said gloomily, "and we'd be no better off than we were a year ago and perhaps much worse off. The question is: Will the Government priming finally take hold? If it doesn't, I can't see but that we'll be worse off than before."

Incidentally the pickup in business in his industry hasn't affected our relief rolls much because his people took care of their own employees — on a loan basis, of course — during the depression. It just means that their own people have gone back to work, most of them owing the company a couple hundred dollars. That's the average, he told me.

Now that shows the state of mind of a big manufacturing executive whose industry has had some Government money. I should add perhaps that I was told that he and all his crowd are Republicans and have been more or less bitterly opposed to everything the President has undertaken. . . .

To Harry L. Hopkins

Houston, Texas, April 11, 1934

Dear Mr. Hopkins:

At no time previously, since taking this job, have I been quite so discouraged as I am tonight.

Texas is a Godawful mess. As you know, they're having a big political fight in Austin. Adam Johnson, administrator, and one of the members of the state relief commission, both, I am told, anti-Ferguson,[1] and both kicked out Monday, are preparing to fight, according to stories I've seen in the newspapers.

And in the meantime — God help the unemployed.

Relief funds in Houston are exhausted. . . . Unless the city and county will underwrite expenses until things get straightened out in Austin, and they get some money down here, they are going to shut off relief.

Lee Hager, retired capitalist and newly appointed local chairman, thinks it won't actually come to cutting off relief — that the threat will spur Austin to some sort of action, although when Perry Moore, the director, telephoned news of the committee's plan to Austin this afternoon it produced no effect. . . .

Trying to spread the money as far as possible, they've got down to the point now where relief in Houston is just a joke. A case worker in charge of single women told me tonight that she had orders today to cut their weekly food allowance down to 39 CENTS! They've been getting less than 50 cents a week for some weeks. To be sure the relief consists of orders on a commissary, and I'm told that at the commissary they get about twice as much for their money as they would get if the orders were issued on retail grocers. But even that is ridiculous. . . .

216

My discouragement goes deeper than that, however. I'm discouraged over the whole damned business — NRA, relief, everything.

I was asking members of the committee today about business and prospects for reemployment in private industry. As a matter of fact, they told me, Houston isn't in such bad shape. The only industry here that has completely collapsed is the building industry. During the boom days, they dug a ship canal up here, took the shipping trade away from Galveston — which must be suffering accordingly — and over-built. Their whole skyline is brand new! They won't be doing any building here for years.

But aside from the building industry, things aren't so bad here. They never have been. The principal industry is manufacture of oil drilling machinery. And it's going right along.

BUT —

Said the head of a company which manufactures oil drilling machinery at lunch today:

"Oh, we can't take on any more men. We've reached the saturation point. Our cost of production has reached the point where we simply cannot take on any more untrained men. God knows we could use trained men if we had them. Our orders are mounting. We have a devil of a time filling them. But we can't take on any more untrained men. It costs too much. It will be six months at least before we can take any more untrained men."

And in the meantime the relief load is 12,500 families with applications coming in at the rate of 1,100 a week.

Later, before dinner, I went over to Hager's apartment to have a drink with him, and we both commented on that statement. Don't you see? Those babies are thinking in terms of 1929 profit. Why, they'll let orders go, dammit, before they'll permit their cost of production to go up and cut into their profit. Now, if that's following the spirit of the New Deal, I'll eat my hat.

Oh, I've kidded myself right along, trying to believe that the codes were working, at least in the big industries — that the textile people, for instance, were complying probably to the extent of 60 percent. But I wonder. I'll bet you right now that 99 percent of American big businessmen are trying to beat them and succeeding. And the little fellows aren't even pretending to live up to them. They can't. The whole damned outfit are simply grabbing everything they can for themselves out of improved business stimulated by Government priming and public confidence in the President. They're not contributing anything. Typical, I guess, is the story told me in Tampa about the department stores that grabbed off jubilantly the Christmas business that resulted from CWA — without putting on one extra salesperson.

Hager, who has spent some time in Italy, believes in Fascism.

"What Roosevelt seems to be trying to do," he said, "is to put over a Mussolini program in a democracy. It won't work. Businessmen won't follow any such program voluntarily. Don't you ever think they will. They're too selfish and too stupid.

"Although I'm a capitalist, I happen to believe in the President's program. Things can't go on as they have. Don't ever kid yourself that they can. We're going to have a change, and, if it doesn't come this way, it will come in another way — like Russia."

He grinned, raised his right hand, and aimed his forefinger at his temple.

"And if it comes to that," he said, "blink-blink!"

Later I noticed behind a framed photograph on his desk about the biggest revolver I'd ever seen.

"There's only one way the capitalistic system can be saved at all in the United States," he said. "That is for the Government to take hold of the situation and by compulsion limit profits and eliminate wasteful competition. That's Fascism, but it's the only thing that will do the trick. If Roosevelt were actually a dictator, we might get somewhere. This way it's hopeless."

And honestly, after nearly a year of traveling about this country, I'm almost forced to agree with him. If I were 20 years younger and weighed 75 pounds less, I think I'd start out to be the Joan of Arc of the Fascist movement in the United States.

I've been out on this trip now for a little more than two weeks. In all that time I've hardly met a single person who seemed confident and cheerful. The social workers are discouraged. Relief loads are mounting. They can't see any improvement. The only bright spot they see is our rural rehabilitation program — but they're wondering where the money is coming from to see that through.

The businessmen . . . are gloomy. Either they're worried because their pickup is traceable entirely to Government priming, or because they have no pickup and can't see any ahead.

Nobody seems to think any more that the thing is going to WORK. . . .

Oddly, I think most of the farmers and businessmen I've talked to these last few weeks would accept anything the President wanted to put over, if they felt he had the power to FORCE them to do it. I think they actually WANT a dictator. I think they'd rather anything in the world would happen than that Congress should get the whip hand. Oh, why did this year have to be an election year? I haven't much doubt but that Congress would have let him do anything he wanted to do if it hadn't been for that.

I don't know. Maybe my thinking isn't clear, but I get that feeling everywhere I go — that they feel they can get away with cheating on NRA — and do — that they do it because "we might as well, for the other fellow will," but that, deep down, they'd be, for the most part, perfectly willing to take orders if they knew they HAD to obey them.

But, like Hager, I can't see much chance for a really effective dictatorship in this country. Not under our present form of government. And so — well, maybe Russia is better off, but the people had to go through a Hell of a lot of suffering to get even as far as they are now.

If we have to have a dictator, I personally would prefer Roosevelt above anyone else. And I wonder if his best chance wouldn't be to go completely red and get it that way. Anyway, the "fat boys" aren't going to play ball with him. Not on any voluntary basis. . . .

1. Miriam A. Ferguson was serving her second term as governor of Texas. Her husband, James Edward Ferguson, was a former governor of Texas.

To Harry L. Hopkins

Houston, Texas, April 13, 1934

Dear Mr. Hopkins:

. . . New Orleans looks pretty hopeless. Your friend Clark[e] Salmon[1] and his publisher, James M. Thompson, of the Item-Tribune, certainly were feeling gloomy enough. What pickup there was from CWA is already falling off. . . . According to Messrs. Salmon and Thompson, the big fellows are beginning to suffer, too, now. For instance, Mr. Salmon had been told by one of the big coffee wholesale houses that their business began to drop very sharply right after CWA ceased. And that despite the fact that CWA hasn't really stopped in New Orleans — all those left being transferred automatically to the Work Division, to be weeded out in the next few weeks.

The intake waiting rooms in New Orleans were jammed the day I was there — as they are most places these days. In any town on this trip I can find the relief office without any trouble at all, by the crowd hanging around outside. The case load March 31 was 8,708. On April 9 it had jumped over 10,000, I was told, and was still climbing.

The white collar problem had not become bad enough yet so that the relief people were conscious of it. So far they've managed to absorb most of the white collar clients in their setup. But Mr. Salmon was worried about it and predicted that within the next few months it might become serious. He says most of the businessmen in New Orleans are more conscious of the fact that a lot of white collar people are in bad shape than they were a few months ago. Former white collar people keep coming into their offices begging for work — any kind of work.

Among the clients — or prospective clients — at the New Orleans intake the day I was there was a man who, Clark[e] Salmon told me, was formerly president of the National Association of Electrical Contractors. Salmon had sent him over, hoping to get him some sort of job if possible, and, if not a job, relief.

"He used to be one of our largest advertisers," Mr. Salmon said. "He was head of a large electrical supply house here in New Orleans. With the collapse of the building industry he went broke. Since then he has gone down and down. He lost his home. He and his wife are now living in a furnished room in the French Quarter. Some months ago he appeared in the office of one of his former business acquaintances, touched him for $25 and offered his watch as security.

"Businessmen around town would have been glad to help him, but he won't accept anything without giving something in return. He has asked them to take him on as a messenger. Anything, to get a little work. He's completely whipped.

"It's not only men like him, who are out of work and broke, that worry me. It's the whole white collar class. They are taking an awful beating. Take our own profession, for instance. I've had to cut editorial expense on the Item-Tribune 30 per cent since the depression hit. That means that all my reporters are getting salaries away below normal. And there isn't much chance of their getting back to where they were. They know it. And when they come in to ask for more money, they invariably start out by saying, 'Of course I realize that if I left the Item-Tribune, I couldn't get a job anywhere else.' That from men who a few years ago, if they couldn't get a raise, would say, 'To Hell with you, Mister,' and take the train for the next town. They're whipped, that's all. And it's bad."

I got one idea out of New Orleans. Everywhere here in the South the Negro case loads are getting to be tremendous. In New Orleans, for instance, EIGHTY-FIVE PER CENT of the load is Negro! The feeling among case workers and supervisors generally seems to be that the Negro load is much larger than it should be. Many of these social workers, remember, are Northerners, not Southerners. There isn't much doubt in my own mind that thousands of those Negroes are living much better on relief than they ever did while they were working. You hear the same stories over and over again — Negroes quitting their jobs or refusing to work because they can get on relief. Perhaps only half of those stories are true, but that's bad enough. And God knows the wages they receive are low, and that their standards of living ought to be raised. But God knows our money is limited, too. And I wonder if it's wise to carry on relief thousands of Negroes — who'd rather get a minimum subsistence from the Government without working for it, or by working only a few hours per week, than to get the same amount by working for it full time — at the expense of some of these white collar people who, I believe, are very apt to make real trouble for us before we get through. If we were not carrying so many Negroes, I wonder if perhaps we couldn't solve the white collar problem to some extent by giving more adequate relief.

Anyway, I'm convinced that it would be well worth our while to have a thorough reinvestigation of all Negro cases. Every social worker I've talked with feels the same way about it. There are drawbacks, of course. If it were ordered from Washington, we'd undoubtedly be up against a charge of racial discrimination. Harry Early,[2] however, comes forth with the suggestion that the states take the responsibility. He suggests that in each of the states where the Negro case load seems to be away out of all proportion, the Negro intake be closed one month, say the month of May, and all Negro cases be thoroughly checked. He believes it would result in a great reduction of Negro cases.

"If they wanted to avoid charges of racial discrimination," he said, "they could close the white intake for a month, too, after they'd checked the Negro case load."

As it is, there isn't much chance of a thorough reinvestigation. Staffs have their hands full taking care of their regular loads plus intake.

"I believe these huge Negro case loads may be due largely to the Negro psychology," said the case work supervisor in New Orleans, a Northerner. "They are children, really. If anything is being given away, they want some, too. We encounter that over and over in our intake. They are accustomed to having things handed out to them by white people. And that's the way they look at relief. Why work, if they can get support from the Government?"

Of course, you can say that the white man is responsible for that attitude, and that it ought to be cured. But, anyway, the way I see it is that our job is to give people relief on a limited amount of money, and, the more people we carry who really could manage to subsist without it, the less adequate will be our relief for the people who really have to have it.

In New Orleans I got another idea of a possible way to handle the intake problem on white collar people. They are trying out there a plan whereby they are permitted to come in by appointment. That spares them the ordeal of having to sit around in the intake for hours. Mr. Hopkins, did you ever spend a couple of hours sitting around an intake? And intake is about the nearest thing to Hell that I know anything about. The smell alone — I'd recognize it anywhere. And take that on top of the psychological effect of having to be there at all. God! I

221

wonder if it would do any good to send out orders to relief administrations to clean up their intake departments, make them less revolting. Probably not. Most of them are so crowded, especially these days, that there probably couldn't be much improvement. But they certainly are AWFUL. If I were applying for relief, one look at the average intake room would send me to the river. . . .

So far, except on roads and some federal projects that have made very little employment, not one cent of PWA [money] has been spent in Louisiana. . . . One project, approved in Washington, is now about 85 per cent completed. It's the only one where work has even started. And on that project the community is still spending its own money. It was a high school to replace one that burned down, and the community's share of the cost was actually in the bank, insurance money, when the project was approved in Washington. So far, however, Washington hasn't sent any of its 30 per cent.

Of the $9,000,000 worth of PWA projects approved in Washington . . . work will start on 19 of them within the next 90 days. That would put 2,700 men to work. And . . . that number represents a little more than one tenth of the men who were on CWA in New Orleans alone. Not one of those 19 projects is in New Orleans, where the work is needed most. . . .

I could go into more detail, but what's the use? If God is good, and the PWA lawyers in Washington get their feet under them and quit acting like a lot of old maids—which they won't—MAYBE 2,700 former CWA workers will go to work on PWA projects in Louisiana sometime within the next 90 days. Twenty-seven hundred men, not one of them in New Orleans where the situation is the worst.

The relief committee in Houston met with the city and county officials yesterday and made their proposition—that the city and county officials underwrite the relief show until they get some money out of Austin, or relief be shut down. The city and county officials chose to underwrite the program up to $100,000—WITH THE UNDERSTANDING THAT NO SALARIES BE PAID TO THE RELIEF STAFF.

It's not so hard, perhaps, on the regular social workers. But a whole lot of those staff people are really relief cases. . . .

In Houston they have a separate set-up for unattached people, including a women's bureau. There are some 500 of these unattached women in three groups, unemployables—that is sick or too old to work—employables, and transients.

The employables are divided about half in half—women under 35 and women over 35. The case worker in charge of them told me that most of the younger ones have lovers or are prostitutes. She is inclined to think—and from what I know of the younger generation I am inclined to agree with her — that most of those who have lovers would anyway, that the depression or the inadequacy of relief would have nothing to do with it. But about those who have become prostitutes — we both wonder.

Recently one of the men in the transient division put on old clothes and went down and mixed with the transients to see how they were getting along. As he walked along the streets in the tougher part of town he was frequently accosted by young women. To one of them he said:

"I can't. I haven't any money."

"Oh, that's alright," she replied wearily. "It only costs a dime."

And here's a story about one of those unattached women who had no lover and is not a prostitute.

She is 28 years old. She worked her way through two years and a half of college. She taught school for eight years. Cuts in appropriations let out many teachers. She was one of them.

She has been on relief off and on, but never when she could get anything at all to do. And that "anything" has included working as a servant. She quit her last job because her employer was giving her only her room and board — for full time work as a servant, if you please. She is now taking care of an old woman in a convalescent home for the magnificent wages of $3 a week.

The case worker, who has been worried about her, was trying to buck her up a bit recently.

"Oh, don't bother," the girl said impatiently at last. "If, with all the advantages I've had, I can't make a living, I'm just no good, I guess. I've given up every amounting to anything. It's no use." . . .

1. Managing editor.
2. Relief administrator for New Orleans.

To Harry L. Hopkins

San Antonio, Texas, April 17, 1934

Dear Mr. Hopkins:

What an empire is this state of Texas! I entered the state a week ago today. Since then I've driven some 700 miles. I've been in the East Texas oil fields where, if they were allowed to run full capacity, they could produce and refine more than a third of the gasoline used in the United States — or maybe it's the world. I've been in Houston, up in Northeastern Texas timber country, in Austin, in San Antonio. I've driven through some of the loveliest, wooded landscape you ever saw and over some of the most uninteresting, flat prairie land I ever saw. I'll leave the state a week from today, and by that time I'll have driven another 900 miles or so and shall have spent a couple of days in Dallas and Fort Worth, shall have met some Panhandle people in Big Spring, and shall have spent a day in El Paso. And I'll have driven 700 miles or so across a vast plain that extends from Fort Worth to El Paso. . . . Their interests are so varied! Oil, timber, cotton, wheat, rice, beef, truck, fruit, and, out West of San Antonio, goats! No kidding. The secretary of the Chamber of Commerce in San Antonio told me today that this town is feeling an improvement because of a pickup in the goat business, furnishing mohair to the automobile manufacturers! Here in San Antonio, too, I ran into a great big needlework industry. It claims to be the largest center in the country for the making of baby clothes! Mexican labor, hand and machine. Until the codes began to come in, the work was done in the homes, women earning as little as 20 cents a day, according to the relief people, although the Chamber of Commerce people earnestly assure me that that figure is too low.

Concerning the state of mind of people I have a little reason for feeling more cheerful than I felt when I wrote you from Houston last week, but not much. Damn it all, this state doesn't seem to be so badly off, really. The oil industry is producing and refining all the oil it's allowed to produce and refine and wishing it were allowed to produce and refine more. Except for a total collapse of the building industry because it's over-built — You never saw anything like these Texas towns, not a sky-line over 10 years old! — Houston isn't in such terrible condition. Shipping is pretty good, mostly oil, out of the Houston and Port Arthur-Beaumont areas. Timber business of course is rotten in this state, as everywhere. Rice not so good because of low price, although the price is double what it was a year ago. Beef the same. Low prices. Cotton, pretty good. Wheat, not so good. Looks like another drouth in the Northern half of the Panhandle. They've had moisture in the Southern half, but it came pretty late. A lot of the seed blew away. They tell me they'll probably have a 30 per cent crop. Here in San Antonio, whose jobbing business with Mexico, they tell me, was ruined by the Republican tariff, things aren't so bad. Mohair business in the West brings in a lot of wholesale and retail trade. Needlework industry going along alright. Even quite a bit of construction. They're just finishing up a $240,000 race track development, and soon after that's completed I understand there'll be jobs opening up on a $4,500,000 building program at Fort Sam Houston and on some of the other Army property hereabouts. PWA! No kidding! Some of the contracts have been let, and the men are being hired. You know they only have Fort Sam Houston, four big Army flying fields, and two big repair depots located here. About 12,000 soldiers. The Army goes a long way toward supporting this town.

And yet, despite all these evidences of an up-turn, you don't encounter a great deal of optimism. Frankly, I wonder if people are as cheerful and confident as they were a year ago at this time. There's so much uncertainty in the air. They don't seem to have that absolute confidence that the President is invincible that they had a year ago. As I wrote you before, they're wondering who's boss. And the average [person] isn't at all enthusiastic about Congress being boss. They seem to feel that, this being an election year, Congress is going off the reservation. They wonder if the President can keep control. It would help a lot, I imagine, if Congress shut up and went home. They're doing too much talking. Of course I'm in Democratic country now, but I certainly get the impression that the business interests down here — even though they do try to beat the codes all the time and probably are — would prefer that the President had more power than less. . . .

The state of mind of the people on relief or applying for relief, in the urban centers at least, is not very good. Those on relief have been on terribly reduced rations for some time. They naturally aren't very happy about it. And everybody — those on relief and those applying for relief — seems to have a false conception of what the new program is to be. They got it apparently from the newspapers, which have played up the work end of it and played down the relief end. The result is that people seem to think that the new program is to be a sort of continuation of CWA — with CWA wages! They get sore as Hell when you try to explain to them that this isn't CWA, but relief — that they aren't eligible unless they're destitute, and that they aren't going to be paid CWA wages, but given relief, a minimum subsistence. To complicate matters, the Texas bond money is tied up to a policy of giving two thirds in kind and only one third in cash. And, right now, two thirds in kind means getting the "kind" at a commissary, although I understand they are planning to get rid of the commissaries as soon as possible. You can say what you like, commissaries, among white people, "just ain't popular."

So, all over the state apparently, you have the white intakes crowded with customers who came in to get, not relief, but jobs. They're plenty mean when they can't get jobs, and they're not particularly happy even when they're eligible for work relief and find that it means two thirds commissary and one third cash, with no rent allowance!

There, apparently, is about one third to half your case load, actual or prospective, in Texas right now, with the white collar load mounting.

The rest of it hasn't any kick at all. With the rest of it, relief is just too popular for anything! They're Negroes and Mexicans, to whom relief, however inadequate for whites, especially white collar people, doesn't mean any lowering of their standards of living at all — in fact, in many, many cases, a BETTER standard of living. They're apparently coming on relief just as fast as they can get on. For them, it's "just swell."

For instance, the case work supervisor here in San Antonio told me today that a white family can't possibly get along on less than $35 a month, especially if you include rent — and rent means a lot to white families, especially white collar families. They need $20 to $25 a month for food. On the other hand, she said, $12 to $15 a month, including rent, represents a fortune to the average low class Mexican family — it's more than they've ever had in their lives before. To them, $20 to $35 a month would be beyond their wildest dreams of affluence.

About half of the case load in San Antonio, actual and prospective, is Mexican. There aren't many Negroes here. If we continue to take on in San Antonio as many Mexicans as we now are — and in other parts of the South as many Negroes — it seems to me that we are forcing white people, especially white collar people, who are very apt to give us trouble, down to Mexican and Negro standards of living. If we had the money, of course, it would be nice to force Mexican and Negro standards of living up to white standards. But have we? The more I think about it, the more I'm convinced that something ought to be done to clean up those Mexican and Negro case loads by thorough reinvestigation and that, as far as possible, we force them to go back to work by withholding relief — even though it may be forcing them back in peonage. What else can we do? Why, in the name of common sense, SHOULD they work — chopping cotton and so on — if we make it possible for them to live without working? I've no doubt at all that the wages paid for farm labor in the South are shameful, and that this condition is due to a surplus of farm labor. . . .

An awful lot of the trouble here in Texas seems to be that Mexican and Negro farm labor won't work for the prevailing wages if they can get on relief. And they've come to town to get relief. If anyone told me that except the social workers, I'd be inclined not to believe it. But they say it's true. Not the higher-ups, in Austin. But social workers out here in the field.

Take San Antonio, for instance. In its population, I'm told, there's a bloc of some 10,000 Mexican families who live here only in the winter, when there's no farm work. Very early in the spring, say in February, they would normally migrate to the truck farms along the Gulf. As the season advances, they move North and West. Right now, I'm told, they should be approaching San Antonio, picking strawberries. A little later, there's cotton chopping North of here. They go on up and work in the Panhandle wheatfields. Some of them stay around and pick cotton in the early fall. Some of them you'll find away up in the beet sugar fields. In the late fall they all come trooping back to San Antonio to stay until work opens up down on the Gulf.

Too many of these people, the social workers tell me, are on relief in San Antonio — or trying to get on relief. Don't you see — there's no point in their going out and working if they can get enough to support them right here, without working for it, or at least without having to work so

226

hard for it? And these people are part of that surplus of farm labor They're not actually needed. The farmers, by paying decent wages, can get along without them, I daresay. As a matter of fact, there's enough of a surplus right at hand so they could get all the help they needed, at rotten wages, without ever calling on this reserve — if it weren't for relief. If we fed all 10,000 families right here in San Antonio, we'd be removing part of the surplus of farm labor, but, with our limited funds, at the expense of white people, with higher standards of living, who are actually unable to get work.

Everywhere the story seems to be the same. I've no figures, because apparently they haven't been thinking along those lines, but I have a hunch that a damned big percentage of those white people aren't ever going to be able to get their jobs back. They're beyond the age limit, for one thing. Do you know that in the oil industry right now they're not hiring men over 35 years old? Quite generally, the age limit seems to be 45 or under. Two reasons for it. One is this group insurance and old age pension business, where the company pays the premiums. They're not good risks. Why, even the Associated Press has that rule — or did have. They didn't hire anybody over 35, because of the group insurance and pension business. The other reason can be traced to the codes, with their minimum wages, whether industry is living up to them or, as I suspect, not. In other words, if they're going to have to pay a minimum wage, they want young people, who can "earn" the minimum wage. It's a business, as I wrote you the other night, of keeping down cost of production. "It's grand to get the higher prices, but we must keep our cost of production down so that it won't eat into our profit." Also, I have a hunch, young people, without experience, are apt to be better satisfied, for the present at least, with the MINIMUM wage.

And so . . . it looks to me as though, before we get through with this business, we're going to have, not only stranded populations, but A WHOLE STRANDED GENERATION. What's the answer? Why, damn it, a man of 45 has a half-grown family! And a man of 35 — in many cases he isn't even married yet!

Add that whole generation to the list of people who aren't going to get their jobs back because of technological advances, and — well, you've got something!

There's no use going into detail about Texas, I guess. But here's the way some of the case loads look.

In San Antonio, population about 280,000, we now have a case load of about 17,500 families. At five to a family, that means 88,500 people. Probably more, because half that case load is Mexican, and most Mexicans have tremendous families. They've been trying to cut down the load, and have been for the last three or four weeks, at the rate of about 350 families a week. BUT the intake, in spite of all they can do, they tell me, keeps pace with the outgo! One encouraging thing is that about half those 350 families they've been dropping every week have jobs. But it doesn't mean so much when for every family taken off because of reemployment, another family comes on for lack of a job. And 60 percent of the new cases, they tell me, are white collar people. Salesmen, for instance, who've been out of work three or four years and have finally come to the end of the rope. I'm not talking now about the number who APPLY for relief, but about those who are shown by investigation to be ELIGIBLE for relief. Well, put it this way: half of those 350 families taken on each week are whites, and 60 percent of that half are white collar people. The case workers know they have no jobs and can't get any. The other half are Mexican. About the Mexicans they're not so sure. They are eligible unless farm work or commonest kind of common labor at wages no higher than relief can be termed a resource. Personally, I think it should be—will have to be.

You'll probably think I'm getting to be a hard hearted old Bourbon. Well, I'm no more hard hearted than are the case workers and case supervisors who are handling this job. They—and I—are thinking about these white people, especially the white collar people. And we are worried. Plenty worried.

Here's another case load. Beaumont and Port Arthur are both in Jefferson county, which has a population of about 135,000, 50,000 in each of the two cities. The case load now, considering the population, is not so high—only about 3,500. It shouldn't be high, for the oil busines is going along producing and refining, I was told, its full allowance. The case load up to now has been evenly divided between Negroes and whites. In the intake, they are trying to limit applications for relief to 75 a day!

"If it's a choice between a white man and a Negro, we're taking the white man," the administrator told me. "We're taking the white applications first and turning away just as many Negroes as we can. We've got to, because of the mental attitude of the whites. We've been threatened with riots here."

In Houston and the surrounding county the case load is 12,500 families, plus 2,700 single persons, of whom TWO THOUSAND—I'm talking about the single persons now—they tell me they've found to be unemployable, because of bad health or old age, that is they're beyond the age limit for industry. New applications for relief have been coming in at the rate of 1,100 a week for the last three weeks. By keeping it down as carefully as possible, they hope to hold their case load to 15,000 families. I haven't figures on how large their Negro load is there, but they were planning to cut it down as low as possible.

There's your case load, and, as far as I can find out, there's not much prospect, for one reason or another, for reemployment in private industry — even in places like Houston and the oil country, where conditions really aren't bad at all. Now what the Hell are we going to DO with these people? Force the Negroes and Mexicans into peonage — and it looks to me as though we'll have to — and make the local communities take care of everyone who is unemployable because he's over 45 years of age? Or what?

In Houston I had a talk with some white collar people. The story was the same — inadequacy and a hatred of the idea of relief, a dread of the intake. Out of the conversation I got two ideas.

1 — "Why," asked one of them, "couldn't white collar people be permitted to apply for relief by mail? Let the investigator visit the home in response to a letter instead of forcing the white collar person to go down and hang around that intake?" The woman who made that suggestion is on relief, a widow with two children. She was some sort of x-ray technician before she lost her job. She said that, when she was finally forced to apply for relief, she wanted to do it by letter, but was told she couldn't. "So I went down there and went through that Hell," she said.

2 — "Why," asked another woman, the mother of two daughters, "don't they give us materials and let us make our children's clothes ourselves, instead of making us take them from the sewing rooms? You've no idea how children hate wearing 'relief clothes.'" Another woman told me her little boy suffered Hell wearing to school trousers she got from the sewing room. "He says every kid in town whose family is on relief wears those pants," she said. "That's how you know they're on relief." The material was striped, quite conspicious, she said, and evidently they got a few bolts of it and made up several hundred pairs for boys whose families were on relief. God, I don't blame the kids! Those stripes suggest a Georgia prison camp. . . .

To Harry L. Hopkins

Albuquerque, N.M., April 25, 1934

Dear Mr. Hopkins:

. . . By and large, I think Texas has felt the recovery program more than any other state I've visited. As I wrote you before, business conditions are not at all bad, apparently in the East Texas oil country, in Houston, even in San Antonio. There's a definite pickup, I'm told, in Dallas and Fort Worth. In Dallas, for instance, the chairman of the relief committee, L.B. Denning, who is also president of the Lone Star Gas company, told me that they were selling more gas now than they'd sold at any previous time in three years and that, for the first time in three years, they were getting new business. . . .

229

Eastern Texas, which is the most thickly populated part of the state, is better off than Western Texas, of course. Apparently there is going to be another drouth in most of the Panhandle. They tell me it will be about the same as last year. There are spots, though, even in the Panhandle where things are looking better. From Amarillo down they've had quite a bit of moisture this year. Generally, they say, it came pretty late, that most of their winter wheat was blown away before it arrived. Through that area they expect to produce about a 30 percent crop. On the other hand, around Lubbock, just South of the Panhandle, between Big Spring and Amarillo, they had enough snow and rain so that things apparently are coming along in splendid shape. The rest of Western Texas, grazing country with some "dry farming," looks pretty dry, except in spots, and they are suffering because of the low price of beef. Wool and goat business is good, on the other hand. San Angelo, in the heart of the sheep and goat country, is sitting on top of the world just now.* * * El Paso is still in bad shape. They had five bank failures there, you know. Their principal industries are all tied up with the mining of silver and copper, which "just isn't being done" these days. They are constantly worried about a heavy case load of alien Mexicans. There are 5,000 of them in the city and county, all of whom came in before the present immigration restrictions were imposed and are not deportable, and half of whom are on relief. They also feel they are carrying a big load of Mexicans who actually live in Mexico! They come across the bridge from Juarez and rent rooms in El Paso, several families going in together on one room, so they can get our relief. To combat it, they've installed an immigration man in the relief office, and they are marking grocery packages so they can be detected on the bridge. It's all pretty much of a mess, hard to control, and, in the meantime, the American population of El Paso is resentful.

But, as I said before, conditions in Texas generally are not so bad. However —

Those improved business conditions are NOT reflected in our relief case loads.

With business improving, the relief load is not decreasing at all. In most places it's mounting.

Furthermore, there doesn't seem to be much chance of any great amount of reemployment, at least for the white skilled workers and white collar men — the class that is getting most restive and that is most apt to cause trouble. There IS work, I believe, for low class Mexican and Negro labor, but at wages so low that they can't compete with relief, however inadequate the relief may be from the standpoint of the white man.

And that, I believe, is the chief trouble in Texas right now, along with the political fighting in Austin that has forced relief standards away down and has given the state administration a bad name. We are carrying on relief in Texas thousands of Mexican and Negro families, to whom relief, however low, is more attractive than the jobs they can get. And the question is:

Should we cut these people off relief and force them back to jobs that actually represent peonage in order that we may provide more adequate relief for a class for which present relief standards are much too low — a class which is absolutely unable to get work at ANY wages and which is apt to give us trouble?

Or should we keep them out of peonage and on relief, thereby, unless we spend a whole lot more money, actually forcing the white man's standard of living down to that of Negro and Mexican labor?

We might, of course, set up two standards of relief, one for Mexicans and Negroes and one for whites. (It's actually been done, quietly, in some places.) But I don't see how the Federal Government could go in for that sort of discrimination.

The mounting case load isn't overwhelmingly Mexican or Negro by any means. There are thousands of white people, notably white collar people, now applying for relief for the first time, I'm told. The difference is that, while thousands of those Mexicans and Negroes COULD get along somehow and be no worse off than they ever were before, these white people CAN'T get work. Some of them — many of them — NEVER will get their jobs back.

I can't help feeling that the only way out is to force those Mexicans and Negroes to go back to work, at whatever wages they can get. I'm mindful of the fact, too, that it's forcing them into very bad conditions and it won't do a thing to bring wage levels up generally. We might give them a sort of semi-relief — surplus commodities, for instance — to supplement their low wages. But if we do that, we are only encouraging the employers, mostly farmers, to continue to pay low wages, even LOWER wages. They'd love to have us do just that, of course. J.R. Martin, NRS man in El Paso, has written for the Department of Labor a confidential report on employment conditions on the irrigated land around El Paso. He has promised to mail me a copy in Tucson, and I'll send it on to you. It will give you an idea of what we are forcing these people back into if we do cut them off relief in large numbers.

In the meantime, I quote a Mexican social worker with a private agency in El Paso:

"All the Mexicans on relief here are perfectly happy. They've got more to eat, they're living better than they ever have in their lives before."

And relief in El Paso in April, Mr. Hopkins, will figure up to $8.86 per month for the average family, wholly inadequate for your whites. In El Paso they have a case load of some 5,000 families right now, with the intake crowded all the time. Sixty percent of that load is Mexican and half of it consists of Mexicans who are not American citizens. The Mexicans are perfectly happy, but the whites certainly are NOT.

The condition in El Paso is exaggerated, of course, but in a lesser degree it exists all over the state.

In addition to the fact that relief is too attractive to thousands of Mexicans and Negroes who might be able to get along without it, there are other reasons, of course, why the case load stays big and continues to grow.

One is that the newspapers have played up the work angle of our program and have played down the relief angle. The result is that there still exists the impression that this is to be "a kind of CWA." It undoubtedly attracts many people who would not otherwise apply for relief. They are mostly whites, however — white collar people and skilled labor. They can be weeded out without much difficulty. Many of them, when they find it's relief, get sore, but refuse to take relief anyhow, whether they need it or not.

There's another, more important reason why the load stays big in spite of an improvement in business conditions. Fred Florence, Dallas banker — who used to be chairman of the relief committee, but quit, the director told me, because the "customers" kept crowding into his beautiful bank to ask him for jobs, to the annoyance of the directors — put his finger on it.

Mr. Florence believes that only half of the unemployed in the country have ever been on relief at all. Half of the unemployed, he figures, have managed to exist — on their credit, by living on friends or relatives, or by their wits — or have been carried along by their employers on a loan basis, as the U.S. Steel Corporation, for instance, carried its people.

Now, as business picks up, he says, that half of the unemployed who never were on relief are getting their jobs back first. The second half won't get a chance until they are absorbed. Sounds reasonable to me.

He cited his own bank to prove his point. When the depression hit, he said, the bank had 290 employees. At one time, a year ago last winter, the number was reduced to 154. So far, he's hired about 30 back — none of whom had been on relief.

"If business continues to pick up," he said, "we'll continue to hire more people, of course. But, don't you see, we'll be hiring back those 106 that are still out before we begin to take people off the relief rolls? They're not on relief. They've managed to pull through so far, and we hope to take them back before they go on relief."

And that may have a whole lot to do with the depressing stuff I get all the time about so little prospect of our relief rolls being reduced in the next 60 to 90 days. It's impossible to tell right now how long it will take for industry to absorb the unemployed who were never on relief. J. C. Capt, the relief administrator in Dallas, doesn't expect more than 15 percent of the relief cases to get jobs, at living wages — living wages according to the white man's standard — in the next 90 days.

Another thing that cannot be overlooked is the age limit in industry and its effect on our relief load. I hear the same thing, over and over again, wherever I go, from employers, from relief workers, and from the clients themselves:

"There's no place for a man over 45 — or 35, in the oil refineries. He's not going to get his job back. They're taking all younger men."

The employers justify it by saying the man over 45 is slowed down, that, especially if he has been out of the shop for sometime, he's dangerous because he's so slowed down. They also point out that we are turning out of our schools and colleges every year some million or so of young men who have got to have jobs. All this is undoubtedly true. AND in addition, you have that compensation insurance and pension business that certainly doesn't make it profitable for an industry to hire old men. You've got the code, with its higher minimum wages, and industry expecting every man to live up to those wages. And you've also got the fact that inexperienced, younger men will accept those minimum wages with better grace than the older, experienced man. Something of a muddle but there it is.

Well, assuming that we clean up our Mexican and Negro case loads and force them back to work at whatever wages they can get, it looks as though we're in this relief business for a long, long time.

1 — The white skilled labor and white collar people on our rolls who ARE acceptable to industry won't get their jobs back until all those who've never been on relief get theirs back.

2 — The majority of those over 45 probably will NEVER get their jobs back.

They're our babies. And what are we going to do with them? . . .

As I see it, we've got to make it possible for them to pay rents, live decently, have enough to eat, be clothed. And we're not doing it — not in Alabama, or Louisiana, or Texas. About all we're doing is to give them something to eat and not enough of that. I'm talking about white people now, people with pretty much the same ambitions and standards of living that you and I would expect to have.

Pardon me for getting personal, but I believe you are a little past 40 yourself. Suppose at 45 you lost your job and couldn't get another one — probably never. How would you like to bring your baby up on relief in Alabama or Louisiana or Texas? I'm over 40 myself. Suppose after this job is finished I couldn't ever get another. How would I like spending the rest of my life on relief — provided, as a single person, I could get relief? I'd be damned rebellious, I tell you. There's plenty of trouble ahead with people like you and me on relief, and there are thousands of them. The number is growing. . . .

In Fort Worth last week I got hold of a copy of a survey made by the Recovery Committee of the Cast Iron Trade. They went to the state fire insurance examiner and got the fire insurance rating of every town in Texas. Then to every town where the rate was above normal they went and found out why. In 537 towns where the rate was above normal they had inadequate water supply. Take Brownwood, for instance. Twelve thousand population. Insurance rate 15 percent above normal, because the size of the watermain should be increased, there should be supply lines, and more hydrants. It would cost about $100,000 to remedy that situation — $60,000 in materials . . . IN 320 TEXAS TOWNS THERE WAS NO FIRE PROTECTION AT ALL! * * * If those towns are to continue to exist, if people go on living in them — God knows why they go on living in some of them! — I should think something ought to be done about that situation! . . .

To Harry L. Hopkins

Socorro, New Mexico, April 27th, 1934

Dear Mr. Hopkins:

After four days of New Mexico, I pause to give you a few impressions. . . .

New Mexico, as you may — or may not — know, is the fourth largest state in the country. It has an area of 78,000,000 acres, of which only 2,000,000 will produce crops! Most of these 2,000,000 acres are irrigated. On the rest there is some sort of natural irrigation or rainfall sufficient to make farming possible. The rest of New Mexico, 76,000,000 acres, is mountain and desert country, worth, I was told yesterday, less than $1 an acre. As much of it as possible is used for grazing, but it is not very good grazing. In at least half of it, I was told, you need 100 acres to one steer or three or four sheep. In the best of it you need 20 acres to the steer or three or four sheep.

A good one third of the state, I am told, is in public domain — national forests, Indian reservations, and vacant public land open for homesteading. None of this land, of course, pays any taxes. It keeps the state poor. Land available for homesteading on July 1, 1932, totalled 13,615,150 acres. A whole lot of this land they think out here in New Mexico ought to be withdrawn from homesteading. Here's what's happening.

In one district alone, 200 homesteading families have moved in to take up land in the last couple of years. They are practically all on relief. More are coming all the time — veterans and unsuccessful farmers from

Oklahoma, Arkansas, and Texas. They failed to make a living where they were, and their chances here are pretty damned slim. The land, I was told, is worthless for anything save grazing. Too dry. And to make a living raising cattle or sheep in this country you've got to have a lot more land than these homesteaders are acquiring even if they had the stock. Furthermore, they are ruining, by plowing it up, grazing land, such as it is. . . .

Scattered about over New Mexico's 78,000,000 acres are only 425,000 people, 60 per cent of them Spanish-Americans. Some of the Spanish-Americans are really Mexicans, but the large majority, they tell me, are actually Spanish-Americans. They are descendants of Indians and the Spanish conquerors, and they were here long before we "Anglos," as they call us, were. We are, more or less, outsiders. They regard this as *their* state. All state business is conducted in two languages, including proceedings in the Legislature. Controlled by American politicians, they swing elections. They are much more politically minded than the "Anglos."

Unfortunately these Spanish-Americans are, from an economic standpoint, helpless people. They've lost control of the land, and of what little industry there is in the state they never did have control. They are easy-going, pleasure loving people, with a standard of living a good deal below our own. They are now the laboring class, sheep herders, section hands, day laborers in the cities, small farmers, who don't seem to know how to take care of their stock or what to do with good land when they have it.

The case load in New Mexico this month consists of some 12,000 families — plus about 1,000 transients, single and families, and 1,750 single men and women. Of the 12,000, between 75 and 80 per cent are Spanish-American.

The population of New Mexico is essentially rural. Only about 16 per cent of the people live in urban centers. And the majority of the Spanish-Americans live in rural areas. But everywhere, even in Albuquerque, the heaviest part of the case load is Spanish-American.

Their relief needs, because of their standards of living, are low, if you want to consider it from that standpoint. In the rural areas, it's largely a matter of supplementary relief — $8 or $10 a month. They all raise a little food. Their adobe houses are cheap and comfortable. A Spanish-American can build a house simply by digging up dirt out of the front yard and molding it into bricks which he dries in the sun. Good houses, too.

They aren't a particularly serious relief problem, except that we'll probably have them on our hands forever unless we try to rehabilitate them in some way. It's largely a matter of education. They need to be taught what to raise, how to raise it, how to take care of their stock. It's going to be a hard job, I gather. They're perfectly docile, but not particularly energetic.

A lot of them will have to be moved onto better land. But there's plenty of good fertile land being opened up by the Rio Grande conservancy project, which is now about completed. I was told that there would be room in the valley for 12,000 families, if we wanted to settle that many there. . . .

The people, business and professional men and the public generally, are most enthusiastic about the possibility of rehabilitating a lot of the relief load in the Rio Grande valley. One businessman in Albuquerque put it this way the other day:

"The Government really has about $9,000,000 at stake in the Rio Grande valley right now. It holds $6,000,000 worth of conservancy bonds, paid outright $1,593,000 for the Indians' share of the project, loaned the First National bank in Albuquerque $400,000, has taken up some $250,000 worth of the bank's stock, has put $1,000,000 into home loans here in Albuquerque. With the Government holding that much of an interest in the valley, it would seem reasonable, wouldn't it, for the Government to put in a couple of million more, rehabilitating relief cases on that land, with the possibility of getting back, indirectly at least, the $9,000,000?"

They're all pepped up about it, really, including the gang at the state agricultural college. But of course it's federal money that will have to be used. The state hasn't any income to speak of.

Well — you've got a case load 75 or 80 per cent Spanish-American in New Mexico. And the other 20 or 25 per cent give more trouble than all the Spanish-Americans put together.

First of all, there isn't a Chinaman's chance of the "Anglos" getting their jobs back. Not right away, at any rate. Industry in New Mexico "just ain't."

The largest industries in the state, before the depression, were the railroads. The Santa Fe in 1929 employed 7,500 men in New Mexico. Last year it employed 3,200. I was told by a businessman in Albuquerque that in June, 1930, the Sante Fe let out every other section crew from Chicago to the Pacific coast. This same businessman told me that in 1930 he sold the Sante Fe $90,000 worth of sand and gravel, as compared with $7,000 worth last year! A woman in our relief setup in Albuquerque, wife of a railroad man, told me that not a single new man had been taken on in the Sante Fe shops there since 1926, and that there are about 600 men working there now, four days a week at wages ranging from $45 to $80 a month, whereas 17 years ago there were 2,200 working full time. And an awful lot of the men thrown out by that curtailment are white skilled workers.

The Sante Fe people have been pretty good sports at that, you know. I was told that in a Northern timber country, up in the mountains, the railroad had gone on buying ties, simply to give the people some work, until they now have enough ties on hand to last them for years.

Well, here's what your Anglo load, 20 to 25 per cent of the whole load, consists of:

Skilled workmen in the cities, principally Albuquerque. Carpenters, mechanics, and so on.

Sick people who have come out here to get well, without enough money to get along, and sick veterans, who will be getting their compensation back now, however, and will be removed from our load. Among the sick people you can include a lot of transients.

A migrant labor class, that used to get seasonal work here and up in Colorado and can't get it any more.

Some miners, both coal and copper, silver, lead, zinc, etc. Not much ahead for them now, especially the coal miners. Here's the mining situation: soft coal mines, cut down to ⅓ of pre-depression production, due to transportation costs and competition from natural gas from Texas; one anthracite mine, employing 200 people one day a week; Chino Copper company, used to employ 2,000 men in New Mexico, now employing 500 three days a week; American Metals company, employing 650 men full time, able to do so because they are producing some silver and gold. The coal mines in 1929 were employing 3,500 men full time, but are now employing less than 2,000, none of them full time.

Some stranded oil workers, left behind by a collapsed boom in the Southeastern part of the state.

Some "dry farmers" in the drouth areas, who will be alright if it ever rains again.

And some white collar people in Albuquerque.

The state crowd aren't conscious of any "white collar problem" as yet, but they are in Albuquerque. And they're worried about it, especially the project engineer. He doesn't know how to fit them into the work division projects. In Albuquerque they now have a relief load of some 1,000 families, including 200 veterans and their families, most of the veterans being sick. The white collar load has been about 5 per cent, but I was told it is growing. They are getting about 50 new cases a week, and a fourth of them are white collar people. . . .

To Harry L. Hopkins

Phoenix, Arizona, May 4, 1934

Dear Mr. Hopkins:

. . . I lost a day this week. On Sunday, driving across desert from Lordsburg, N.M., to Tucson, I turned over in loose gravel on a road which seems to be a sort of political football. The towns of Douglas and Bisbee, wishing to keep the road as bad as possible, have enough influence at the Statehouse to prevent its being repaired. The result is about one wreck a week, with a couple of fatalities every month or so. Douglas and Bisbee are interested because it diverts traffic away from them. * * * So, since I had apparently carried most of the weight of the car on the back of my neck during the split second while it was rolling over, the doctor seemed to think it might be a good idea for me to spend Monday in bed, which I did. Incidentally, sir, you have to have a darned good neck to get away with anything like that. I think mine had no doubt got toughened up these last five or six weeks from carrying the weight of the world on it. * * * Since Monday I've been moving fast, with little opportunity to write.

Anyway, I haven't felt much encouraged to write. Damn it, it's the same old story down here, wherever I go.

Two classes of people.

Whites, including white collar people, with white standards of living, for whom relief, as it is now, is anything but adequate. No jobs in sight. Growing restive.

Mexicans — or, East of the Mississippi, Negroes — with low standards of living, to whom relief is adequate and attractive. Perfectly contented. Willing to stay on relief the rest of their lives. Able, many of them, to get work, but at wages so low that they are better off on relief.

So many Mexicans and Negroes on relief that, with a limited amount of money, we are compelled to force the white man's standard of living down to that of the Mexicans and Negroes.

I believe that in the whole Southern half of the United States you will find this to be the big relief problem today. Certainly it is in every urban community. I've encountered it everywhere I've been on this trip: Alabama, Texas, Louisiana, New Mexico, although not so bad there, and Arizona.

Add to it newspaper publicity — carried out of Washington by the press asssociations, I am told — that has led the population to believe that everyone in the state on relief is going to get $21 a month cash, no more and no less, under the new program, and you have Arizona's problem. The Mexicans all want "the $21 a month the Government has promised us." The whites, who have actually been getting more than that on direct relief, don't see how they can get along on it and are worried stiff. It represents a "raise" for the Mexicans, from relief with which they were perfectly satisfied and which apparently was adequate, and a "cut" for the whites. . . .

I have been writing you right along that the only way I could see to clean up this Negro-Mexican business would be to reinvestigate thoroughly the Negro and Mexican case loads, closing the intakes to get them out of the habit of registering for relief for a few weeks and to turn the case workers loose for the reinvestigation, and to force every Negro or Mexican who could get any work at all, at WHATEVER wages, to take it and get off the relief rolls. * * * I must admit that there are people in the set-up who don't agree with me on this. They argue first of all that we are forcing these people into peonage. Employers, particularly farmers and housewives — the two worst classes of employers in the country, I believe — will take advantage of the situation. I've written you about housewives who think Negroes, Mexicans, or even white girls ought to be glad to work for their room and board. And last week in New Mexico I heard about sheep growers who want to hire herders at $7 a MONTH! It is also argued that, particularly in cities, thousands of the Mexicans and Negroes actually CAN'T get work — that, if there is any job, no matter how lowly and how poorly paid, a white man will take it, and that there would be Hell to pay if a Negro or a Mexican got it. I don't believe that, however, to the extent that some people do.

It's almost impossible to get to the bottom on this farm labor proposition. The farmers — sheep and cattle men, cotton growers, and so on — are all yelling that they can't get the Mexicans to work because they are all on relief. But when Mexicans and Spanish-Americans won't go out and herd sheep for $7 a month because they can get $8 or $10 on relief, it seems to me that the farmer ought to raise his wages a little. Oh, they don't admit trying to get herders for $7 a month. If you ask them what they are paying, they will say, "Anywhere from $15 a month up." But our relief people looked into the matter and found out what they actually were willing to pay.

A thing that complicates the whole situation right now is our hourly rate under the new program. In Arizona, for instance, the minimum is 50 cents an hour. We adopted it because it is the hourly rate on public works in the state of Arizona. But, don't you see, it's a "political" hourly rate? Jobs on highways on public works in Arizona are dealt out as political patronage. The ACTUAL prevailing wage in Arizona is nowhere nearly that high. Up to now there haven't been many people getting 50 cents an hour in Arizona — and damned few Mexicans. Now we come along and announce we are going to pay everybody on relief 50 cents an hour. You can imagine the furor.

You've got the Latin temperament to deal with down here, too. Latin and Indian. They don't "want" things. They haven't any ambition. A man who is half Spanish and half Indian has an entirely different slant on life from ours. To begin with, it's a semi-tropical country. The Spaniards came here generations ago. They are easy-going, pleasure loving. It isn't in their makeup to "get out and hustle." And the Indian in them certainly wouldn't make them ambitious. The Indian never was a hustler. He wanted just enough, no more. Your Mexican, or your

Spanish-American, is a simple fellow, with simple needs, to be obtained with the least effort. And if he could work five days a week at 50 cents an hour or three days a week at 50 cents an hour, he'd work three days, even though it meant less income. His attitude is: "Why work any more after you've got enough?" And when it comes to working seven days a week, 10 hours a day, for no more than, or even less than, he'd be getting on relief — well, he just can't see that at all. * * * And so, this 50-cent hourly rate is just swell for a Mexican, even though the number of hours he can work and the amount of money he can get per month on it are limited. And $21 a month, earned at the rate of 50 cents an hour — why, that's just Heaven to him! He'd have a grand time on $10 or $12. And has been.

The Mexican or Spanish-American diet is so different from ours. Chili beans, red beans, a little grease, flour or cornmeal, a few vegetables and a little fruit in the fall. It's a cheap diet. But they've thrived — or would it be "thriven"? — on it for 500 years. We're silly to try to change it. As a matter of fact, doctors over in New Mexico have been making a study of that diet, observing the effect on the children. They've had the surprise of their lives. Those children are a darn sight better off physically, on that diet, than most of our white children are in families living on minimum subsistence rations.

In Tucson not long ago arrived a huge shipment of surplus commodity butter. They had no place to keep it. They had to ration it out to Mexicans and Indians as well as whites. The Mexicans and Indians had never tasted butter before. They didn't even like it. They tried to fry beans in it — and came back yelling for lard!

Now if these people can live on $10 or $12 a month and be reasonably healthy and so contented that they won't even take work when it is offered them, let alone go out and look for it, why, in the name of common sense, raise them above that? Especially when we have a limited amount of money. I'll grant that the work that is offered them pays darned little — that it's practically peonage — but it's all they've ever known, and I doubt if the Relief administration is financially in a position to battle low wage scales all over the South and Southwest.

There is a way of handling the problem, other than throwing the Mexicans and Negroes off relief — and the local relief administrations have been doing it. Discrimination. Two standards of relief. The idea will sound horrible in Washington, but — I'm beginning to wonder.

The only place where they've come right out and admitted to me that they've been doing it is in Tucson. They were doing it before Federal money came in, there, and during April, between CWA and the new program,[1] which went into effect May 1, they went back to it. They said April had been the smoothest month they'd had for a long time.

In Tucson — without any publicity, but so quietly that people didn't even know they were being classified — they divided their case load into four groups, Classes A, B, C, and D. They have about 2,800 families on relief there: 1,200 Mexicans, American citizens, but with a low standard of living; 800 Yaqui Indian families, political refugees from old Mexico; 800 white families.

Into Class A went 60 families. Engineers, teachers, lawyers, contractors, a few former businessmen, architects, and some chemists who used to be connected with the mines. They and each of the other three groups had their own intakes. No mixing. They gave this group a $50 a month maximum, 50 per cent cash. It took care of them fairly adequately, rents, clothing, and everything. They set up projects for them, manning their auxiliary staff with them. Although they were required to work only a few hours a week for what they were getting, these people have been giving full time, voluntarily.

Into Class B went 250 families, on a maximum of $36 a month, from 33⅓ to 40 per cent cash. It consisted of some white collar people — clerks, stenographers, bookkeepers, and so on — and skilled labor. Many of these people were able to augment their incomes by a few days work now and then.

Into Class C went 1,000 families, on a $25 maximum, 30 per cent cash. It consisted of white unskilled labor and Mexican and Spanish-American unskilled labor with standards of living higher than those of most Mexicans.

And into Class D went 1,490 families, on a $10 maximum, all in kind. These were the low class Mexican, Spanish-American, and Indian families.

They have a commissary in Tucson — and I'm beginning to wonder, too, if a commissary IS such a bad thing where you've got a large crowd of people with low standards of living to feed. As a work project, they raise two-thirds of the vegetables distributed through the commissary. They buy milk wholesale, giving it out at 8 cents a quart instead of 15 as charged retail. Incidentally, from school districts where these low class Mexicans and Indians live and where distribution of milk to children has been going on for years there came a few weeks ago word that the health of the children had improved to such an extent that they no longer needed to distribute the milk!

"Now this all may seem pretty bad to you," the relief administrator told me, "but you're going to quit some day and leave us, here in these communities, to carry on. We'll never be able to carry on under the conditions Washington is imposing on us now."

And so — I'm wondering if perhaps we should try to set up a national standard and impose it on a state like Arizona, a town like Tucson. I'm wondering if we shouldn't give these state and local committees a little more latitude, a little more discretionary power. * * * Don't think I can't see the dangers in it. And I realize the terrific pressure brought to bear by the Labor crowd on those wage scales. But, dammit, man, our job is to feed people and clothe them and shelter them, with as little damage to their morale as possible. And that's all, as I see it. We haven't got the money to do any more. I can't see — I've never been able to see — that it was the job of the Federal Emergency Relief Administration to fight the battle of the American Federation of Labor. We ARE feeding people, clothing them, and providing shelter for them as best we can. But what are we doing to their morale? I've been on the road nearly a year now. More and more I've come to the conclusion that, the less we interfere with the normal lives of these families, the less damage we're going to do to their morale. If, by relief, we raise a family's income beyond whatever [it] has been before or beyond what it has any chance of becoming normally, we are damaging the morale of that family. And if we lower a family's standard of living too much, we are going to ruin its morale, too — or make a rebel out of the head of that family.

In Tucson, if we enforce that 50-cent hourly wage rate with the limit on hours, we're going to do both of those things, I'm afraid.

I was in Tucson May 1, the day the new program went in.

All the Mexicans who could read — and even more who couldn't — were over at their intake, demanding the $21 a month "the Government has promised us."

In the office of the administrator, I sat talking for an hour with half a dozen white collar clients. Among them were a landscape painter, a certified public accountant, a former businessman, an architect, a former bank cashier. All save the artist were men of 45 or thereabouts. All had been in the group of 60, Class A. We went over their budgets, to see if they could possibly get along on that $21 maximum.

Said the painter:

"I pay $6.50 a month rent. There are three of us, my wife, my 18-months-old baby, and myself. We have three rooms in a garage. No water. An outside toilet. The baby's food costs us $6.03 a month — $4.11 for milk, .46 for Cream of Wheat, .26 for prunes, $1.20 for vegetables. He should have more, but he can get by on that. Our lights and coal oil for fuel come to $4.30 a month. Add $6.50 for rent, $6.03 for the baby's food, and $4.30 for light and oil, and you get $16.83. Subtract that from $21, and you see my wife and I will have $4.17 a month for food for ourselves. Can't do it."

The certified public accountant was trying to hang onto his home. "If I lose that," he said, "it's the end — that's all." He has a Federal Home

242

Loan, which requires that he pay $10 a month interest. That leaves him an $11 balance, and he has six in the family and a baby coming. In April he got $40 and managed to get by, although, of course, he had to keep one of the children out of school to help his wife because he couldn't hire any one. He wasn't kicking about that, however.

The former bank cashier also had six in the family — himself, his wife, his parents, his crippled sister, and her child. He wasn't paying rent. They had moved in with friends. But they were paying half of the electric, water and fuel bills.

"I'm afraid for my parents," he said. "Lord only knows how we'll get along. They are unhappy now and feel they are in the way. It's a bad situation."

The former businessman, who told me that, when the depression hit, he was worth $60,000 — and other people told me he was telling me the truth — had only three in his family, his wife, himself, and a son, who had to leave college, but who has been unable to get steady work of any kind. He is paying $15 a month rent, having recently moved out of a $25 apartment. That leaves $6 a month for food for the three of them.

"All this — it breaks you down," he said quietly. "We men who have been the backbone of commerce, who have had ambitions and hopes, who have always taken care of our families — what is going to become of us? I've lost twelve and a half pounds this last month, just thinking. You can't sleep, you know. You wake up about 2 A.M., and then you lie and think.

"Why, I've sat across the tables from Jesse Jones[2] and talked contracts with him, running up into many thousands of dollars! But I'd be afraid to face him now. You get so you feel so whipped!"

There was a moment's silence. Then the former bank cashier spoke.

"Yes," he said, "all those years of practical experience you and I have had don't count for anything now.

"When you're 45 and trying to get a job, they say to you, 'I'll get in touch with you later, Mr. So-and-So. Mighty glad you dropped in.'

"But you never hear from them."

In Albuquerque the other day, I was talking with a lawyer, a former judge, who is one of the big men in the town.

"The Government has got to take care of these people," he said, "if it takes your hat and mine. Why, we don't know the beginning of taxation in this country yet. And if society, as it is now organized, can't give a man a job, then the Government, representing all the people, must do it — a decent job, at a living wage." . . .

1. PWA.
2. Texas banker who headed the RFC.

To Harry L. Hopkins

Phoenix, Arizona, May 6, 1934

Dear Mr. Hopkins:

The chief trouble with our transient care, as I see it, may be that it's too good. Transients on relief get better care than residents on relief.

Especially is this true of single, unattached men. Women, too. Any unattached person "in the know" would be a damned fool NOT to go transient. Of course, that MAY be the solution to the unattached person problem for us. I don't know.

The same is true, but perhaps not to so great an extent, of families. I visited Friday afternoon the camp for transient families near Phoenix. It is an old auto camp, kept scrupulously clean, with small, but comfortable, cabins. There are electric lights, bath houses, laundry, plenty of hot water, plugs for electric irons. The families get pretty adequate food orders, slightly higher than those given to residents. Plenty of milk. Some clothing. * * * In other words, that camp represents what we'd LIKE to do for the great masses of our clients who live in these towns. It's the ideal — which we have never reached in most places. Good housing. Clothing. Medical care. Adequate relief.

Now why wouldn't any family that got wise to this — and the grapevine, I'm told, is developing marvelously — prefer going transient than living on relief in, say, Oklahoma or Texas?

The fact that they are better treated may be due to several reasons. In the first place, it's a federal program. No local politics mixing in, tying up funds, and that sort of thing. They have regular allotments, know where their money is coming from and that they are going to get it. They can budget. That makes a lot of difference. They can do a better job, with less cost. For instance, the engineer who was in charge of CWA projects in San Antonio told me that materials on one job had cost a couple of hundred dollars extra because they didn't get their money in time to pay cash and get the discount. That sort of thing probably doesn't happen in the transient setup. * * * Then they have their clients bunched. I guess you can always handle the feeding proposition better and more cheaply when you feed a lot of people at once, in one place. Not so good from the social standpoint, but that doesn't enter into the single man situation. He hasn't any family life anyway. And with families on relief, food and shelter should come ahead of social problems, I reckon.

The great weakness in the transient show seems to be that it isn't stopping transiency. . . .

It has stopped it to some extent of course. Roads parallel the railroad lines a lot out here. Since leaving Fort Worth, I've been watching freight trains, as they passed. . . . It seemed to me that there were a good many boys riding the trains, but said the relief director in El Paso:

"Three hundred used to drop off a freight train when it came in here. Now we get about fifty."

However, in the last few weeks since it's begun to get hot in the desert and in Southern California, the Arizona transient camp at Flagstaff, up in the mountains where it's cool, reports an increase of THREE HUNDRED PERCENT in its registrations! Miss Hawes[1] brings a gloomy story from Denver. Six weeks ago, she said, there were about 40 registrations a day. Now it's jumped to 80. * * * All that means only one thing. They're still traveling. Wintering in the South, summering in the mountains—at Uncle Sam's expense. Perhaps it's just as well. I don't know. We'd have to support them somewhere.

Undoubtedly the railroads are not cooperating with us as much as we had thought they would in trying to stop this transiency. Well, they have their difficulties, too. In most of these states, I'm told, there is a law prohibiting throwing a man off a moving train. Very well. You stop your freight train and throw them off. Then what happens? A freight train starts very slowly. By the time it's under way, they're all back on again! One of the roads tried leaving with the bunch that was thrown off a couple of railroad detectives, who could see that they didn't climb aboard again and would themselves flag the next passenger train. Results—several detectives were badly beaten up, and in some cases the men thrown off walked along the tracks breaking every switch light they came to. So, you see it's not at all honey for the railroads.

That's only a minor cause anyway. The real difficulty seems to lie in a lack of uniformity between the various states and communities.

For instance:

Arizona has no transient shelters. If a man comes in here, he is taken into a camp at once. He must sign up for two weeks in the camp. If he isn't willing to do that, he's just sent on his way—but with no shelters to stop at over night, with free food and lodging. . . . Transient families are taken into camps or, if there is a sick person in the family, given housing in the towns, and as fast as possible they are sent home—NOT on free gas tickets, but on the train.

But the states around Arizona have transient shelters. Their camp rules are different. They provide gasoline tickets. And so on. . . .

The general level of the transient camps and shelters is, I believe, good. But naturally some camps and some shelters are better than others. The result is that you have transients, both unattached persons and families, "shopping around." Their pet story at the transient family camp here is about a woman who came in, was dissatisfied with the accommodations, burst into tears, and sobbed that in Texas they had given her a hotel room with a private bath! . . .

Maybe what the transients need is a field staff of their own. Except for Margaret Reeves, in New Mexico, and Florence Warner here in Arizona, none of the state relief administrators I've seen seems to know very much about the transient situation — or care. State transient directors are left pretty much to their own devices, by everyone, including Washington, as nearly as I can find out! . . .

Arizona and New Mexico have an added problem, as you know, in that large numbers of their transients — particularly the families — are attracted here by the climate, because of illness.

Doctors and relief people in both states all protest that the great majority of these families shouldn't come at all. Some member of the family has tuberculosis. The family doctor says, "You might get better in Arizona or New Mexico." So they climb into an old car — usually worth only about $25 or $30 — and out they come, getting free gasoline at transient centers on the way. They hardly get here before they're broke. Then we take them on. It is the contention of the doctors out here that, with proper care and food, they'd stand just as good a chance of getting well at home as they do out here. Probably better. They could probably get free hospitalization at home. They can't here. These states are too poor to provide hospitalization for their own people, let alone transients.

With your background you must be a whole lot more familiar with this tuberculosis business than I am. But anyway, doctors and relief people here say of the majority of the people who come out here with tuberculosis and no money that they would be better off back home. They feel that Eastern physicians are highly irresponsible to recommend their coming out here, without funds. As a matter of fact, I'm wondering if doctors in the East really do recommend it. I suspect a good many of these people of coming "on their own."

Arizona gets tough with them. I can't say that I blame Arizona. As that man in Tucson said to me the other day, the Federal Government is going to get out of this relief business some day. And what a fine crop of unemployables Arizona would inherit, if they let these people stay.

So they examine carefully all the people who come rattling out here in Model-T Fords for their health, without anything to live on after they get here — people with tuberculosis, asthma, sinus trouble, arthritis, heart trouble, and all the rest of it. And they permit to remain only those the doctors feel cannot safely be sent home. That's a small number.

About 40 percent of the transient families they get in this state have come because some member of the family is ill. And of that 40 percent only about 15 or 20 percent, I'm told, really have to stay. They're mostly victims of asthma. Not many of those with tuberculosis actually have to stay. Living in Phoenix right now, on transient relief, are eight families in each of which there is someone with tuberculosis. They are the only families out of several hundred that have appeared since the transient relief started that have been allowed to remain on account of tuberculosis. All the rest have been packed up, baggage and all, on the train.

They don't simply buy them a few gallons of gasoline and start them back in their rattletrap old cars. They send them on the train. A family before it can get transient relief in this state has got to turn in its car. The cars are appraised, and the value of the car balanced against the cost of relief and transportation home. Most of the cars aren't worth anything—$15 to $30. They haven't yet taken a car the value of which was worth more than the relief and transportation home. Some of the families give them up willingly enough. There have been about 160 families that have refused and have gone without relief.

At first glance, this may look pretty tough, but I don't think it is, really. Why should we buy gas for transients to tour the country on? The whole purpose—or at least one of the major purposes—of this transient program was to discourage transiency, wasn't it? We aren't discouraging it when we buy gas for them, are we? It isn't only families with tuberculosis or other health problems that come tootling in here on free gas, you know. There are in Arizona now about 5,000 transients who are our clients. Of these some 1,200 are in family groups, between 300 and 400 families. Less than 40 percent of them are out here for their health. The rest are "just traveling." Looking for work, some of them. Some of them, I suspect, taking vacations. Some of them on the road because relief in their home states is inadequate. Just "shopping around." In Phoenix there are eight families that have been allowed to stay because of illness in the family. In a camp outside the city are between 30 and 40 families in which there is no health complication at all. These are due to go home as soon as arrangements for their return can be completed. Most of them came in here in automobiles—on free gas. Why, they even drop in at transient headquarters to pick up gas books that have been sent on for them from other states! Most of them never would have got here if it hadn't been for free gas books supplied by transient shelters. Honestly, I just can't see that system at all.

There is one angle to the situation that troubles both Miss Reeves and Miss Warner a little. That is, the way these families feel when they are sent home. Some member of the family is ill with tuberculosis. Some doctor in the East, maybe, has said, "If you go to Arizona, you may get well." So they've come to Arizona. And now, when we tell them they've got to go back, both the patient and the rest of the family feel as though we were signing his death warrant. It's so hard to make them understand.

For this reason, I think, New Mexico is somewhat more lenient with them. But New Mexico doesn't get so many as Arizona gets. In New Mexico they are considering a plan to colonize some 150 of these families somewhere in that Rio Grande conservancy district.

Miss Warner, here in Arizona, feels that perhaps some way could be worked out whereby they could be permitted to stay, but their care and relief charged against the states from which they came. The main thing is that they should not be allowed to remain here, establish residence, and become permanent charges on the state of Arizona, don't you see? I don't blame Arizona for kicking on a proposition like that.

The matter of hospitalization is aggravating. Although you find comparatively few unattached transients who say they have come out here for their health, they find a good deal of tuberculosis in the camps. Some of the men are very ill. Anyway, they probably should be isolated. Also the men with venereal diseases. And they are being isolated, of course. Most of the camps and shelters have infirmaries.

Mr. Paul Murphy, the Arizona boy with a flare for spending money, has gone further. He has two big infirmaries, that are really hospitals. All the men with venereal diseases are concentrated in the clinic and infirmary at the camp here at Phoenix. Those with tuberculosis are sent to the camp at Nogales, on the border. Incidentally, no man under 40, unless he's flat on his back with tuberculosis, is permitted to register at that camp, because of social complications!

I went through his hospital at Nogales. It's a peach. Operated almost entirely by the transients themselves, at a cost, for care and everything, of a little less than a dollar per day per man. * * * There are about 60 men in the hospital down there now.

One of the big problems in the camp at Nogales is death. They've had 15 deaths down there. They owe the undertaker $320, and he says he can't afford to bury any more of them. Murphy, Miss Warner, and I talked out a plan whereby they can get around having an undertaker. Making coffins can be a work relief project. Not for the men in the camp — it would be damned bad for a man of 40 or over, in a transient camp where there was a tuberculosis hospital, to make caskets — but by resident relief clients, who could also dig the graves. Priests and preachers will conduct funeral services for nothing. But the question is: what to do about that undertaker's bill. Certainly he ought to be paid, some way. He's just a little fellow. He can't afford to lose that money. Can't get any money from the state. They're non-residents. And can't get any money from the county, which has all it can do to take care of its own pauper burials.

I found Miss Reeves, in New Mexico, longing to do something about hospitalization, too. Both for the people with tuberculosis — they have a good deal of it among their children there, too, and no free hospitals — and for people in isolated places in the state, where there are no doctors, no hospitals, nothing. They could take over one of the abandoned institutions in Albuquerque — five out of seven are closed for lack of paying patients — and they could, in two or three isolated spots about the state, set up small emergency clinics, at least places where children could be born and emergency operations performed. They've got unemployed nurses enough to staff them. And what about some of these doctors we're carrying on relief? Why not subsidize them a little maybe and get them to come out to New Mexico? Probably sounds pretty wild to you. . . .

1. Mary Houston Hawes was a statistician for Corrington Gill, chief of the Division of Research, Statistics, and Finance for FERA.

To Harry L. Hopkins

Enroute to Washington, May 8, 1934

Dear Mr. Hopkins:

Now as to prospects for employment in Arizona and New Mexico and the state of mind of people generally.

In New Mexico, as I have already written you, the prospects for jobs, except for Mexicans and Spanish-Americans to work for less than they are getting on relief, are not so good. Can't see much reduction there in our relief load, except through reinvestigation of the clients. That may help a good deal, however. For the reason that in many of the counties they haven't had until now any trained or paid administrators. Where you depend on a volunteer, local committee to handle relief, I think your case load is apt to be high — everywhere except in New England, at any rate. A trained case worker recently installed in one New Mexico county told me that through investigation she was removing about four out of every five of new families from the rolls. Most of them, it is true, were being removed because they could get farm work, at however low wages, were being sent to seasonal work, and probably will be back later. Well, even that will ease the load for the time. And a substantial number, she said, really had resources and probably won't be back. * * * As fast as she can wangle money out of the counties to pay their salaries, Miss Reeves, the state administrator, is installing trained county administrators throughout the state. It's a question of money rather than opposition to trained workers.

Prospects for reemployment in private industry are, I should say, less encouraging in New Mexico than in Arizona. Their only industry, outside of Government work, of which there is a good deal normally, in the National forests, about the Indian reservations, and so on, is the railroad business, and, although the state NRS director thought the Santa Fe might be putting some men back to work in July, I didn't get any such story from anyone else. The Santa Fe is economizing. It took off three passenger trains through Arizona this week. I was told that not a single new man had been hired since 1926 in the shops in Albuquerque, and that the prospects of any being hired were damned slim, and that the road had laid off every other section crew from Chicago to the coast, that they're still out, with no prospects of going back. Relief people estimate that employment on the railroads in New Mexico is now about 40 per cent of normal.

Take out your Government and railroad payrolls in New Mexico, and you have left: the sheep industry, which is doing without labor right now to a large extent, I was told, rather than try to compete with relief (they're the babies who want to pay herders $7 a month and board); the cattle industry, which is in a bad way owing to low prices and drouth conditions; some dry farming, little fellows who do their own work; some cotton growing on irrigated land, which will provide quite a bit of seasonal work; potash mines in the Southeastern part of the state, which, I have been told, will be closed down if, in our trade agreement with Russia, we let potash in free; and some copper, silver, and gold mining, also zinc and lead, in which there isn't much doing right now.

Because it affects both states — in Arizona, of course, it's the only industry — I may as well go into the mining business now. And that's what makes the prospects look better in Arizona than in New Mexico.

In the copper business, there's something in the air. The dope, as I get it, is that the mines are beginning to open up — to produce copper for munitions factories in Japan and Europe. There's some mystery about it. No copper man of course admitted to me that they are selling copper to foreign munitions plants. But that's what they tell their friends. It's just one of those things that seems to be known all over Arizona, without anyone saying anything about it publicly. I've heard it repeatedly. A businessman up in the town of Globe told me yesterday that one Arizona copper mine had sold all its last year's production to France, and that its export trade with France had jumped 50 per cent in 1933 over that of 1932. A mining man told a friend of mine in the state that Japan, once an exporter of copper, has become an importer, buying heavily.

The New Cornelia mine, at Ajo, near Tucson, is opening up. It is predicted that 400 men will be at work there by July 1. Some are already at work. I understand the superintendent of that mine is telling his friends its all foreign munitions business.

There are rumors — pretty well founded — that the Miami mine, at Miami, which has become almost a "ghost town" these last two years, is going to open up. Some men had been taken back yesterday, in an experimental leeching plant they have there.

Yesterday morning in the lobby of one of the hotels in Phoenix Miss Warner, the state relief administrator, ran into the Governor.[1] He told her confidentially that the Miami mine IS going to open up, but that "they are going to ease the men back gradually, a few at a time, to avoid labor trouble." The Miami mine, in its various activities, used to employ 3,000 men.

The effect, if the Miami mine actually does open up and start running full blast, on the two towns of Miami and Globe, should be marvelous.

Tucked away up in the mountains East of Phoenix, there they lie, two towns built on copper. There are three mines there: Miami, independently owned, which used to employ 3,000 men; Inspiration, which is rated as a subsidiary of Anaconda, although, I was told, Anaconda actually owns only about 30 per cent of its stock; and Old Dominion, which apparently is down for good. Inspiration, I was told by mining men, used to employ around 3,600 in its heyday.

Nobody seems to know just what the populations of the two towns are now. They used to be 8,000 or 9,000 each. Miss Warner thinks they are both down under 5,000 now. Registration figures and school enrollments, on the other hand, show only a slight decrease. One thing did happen. After they all closed down, hundreds of Mexican aliens who had been working in those mines were deported. Shipped back to Mexico.

You never saw more dejected looking places than Globe and Miami right now. Seventy per cent of the people are on relief, and God only knows what the rest are living on. Instead of thousands of men working in the mines, you have now a handful—100 or 150 superintendents, foremen, technical men, white collar men, key people, whom the companies don't want to lose—working as "watchmen," at from $50 to $100 a month. A man who once held a high salaried office position in one of those mines took me up there. He is now disbursing officer in the state relief office—and drives a 1926 Studebaker.

Half the store buildings in Globe and Miami are vacant—and apparently about half the houses, too. Those who haven't moved away have doubled up, to save on rent. Everything is going to ruin. Thousands of tons of rusted machinery. Old cars. The only new cars you see on the streets are those with out-of-state licenses, driving through. One of the most pathetic things I noticed was the showroom of the Cadillac-La Salle company. Not a car in it! And I'll bet they used to sell plenty of Cadillacs in Globe and Miami! * * * Nobody seems to have anything to do. They just hang around, moving listlessly along the streets. Why, on the main street of Miami you can hear an automobile start a couple of blocks away. * * * They tell me there are other mining towns in the state even worse off. In one of them is the wreck of what was once a good hotel. If you stay there now, they send up a wash bowl and a pitcher of water, although the place has modern plumbing. They don't get enough business to pay for the water to keep the plumbing going!

"We're just about at the end of our string," the relief administrator in Globe told me yesterday. "Our people just take whatever you give them. They don't even kick about it any more."

I got something of the same picture down at Bisbee and Douglas, in the Southeastern part of the state. There used to be two mines in operation at Bisbee and two smelters at Douglas. They merged, and now you have one mine and one smelter, working part time and employing, part time, less than 2,000 men, instead of 7,000 or 8,000! Because of the merger, the county relief director estimates that there are 1,200 stranded families in those two towns — 1,200 heads of families who never will get their jobs back, no matter how much the copper industry picks up. It's probably larger. Harry Clark, superintendent of the smelter at Douglas, is a member of the state board of public welfare. He told me that in Douglas alone there were between 600 and 700 men who would never get back into the smelter. And 75 per cent of these people are white American citizens.

"At first they tried to find work in other places," the relief director told me. "Many went up to Boulder Dam, and hundreds of them did get work there. Many started wandering. They're coming back to us now — some of them have been from Coast to Coast — penniless, tired out, old, discouraged."

The state of mind of people living in those towns could hardly be happy. I should think they'd go crazy. I would. Mostly they seem to be apathetic. There wasn't even much discussion of the copper code, which went into effect a week or so ago. * * * The publisher of a newspaper in Bisbee, owned by the Phelps-Dodge corporation, earnestly assured me that he believed Dr. [William Albert] Wirt[2] was a patriot! Don't you see? That man is AFRAID. He and his little job face extinction. There was fear in his eyes as he spoke. They're afraid of everything, including the New Deal. I suppose he is afraid that, if the New Deal goes through, it will put the corporation out of business, and he'll lose the little job he's hanging onto so desperately in that hopeless little town. And he is therefore quite willing to believe anything he hears about the New Deal and anyone connected with it.

And so, you can see what it's going to mean to these towns like Bisbee and Douglas and Globe and Miami if the mines open up — to sell copper abroad, for munitions. To the whole state, for that matter. . . .

Anaconda Copper company keeps the Inspiration mine closed. Although it owns only 30 per cent of the stock, it got the Inspiration mine listed as its subsidiary under the code and in the production allowance. Production was allocated, not on a basis of the output of each mine, but to the Anaconda Copper company as a whole. On the ground that they can mine copper more cheaply in Montana than in Arizona, they keep the Arizona mine closed and mine their allowance in Montana. Therefore, Inspiration mine isn't very apt to open up right away!

Aside from mining, there isn't much to look to in this state. If the mines are running, the state is prosperous, and everybody has work. If they aren't, the state is in bad shape, and there aren't any jobs. That's about the situation.

Some stock raising and farming—the second-ranking industry in the state. Bad now, both because of low prices for beef and because of drouth. This seems to be another of those states that are drying up! Water getting scarcer all the time and more expensive. Marvelously fertile land—when they can get water. Otherwise, desert.

So much for private industry's prospects for providing jobs for people.

On PWA, here, in New Mexico, in Texas—I can't see much to cheer about. Where there are Federal projects, there is more hope. Texas is benefitting greatly in that respect. Down at San Antonio, for instance, where they are about to start $4,500,000 worth of construction on Army property. Several other big Federal projects will help some. There's some PWA road work going on, too. That helps. But, on the whole, PWA really isn't being felt here.

. . . In Albuquerque, where there are right now 1,000 families on relief, 23 men are now working on a PWA job. Between now and about September 1, 60 will be employed. And the job will be finished about September 1. Sixty more MAY get PWA jobs for a few weeks if two other projects, approved, but unable to start because the legal and financial negotiations are not yet complete, really get going. And in the whole state, 78 now employed, with the prospect of jobs for less than 500. Certainly can't see anything to cheer about in that.

They certainly aren't doing any cheering about PWA in Arizona. The state PWA chairman, I was told, spent SEVEN MONTHS in Washington trying to get things going and finally gave up in disgust and came home.

Arizona, I understand, is listed as having been allotted $40,275,000 of PWA money. Of that, some $14,000,000 is charged against the state for Boulder Dam. Miss Warner made a special trip up there to see if she could get jobs for some Arizona unemployed. She had no luck at all. Another $10,000,000 is a road grant. That is mostly spent or under contract now. It hasn't provided enough jobs so that it's even felt. Four million goes into the Verdi irrigation project, a federal project. That's doing some good. Sixty-five men are working now, engineers and the like, on preliminary surveys. Work will probably start sometime within the next three months. No estimate available on the number of men to be employed. I was told PWA is putting several million into the Indian reservations in Arizona. Doesn't help us a darned bit. The work is given to the Indians themselves—enough I was told, so that they are quitting Navajo rug weaving. . . .

1. Benjamin B. Moeur.
2. Superintendent of schools in Gary, Indiana, who made headlines in 1934 when he charged that Roosevelt was "the Kerensky of our American Revolution" and that the New Deal was planning to overthrow American institutions.

To Harry L. Hopkins

Dayton, OH, May 25, 1934

Dear Mr. Hopkins:

I visited yesterday for the first time a subsistence homestead unit.

I can hardly describe to you its effect on me. This may sound awfully egotistical, but one must have seen what I've been seeing these last few weeks and heard what I've heard to understand, that's all.

The homestead, backed by the Department of the Interior, but tied up with the cooperatives here, which are operating on a grant from us, consists of 160 acres of land in the gently rolling country just outside of Dayton. Thirty-five families are to live there. Some of them are already there, living in temporary shacks which, as soon as their houses are finished, are to be turned into outbuildings. All of them have got their land in shape and their crops planted. Several of the houses are nearing completion, and I visited one family whose house was completed and occupied.

These families are of the same type as the white collar people I've been talking with these last few weeks — the people I've been so worried about. And what a contrast!

Instead of hopeless, afraid, whipped people, yesterday I found people busy, smiling, planning — actually happy! Honestly, the contrast simply bowled me over!

We visited first the family living in its new home — a neat, clean five-room cottage. You should have seen the expression of contentment on that woman's face as she showed me around her new house, with its roomy fireplace, its wide, clear windows, rugs on the floor and a cover on the couch that she had woven herself, on a hand loom!

Outside, their garden and feed crop were well started — strawberries almost ripe. There was a big flock of chickens, all in grand condition, some ducks, a sow with four fat, healthy looking pigs, some rabbits, which they are raising for meat. It all looked wonderful.

They've worked hard, these people. They moved out there last fall and spent the winter in what is now their barn. Dr. Elizabeth Nutting, head of the cooperative units here, told me that the woman was sick for several weeks. But they pulled through, and, as the woman said:

"It's no picnic, but we're coming out alright, and, when we get through, we'll have something."

Everywhere, as we drove around over the farm, they were at work in their gardens, men and women, and, I tell you, it was grand to see them grin and wave as we went by, to feel their firm handclasp when they came over to talk with us. Gosh, you've no idea what a difference between them and those poor devils I talked with in Montgomery and Houston and Tucson and Albuquerque! I just can't describe it!

One of the best things about this particular unit is the low cost of their homes and land. I don't know that this is actually true,* but, judging by the figures different homesteaders gave me, I imagine not one of those thirty-five families will be in debt over $1,000 when they move into their houses! And there's where the cooperatives, in which we are interested, come into the picture.

The thirty-five participants purchased the land as a unit. Each family has been assigned about three acres, which, according to the state college of agriculture, will supply enough garden truck for a family of five and feed for "three goats or half a cow." Most of them are getting goats. Some of the land is being held for community pastures, a park, roads, school property, and a community house. To amortize the debt and pay taxes, each family pays rent for its land.

On their buildings they go into debt only for the materials. The houses are being built BY THE PEOPLE THEMSELVES, under skilled supervision of course. They have made themselves into a sort of building unit, everybody putting in a certain number of hours per week until all the buildings are finished. The average cost of those houses — and they are good houses, too — is somewhere in the neighborhood of FIVE HUNDRED DOLLARS. Outbuildings, seed loans, loans for the purchase of stock, and so on will bring the debt per family up to a little over $800, on the average.

All the carrying charges — land rent, house, insurance, everything — total, on an average, around $20 a month! And I believe they are given fifteen years in which to pay off the debt. Actually a family with a very small income has got a chance out there.

One of the homesteaders, a former teacher, figured out with me that with careful management a family of five could get by out there on $40 a month cash! That allowed $10 a month for staple groceries, the things they can't raise, and $10 a month for other things, including shoes for the children. Most of their clothes they can get through the cooperative units here in Dayton. . . .

Dr. Nutting tells me that none of the families out there will have a cash income of less than $50 a month.

While I was jubilant, I found Dr. Nutting and the others in charge of the cooperative units and the homesteads here most unhappy yesterday. They've struck some pretty tough snags. Their chief worry right now is that, after being told to go ahead, select their homesteaders, and buy four more farms for four more units, they received yesterday from Washington a wire telling them to hold everything up, pending an investigation of their whole set-up. They haven't had the courage yet to tell the prospective homesteaders.

I don't know yet exactly what the trouble is, but apparently they've

* It *is* true, I am told.

run into opposition politically here in Dayton. Dr. Nutting and Mrs. [George] Wood, who have been in this thing now for nearly two years and have taken some awful beatings, are worn to a frazzle. They've become so sensitive that everything seems worse to them than it probably really is.

Dr. Nutting hasn't given me a complete account of their side of it yet. Last night, however, I dined with Mrs. George Shaw Greene, one of the most prominent women in Dayton, who gave me a fairly objective account. Mrs. Greene's role in all this business is more that of an observer than of a participant. She is on the board, has had plenty of chance to watch developments, but hasn't become so deeply involved that she is apt to get too excited. Incidentally Mrs. Greene is a businesswoman — a broker, of all things!

"The whole thing is absolutely sound," she assured me, "both the cooperatives and the homestead plan. The cooperatives may not have been managed as efficiently as they might have been, but there's been no willful waste of money. One of the difficulties has been that we tried to develop leadership among the unemployed themselves, to run the cooperatives. It proved disappointing. In time that leadership may develop. The ideal way would be for the unemployed to take over the management of their cooperatives and run them themselves. But they apparently are not ready yet. I don't think that is a thing to worry about, however. And what Dr. Nutting and Mrs. Wood have done for the morale of those people, with their cooperatives, is almost beyond belief. I honestly think we might have had trouble here, such as they've had in Minneapolis and out in Kansas, if it hadn't been for the cooperatives. They've certainly made themselves felt.". . .

In the meantime, nothing can go ahead on the other four homestead units, the homesteaders can't get their crops in — after being promised that they could, on the authority of representatives of the Department of the Interior, they say here — money that has actually been allocated to the unit now under way is slow coming, with the result that their credit is being hurt, purchase of materials is delayed, and work on the houses is held up, and Dr. Nutting, Mrs. Wood and others who have put in nearly two years working on this thing are heartsick and about ready to give up. There seems to have been a stream of investigators of one sort or another out here, but nothing happens.

Of the cooperatives — I've seen a couple now, in Richmond and here — my feeling, so far, is that "it's just a baby, clumsily learning to walk, but a darned healthy one." I'm getting a closer view of the show here this afternoon and tomorrow, and I'll write you again in a day or two.

I'll say this much — that in the cooperatives, here and in Richmond, I've seen in the last few days more smiling faces than I'd seen in weeks before. . . .

To Harry L. Hopkins

Dear Mr. Hopkins:

Herewith a few observations on self-help cooperatives.

Of course I don't know much about them yet, but, after looking over a couple of them pretty carefully — the Citizens' Service Exchange in Richmond, Va., and the Dayton Association of Cooperative Production Units, at Dayton, O. — I have reached a few conclusions which, however, I freely admit I may have to drop as I see more of the cooperatives.

My approach to them has been that of one looking for some way out for the big load that I am convinced, after conversations with many employers, is never going to get back into private industry — that stranded generation I've been worrying about.

Incidentally, here is some more dope on that subject. In Dayton the relief administration has taken on a former personnel manager with General Motors to go over the relief load to weed out those who are employable and try to get jobs for them. She approaches it with a practical knowledge of the kind of people that are wanted in private industry. She hasn't gone far enough with the survey yet to have any figures, but I was told that she was simply flabbergasted at the large number of heads of families on relief who haven't a Chinaman's chance of getting back into private industry. And in the majority of cases, I was told, they are to be considered unemployable because they are beyond the age limit, which around Dayton — in plants like Frigidaire and the National Cash Register Company — is 45.

It's probably too early to tell whether the self-help cooperatives offer any solution of this problem. Those I've seen are still in a highly experimental stage, apparently. There's an idea there, I believe — and a promising one. But it hasn't been developed very far yet. . . . The Dayton outfit certainly has suffered from too much publicity.

Walter Locke, editor of Jimmy Cox's Dayton News, puts it something like this:

"It's an experiment, along a line that the American doesn't follow easily. It's hard to fit an American into any cooperative enterprise. He's too individualistic. He wants to set his own goal and attain it himself, in his own way. He doesn't like the idea of being regimented. I think that's fairly evident if you consider the reaction of many businessmen toward NRA.

"The American also wants to achieve things quickly. He has little patience. These cooperatives, if they are going to amount to anything at all, will have to be developed slowly. They're breaking new ground. But I think you'll find that your businessmen and your participants both are apt to get impatient with them — to look upon them as being too visionary because they don't attain perfection right away."

He may be right. I have encountered a good deal of distrust toward them — on the part of businessmen, participants, and social workers. There is a tendency to look upon them as "pipe dreams." And the fact that some of the people who are trying to put them over are a bit too zealous and ambitious, talk too much theory, perhaps, doesn't help them a bit. That's one of the troubles in Dayton.

It would seem to me at the moment that, if the self-help cooperatives are to offer any solution to the problem of those who are never going to get back into private industry, they must do two things: they must become self-sustaining, and they must be run by the participants themselves.

Those I've seen so far would appear to be a long, long way from becoming self-sustaining. The trouble is that they've got to have working capital. They might acquire that cash by selling their surplus if they had any market, but — they really haven't any market. And I don't see just where they'd be apt to find a market. It's a cinch they can't compete with private industry on a mass production basis, even if it were desirable for them to do so. And so far I haven't much faith in the idea of trying to earn a living by weaving on hand looms or making gadgets of wrought iron or wood. The market for that sort of thing, I should say, is pretty limited.

To illustrate how necessary it is to have a market:

The Dayton production units were going along pretty well — as long as the Dayton relief administration was running a commissary and was buying their output either for cash or on a barter basis for coffee, tea, sugar, and some of the other things the participants could not produce for themselves. But when the commissary was closed in January, it just about ruined the cooperative. They've lost their market.

The Exchange in Richmond is severely handicapped — or would be, if we weren't supporting it — by lack of a market. It hasn't a chance in the world of ever becoming self-sustaining unless it finds a market. And until it can supply EVERYTHING a family needs it will have to have some working capital. . . .

There appears to be among the participants a lamentable lack of what I term, for lack of a better expression, "good, sound business judgment." They want to proceed too fast — run away from themselves, so to speak. For instance, in Dayton, one unit used up a lot of the capital and ran into debt putting up a building! They didn't need the building, really. I don't think they should have been allowed to put it up. Another Dayton unit, consisting of eight families, has taken on a poultry farm outside the city. The man in charge, a former railroad worker, is extremely interesting. He was making bombs in his cellar, preparing to blow up one of the Dayton banks, I was told, when someone got him interested in the cooperative. The cooperative has done wonders for his morale, but — ye gods! He and the other seven families have gone something like $20,000 into debt — a lot of it to the cooperative — to buy and equip that farm. The man has apparently gone crazy on the subject of stock and equipment. He's got 7,000 chickens out there now — and God only knows how many he'll have when the eggs now in his huge incubator all hatch out. He's put up three buildings and wants to put up a fourth. He's talking about buying a herd of Jersey cows. And he wants a Diesel engine and an electric milking machine! These may be extreme cases, but I'm told, even by Dr. Elizabeth Nutting, that that's one of the reasons why you can't let the participants run the show themselves.

Another reason would seem to be human nature itself. There's no use talking — the strong will exploit the weak, if they get a chance, and human beings will play politics. . . .

So there you are: they haven't yet found a way of becoming self-sustaining, apparently, and, judging by Dayton's experience, the unemployed so far have not developed leadership capable of running them.

If they are to continue with working capital coming in from the outside, it seems to me that they must have public opinion behind them.

There may be something in what Walter Locke says about the natural distrust of the American businessman for anything as slow-moving and as visionary as a self-help cooperative. But I think public opinion will depend largely on local situations. Certainly the idea of people on relief working for what they get should appeal to the public. There may be a certain amount of resistance from retail merchants — they tell me there was here in Lansing at the start — but that can be worn down. The self-help idea shouldn't be hard to "sell."

As a matter of fact, public opinion in Richmond seems to be strongly behind the cooperative there. In Dayton it is not. Here's why:

The two dominant figures in the Dayton cooperative unit have been, as you may know, Dr. Nutting and Ralph Borsodi.[1]

Borsodi, right from the start, would be at a disadvantage in a city like Dayton. His name is against him. Dayton is in the Hinterland. It doesn't trust "foreigners." Borsodi apparently failed to "click" with Dayton businessmen. They think he's visionary, too much of an idealist, although all of the people who have given me this slant believe he is absolutely sound and, on the subsistence homestead plan, with its low cost houses, has done a swell job. But Dayton would have to be shown, and it isn't willing to wait for results.

Both Borsodi and Dr. Nutting apparently talk too much — in an idealistic sort of way that is over the heads of the people of Dayton. For instance right at the start, says Mr. Locke, Borsodi talked about FIFTY subsistence homestead units in the vicinity of Dayton. Here was the reaction:

The real estate men, with plans for developing suburban residence districts, yelled:

"Hey, where do we come in? This is going to ruin us!"

And the contractors, seeing all that business slip out of their hands, and the building supply people, assuming that, if subsistence homesteads were to be built on that scale, the supplies would be bought wholesale, and they wouldn't get any of it, joined in the wail. Get the idea? . . .

It's this sort of thing — a kind of failure to understand the public opinion of a town like Dayton — that gets these people into trouble. Then, when a lot of soreheads, believing a lot of lies which they've never taken the trouble to investigate, run down to Washington and yell, they can't get the support they need from the really solid, dependable citizens. That, in a nutshell, is what is the matter in Dayton.

Some of the good, solid people, like Locke and Mrs. Greene, who really know what Borsodi and Dr. Nutting are doing, believe in them. They think they should be permitted to go ahead and finish the job. But a lot of people in Dayton look on Borsodi and Dr. Nutting as "theorists," "visionaries," and so on. They don't trust them. I daresay that, if the subsistence homestead unit they have started works out as well as it promises, the time may come when people in Dayton will say Borsodi and Dr. Nutting were right. But in the meantime, they should be protected — from themselves, I guess. In other words, they shouldn't be allowed to talk.

Of course you're going to get that charge that the people running the cooperatives are "visionaries." Well, they are. You have to be a visionary to run a cooperative.

I daresay there has been a good deal of inefficiency in the management of the cooperatives, both in Richmond and in Dayton. The only enemies that the cooperative in Richmond has, apparently, are the politicians who run the Department of Public Welfare. For one thing, they're sore because it wasn't turned over to them I daresay. . . .

I have the feeling that many of them regard the cooperative as only a makeshift. Just something to carry them through until they can get jobs. I have the impression that the majority of them, were they offered jobs in private industry, would say, "To Hell with this!" and rush to the job. Perhaps that's just as well, but, if that's the way they feel, I wonder how happy the permanently unemployed would feel in cooperatives. Some of the participants struck me as being a little wistful — still hoping against hope that they might be able to get their "real jobs" back. Of course they faced a test when CWA came in. In Richmond, I was told, relatively few went over. In Dayton, I gather, they all tried to get CWA jobs!

One of the things that interested me most in Richmond was their turnover. They carry in the Exchange there about 600 families. In 1933 200 of the participants — about a third of the membership — got permanent jobs in private industry! Mrs. Amy A. Guy, who runs the cooperative, is building up one of the most effective free employment agencies you ever saw. You see, in the cooperative the workers are able to maintain their occupational skills. Also, she is in a position to KNOW whether a man can fill a job or not. Apparently employers have grown to trust her. Many of them call her up regularly whenever they have a job to offer.

One thing — the cooperative offers a grand way to provide adequate relief cheaply. In Richmond, for instance, they get three dollars of relief for one dollar expended! In April, the average family on relief in Richmond got something like $8.86 for the month. Families in the Exchange got about $20 worth of relief — at a cash cost of around $7 per family! And on the whole — although they may regard the Exchange as a stop-gap and wish they could have a little money in their pockets once in awhile — I can well believe that the morale of the people in the Exchange was better than that of the people on relief. One trouble is, though, that most of the families in the Exchange — no, I beg your pardon, about a third of them — have to have relief orders for things like coffee and sugar and tea. The others manage to pick up enough work for cash outside to get those things.

The one thing I have seen that I'm absolutely sold on is that subsistence homestead unit at Dayton. I guess I talked with practically all of the homesteaders. They are grand. And the thing that gave me the biggest kick of all was the fact that EVERY DARNED ONE OF THEM stands a swell chance of paying out. None of them will be in debt $1,000 when they move into those new houses out there. They can see how this thing is going to work. And so can I.

A lot of the antagonism toward subsistence homesteads in Dayton developed among wealthy people who live just outside the city, in Washington township. They all have fine estates out there. They were given all sorts of misinformation — for instance, that the Negro unit, very unwelcome to Daytonians anyway, was going to be out there, that the people weren't going to pay any taxes, that the houses were going to be shacks. They even went so far as to hire a lawyer and start injunction proceedings, I believe.

Last Friday Walter Locke, who is very enthusiastic about the unit, took half a dozen of the most antagonistic of those gentlemen out to see the place. All the way out, he said, they kept talking about shacks, rural slums, and all that sort of thing. He said they got the surprise of their lives.

They were looking over one of the houses — a very attractive stone cottage — when Mr. Locke turned to a bank president, one of the group, and said:

"How much money would you be willing to lend on that house when it is finished?"

"Twelve hundred dollars," the banker, one of the most bitterly antagonistic men in the crowd replied.

"And how much," asked Mr. Locke, "do you think the owner could have got from a building and loan association back in the boom days?"

"Five thousand, easily," the banker replied.

"Well," said Mr. Locke, "the owner of that house will actually be in debt for it a little over $500 when he moves in."

They ran into one young chap out there among the homesteaders whom they all knew. He had been a friend of the son of one of the men, but, with the loss of his job, had dropped out of sight. They had a long talk with him. He showed them, as he showed me, all his plans, his ground, with the crop all in, talked the whole thing over — enthusiastically, hopefully. Oh, gosh, you've no idea of the contrast between the way those people feel and the way our white collar and skilled labor clients feel!

On the way back to town, Mr. Locke said, one of the men said:

"Well, I'd hate to put myself in the position of preventing that chap from carrying out his plans!"

I spent one hour in the relief office in Dayton Saturday. It was enough. Same old story.

"They're restless," I was told. "They're tired of being out of work. They want jobs, salaries, a normal way of living. We don't know what's going to happen. Many of them are realizing now that they aren't going to get back into private industry. God only knows when they'll break loose!"

You feel that restlessness all through this part of the country. It just seems to be a settled thing in people's minds that there's going to be a lot of trouble — strikes, riots.

Take that Toledo situation.[2] The papers said that out of a mob of 3,000, only 300 had ever worked in the plant, were actually strikers. Undoubtedly there were some outside agitators, but certainly not 2,700 outside agitators. Who were, then, those people who were so desperate that they were willing to get out there and face National Guards' rifle fire over something that was none of their business — people who never had had jobs in that plant and never would have?

I'm afraid most of them were our relief clients. And I think most of the relief workers would agree with me on that. . . .

It's nice, for a change, to see things that are a little promising, even if they aren't perfect.

1. Economist and author actively concerned with moving urban dwellers into a cooperative rural or suburban setting.
2. Hickok was referring to the Auto-Lite strike.

To Harry L. Hopkins

Enroute to Knoxville, Tenn.   May 31, 1934

Dear Mr. Hopkins:

I read with interest and pleasure in the morning paper Tuesday that the Michigan relief load had gone down a bit.

That afternoon, however, William Haber, the state relief director, bowled me over with the news — which the papers have NOT published — that the automobile industry in the last week had laid off more than 16,000 men: Ford, 7,000; Buick, 5,000; Hudson, 4,000; Oldsmobile, somewhere between 500 and 1,000.

The feeling seems to be that industry generally is in revolt against NRA and is throwing down the gauntlet to the President. Everybody apparently expects a lot of trouble along the industrial front this summer. In Michigan it's accepted — with a sort of curious calm by the relatively few people I met — that there will probably be a good deal of disorder before the summer is over. And some people think that the textile industry's request for a production curtailment was part of a general revolt, since it, too, may precipitate a big strike. A kind of sabotage, perhaps, on the part of industry? . . .

The main purpose, however, of my trip to Lansing was to have a look at Community Cooperative Industries, Inc., and that is what this letter is about.

Of the three self-help projects I've seen this one strikes me as being the strongest and the best. If it is permitted to go ahead with some encouragement and not too much interference, it may show the way whereby these things can be of some help in solving the problem of the permanently unemployed.

Its set-up is, of course, quite different from those of the other two I've seen, at Richmond, Va., and Dayton. It meets the objection I had against the other two, in that it actually is run by the unemployed — unemployed white collar men — and yet really it is less democratic than either of the others.

The Lansing unit is really modeled along the lines of private industry. It is run by a board of six unemployed white collar men, former business executives. They really play the role of employers. All the other participants are actually employees. The board has the right to hire or fire. The board members are not elected by the participants. Theoretically at least, they are selected by the advisory board of citizens. Everybody gets paid in scrip, including the board members, who are paid, not as directors, but for the work they do heading up the different departments.

One of them, F. H. Sawyer, a former industrial engineer, with a rather wide background as a business executive and employer of labor, is general manager — active boss of the whole show. A former state sales manager for an insurance company is assistant general manager. When I was in Lansing he was up in Grand Rapids, helping to reorganize along the lines of the Lansing unit the Grand Rapids outfit, which had not functioned very well. Another director, a former clergyman, is production manager. And so on down the line, each of the directors contributing his service in an executive capacity as head of a department and being paid entirely in scrip.

As originally set up the organization had nine of these working directors, including, in addition to those already mentioned, a former sales executive, a former banker, a former factory superintendent, a couple of former merchants, and a representative from one of the unemployed citizens' councils. There was a reorganization, several of the directors going back into private industry, and the present members of the board — led, I gather, by Mr. Sawyer — kicking out the representatives of the unemployed citizens' council and cutting the board down to its present size.

This may sound arbitrary. I think it was. But it undoubtedly has resulted in a good deal more efficiency in the unit. At least this unit impresses me as giving some promise of becoming eventually a self-sustaining, going concern. The others have not.

Here you have three kinds of self-help organizations:

Richmond, Va., in which the participants have no actual voice in the management and never have had, but who do have an organization that is permitted to work up ideas and make suggestions, to be decided upon by a board and management consisting of outsiders. In other words, in Richmond it's a matter of "doing something for the unemployed."

Dayton, where the participants themselves have tried to run the enterprise and have failed, apparently because they didn't have among them the proper leaders, with executive and business experience. The whole thing is now being reorganized, with control being taken away from the participants.

Lansing, where the participants — or rather a small number of the participants — are running the show, along private industrial lines, with

264

former executives serving as executives, with former employees serving as employees.

The idea of complete democracy in these units is perfectly lovely, but I'm skeptical about its working. Somebody's got to be boss that's all. People don't change fundamentally, even though they are unemployed. Their ambitions, their natures remain the same, and I can't see that being unemployed is going to make a business executive out of a man who has never had any training along that line at all.

Therefore, it would seem to me that a unit organized along the lines of that in Lansing would have a much better chance to succeed than one in which the rank and file of the participants were trying to manage it. One criticism might be that the former executives now out of employment and available to run these units really are not successful executives — that they wouldn't be out of work if they were. I don't think that's true. Not right now. It may be that, if things continue to improve, the best of the unemployed executives will get their jobs back, but right now I believe there are plenty of them out of work, good men, perfectly capable of handling this thing. And incidentally these are the people who are hardest to fit into any work relief program. Well, here's a chance for them.

I have gone into this at some length because a good deal of pressure is being brought to bear on the Lansing unit to reorganize, along more democratic lines. They are considering taking on another director, out of the ranks, so to speak. Mr. Sawyer — who told me he had recently turned down a good job in private industry to stay with this thing, "although my wife would kill me if she knew it" — says he's through if anything is done to take control out of the hands of the type of directors now running the project. . . .

The Lansing unit is facing a lot of problems constantly. They all are. Sawyer says they have made many, many mistakes. Well, that's bound to happen. But there was a businesslike air about that place that impressed me greatly. I believe those people have a chance to succeed.

They haven't so many activities as some of the others. They've gone through that period. Some of their activities were wiped out when they came under a federal grant. A garage, for instance, where they did work for the public on a cash as well as a barter basis. One of their best stories is about paying an undertaker's bill by repainting the undertaker's hearses!

They have a very good bakery, which was almost wiped out by the new relief set-up a few months ago. When the city of Lansing was handling relief, it bought, on a basis half cash and half barter, some 3,500 loaves of bread a day from this bakery. Under the new county set-up, the social worker in charge has ruled that this cannot be done — that the unemployed must have grocery orders which they can cash anywhere they please. In other words, no commissary of any sort.

Even so, the bakery stands a chance of becoming a well paying proposition in time. They have developed there a new kind of health bread out of dehydrated vegetables. It's good bread, too. I ate some of it. Batten, Barton, Durstin & Osborne, Bruce Barton's big advertising firm, has a branch office in Lansing, and its management has become interested in the possibilities of developing this product. I understand that Bruce Barton is going to be out in Lansing sometime next month to take a look at it. Sawyer and the others seem to think this bread could go on the market, in spite of the federal grant, because there is no other bread like it now on the market. Well — there's a possibility, you see. Just how long the man who developed the formula — an old, broken down baker, with asthma and no capital — would be willing to stay in the unit if he saw a chance to make a lot of money for himself is something I'm wondering about. Sawyer thinks he'll stick. If they are going to get anywhere, I should think the unit better get a patent on the formula.

They aren't making clothes in the Lansing unit any more — cheap, shoddy, badly made "relief clothes." They are doing very little hand work. Instead, they've borrowed a power loom from a woolen mill and have set it up in their shop. The mill has lent them a man to show them how to use it, and they are starting out to make real, honest-to-goodness blankets and suiting. At Owosso there is a big, cooperative colony some years old, where they raise a lot of sheep. Negotiations are about to be started whereby the Owosso colony is to furnish the wool, to be carded there or in Lansing, in return for cloth. In time a tailor shop may be set up — but not unless they can find people to do the tailoring who know how. If that isn't done, they'll work out some sort of barter plan with a tailor — so much cloth, for so many suits. It has possibilities, I think.

One of the commodities that is bothersome in Richmond and Dayton is sugar — how to get it without paying out cash from the working capital. The Lansing unit has put in a big crop of sugar beets on its farm this year. Arrangements have been made to have the crop converted into sugar at a privately owned mill, on a barter basis. They are also counting on being able to exchange a surplus of canned vegetables from their farm with local grocers for coffee and tea, cleaning powder, and so on. As a matter of fact, they've got the barter idea worked out so far that they do pretty well toward supplying all the needs of the group, putting every cent of their grant money that they can into equipment and stock. They will succeed only as they reduce the amount of federal money they have to put into "working capital," they feel.

Their future depends on two kinds of market — one furnished by other units around the country, the other by the general public whenever federal aid is withdrawn. By reducing his payroll, now around 150, one half, Sawyer thinks he probably could get by now without federal aid, except what is needed for buying equipment, but Haber thinks they wouldn't last over six months. Haber is probably right. But I can see where they might get on a self-sustaining basis in time.

Right now they are concentrating a good deal on their farm — which also constitutes something of a problem. The farm, formerly used as a state training school for boys, has been offered to the Federal Government by the state for use for subsistence homesteading or allied projects, with the provision that, if the Government ever ceases to use it for any of those purposes, it reverts back to the state. They took on the farm with the understanding that they were to have a grant from the Department of the Interior to set up a subsistence homestead project thereon. Now, it seems, the Subsistence Homesteads division questions the terms set by the state. They want clear title to the land, and the state's terms, they said, do not provide it. So the whole thing is a bit up in the air.

So far, the Lansing unit has invested about $3,500 in the farm — seed, stock, and equipment. There are some grand dairy buildings on it, in good shape. They have bought carefully, Sawyer says, always with the possibility that they might have to get rid of the stuff a year from now, in mind. For instance, they bought eight big black Percheron work horses. Good stock. But when they bought them they had an understanding with a dairy, that uses exclusively horses of that type for its delivery wagons, that it would take them over if they ever had to dispose of them. By a dicker with the John Deere Plow company they got their machinery at a very low cost. By repainting it and taking good care of it, Sawyer says, they could undoubtedly sell it next spring for very little less than they paid for it. They're going slowly out there on their farm, it seemed to me, and on a sound basis. For instance, instead of buying thousands of chickens, they are starting with a small flock of very good Rhode Island Reds and will let the flock build up of itself. It sounds and looks sensible. Of course I'm only a novice, but it seems to me that the things they are doing are well balanced, sane. And that's what you get when you have people with some business background running a thing.

Their subsistence homestead project sounds interesting. The first unit is to consist of 50 families. To be eligible, a family must be on relief or eligible for relief, and preference is to be given to families where the wage-earner is beyond the age limit for employment in private industry. They've set the ages from 40 to 55. The management will consist of the directors of the Lansing cooperative unit, plus one director selected by the Government. All land not used by the homesteaders — is to be used by the Lansing cooperative unit as a farm. The number of homesteaders would be increased eventually up to 325.

Each homesteading family is allotted one acre of ground. This was done on the advice of the agricultural experts of the University of Michigan, who said one acre was enough if they don't have stock. They are to be allowed to have goats if they like, but the cooperative farm will maintain the dairy cattle and produce the major crops.

An agreement was made, Sawyer said, whereby the relief administration, as a works project, was to build the houses. Sawyer says he understands that this may be out because Washington has ruled that the state of Michigan cannot start any more work projects. I have a hunch, however, that it was just an oversight somewhere, and that it can be straightened out.

The houses, with electric lights, gas, and running water, are to cost about $1,900 apiece. The plots of land are to be permanently leased to the homesteaders.

Now here's how a man on the relief rolls, with no income at all, can get out there on a homestead:

The cooperative gets the cash from the Government and advances him credit for his house. The 50 homesteaders are to be covered by a group insurance policy, the premiums to be figured in their annual carrying charges.

The cooperative employs the homesteader, paying him in scrip enough to provide his living and his carrying charges. He pays back in scrip the amount of his carrying charges, about $30 a month covering his land rent, loan, taxes, insurance, repairs and upkeep. Out of some of the federal grant, the cooperative sets up a sinking fund, which it pays in cash. The homesteader doesn't handle any cash in the transaction at all. It is all handled by the cooperative. Of course, if he should get a job, he can pay in cash instead of in scrip. But if he never does get another job, he can still pay off in scrip to the cooperative.

It's a bit involved, perhaps — I'm wondering as I write just how that sinking fund is to be managed — but it's an interesting idea.

In addition to troubles about their land and pressure to democratize, the cash problem is bothering the Lansing unit, as it is the others. And this, I think, is the chief weakness in the whole system.

The participants are getting restless. They want some CASH. And that goes right up through to the directors. Sawyer is trying to make some arrangement whereby out of federal money his people can be paid 25 per cent cash for their work. And he rather wistfully suggested to me yesterday that FERA might take on the executives on a cash basis.

Well — there you are. You can't get away from it. That's the whole weakness of the cooperative. People — even people like Sawyer — get to wanting cash. And I'm afraid that is going to be the undoing of the cooperative.

All this stuff sounds a bit muddled, doesn't it? Well, the whole thing is new — and muddled. But it's damned interesting. And somehow I feel that, even if they expire when Federal relief is withdrawn, these cooperatives will have served a grand purpose. They haven't cost us much, and they were a whole lot better for the participants than relief would have been. Their morale undoubtedly is away above that of people on relief in the ordinary way. . . .

To Harry L. Hopkins

Florence, Alabama   June 6, 1934

Dear Mr. Hopkins:

A Promised Land, bathed in golden sunlight, is rising out of the grey shadows of want and squalor and wretchedness down here in the Tennessee Valley these days.

Ten thousand men are at work, building with timber and steel and concrete the New Deal's most magnificent project, creating an empire with potentialities so tremendous and so dazzling that they make one gasp.

I knew very little about the Tennessee Valley Authority [TVA] when I came down here last week. I spent part of my first day, in Knoxville, reading up on it. I was almost as excited as I used to get over adventure stories when I was a child. This IS an adventure!

Since then I have been traveling through the Valley and the state—a couple of days in Knoxville, a trip to the Norris dam and the town of Norris, a day's motoring across to Nashville, stopping enroute to look over a subsistence homestead colony a few miles from the Valley, a day in Nashville, a day's trip down here, visiting with farmers, relief workers, county agents in little towns along the way.

Today I saw the Wilson dam and went down into the power house—which is the best way, I found, to get an idea of how big this thing really is—and drove 20 miles on up the river to watch workmen drilling in rock to lay the foundations of the Wheeler dam.

I've talked with people who are doing this job, with people who live in the towns and cities that are going to feel the effects of this program, with ordinary citizens, with citizens on relief—as many kinds of people as I could find.

They don't all get so excited about it as I do. They criticize some features of the program. I have an impression that thousands of people right here in the Valley don't really know what it is all about. But the people—the people as a whole—are beginning to "feel" already the presence of TVA, even though it hasn't made any dent on our relief rolls.

Nearly 10,000 men—about 9,500—are at work in the Valley now, at Norris and Wheeler dams, on various clearing and building projects all over the area.

Thousands of them are residents of the Valley, working five and a half hours a day, five days a week, for a really LIVING wage. Houses are going up for them to live in — better houses than they have ever had in their lives before. And in their leisure time they are studying — farming, trades, the art of living, preparing themselves for the fuller lives they are to lead in that Promised Land.

You are probably saying, "Oh, come down to earth!" But that's the way the Tennessee Valley affects one these days.

Ten thousand men at work may not seem like so many when Tennessee still has a relief case load of 68,000 and Alabama around 80,000. But it's something. And there's no "white collar problem" in Knoxville these days. And people say to you, "Oh, we're lucky down here in Tennessee. TVA's a help!"

"Oh, I haven't heard anybody say anything about the Depression for three months," remarked a taxicab driver in Knoxville the other day. "Business is three times as good as it was a year ago. You ought to see the crowds at the ballgames."

Over in Nashville the attitude seems to be:

"Maybe we don't get so direct a benefit out of TVA as they get in Knoxville, but it will be coming eventually. And in the meantime, at least, Roosevelt is trying. He's doing something!"

Another way by which people hereabouts are being made aware of TVA is in the lowering of rates for electricity. They've been forced down already, even where the distribution is still in the hands of privately owned companies.

"I put in an electric hot water heater sometime ago," one man told me, "but I haven't been able to use it because it cost too much. But now, with this new rate, I can. I can run that, with all my other equipment — range, iron, mangle, vacuum cleaner, lights, and radio — for the same cost as I went without it before."

Before I leave the Valley, I'm going down to Tupelo, Miss., the first town to start buying its electric power directly from TVA, and see how they get along. Up here, one hears enthusiastic reports.

Well * * * Tennessee has got a huge job of rehabilitation on her hands. And with TVA setting up standards in rehabilitation, the rest of the state has got a long, long way to go.

Out of nearly 70,000 families on relief in Tennessee, probably 30,000 or more live in small towns or in the country. Many of these are in abandoned lumber and mining camps. Most of them who are farmers apparently are living on sub-marginal or marginal land.

Fairly typical, for Western Tennessee, I gather, was a district I visited yesterday. Table land. Thin soil. Terrible housing. Illiteracy. Evidence of prolonged undernourishment. No knowledge of how to live decently or farm profitably if they had decent land. . . .

Crops grown on it are stunted. Corn, for instance, grows only about a third as tall there as it does in Iowa. They tell me it isn't even good timber land. Just a thin coating of soil over rock. A county agent said it might make good orchard land, but any farming operation there should be under skilled supervision with authority to make farmers do as they were told.

Eastern Tennessee is worse, of course. There you see constantly evidence of what happens when you cut timber off mountain sides and plant crops there. There are great "bald patches" of rock on those mountains!

What to do with these people makes a nice little problem. Whether to move them off — and, if so, where to put them — or, on table land, for instance, where with careful and authoritative supervision they might eke out a living, leave them there and take a chance on their being absorbed in the industries that should be attracted down here by the cheap power furnished by TVA.

There might be, I should think, the possibility of a sort of temporary supervision. Rehabilitate the present adult generation where they are. Try out orchards instead of corn on the table land, for instance. And have it understood that their children are not to inherit that land, but that it will be taken over by the Government as they die, the Government to pay the heirs for it, either with cash or land somewhere else. The idea was advanced by Grace Falke, Secretary Tugwell's assistant, who has joined me on this trip. Help the parents to get at least a fairly decent living now and do a bang-up job of public health and education on the children.

This may sound wild, but I doubt if in Tennessee there is enough good land available for all of them.

Near Crossville, for instance, a subsistence homestead unit, with some of the loveliest little houses you ever saw, is being set up on about 12,000 acres of new land. They are starting out to raise mostly vegetables on it. The farm expert in charge says that the soil won't stand up under anything heavier, although it's good soil if handled expertly. They haven't been able to dig cellars under those houses because, if you go down 20 inches below the surface, you hit rock! I wonder if any sort of farming can ever be carried on permanently on soil that thin.

That homestead unit has the nicest houses I've seen anywhere. They are building them of a beautifully colored rock found on the place. They are grand houses, really. But it's the same old story. Each family moving in there will be somewhere around $2,500 in debt, and any definite plans for enabling those people to pay off those debts aren't in evidence. They seem to be trusting to God — and the Government.

Well — so far, Tennessee hasn't got far with any rural rehabilitation program. As you know, they've had a lot of administrative trouble.

They've at last got a rural rehabilitation man, out of the agricultural extension serivce. He's just finding himself. They're not thinking of rural rehabilitation in Tennessee for this year, but next year.

And all over the state, in the rural areas, the story is the same — an illiterate, wretched people, undernourished, with standards of living so low that, once on relief, they are quite willing to stay there the rest of their lives. It's a mess.

But then — there's TVA. It's coming along. My guess is that, whatever they do or don't do about rural rehabilitation down in Tennessee, in another decade you wouldn't know this country. And the best part of it is that here the Government will have control. There's a chance to create a new kind of industrial life, with decent wages, decent housing. Gosh, what possibilities! You can't feel very sorry for Tennessee when you see that in the offing.

To Eleanor Roosevelt

Florence, Alabama   Wednesday, June 6 [1934]

Dear You:

. . . Today has been strenuous. A field representative of the Tennessee relief administration came down with us, and this morning a field representative of the Alabama administration and the Alabama state transient director joined us.

We spent the morning in conference, took a quick look at the transient setup — thousands came here looking for work, you see, and present quite a problem — and spent the afternoon looking over Muscle Shoals — Wilson dam and power house, Wheeler dam, the houses they are building there for the engineers and their families, the construction camp, and so on. It's all on such a huge scale! But darned interesting. Always in the background, though, is this dreadful relief business — dull, hopeless, deadening. God — *when* are we going to get out of it? As nearly as I can figure it out, most of the relief families in Tennessee are rural, living on sub-marginal or marginal land. *What* are we going to do with them? And, so low are their standards of living, that, once on relief, low as it is, they want to stay there the rest of their lives. Gosh! TVA is now employing some 9,500 people. But it doesn't even make a dent! . . .

To Harry L. Hopkins

Florence, Alabama   June 7, 1934

Dear Mr. Hopkins:

Today I had my first look at our rural rehabilitation program actually under way. It was the most encouraging day I've had in many weeks.

Whereas Tennessee hasn't got a darned thing done on rural rehabilitation so far, Alabama's "victims" have their crops in! Their mules and steers have been bought and turned over to them. They're on their way.

Right here in Northwestern Alabama, in two counties, 83 farm families, colored and white, are now undergoing the process of rehabilitation. I visited half a dozen of those families today, saw their crops and their livestock, talked with them about their plans.

Alabama, as you doubtless know, has gone at this rehabilitation business on a very simple and, I think, practical basis.

First of all they set up a loaning organization, through which the money is distributed to the families on a loan basis. The farmer can pay back this loan in any one of three ways — cash, work, or surplus produce which the Relief Administration takes over and distributes to its clients in the towns as it distributes Federal Surplus commodities.

The loans are kept as small as possible — just enough to give him a start. Perhaps he needs a work animal. If he does, he is provided with a mule or a steer. Simple tools are provided. Fertilizer and seeds. And, of course, groceries and stock feed to carry him through until he harvests his crop. All these are figured in the loan. Loans to farmers I saw today ran from $49 to $165. I understand that they average around $80.

No land is being bought, for the present. Most of the families are being put on land that has been taken out of production and leased to the Government. Most of the families are tenant farmers. Before they are taken on, the landlord must sign a waiver, agreeing not to take any of the tenant's crop or profit this year for debt. The agreements extend from January to December, 1934. Landlords, on the whole, have been quite willing to sign the waivers. In return, their land is improved, under skilled supervision, houses repaired, and so on. None of the tenants is allowed to plant cotton, unless he agrees to turn it over to the relief administration. He will be allowed to sell none of his surplus crop. It all goes to the relief administration, to be counted against his debt. As a matter of fact, most of them will pay off their debts entirely with surplus produce and labor.

For his cash income, for clothing and so on, each of these farmers will be given preference on county road work, paid out of county funds. It's all arranged. Most of them, I understand, will be given a chance to earn about $60 or better in cash.

For the most part, the farmers to be rehabilitated this year have been selected carefully, by county rehabilitation committees, made up of the county relief director, the county agent, one businessman, and one farmer. The candidates were selected after a survey of all farm families on relief, made back in April. The idea is to start out this year with those most likely to succeed. These will be given further opportunities next year, if they make good this year, and next year, if the program goes on, less likely candidates may be taken on. It's all experimental this year, of course, and they want the best possible material to work with.

Supervision is supplied, under direction of the county agent — and they tell me that, in Alabama, the county agents are working into this program much, much better than the relief people had ever expected — by "cotton committeemen." These are farmers of the community who were selected to assist the county agents with the cotton reduction program. Good, practical farmers, who understand the people they are to work with. They are on a per diem basis and are supposed to visit the farmers under their supervision a certain number of times each month. Many have become so interested that they are working way overtime, without pay. . . .

It may seem to you that the Alabama plan is a bit niggardly — $40 mules, steers, borrowed land. But the thing does look practical. Instead of starting out with $2,500 houses, a lot of brand new, expensive equipment, and stock, these people are being given the things they actually need to get started — and on terms which they can meet. If the plan lives up to its promise, you see, these other things will come in time. Instead of starting out with them — and a heavy debt load — these people are going to be given a chance to earn them.

"What they all need mostly," the supervisor told me, "is somebody to handle their business affairs for them. Most of them can't read or write, you know. Never until this year have they been so situated that they actually knew what they owed. The landlords have kept the books on them. Now our job is to see that they get a new start, with someone to protect them."

Whether the landlords who have signed debt waivers this year will be in line trying to collect next year is a matter for conjecture. Many of them, however, have agreed to waive the debts entirely.

One feature about the Alabama program that may not be so good is that much of the rehabilitation is being done on borrowed land. No promise is held out to the farmer that he may be able eventually to buy that land. But there's no reason why, if he makes good, he shouldn't be enabled to buy land eventually. He is now being given a swell chance to establish his credit. As a matter of fact, businessmen are watching the experiment with keen interest. Frankly skeptical when I was down here in April, their attitude is beginning to change, I was told. Public sentiment is getting behind this thing. They're even beginning to believe in steers again!

As evidence of public interest, they cited me today the case of one wealthy landowner near Florence who has turned over a large tract of timber land for the use of rehabilitatable families for four years, free of charge. They can have all the timber they want, to build their houses, and the use of the land they clear. The plan is for the men themselves, under trained supervision, to build their own houses — log cabins. Those who at the end of the four-year period show promise of making good will be permitted to buy the land or take it on a long term lease.

I think one of the grandest things about all this is the attitude of the people themselves.

"You can hardly appreciate it, without having known them before," a county relief director told me. "They're off relief now, and there is in them a new kind of independence and self-respect."

One thing the Alabama Relief Administration has done that may seem a bit harsh. Where a tenant has been selected for rehabilitation, and the landlord refuses to sign a debt waiver, they take that family off relief and tell the landlord he has got to carry them. They are counting on public opinion to back them up in this stand. Too early to tell yet how it's going to work.

I also looked over today the transient setup here at Muscle Shoals. As might be expected, thousands of workmen have come in here in the last year expecting to get work in the Tennessee Valley. They seem to concentrate here, rather than up at Knoxville. Since last August, nearly 7,000 workmen have come here, registering at the transient bureau. More than 1,200 of them brought their families.

Right now in this area the transient bureau is caring for 700 single men and 300 family groups. During April 883 single men and 222 men with families registered at the bureau. But also during April 593 single men and men with families were sent home — many of them to jobs. A dozen or more, skilled men, actually did get TVA jobs.

They have a peculiar type in here — men who follow the big construction jobs, wherever they are, and have no legal residence. Skilled workmen, most of them of a high type.

Only a few of the single transients — about 90 — are quartered in barracks. All the rest are boarded in private homes in the towns. Families are placed in rented houses.

There has been very little trouble over them. This, probably, is why:

They have for work superintendent for transients in this area a landscape architect. He is a good one. Among other jobs, he did the Sesquicentennial grounds in Philadelphia a few years ago. A very high type of man. They got him off the relief rolls in Birmingham! . . .

Florence had only one small park when he came here — a dusty little park, right in the center of the town. But land has been set aside for parks in Florence 120 years ago.

The story is that Andrew Jackson, stopping here enroute to the Battle of New Orleans, picked this site for a town. He organized a land company and later brought over from Italy a man to lay out the city, which, incidentally, was named after the Italian's home town in Italy! In his plan was a park along a creek on the outskirts of the town. And that was the end of it until last fall, when the landscape architect came up here from Birmingham and began to look around for work for transients to do.

Today he escorted me through that park — a beautiful place, with its swimming pool, barbecue pits, excellent drainage system, lovely walks and bridle paths. And this is what the transients have done for Florence — this and two or three other smaller parks. As a result, transients are not unpopular in Florence! And — possibly another result — they have here transients who have been here for a year. Apparently, too, the residents of Florence regard them as perfectly acceptable citizens. It struck me as nice handling of what might have been a bothersome situation. And certainly the work they have done is beautiful.

I saw also today what became of some of the CWA wages paid in Florence.

There is a terrible housing shortage here. Families live all crowded up — sometimes two or three families in a couple of rooms. I saw families living in abandoned boxcars, shacks, tents — one family living in an abandoned trolley car, for which they pay $8 a month. It's all rather grotesque if you've driven first through the elaborately laid out subdivisions — the dream of real estate promoters back in the Muscle Shoals boom days — away out in the country, with streets laid out and marked with markers just like those in New York City, an abandoned country club, beautifully lighted boulevards, sidewalks away out in the country in cotton fields!

Well, after looking at some of this awful housing in the town, we drove out into a deep sort of canyon, along the railroad tracks. And there we found about 100 families, living in brand new shacks. No water. No sanitation. An awful mess, should any sort of epidemic start.

"All these men," the relief director told me, "were on CWA. And this is what they did with their money."

Some of them, on relief wages, are still working, finishing up a CWA job on the campus of Teachers' College in the town.

They are putting the finishing touches on a very handsome amphitheater, which will be a nice place for college theatricals when it doesn't rain.

When you think of the shacks they come from — shacks they built out of their CWA wages because they had no roofs over their heads, shacks so bare and uncomfortable and in such terrible surroundings — to work on an amphitheater that nobody is ever going to live in, that will hardly ever be used for anything —

Well, it all seems sort of silly, doesn't it?

To Harry L. Hopkins

Enroute, Memphis to Denver, June 11, 1934

Dear Mr. Hopkins:

. . . I wound up this last weekend in Memphis, where I saw several kinds of people, including:

One wealthy cotton man and banker who gives the impression that he thinks all tenants are lazy beggars and should be treated as serfs and would rather see the price of cotton stay down at 5 cents a pound forever than be boosted with Government control and Government insistence on any sort of fair play for sharecroppers and laborers.

The local political boss,[1] who assured me that everything was just too hunky dory, but who wasn't at all enthusiastic about the possibility of 3,000 transients now in Memphis remaining there forever.

A flock of social workers, who would like to see Tennessee have a good, strong public welfare department and are, they said, working toward that end, but whose approach to the relief problem is so typical of the old line social worker, supported by private philanthropy and looking down his — only usually it was HER — nose at God's patient poor, that it made me gag a little.

The conservative editor of the conservative Memphis Commercial-Appeal,[2] who thinks we've got a big rural relief load that will stay on our hands forever, if we don't drop 'em pretty soon, and who wonders if the people down in Tupelo, Mississippi, who are now getting their electricity for one third of what it used to cost them, aren't going to have to make up for it later on in higher taxes.

And the liberal editor of the Scripps-Howard newspaper,[3] who thinks the New Dealers aren't aggressive enough — don't do enough propagandizing.

One thing I've noticed particularly. That is that people outside the relief business aren't thinking much about it. They are more like they used to be last summer, when things were booming and, if they were conscious of relief at all, they were bored by it, not critical, just bored. CWA apparently aroused public interest in relief for a time. Now that's gone, and they've lapsed back into indifference. The comment you usually hear is, "You've got a lot of people on relief who are there to stay as long as you'll let 'em." And that's all they have to say. No criticism. No commendation. They're just indifferent.

On this trip I've tried not to be too preoccupied with relief. I've tried to find out what the people as a whole are thinking about — people who are at work. I carry away the impression that all over the area, from Knoxville, Tennessee, to Tupelo, Mississippi, and on up to Memphis and Nashville, people are in a pretty contented, optimistic frame of mind. They just aren't thinking about the Depression any more. They feel that we are on our way out and toward any problems that have to be solved before we get out their attitude seems to be, "Let Roosevelt do it." . . .

Outside of one town, there isn't any particularly militant labor leadership in Tennessee, apparently. So Toledo, the threatened steel strike, the labor difficulties elsewhere in the textile industry, and troubles down around Birmingham seem to make little impression in Tennessee. You don't see much evidence of restlessness.

There apparently isn't much among the people on relief, either. That may be due to the fact that in Tennessee the number of skilled workmen and white collar people on relief is relatively small. The load is largely rural, of a class of people whose incomes normally and whose standards of living are so low that relief does not seem inadequate to them at all. They are quite satisfied with it. The problem is going to be getting them off.

Everywhere, even though the relief loads remain large, you hear the same story. Business has picked up. Retail sales and advertising in Memphis, for instance. I was told that no city in the South has received greater benefits from the cotton program than has Memphis, a shipping and trading center. Down in Tupelo everybody seems to be feeling grand. Garment factories and a textile mill are going peacefully along under the code, the Chamber of Commerce is getting inquiries from industries attracted there by the low power rate, and the proprietor of a 38-room hotel relates with satisfaction how she operates her hotel, with lights, fans in all rooms, two vacuum cleaners, two electric irons, refrigerator, and radio with an electric bill of around $20 a month.

Incidentally there are now in Tupelo six companies selling electric equipment, including both the expensive kinds and the new, cheaper models put out by the manufacturers in agreement with TVA. They say that in 17 days, after the new models were brought in, 137 refrigerators were sold and 17 ranges — that one dealer sold in one week 21 units, i.e., stoves or refrigerators.

Differences in prices between the regular equipment and the new models, not quite so deluxe, run something like this: electric refrigerators, top standard price $137, new price $80; hot water heaters, top standard price around $95, new top price $60; ranges, top standard price $137, new top price $80.

When I was in Tupelo they had no figures to show just how much electric equipment had been sold, but I was impressed with the figures of one dealer, who handles only the high priced stuff. In less than a month he had sold ten refrigerators and five ranges. And Tupelo is only a small town, about 6,000 population.

It is still a little early to see what the new electric rate is going to do for householders and farmers in and around Corinth and Tupelo. I went down there thinking perhaps I could see some urban housewives and farm wives actually using the electric refrigerators and stoves that they'd never have had in their lives if it hadn't been for TVA. But it hasn't reached that class yet. New wiring is just being begun — 10 miles of it in Tupelo! But it's going along. Dealers say they are taking orders from farmers right along. One thing they are doing is to cut down greatly the cost of wiring a house. For instance, in Tupelo it used to cost as high as $60 to have an electric stove installed in your house. It now costs $5.

Even though I was disappointed in not being able to find in Tupelo and the surrounding country housewives using electric equipment that they had never expected to have, I felt that my trip was not in vain. Private industry, to a large extent, in Tupelo has actually tried out the subsistence homestead idea! And it seems to work!

It began back in 1923 with one garment factory, the management of which adopted a policy of hiring only workers who lived out in the country, on their own little farms. The movement spread. There are in Tupelo two garment factories and a textile mill that employ a total of around 2,000 people, and of these, I was told, only 700 or 800 live in town. Busses collect the workers from their farms, averaging around 15 acres each, every morning and bring them to work. And each evening take them home. As a matter of fact, they are school busses. They bring the workers into town first, then take the children to school, and in the afternoon they take the children home and then come after the workers.

People generally around Tupelo are pretty keen about the idea after having seen it in operation for several years. Relief workers told me that very, very few of the workers who lived that way had appeared on the relief rolls. One young man, a clerical worker in one of the garment factories, told me how it works out for him. He has a 10-acre farm, about three miles from town. Has a cow, some pigs and chickens, garden, some pasturage, a good comfortable house. Raises practically everything he eats.

"As a matter of fact," he said, "except for what I pay out for clothes and the upkeep of my car, the salary I earn here in the factory is just about all net profit! And I've got the place, all clear of debt, to go to if anything happens to my job."

They are setting up near Tupelo a subsistence homestead unit to which no one will be admitted who hasn't a job. Most of them are employed in the garment factories. Well, at least those people have a reasonably good chance of being able to pay their way out. . . .

You certainly don't hear much about the drouth down here. We are now traveling through Arkansas, and the country looks grand. They're harvesting, winter wheat apparently. Cornfields look good, and the stock is fat.

Well, despite drouth and pig-headed capitalists and labor leaders, people who don't have to be on relief but want to, and people who have to be on relief and hate it, the machine that takes jobs away from men, stupidity and indifference on the part of the public toward what we are trying to do, and all the other things there are to worry about — it's

279

funny, but I believe that probably in many large areas of the United States right now 90 percent of the people are perfectly happy and contented, working along, thinking, as Rex Tugwell says, "mostly about baseball and the races!"

That's probably true in much of the territory I covered in my last trip before this one. Only I stuck too close to the relief picture, I guess, and couldn't see anything else.

1. Edward H. Crump.
2. An apparent reference to Thomas Fauntleroy, managing editor.
3. Edward John Meeman of the *Press-Scimitar*.

To Eleanor Roosevelt

Akron [Colorado], June 15, 1934

. . . Well, we entered the Colorado drouth area today — in hail and a cloudburst! It was very funny really. As we drove out of Fort Morgan, about 35 miles west of here, young Terry Owens, one of the field engineers who is driving us about, announced with a flourish, "You are now in the drouth area." He had hardly got the words out when simultaneously we got a flat tire and it started to pour! Hail, too! And there has been a severe electric and hail storm here tonight, with a regular cloudburst. They had one last night, too, and they now consider the drouth broken in this part of the state. Too late to save the small grains, but they think there will be plenty of good grazing and possibly some corn. The rain, after its long delay, brought tragedy to some. One farmer, living on lowland, lost all his stock in last night's rain. Forty-two head of cattle, all drowned. Isn't it ironic? Yesterday he was worrying about his cattle starving to death because the drouth had burned up all their food. Today his stock was all dead anyway, drowned, and everything else swept away — his house and his barns under water. The heavy rains may change our itinerary. They have only dirt roads down where we had planned to go tomorrow. They don't look promising now, and, if it rains all night, as it seems about to do, we can't get through. That means we'll go back to Denver tomorrow instead of Sunday. . . .

We spent most of today tramping around in the beet fields. I had my first look at child labor — children 8 and 10 years old working in the beet fields. It was not a nice picture. I ought to write a report tonight, but I've gritted my teeth so much these last two days that the roof of my mouth is all raw. So I think I'd better take said teeth out and go to bed. If I don't I may not be able to wear them at all tomorrow! Tired tonight, but not nearly so tired as last night. . . .

To Harry L. Hopkins

Denver, Colorado, June 17, 1934

Dear Mr. Hopkins:

I came back to Denver yesterday a day earlier than I had planned — because it had rained so hard in the drouth area that the roads were impassable! . . .

They had regular cloudbursts up there both Thursday and Friday — in an area about a hundred miles North and East of Denver. In that country the wheat grew only a few inches above the ground, if indeed it came up at all, before it was burned brown. Much of the corn never did come up because the soil was so dry that the seed failed to germinate. For a couple of weeks in that area the cattle have been searching around between clumps of Russian thistle for bites of dry buffalo grass so short that they got mostly sand. And just West of where we were they say the farmers trying to plow this year have in more than one instance broken their blades on rock. Apparently most of the top soil had blown away, and they were down to bed rock!

But in much of that area it's all changed now — with two good heavy rains. The clouds last night indicated they might be having still another.

The rain isn't going to help their wheat crop any. In most of the area they don't expect more than a five per cent crop. A Government wheat inspector reports that in one of those counties they expect to get only 300 bushels off from 2,560 acres of land!

But it is going to help their livestock situation tremendously, and they were all going around grinning yesterday. Funny how people will cheer up if given half a chance! The relief administrator in one of those counties is a farmer and cattle grower. . . .

Some queer things happened. One farmer, for instance, who had undoubtedly worried all day Thursday about how he was going to keep his cattle alive without any food, woke up in the night to find most of them drowned! He and his wife and children managed to get to a little hill before they were drowned. By daylight their house, barns, livestock, everything was gone, swept away in a swirling torrent of brown flood water. They were finally rescued from the hillock, with great difficulty, by the fire department from a nearby town.

They tell me this isn't the worst drouth section in Colorado. As a matter of fact, it doesn't look so bad as pictures from South Dakota that I saw in the newsreels last night — nor so bad as things I saw in South Dakota myself last fall. You drive through miles and miles of bare plowed fields, where the crop never came up at all. But the stock isn't in such bad shape, and this rain will undoubtedly save it.

However, this is the FIFTH year of drouth in that area! Not a crop in 1933, 1932, 1931, or 1930! The relief director in one of those counties told me that in the last few months several farmers have gone insane. Applications for relief have been increasing. Everybody is broke. Eighty-five per cent of the cattle are mortgaged. Land values have dropped to less than a dollar an acre in some sections. Mortgage holders refuse to foreclose. They don't even bother to have tax sales. The land isn't worth it.

It's the same old story. Farmers came in from Nebraska, Kansas, Missouri, homesteaded, and plowed up range country. For a few years they had phenomenal wheat crops. Then came the drouth. This may sound a bit encouraging:

"Many of us have decided," said the relief administrator who is also a farmer, "that this land better be turned back to grazing. We're doing a good deal of it."

But he added that, should wheat go up to $2 a bushel, a lot of them would undoubtedly go back to plowing again, gambling on the weather. Cattle control program may encourage them to leave wheat alone, though, if it brings the price up, or if they get allotment checks.

The more I see of the workings of the AAA, the more I become "sold" on it. Wheat allotment checks represented the only income many of those farmers got last year. Of course it was only another form of relief — paying them for cutting production when they didn't produce anything at all. It's giving them relief out of the pockets of the processor and the consumer. Well, why not?

Naturally, those farmers are strong for the program. So are the small town merchants with whom they trade. The capitalist group — sugar barons, bankers, both city and small town — don't care for it. But then, they don't care for anything the Administration is trying to do anyway. . . .

Most of this week, however, I've given to trying to find out about the sugar beet industry.

It's just one big complicated mess, isn't it?

So far as the people down at the bottom are concerned — their plight isn't much different from that of the Negro and poor white tenants and sharecroppers in the Cotton Belt. The chief difference seems to be that in the Cotton Belt the exploitation isn't so well organized. It's the same sort of peonage — Negroes and poor whites in the cotton fields, and in the beet fields Mexicans, for the most part, brought up here by the Sugar companies.

The charge has been made, I believe, that the beet sugar industry is "inefficient." Well * * * from the standpoint of the Sugar companies, it appears to be anything BUT inefficient. They've got the most perfect system of gouging both the farmer and his labor you ever heard of. It's marvelous!

The arch villain would seem to be the Great Western Sugar company, which, I'm told, controls most of the others. This company — I'm told it is a matter of public record — has been paying good fat dividends while other industries were going broke during the Depression.

In 1933 — the year they couldn't afford to pay the grower more than $4.50 a ton for his beets, with the result that the average Mexican family, father, mother, and children, who actually got out into the fields and RAISED those damned beets, got considerably less than $100 per family for their labor and some of them haven't been paid yet — the Great Western Sugar company not only declared nice, juicy dividends, but it set aside in some sort of holding company $8,000,000 or $9,000,000, presumably to avoid having to pay income tax on it!

What we really did, I guess, was to subsidize the Great Western Sugar company by carrying practically all of the Mexican labor and a good many farmers, too, on relief last winter!

Boy, ARE these Sugar companies sitting pretty! They get theirs, anyway you look at it. On wretchedly paid peon labor, on farmers who have been virtually serfs, too, they have made, I'm told, out of an original investment of $13,600,000, a profit of $100,000,000 since 1905, have acquired some $80,000,000 in assets! Apparently they've dug into the pockets of the consumer, too, PLENTY, by fixing the price of sugar pretty much to suit themselves. And then they've got the nerve to weep about being hard up and demand a tariff, even against the Hawaiian Islands and Puerto Rico. Phew!

Take the Great Western Sugar company, for instance. They've got themselves into the sweet spot where they have no responsibility whatever toward anyone — farmer or labor.

The company is the boss. The farmer is his hired hand. He doesn't get wages, of course. He gets what the sugar company wants to pay him for his crop, that's all. Why the sugar company even has field men who go out and actually boss the farmer — tell him how to raise his crop. If the company's field man doesn't like the way the crop is coming along, he can direct the farmer to take on more help, which, of course, the farmer does, charging it against what he has agreed to pay the Mexican. Gosh!

The farmer's lot, as a matter of fact, isn't much better than that of the Mexican. Plenty of Mexicans didn't get paid last fall for the simple reason that the farmer — after he had paid the sugar company for his seed and had paid the bank, which wouldn't lend him any money unless he raised sugar beets, "cash crop" — didn't have anything left. They tell me the turnover among beet sugar farmers is immense. It's got now so that Japanese are about the only farmers who can raise sugar beets and make a living. They came in here first as laborers. In many cases they are now the farmers, hiring Mexican and even white labor to work in the fields! I visited one farm the other day run by a Jap.

The sugar companies even have a sort of "company union" among the farmers. It is called the Mountain States Beet Growers Marketing association. I was told — and reliably, I believe — that it represents about 40 per cent of the growers and that it apparently exists only to "yes" the sugar companies.

For instance, this year — and I suppose in past years — the association has put out contracts for Mexican labor to sign. The charge is made that the contracts were drawn up by the Great Western Sugar company. They just run the whole show, that's all, tell the farmer what to do, how to manage his help, what to pay, everything. They certainly have control of the situation, I'd say.

And away down at the bottom you have Mexican families working in the fields — children, some of them, 8 years old — most of the summer without pay in many cases, piling up bills which will take all their small earnings at the end of the season, if they get anything at all! Living on relief in the winter.

As nearly as I've been able to find out, the great majority of the beet workers in Colorado have gone back into the fields this season without any idea of what they are going to be paid for their labor, or whether they are ever going to be paid at all!

I myself have talked with families who are out in the fields working, living on credit, hoping they may get a little money after the thinning is completed, hoping they MAY get paid in full sometime next December! And many, many of these people haven't been paid for last year's work yet!

You hear a lot of talk out here about how the Mexicans refuse to go back to the beet fields this year, from farmers, sugar company officials, some relief people. But up in the area where I've been, the figures don't show it.

In one place the case load, including men working on Emergency Works Division [EWD] projects as well as families on direct relief, dropped from 600 in May to 350 at the present time. Most of these men, I was told, went back to the beet fields — to live on credit all summer and with very little prospect of having enough at the end of the season to carry them through the winter. The county administrator sent out a notice that jobs on Works Division projects were really relief, and that every man who accepted such a job, when he could get work, was keeping somebody else from being helped. The next day, in that one little district, 12 Mexicans came into the relief office, turned in their work slips, and said they were going back to the beet fields. Only three or four men in the district have refused to go back to the fields, the relief director told me. . . .

284

To Eleanor Roosevelt

[Enroute, Denver to Los Angeles]   June 23, 1934

This has been rather a nice day on the train, through beautiful scenery. And I've done quite a bit of work. . . .

The Royal Gorge was a bit disappointing. The day was cloudy and it needs sunlight to bring out the shadows and the colors. . . . All afternoon, though, the mountains have been very majestic even though there isn't much snow on them, and now, after crossing through Tennessee Pass — more than 10,000 feet altitude — we are going down the Western slope of the Continental Divide through some very beautiful mountains all covered with pines. The loveliest, clear, green river rushes over rocks beside the train, and flocks of sheep are grazing on really *green* pastureland and just below the timber. This road bed is pretty rough, but the scenery more than makes up for it. I've never seen any lovelier. Especially after so many, many weary miles of drouth and desert in Colorado.

I'm feeling much, much better tonight than I have for a week or so. I got terribly tired — more tired than I've every been on any previous trip — and it was all so depressing. Sugar beets, drouth, abandoned coal camps. And administration of relief in Colorado has been until recently such a mess. All sort of corruption, apparently, in Denver. And out in the state inadequacy, intolerance, complete domination by industry, using us to subsidize itself. We are still carrying on relief in Pueblo 430 families employed in a steel mill operated by the Colorado Fuel and Iron Company, as you know, a Rockefeller company!

The "pay-off" came the other night in Canon City, when a member of the state prison board told me all about the case of a young man who was executed there last night for murder. He and another boy were convicted of killing a rancher in a holdup, which netted them only two cheap pistols. The other boy's family were able to raise $200 to carry his case to the Supreme Court — so he is still alive, with the possibility that he may be granted a new trial and acquitted. Kelley, the man who was executed last night, couldn't raise the $200 — so he got no appeal. And last night they killed him. The member of the prison board told me that both boys were undoubtedly guilty — the one who is still alive every bit as guilty as the one they executed last night.

The thing has nearly driven me crazy. How *can* you have any faith or hope in us if we do things like that in this supposedly enlightened age? My first impluse was to hand over the $200 that night — I still had most of my pay check — and see if we could get him an appeal, too. And I still think I should have. I think the impulse was *right* and that I should have done it. The $200 was needed to get a transcript of the evidence in the trial. The field representative of the state relief administration, who was with us, talked me out of it. She pointed out that there'd certainly be publicity on it, and, because of my Government connection and my connection with you, it might embarrass the President. Feeling against the two has been pretty strong in the state. People feel that the other boy shouldn't be allowed to appeal, that he should be executed, too, but it didn't seem to occur to them how terrible it was that one should die, while the other, because his family could raise $200, was permitted to go on living even for a few months. Why the governor[1] wouldn't grant him a stay I can't imagine. I feel as though we were living in the Dark Ages, and I *loathe* myself for not having more courage and trying to stop it, no matter what the consequences were. *You* would have *done* it. Well — I guess I'd better not think about it any more. . . .

1. Edwin C. Johnson.

To Harry L. Hopkins

En route — Denver to Los Angeles, June 23, 1934

Dear Mr. Hopkins:

. . . I may as well finish up with the beet sugar business. . . .

Some of the confusion this year seems to be due to the fact that a lot of people have the impression that the Department of Agriculture is going to do something about a minimum wage, or rate per acre, to be paid to labor. You hear over and over again of farmers having said to the workers, instead of offering them any sort of contract, "I'll pay you whatever the Government decides." And on that promise many families have gone to work. . . .

I believe I wrote you before that apparently there has been very little rebellion on the part of labor against going into the fields, under even the most unsatisfactory terms. Those who are rebellious are making a lot of noise about it, of course, but for every one who refuses to go into the fields probably a hundred have gone and under most unfavorable circumstances.

Leading the rebellious souls is Thomas F. Mahoney of Longmont, who as head of some Knights of Columbus committee formed to look after the interests of the Mexicans, has spent twelve years on the sugar beet labor problem. State relief people, who are all on the side of labor in this situation, say that on the whole Mahoney is right in anything he tells you, although he is inclined to get pretty emotional about it. The local relief officials are divided. In one town for instance, they spent most of their time assuring me that, even if the Mexicans did collect any money in the fall, they'd spend it all on second hand automobiles and then come on the relief rolls for the winter. The truth undoubtedly lies somewhere between what Mahoney says and what some of the relief people say. . . .

Two things make it difficult to make people give up relief or EWD jobs to go to work, particularly where the work consists of the most casual, irregular sort of employment, such as most of this farm work around here is. People on relief have learned — they were beginning to find it out even last summer in Pennsylvania — that, if you take a few days' work, you're cut off relief, and you've got to go through a lot of red tape to get back on. They're afraid to take a chance. Except for the beet fields — and then they don't, most of them, get any money until sometime in the late fall — the jobs these people are offered aren't REAL jobs at all. Just a few days' work here and there, harvesting vegetables, working in canning factories, and so on. AND THEY HAVE NO ASSURANCE THAT THOSE TWO OR THREE DAYS' WORK WILL CARRY THEM THROUGH UNTIL THEY GET SOME MORE. Why, in the name of common sense, SHOULD they turn in an EWD work card for that sort of job? . . .

And in the meantime, they are out there in the beet fields working this summer, thousands of them — men, women, and children.

One of the most vicious things about the whole business is the way the sugar companies and the farmers have managed it so that they have no responsibility whatever for child labor that exists in the industry.

You see, the Mexican who works in the beetfields isn't hired by the farmer or the sugar company. Neither are his wife nor his children. The husband and father enters into a CONTRACT with the grower to thin, weed, pull, and top a certain number of acres of beets. He is paid — if he gets paid at all — by the acre. And the terms are so poor that he's just about GOT to work his children to make even the barest sort of living. . . .

If the United States Government or any state government should try to stop child labor in the beet fields, the only person they could "crack down on" would be the Mexican laborer, who could rightly say, "I can't make a living without working my children." Both the sugar companies and the growers piously refuse to hire any day labor younger than, I believe, 16. But the one thing that would keep the children out of the fields they don't do — that is, see to it that labor is adequately paid, so that there is no need for the children to work.

These Mexicans are interesting people. Most of the adults seem to be illiterate peons, very low grade mentally. Sort of childlike. They grow old very rapidly, apparently, especially the women. But the children are unusually bright and attractive — more so than American children on the whole. Somewhere, in the process of growing up, they seem to

287

lose it all! And one of the most pathetic things you ever saw is the anxiety of some of the Mexican fathers and mothers that their children should be educated.

In a blazing sun the other day I stood out in a beetfield talking with one of those Mexicans. His four children were working in the field with him, the youngest 12 years old. All girls, the two older ones, 15 and 16, with lips and nails brightly rouged! They were weeding. Don't ever get the idea that ANY work in the beetfields is fun—even though farmers will tell you, they DID tell me, that "working in the beetfields doesn't hurt kids any. It's good for them to be out in the sun!"

Whether it's good for them or not, I certainly did not enjoy seeing that 12-year-old—undersized, with a droop to her shoulders that no 12-year-old should have—working her way up those rows, alternately hoeing and stooping over to pull weeds.

"We go to Denver in the winter," the father said, "because the schools is better in Denver. I want these kids to get better education than I got."

I daresay everybody who comes out to Colorado is horrified by the child labor in the beetfields. I suppose the farmers have built up a sort of defensive attitude on the subject. Perhaps that is why that farmer said to me that it didn't hurt them—that it was good for them. And possibly the impression has gone abroad that the children are younger than they really are. They are all so undersized.

We stood in the yard of one Mexican beetworker's shack and watched the family come home for the midday meal—father and five children, two girls and three boys. As he came trailing along across the field, the youngest child didn't look over 6 years old. But he told me he was 9.

"It's all a lot of rubbish that 5-year-old children work in the beetfields," one farmer told me. "A 5-year-old child wouldn't know the difference between a beet and a weed."

And yet—

One Mexican mother told me that her children had started working in the fields when they were 6.

And a little Mexican girl—a bright little thing, with the keenest brown eyes—told me that she started working "in the beets" when she was 8. She is 10 now and is working this summer, along with her older brothers and sisters.

"How do you thin beets?" I asked her. "It must be hard on your back, stooping over that way all the time."

"It's better," she said, "if you go on your knees."

"What time do you start in the morning?" I asked.

"Oh, maybe 6 o'clock, maybe earlier," she replied in the most matter-of-fact way.

"And what time do you get through at night?"

"Six o'clock," she answered, "only sometimes it's 7, and sometimes it's dark. I get pretty tired sometimes when it's getting dark."

Farmers will tell you, too, that the children don't really work. But one Mexican father said:

"Oh, these kids — they're the best workers of all!"

He said it as though he was proud of his children!

I was told that heart disease is common among children of Mexican beetworkers. From Weld county — which was settled by the young men whom Horace Greeley advised to "go West and grow up with the country" (the Boettchers, Great Western Sugar company barons in Denver, were among the lot, incidentally) — the relief worker sent a young Mexican, 18 years old, to a CCC [Civilian Conservation Corps] camp a few weeks ago. He was sent home. Bad heart. His mother said he had worked "in the beets" all through his childhood.

I ran across two cases of blindness which the relief workers said were due to "working in the beets." Having been out in some of those fields in a blazing sun, I can certainly understand how that happens. The shiny green leaves throw up a glare that is simply blinding.

Oh, Lord, it is an awful thing to see — the beet sugar business! And you can't help wondering if, given half a chance, those children wouldn't grow up to be so much superior to their poor, illiterate, stupid, physically inferior parents. As it is, they'll be just peons, that's all. And the families are so large. Twice as many Mexican peons a generation from now as there are now! Gosh.

And on this sort of thing is built up one of the most powerful industries in the country. An industry that in 1933 had $78,000,000 in assets and no debts, an industry that has gained $166,000,000 in less than 30 years.

Our relief administrator in Weld county is a former employee of the Great Western Sugar company. He used to be manager of the plant in Greeley, the county seat.

"I used to think the sugar company was right — that it really was abused by its critics," he told me. "Since I've been on this job, though — I've learned a lot."

Incidentally, in that county until a very few months ago, a beet worker's family, to get on relief, had to be okayed by the field man of the Great Western Sugar company! . . . That was one of the first situations Captain [C. D.] Shawver cleaned up after he went in as state administrator. It was the system all last summer and most of last winter.

The present relief administrator, who formerly worked for the company as manager of the local plant, was put in by Captain Shawver. He figured out for me when I was there just who got the money from last year's beet crop. It works out something like this:

"Last year," he said, "the Great Western Sugar company paid the grower $4.50 a ton for 15 percent (standard) beets. Out of a ton of 15 percent beets, the company got 300 pounds of sugar. At 6 cents a pound, the company got $18 for the 300 pounds of sugar produced from the ton of beets for which it paid the grower $4.50. That's just the sugar. The company also got something for the residue — they feed the pulp to livestock around here. But we'll not figure that in.

"To produce the 300 pounds of sugar that brought in $18, the company had to spend $9. Of course any official of the company would figure it out so that the company got no profit at all. But I know the sugar business, and I tell you that the cost of the beets, all labor cost — the sugar company runs its business entirely on seasonal labor, laying off even its technical people during the dull season — depreciation, new equipment — it doesn't run over $9 per ton. That gives the company a net profit of $9 on the ton of beets for which it paid the grower $4.50.

"The grower got $4.50 per ton for his beets. His yield averaged 13 tons to the acre. That would give him $58.50 per acre for his beets. He also got a by-product credit of $3 per acre, bringing his gross income per acre up to $61.50.

"Now here is what it cost the farmer to produce those beets: for preparation of the ground and planting, $7.76 per acre; for cultivating, $4.43; for irrigation, $7.38; for harvesting somewhere around $10 an acre; for manure, $7.09; for seed, $3.12; taxes, $2.56; interest on his investment, depreciation, and so on, about $9. That brings the production cost, WITHOUT labor, up to around $50 an acre. Add $12 an acre for labor onto that — and you'll see why many beet workers didn't get paid last year.

"In other words, while the company made $9 a ton on the beets — $117 to the acre, on the basis of 13 tons to the acre — the grower just about broke even if he didn't pay his labor!"

Well, there's the situation. It's a bad business. Apparently it's always been a bad business. And for years the Government has been investigating and reinvestigating, without ever actually doing anything about it. Just what is going to happen next nobody seems to know — nobody out here. And in the meantime, we're subsidizing the industry, although to just what extent I can't say. There are no real figures.

What I've written is, I realize, pretty sketchy. But, if I had stayed there two or three weeks instead of two or three days, I daresay the impression would be the same.

To return to the statement that we are subsidizing the industry — there seem to be no real figures on how many beet workers now in the fields are getting supplementary relief from us. But of course we carried most of the beet labor in Colorado on relief through the winter. . . .

To Harry L. Hopkins

Enroute to Los Angeles, June 24, 1934
Dear Mr. Hopkins:

. . . One of the most interesting things I saw in Colorado was the following:

In Pueblo, as you may know, there is a large steel plant operated by the Colorado Fuel & Iron Company [C.F.& I.], one of the Rockefeller interests, employing normally between 4,000 and 5,000 men.

And to the families of 430 men employed in that plant the Colorado Relief Administration, dispersing through the county setup Federal relief funds, is granting right now supplementary relief!

In other words, we are right now in the position of subsidizing John D. Rockefeller!

Here is the whole story:

Back in 1929, when things began to go bad, C. F. & I., as it is known out in Colorado, began doing welfare work, so-called, among its employees in the steel plant who were not working or employed on a very limited part time basis.

The "welfare work" was of the same sort as that done by the U.S. Steel Corporation among its employees — i.e., it consisted of extending credit at the company store. I have it from an official of the company that some of those workers, under that system, got themselves in debt to C. F. & I. as much as $1,000.

In 1932 R.F.C. relief funds came into the county, and a relief committee, dominated by C.F.& I. officials, was set up to administer these funds.

This committee continued to function, handling FERA funds, until February, 1934, about four months ago.

Last February, soon after he became state administrator, Captain Shawver changed the setup in Pueblo, removed control from that committee, and put in a new administrator, a member of the state staff.

"When I went in," this new administrator told me, "I found to my surprise a large number of workers, employed full time at the steel plant, getting supplementary relief. The average was $10 to $20 a month, in the form of dispersing orders for food and clothing, to be cashed at the company store!

"These men were back working full time in the mill. When I investigated I found out that the company, collecting the money the men owed them for its 'welfare work' before the Federal Government relief came into the picture, was withholding their salaries and having them carried on relief until the debt was paid up!

"The relief committee, dominated by company officials, had worked out a budget for each of these families. Supplementary relief was granted to fill out these budgets after the company had taken out of the men's pay checks what it deemed a fair amount toward payment of their debts. In most cases the men had only a few cents left each pay day after the company had collected on the back debt. The relief administration was putting up the rest.

"Not only was the relief administration supporting these men while they worked out their debts to C. F. & I., the company was also getting through its company store most of the money put out by the relief administration for the support of these families, the heads of which were working in the mill. Dispersing orders are issued on stores selected by the clients. In the great majority of cases, these clients chose the company store. They knew darned well that they stood a chance of losing their jobs if they didn't!"

The new administrator's first step was to get a new committee. The company declined representation on the committee, on the ground that "relief in Pueblo was being thrown into politics!"

He next set about to try to stop subsidizing the Rockefellers. It's now developed into a grand fight, with the workers somewhere in the middle of things. . . .

For instance, if a man is earning in the mill less than his budgetary requirement, the relief administration will supplement that amount and bring it up to his budgetary requirement, and that is all it will do, no matter how much the company is holding back in payment of the man's back debt. If the amount a man earns, regardless of how much the company is holding out, meets or exceeds his budgetary requirement, the relief administration will not grant supplementary relief.

That means that the company has to extend further credit to the family at the company store—which certainly doesn't help the family much! But—gosh!

The administrator told me a steel worker came to his office the other day and told him that, while he was earning $60 a month in the mill, the company was holding every cent of it back in payment on his debt and limiting him to $20 a month credit at the company store to live on. In other words, the man worked full time in the mill, earned $60 a month, never got a cent of it, and was allowed to live on $20 a month—increasing his debt by that amount each month!

It's the darnedest situation you ever saw! The local merchants, among others, have been jumping on the relief administrator. They know the company is holding back the salaries of the workers in payment of their debts. That is just about ruining the local merchants, because the workers haven't any money to spend. They think the relief administration ought to be more generous, if you please, supplement the workers' net incomes, instead of their gross incomes, and in cash—so that they can get some business!

One of the most unique suggestions made by the company officials to the former relief administrator — and turned down — was this: that the relief administration put some of its clients, who were mill employees, to work painting the company's buildings. The relief administration would carry them on relief while they were doing this work, and the company would credit the work against the men's debts!

This whole problem of granting supplementary relief — and thereby subsidizing private industry — is causing a good deal of worry and concern to the state staff. They don't know what to do about it.

Some of it is being done in the sugar beet industry, as I have already written you. It is also being done in coal mines — some of which are owned by C. F. & I. — where miners do not get enough work so that they can live on their wages. Nowhere else, so far as I heard, is it being done because employers are holding back the men's wages in payment of debts.

In one C.F.& I. mine a plan was worked out whereby the company, instead of employing more men on part time, employed only a few, on full time at a living wage, and all the others went on relief.

But when this plan was tried out in another mine, not owned by C. F. & I., the United Mine Workers raised a terrible howl, and it didn't go through. I hate to sound like a Tory, but it's fairly obvious to me what the United Mine Workers were interested in. Dues. Capital and Labor — they all play us for "a bunch of suckers."

One's first reaction is that the relief administration ought to quit supplementing incomes of people who are at work — at once and entirely. But what are you going to do? Let the families go hungry? And suppose, unable to live on what they are earning, they all quit and come on relief? . . .

Just to get their reactions, I went to see officials of C. F. & I. in Pueblo the other day. Using tactics one learns in the newspaper business, I was very innocent and very "dumb" — tried to let them think they were pulling the wool over my eyes.

I was unable to see the superintendent — don't know whether he ran out on me or not — but I had a fairly extended conversation with his assistant and a company welfare worker. (They have at the plant in Pueblo, all boarded up and closed now, because they say they can't afford to run it, a very handsome Y.M.C.A. building, the gift of John D. Rockefeller, Jr.!)

I heard a lot of very pathetic talk about the company being in the hands of receivers and the stockholders not getting any dividends, and a lot of very enthusiastic talk about the "happy cooperation" (this from the welfare worker, an awfully sissified sort of chap) between the company and the relief administration. Typical, from the welfare worker:

"At one of our mining camps in Wyoming we know just how much employment we are going to have and how long it will last, and, through our very happy relationship, the relief administration is able to forget all about that county for the next few weeks. And then when we get through, we'll notify the relief administration, and they will take all the families on relief." . . .

I was told all about the company's sewing classes — in which they made clothes for themselves out of material sold to them at the company store on credit. All the workers, I was assured, were very happy, knowing they had the great big beautiful company, with all its resources, behind them — to permit them to pile up debts so that they'd never be free again in their lives, apparently, unless we carry them on relief while they are paying their debts.

"My, but they must owe the company store a lot of money," I said sympathetically. "Will you ever get any of it back?"

"Well, we regard it as a deferred debt," I was told complacently. "Some of them have paid back most of what they owe. But some of it we'll never see again. Some of those families owe us as high as $1,000."

"Are you trying to collect any of it?" I asked.

"Oh, no," I was told, "not unless we feel that the man can AFFORD to pay some of it back!"

That was a bit hard to take, but I didn't say anything.

They told me they now have between 3,000 and 4,000 men working.

"All on full time?" I asked.

"No — not all on full time," I was told. "We try to spread the work, to give every man a chance."

"Are any of your people here in the mill getting any supplementary relief?" I asked as innocently as I knew how.

"Oh, no," I was piously assured. "We don't believe that men who are back at work should get relief!"

And that — was — that! . . .

To Harry L. Hopkins

Los Angeles   June 25, 1934

Dear Mr. Hopkins:

. . . I didn't get out into the real drouth area. Rex Tugwell's assistant, Grace Falke, who is still with me, and I attended in Denver a session of the Colorado Drouth Relief committee. Mr. [E. W.] Sheets, the man who heads the Department of Agriculture's livestock relief show, had a session of cattlemen from all the Southwest and Mountain states on while we were there, and we saw something of them, too. We decided that certainly both the Department of Agriculture and the Relief Administration in Washington were hearing plenty about drouth, so we didn't take the pretty long trip we would have had to make to get into the toughest drouth area in the state. On both our trips out into the state we drove through some counties that were in "secondary drouth" areas. In one of them, as I wrote you, we darned near got drowned in cloudbursts!

Attending Mr. Sheets' conferences was a gentleman named [M. T.] Morgan, who represents the Surplus Commodities Corporation. Grace Falke and I had breakfast with Mr. Sheets one morning, and he complained to me that the Surplus Commodities people were not moving fast enough in taking over the cattle purchased by AAA. Farmers were complaining, he said, that their cattle were driven to designated points, where they had to remain too long because the Surplus Commodities and Rural Rehabilitation people were not ready to take them over.

Later I had a talk with Mr. Morgan. He said this was not so — that we had kept up with AAA on the cattle program so far. He was afraid, however, that we might get behind because of an apparent lack of coordination between Washington and the state relief administrators. The state administrators, he said, seemed not to have any very clear idea as to what they were supposed to do with the cattle — both the "canners" and the cattle that were to be distributed to families being rehabilitated. This seemed to be the case in Tennessee when I was there. The state administration had received word that a lot of cattle — I think it was 80,000 or 90,000 head — were to be shipped into the state. They didn't know what to do with them. I talked with one county administrator who said he had received a wire from Nashville asking him if he could place 12,000 head of cattle on farms in the county. It apparently had knocked him goofy. Morgan thought the state administrators should be given clearer instructions. He thought that the state administrators should have been present at the meeting in Denver. He apparently did not feel that he had the authority to instruct them himself. But he said he was going to talk the whole matter over with Colonel [Lawrence] Westbrook.[1] No doubt he did, and probably the whole thing is straightened out by this time.

Mr. Sheets at the conference in Denver was talking about the possibility of having to move as many as 8,000,000 head of cattle out of the drouth areas this summer — either to be slaughtered or turned over to families being rehabilitated. Morgan said he didn't think the number would be anywhere nearly so great — possibly between 4,000,000 and 5,000,000. He told me confidentially that he thought Sheets was saying some of those things to scare the Relief crowd into action. He said he didn't see, however, how we were going to take care of all the cattle through Surplus Commodities and Rural Rehabilitation. He thought we'd probably have to think up something else to do with some of them.

Sheets had an idea of turning back some cattle to farmers whose herds had been wiped out — i.e., farmers whose whole herds had been bought by us, probably in such bad shape that all we could do was to slaughter them. Neither Morgan nor I could work up much enthusiasm over that idea, however. Boy, the newspaper headlines I can see in such a program! However * * *

The most disquieting drouth stuff I heard in Colorado was in Canon City last Thursday night. Canon City is in Fremont county, just a few miles from the Royal Gorge. It is in the center of a very fertile irrigated district along the Arkansas river. Apparently, even that irrigated area is going dry this summer!

As I have written you before, I think, there is very little snow on the mountains this year. Only one little patch on Pike's Peak, for instance. On the way to Salt Lake City on the train Saturday, we went up over Tennessee Pass, more than 10,000 feet altitude, on the train. Even up there, the mountains were almost bare. At this time of the year they should be white.

The Canon City correspondent of the Federal Land bank gave me this material. The normal flow of the Arkansas river at Pueblo at this time of the year, based on figures over a period of 21 years, is 2,240 "second feet" — i.e., feet per second. The flow on June 21 — that is, Thursday — was 138 second feet.

One of its largest tributaries in that area, Miles creek, should have at this time a flow of between 30 and 40 second feet. The flow Thursday was 3½ second feet. Water from Great creek, another tributary, was shut off last week, meaning that crops depending on irrigation will get no more water unless it rains. One reservoir had gone entirely dry. In several parts of the area all water was being held for stock. None was allowed for irrigation. There are many orchards in the area. He said he thought they would survive, but that all garden and feed crops would die unless they got water within the next two weeks. Which means big relief loads for us. Someone else told me that more than half the irrigated land in Fremont county had no water last week.

The Denver city and county relief administration was to me something of an enigma. It is in very bad odor with the state administration, with the new acting administrator, for the city and county, and with the newly appointed postmaster, Mr. [James O.] Stevic, who formerly served on the committee. On the part of outsiders I found nothing much but indifference. The Denver Post attacks it regularly, but then — the Denver Post attacks everything, especially everything connected with the present administration in Washington. . . .

The Colorado transient bureau has recently undergone a reorganization, and a new chief is going through in the transient service, I gather, what Captain Shawver has been going through in the state relief adminstration. The Denver transient shelter is awful. One of the worst I ever saw. But out in the state they have some decidedly promising camps and their campsites are marvelous — about the best I've ever seen. They have one in an abandoned coal camp up in the mountains, where they expect to put 1,000 men eventually. It is marvelous, a perfectly grand camp. I also visited the Black Forest camp, near Colorado Springs, where they are thinking of setting up a kind of rehabilitation camp for men who are sick and for older men. I was crazy about the place, although it isn't very large and will probably have to be abandoned unless they do use it for a rehabilitation camp caring for a limited number of men. It certainly is a beautiful place.

After seeing the transient set-up in Arizona, where there are no shelters in the cities at all, and the Denver shelter — I believe in camps! I think that Denver shelter ought to be abandoned! Perhaps I'm unfair I spent very little time in it — didn't go through the dormitory at all. But the very odor and appearance of the place was enough for me. Gosh! As a matter of fact, the worker who took me over there had nothing but apologies for it.

The transient problem in Colorado is, to be sure, a bit overwhelming just now. They gave service to 14,000 cases in May. In April there were 11,000, last January only 800, and last autumn only 200! Single men are registering in Denver at the rate of about 125 a day — and too many of them just use the shelter as a free hotel, coming in on freights late at night and leaving early the following morning, immediately after breakfast. They say they can't hold them. Well, you'd have to rope me and give me knockout drops to make me stay in that place! Their camps, among the best I've ever seen, seem to be too far away from Denver. I understand, however, that they are planning to set one up nearer the city. One thing that has held them up has been lack of a proper site. Well . . . young Mr. Paul Murphy, down in Arizona, may be a big spender, but he's running the best transient show I've seen. Except in Florence, Ala. — and they've got a genius in charge of their work projects there. . . .

They do one very interesting thing at that camp in the abandoned coal town. They give them the rudiments of mineral mining, grubstake them, and let them go out into the hills prospecting for gold. They've had pretty good success with it, too.

One thing that is worrying the Colorado transient people a bit is the way the number of transient families is increasing. The load used to be 30 per cent families and 70 per cent single men. It's now nearly fifty-fifty. They are getting a lot of families from the drouth areas in the Dakotas, Nebraska, and Minnesota, they say.

This transient thing is funny. Men, unable to get work in California and enroute to the Kansas wheatfields, actually meet up in Denver with men unable to get work in the Kansas wheatfields and on their way to California! . . .

1. Assistant administrator, FERA.

To Harry L. Hopkins

Los Angeles, June 27, 1934

Dear Mr. Hopkins:

Well, I am now in what has been described as "the blackest spot in the United States," from the relief angle.

Oddly enough, though, I have seen and heard here in the last two days some of the most encouraging things I've encountered on this trip. I really think things are improving in the relief picture in Los Angeles.

Of course, I've heard plenty about those indictments. I had a long talk yesterday with [Ray] Branion,[1] who of course is very much excited. I think I'd be excited, too, were I in his position. He says it will cost him $10,000 — which he hasn't got — and even then he may be convicted and sent to prison. One of the defendants, a former county CWA administrator, is actually on a work relief project now, getting $9 a week, they tell me! He was a relief client to begin with.

Branion and some of the state staff say it is just a big political frame-up — that John B. Elliott, one of the Democratic leaders, who claims, I am told, a great friendship with the President, which I cannot understand, since they also say Elliott has been a sort of man Friday to [William Gibbs] McAdoo, and Rheba Crawford Spivilan, state welfare director (remember the "Angel of Broadway," who came out here to go into the movies and ended up preaching in Aimee McPherson's Temple?) have sworn to "get" Branion and have succeeded. They say Elliott's animosity and that of McAdoo was aroused by Branion's failure to "play ball" with them and let them use relief for political purposes. It's all a bit confusing. Although Elliott is supposed to have been one of his strongest henchmen and although Elliott is supposed to have had gubernatorial ambitions, McAdoo, I am told, has endorsed George Creel for the Democratic nomination. Branion's story is that all the Democrats in California expect McAdoo to die shortly, and that Creel has agreed to appoint Elliott to fill out his term in the Senate. Branion told me he met McAdoo outside the hotel here yesterday and greeted him with, "Well, Senator, you look like a pretty lively corpse! I understand all the boys expect you to die." He said McAdoo rather stiffly replied that he was feeling better. Well, anyway * * * the theory of Branion and his staff is that Rheba and Elliott are out to "get" Branion and are fairly well succeeding.

298

Less passionate about it are one newspaper reporter who has covered the story from the beginning until very recently and Frank Y. McLaughlin, Los Angeles county relief administrator, who, as a division chief of Mr. Ickes' investigators, had charge of several investigations of relief and CWA in Los Angeles, city and county.

They both admit the presence of politics in the mess, but also say that the CWA administration down here, before the Army took it over, was appalling in its utter incompetence. Neither of them feels that Branion or Pierce Williams[2] was to blame, although the newspaperman is inclined to think Branion had a positive genius for picking incompetent men to run his relief and CWA activities down here. On the other hand, Branion picked McLaughlin as administrator, and the newspaperman and I agree that McLaughlin is a wonder. . . .

In spite of all this mess, however, I can't help feeling very much encouraged about the Los Angeles situation.

McLaughlin has started right in at the bottom to straighten out Los Angeles, and I think he is going to do it.

First of all, he is having a complete and thorough check of the case load. It now totals 110,985, with the relief administration carrying some 85,000, of which about 25,000 are on EWD. It's pretty much of a mixed-up affair. The county is not carrying its full load of widows, orphans, indigents, and so on.

His survey will straighten that out, turning the unemployables back to the county, where they belong. He hopes to cut his case load down perhaps to 53,000, although he isn't making any estimates yet. The check has barely started. It probably won't be completed before September. When he gets through, he is going to know all about his clients, their availability for employment, and so on.

At the same time . . . he is having made a very careful economic survey of the city and county. This, he says, isn't going to be a bit popular with the Chamber of Commerce, which has for years — and still does — urge people to come out here. His idea is that the whole economic structure here is about to topple over because there are too many people in Los Angeles for the amount of employment that its industries, even under the most favorable circumstances, can provide.

A whole lot of these people undoubtedly have got to be moved out of Los Angeles. And he believes that this will have to be the next step after he gets his relief case load "sorted out," so to speak, and gets from his survey a complete picture of the economic situation.

He is thinking now of placing some 5,000 migrant farm laborers and their families on subsistence homesteads in the San Joaquin and Imperial valleys. He believes they can earn their cash incomes, about $400 per year per family, working for the farmers during their busy seasons, that such a project will stop some of the migration and some of the labor troubles in those areas. He has worked out a scheme for financing it, partly with private funds and partly with relief funds, the details of which he is going to give me later. These 5,000 families, he says, normally work in the fields in the summer, traveling up and down the coast, and winter in Los Angeles — just now, on relief.

He has another idea, which I think is most interesting, for getting some of the Mexicans, a terrific problem in this county, out of the labor market. He wants to build them a pueblo town and put them out there making glass and other Mexican wares, to be sold to the tourists. I'm to get more details on this later, too.

I certainly am impressed with Mr. McLaughlin. And everywhere I go I get the impression that he is bringing order out of chaos. Really, he stands extremely well with people here.

Right now he is concentrating on trying to separate the employables from the unemployables. He wants next, for the time being, to get as many as possible of the employables at work. . . . By the time you get this, he will have 25,000, his full allotment, at work. He is hampered and bothered, however, by uncertainty. He doesn't know how much money he is going to have after July — if any. He'd like to know so that he could do some planning.

I had my first look today at a part of the biggest transient show in the country. Mr. [H. A. R.] Carlton, the state transient director, took me out to see a couple of the boys' camps. They are grand!

Up in Colorado I saw boys in the same camps with the men. They were segregated to some extent — housed by themselves. But somehow I couldn't help feeling a bit uncomfortable at the spectacle of those kids mixing with the older men, many of whom are such derelicts. Pretty hopeless and bitter, many of those older wanderers. About all we can ever hope to do with them is to "save the pieces," so to speak. I hate the idea of youngsters, some of them in their early teens, mixing with the older men, getting their bitter, hopeless slant on life.

The atmosphere in the two camps I saw today was so different! You never saw such pep in your life! Two camps. One had boys from 14 to 19 years old, the other from 18 to 21. About 200 in each camp. All of them had been riding the freight trains. Almost all of the 48 states were represented. One boy of 12, for instance, had ridden all the way out from New York in box cars. He said he was 14 when he registered, but finally admitted to the camp director that he was 12.

The procedure is to keep the boys in camp and let them earn their transportation home, plus some money to take with them. Most of them stay about three months. And not a single boy has ever been turned loose unless he went home or to a job.

The kids look on the camps much as boys look on private schools!

They have a sort of alma mater feeling after they leave! You should see some of the letters they write back! Most of them leave unwillingly. Some of the younger boys have been known to cry. To many of them the camp is better than any home they've ever known.

I think they have an excellent education program for them, and the enrollment in classes is almost 100 per cent. They give them everything from mathematics and languages to aviation and work on Diesel engines! The camps are almost self-governing, too, and they tell me they have practically no disciplinary problems. You should see the way those youngsters enter into the spirit of the thing. It's swell! And, once they get some food in them and get them tanned up, they are marvelous looking youngsters.

I think the thing that really impressed me about those camps was the optimism you saw on the faces of the youngsters. They're not beaten, these kids. They're busy and happy and interested, planning for the future. The contrast between them and the older transients is enough to knock you over. And I am convinced that, by removing them from the influence of those older, defeated wanderers, we're going to make something of these boys. I think we may have caught them in time to prevent their becoming professional tramps.

A great majority of them come from families on relief, I was told. Many of them from Texas, where — in April, at least — relief was woefully inadequate. . . .

I think that one of the best jobs of social work I've ever seen is being done right now with those kids.

They've done some really good work, too — the older boys supplementing the work of the CCC camps in one of the national forests. And you ought to see the gymnasium the younger boys built for themselves. And it's all done with such vim and enthusiasm. Well, you just can't understand unless you've seen several camps for older men and then a couple of these boys' camps.

I understand that, at first, the boys' camps cost more than the camps for adults, but they've been scaling that down. Now the cost runs about 40 cents a day per boy, of which about 30 cents goes for food.

I've seen some excellent transient camps these last few months. Good physical surroundings. Good supervision. Some good work projects. But I'm telling you those camps today were the best I've ever seen. About all we can do for those adults is to keep them off the road for a little while. Perhaps work a few of them back into some kind of normal life. But here — why, we're making honest-to-God citizens out of those kids! . . .

1. California FERA and CWA administrator.
2. Field representative for FERA and CWA.

To Harry L. Hopkins

Dear Mr. Hopkins:

I returned late last night from a three-day trip into the desert. The impressions I have brought back with me are somewhat confused and not too cheerful. They consist of heat, depression, bitterness, more heat, terrible poverty, confusion, heat again, and a passionate longing for some sort of orderly plan for procedure.

As I look back on it all this morning, I am inclined to believe that everything I heard out there was affected by the heat and dust — both in the way people feel out there and in the way I felt myself. Why in God's name anybody ever wants to live out there!

Well, it looks like a pretty hopeless mess to me. I've yet to see an irrigated district in California where the people generally are making a living. It all looks like sub-marginal land to me.

To begin with, even under the most favorable circumstances, they are farming at a disadvantage. They can't farm without water. And they've got to pay for their water. How much they have to pay depends on the will, usually, of private interests that happen to control the water itself and its distribution. On a five-acre tract, for instance, it may run to about $100 a year. They get caught two ways. They have to pay a private company for the water itself, and they have to pay a power company to distribute it! A big farmer, who can afford a Diesel engine to do his pumping, may get it for as little as $1 an acre per year. But there aren't many farmers who can afford Diesel engines. Most of the people out there are on small tracts — one to 20 acres. They average about five.

Now as I see it, even taking into consideration the fact that they can produce, with water, a great deal more on their land than can farmers outside irrigated districts, these people are always at a disadvantage. They always have to pay for their water before they can farm. Even if they are out of debt, own their land completely, they have that burden.

Most of them are not out of debt. Everything they've got is mortgaged, including their water rights! They are away in over their heads. I can't see how they are ever going to get out and have a chance to make a living where they are unless somebody steps in and wipes their debts clean and forces a reduction in cost of water and its distribution. That "somebody" would have to be the Government. It would be a terribly expensive business, and then I wonder whether they could support themselves!

For instance:

In a section of that desert company we visited yesterday they raise alfalfa. Marvelous alfalfa, and with water a great deal of it. Owing to transportation cost, their only market for alfalfa is in Los Angeles. It sells for $15 or $16 a ton down here, brought down by truck. The farmer out in the desert gets $11 or $12 a ton. With his water cost and so on, it costs him a little more than that to raise the stuff! . . .

How did they ever get out there into the desert, anyway? Well, here's the answer.

Some smart businessmen went out and bought up a lot of desert land, with its water rights. They developed some sort of irrigation system, just enough probably to bring water in, probably not enough to take care of the situation if the land was ever actually settled. Then they persuaded a lot of poor suckers to come out there and buy little pieces of that land—former service men, families of which some member had tuberculosis or asthma, people out of work, and so on. They sold it to them at good fancy prices, too.

They formed the victims into "irrigation districts," cooperative organizations, so to speak. These cooperative organizations bonded themselves to pay for the land and water rights. Bonds were unloaded on another bunch of suckers, who by buying the bonds furnished the money to pay the company that started it all. The company slid gracefully out of the picture then, leaving two sets of poor suckers—the farmers and the bondholders. The power companies got in, however, setting their own price for the distribution of the precious water.

And so they started to make the desert bloom—a lot of poor fools, head over heels in debt. They couldn't make a go of it, naturally. In addition to carrying impossible burdens, most of them had no idea in the world of how to farm on irrigated land, if, indeed, they knew anything about farming at all. In one district at least—the Palo Verde valley, along the Colorado river, the irrigation equipment put in by the development company was so poor that the farmers in the "irrigation district" had to bond themselves some more to provide adequate irrigation. Now I ask you—what chance did they ever have to make a go of it under those conditions?

The situation now is that the bondholders hold most of the land. It's no good to them, either. And the poor devils who went out there to farm are still on the land, unable in many cases to get water so they can even raise a vegetable crop. They are our relief load.

Some of them have succeeded in getting Federal Home Loans. The Federal Home Owners' Loan Corporation took over the mortgages on their land, but failed to take over their water problem. So you have this picture, as presented to me by one of our clients yesterday:

He has a five-acre tract, on which he had hoped to raise chickens, some fruit, and alfalfa. His chickens are all gone. He had to get rid of them because he couldn't afford to feed them and the relief administration couldn't help him because that would be subsidizing a private industry, God save the mark! After what I heard in Colorado about the

beet sugar industry and the Colorado Fuel & Iron outfit, you can imagine that this didn't go down so well with me. He is supposed to pay
$5.15 a month in interest on his loan to the Federal Home Owners' Loan
Corporation. He is six months in arrears, and they are beginning to
write him polite, but firm, letters. They have also called to his attention
the fact that he is in arrears in payments for his water stock—i.e., his
water rights, without which his land would be worthless and a very bad
investment for the United States Government. Those payments amount
to $45 a year, and that doesn't even touch distribution. If he wants to
have any water to use, he pays about $50 a year more. * * * So there he
sits, on his five acres, without any water and therefore unable to raise
anything, without any stock, no way to make a cent of money, with the
United States Government feeding him and demanding that he
somehow raise $5.15 a month to pay on its loan to him and $45 a year to
protect the Government's investment. Naturally—he's not so very
happy. It does seem to me that, being there, he might at least be permitted to raise some food to feed himself and his family. But who is going to
put up the $100 a year for water? And who is going to put up the $5.15 a
month which he is supposed to pay the Government? . . .

My impression of the California Emergency Relief Administration is,
so far, very bad. WHY didn't they get started on their rural rehabilitation program? The counties are beginning to set up work programs
now, most of them probably not so very good, out of their limited funds
because the people are desperate and won't have relief. WHY were the
utilities permitted to insert in the law authorizing California's
$24,000,000 bond issue for relief a joker whereby the whole thing is
unloaded onto the counties, already broke? The utilities are the big state
tax payers. So what did they do? They "fixed" the law so that the bond
money is loaned to the counties, which are to pay it back out of their gas
tax allocations for ten years beginning in 1937! Isn't that a peach? The
counties, broke and desperate, are now mortgaging what little financial
future they have to carry a burden that ought to be carried by the state.

It's a mess. Nobody seems to think it's Branion's fault. They regard
him simply as a victim. It's California politics, that's all. God damn it, I
think we ought to let Japan have this state. Maybe they could straighten
it out. . . .

To Eleanor Roosevelt

El Centro, California, July 3, 1934

Phooie, but it's hot here! Someone said it was 128 yesterday, and I
believe it. Yet the only thing I really mind awfully is the cooling system,
which won't let us open windows. . . .

This valley is the damnedest place I ever saw — except Southern West Virginia and Eastern Kentucky. There is the same suspicion and bitterness all through the place. An unreasoning, blind fear of "Communist agitators." If you don't agree with them, you are a Communist, of course. There is a rumor about here that they beat General [Pelham Davis] Glassford[1] up before he left the valley. There is also a story that they gave him knockout drops in a cocktail. He himself told one of our field people that the county agent — respresenting the Department of Agriculture in the valley, if you please — threatened him with the possibility of being "taken for a ride" if he didn't agree with "public opinion" in the valley! We have a new relief administrator in the valley, and he hadn't been here two days when a committee of citizens who call themselves the vigilantes called on him and told him there were "two ways to play this game — the valley's way and the Federal Government's way" and that he'd better "choose right."

They have no use for the Administration. One of the leading citizens told the state field man for the relief administration that he'd like to lead the pack and give Rex Tugwell a beating if he "ever showed his face around here." He *was* here last summer, as a matter of fact, but they were never aware of it. And they call Harry Hopkins a Communist. . . .

1. A retired army officer and former superintendent of the Metropolitan Police Department, Washington, D.C., who unsuccessfully served as a special labor conciliator in the Imperial Valley.

To Aubrey W. Williams[1]

Bakersfield, California, August 15, 1934

Dear Mr. Williams:

. . . To begin with, if you would believe the newspapers, California is setting out on a campaign of "red-baiting." Ever since the "Vigilantes," the majority of whose members I am told are American Legionnaires, went out in San Francisco and raided so-called "Communist" headquarters, herding together a lot of poor devils who weren't Communists at all and having them thrown into jail, there have been big headlines in the San Francisco papers every day about ridding the state of Communists. They are having a grand time there now, with the state convention of the Legion in session there, demanding a peacetime death penalty for treason — i.e., "Communism" — and considering a move to censure Frances Perkins.[2] The motion never got out of committee, however, and today, after big splurges in the newspapers, they took it all back and admitted that perhaps Miss Perkins knew her business and was able to handle the "undesirable alien" problem.

Now just how much of this is "newspaper talk" and how much the rank and file of the people of California are interested in it is hard to say at this time. My own impression is that the majority of the people of California, while they hate Communists and are afraid of them, do not believe quite all that the newspapers have to say on the subject. There are, of course, spots — the Imperial Valley, for instance — where they are simply hysterical on the subject. But by and large I don't believe they are. Not now, at any rate.

The metropolitan newspapers, of course, with the exception of the Scripps-Howard papers, are violently anti-administration. . . . In addition, one of the leading publishers of the state, Mr. [Harry] Chandler of the Los Angeles Times, has been a "red-baiter" for years, ever since his plant was blown up, and he has in the Imperial Valley and in adjacent Mexico large interests by reason of which he has no love for this administration.

I was informed — and I got this from several pretty reliable sources — that all over the state in the last few weeks newspaper publishers have been getting together in more or less secret sessions and laying plans publicy to put on a campaign to rid the state of Communists, but privately to fight Roosevelt. I should add that while I was in San Francisco I saw, among other persons, a man who ranks next to the general manager of the Associated Press. He had been on the road for a month, talking with publishers, all the way across the continent. He told me that, almost without exception, they are very bitter against the President. He is not friendly himself. So, I imagine, that what is happening in California may very likely be going on all over the country.

Allied with the newspapers in this little effort, you find, of course, most of the big business interests, the Chamber of Commerce, the Republican candidates for office, and, in California at least, the American Legion.

To date, the Chamber of Commerce crowd have been doing the most effective work. They are putting on a little under-cover compaign of their own. It's a whispering affair. They don't say much about the President. It's aimed mostly at Mrs. Roosevelt, Henry Wallace, Rex Tugwell, and what they rather vaguely describe as "the rest of the New Dealers." Mrs. Roosevelt especially is supposed to have strong Communistic sympathies and a tremendous and very bad influence on the President. What they are doing — or setting out to do — is gradually to plant in the minds of the conservative, middle class of Californians the idea that all those about the President in Washington are Communist sympathizers, if not actually Communists. I should have included in that list Miss Perkins. Down in the Imperial Valley they also include Harry Hopkins — but down there everybody in Washington is supposed to be a Communist, including the President himself. . . .

Carl Mydans, FSA

A mother with some of her children who were living in a shack in a field near U.S. highway 70 and the Tennessee River.

"A Promised Land, bathed in golden sunlight, is rising out of the grey shadows of want and squalor. . . . Ten thousand men are at work, building with timber and steel and concrete the New Deal's most magnificent project." TVA's Kentucky Dam.

Lunch time at a CCC camp, designated as TVA 22, near Esco, Tennessee.

Members of a Missouri family, stranded near Tracy, California, described their situation as "broke — baby sick — car trouble."

"One of the principal causes of labor trouble [in parts of California] lay . . . in the unspeakably bad housing provided for the seasonal, migratory workers." Families looking for work in the pea fields of California.

"[These people] are squatting on the outskirts of towns . . . with no sanitary facilities whatever, in the most miserable colonies of tattered tents, shacks built of pieces of tin and paper cartons, and crude shanties you ever saw." Squatter camps in California (*top* and *bottom*).

"Some of the more liberal growers" undertook to provide better housing for the migrant workers they employed.

Six thousand men worked on this CWA street project in San Francisco.

"We are the men whom Life has beaten down." Howard Street in San Francisco's skid row.

The Associated Press man who covered the strike — and who has been covering labor for a long time — also knows some Communists, although from him I got mostly the slant of the conservative labor leaders. . . .

"The Communists — what few of them there actually are out here — are of course very bitter against the President," he said. "They thought back in the late winter of 1932-33 that the revolution was right at hand. Now they say Roosevelt has postponed it for five or six years. In the meantime, they'll frankly tell you that they are out to do as much damage to him and his New Deal as they can. This recent fracas in San Francisco delighted them.

"They haven't much hope for a revolution in the near future, but in the meantime they feel they may as well embarrass Roosevelt all they can by stirring up trouble, particularly among the unions and the unemployed. They aren't bothering much about the unemployed out here because they've found labor such a fertile field.

"When NIRA[3] was passed, union labor — particularly the longshoremen and the seamen — was pretty much down and out. Many of the unions had lost their charters. It all goes back to the [Warren G.] Harding administration, when the Government, controlling the merchant marine, really crushed those unions. They had lost caste completely. And the shipowners had complete control of the hiring halls. Conditions were awful. Believe me, there was plenty of reason for labor to be sore.

"Along came NRA with what they interpreted to be a promise of Government support for a closed shop. Organizers came out here. The union membership jumped way up. They got their charters back.

"Having joined the unions, they now began to want to better their condition. Their first thought was to get control of those hiring halls. That, of course, would mean a closed shop. They found their conservative leaders, however, none too anxious for a strike. They held back. And here's where your Communists came into the picture.

"They got a following. It grew and grew. Most of these men who went on strike aren't Communists at all. All they wanted was a square deal. They'd follow anybody who would try to get it for them. They lost faith in their leaders. The Communists promised to lead them to success. So they followed the Communists. And out of that grew the General Strike.

"The public seems to think the General Strike was a flop. The Communists don't. They are well satisfied. And they are convincing most of their followers that it wasn't. 'Labor showed its strength. We had 'em scared to death.' That sort of thing. This fellow [Harry] Bridges who led the strike and who is a Communist never intended that the General Strike should last more than a few days. And, believe me, he has by no means lost his following among those fellows, even though he is keeping quiet now."

The Associated Press man gave me the impression that the conservative labor leaders, back in control now, for the time being at least, do not really appreciate the strength of this radical move in the ranks. . . .

And there's the situation. In the meantime I haven't yet talked with a person who doesn't think Upton Sinclair is going to win the Democratic nomination for governor — and that he will be defeated, and by Old Man [Frank] Merriam. Sinclair will be labeled "Communist," and that middle class that's afraid of Communists will vote for Merriam, even though, for the first time since the state was admitted to the Union they tell me, registration has indicated a Democratic majority in California.

I have tried to give you the state of mind of the liberals and labor.

It's rather hard to get any really frank statements out of the conservatives. It's fairly apparent, though. Mayor [Angelo] Rossi told me that he thought the businessmen and the Chamber of Commerce crowd — who were almost ready to murder him because he stood out, and almost alone, against martial law in San Francisco — were "feeling a little better now." Mr. [Frank] Foisy[4] certainly wasn't. He is very bitter against Frances Perkins, [Edward F.] McGrady[5], and everybody else who has had anything to do with the situation, including General Johnson. He charges McGrady and Miss Perkins with cowardice. He cited this as what he termed McGrady's attitude.

The bitter fight is, of course, over control of the hiring halls. A compromise agreement, whereby labor and the employers were to have joint control, with a federal representative to arbitrate if they got into a clinch, was accepted by the conservative labor leaders, but rejected by the left-wingers then in control of the membership. . . .

Business conditions in San Francisco aren't so bad, really. As a matter of fact, they tell me San Francisco never was hit so hard as most cities. But most of the businessmen and bankers, with the exception of [Amadeo P.] Giani[6] (or however you spell his name), who has always been a strong Roosevelt booster, I am told that most of them are really not at all friendly. They just don't like the New Deal, and that's that, even though some of them accept it with resignation and some give "lip service," but now and then throw in a bit of what they call constructive criticism. This from a newspaperman who covers the financial run.

They are complaining of course about Government expenditures. And at the same time some of them — the retail merchants — would like to see CWA come back! It meant money in their pockets. They are somewhat like that gang down in the Imperial Valley, including members of the relief committee, who say Harry Hopkins is a Communist, but — sent a special representative to Washington to get all the drouth relief they could out of him!

It's rather difficult to get in San Francisco much of any comment on the relief show. They're too much interested in this "red-baiting." Or else they simply aren't interested in anything at all, outside their own personal problems.

"What are people thinking about?" I asked everyone I saw. Again and again the answer was:

"Their jobs, and whether they are going to keep them or not. Or if they're going to get a raise." . . .

1. Williams was acting administrator while Hopkins spent July and August in Europe, chiefly investigating housing, social insurance, and relief programs in several countries, instead of vacationing as the president had hoped.
2. Secretary of labor.
3. National Industrial Recovery Act.
4. Employers' representative in the longshoremen's strike.
5. Assistant secretary of labor.
6. Giannin, board chairman and founder of the Bank of Italy, which later became the Bank of America.

To Eleanor Roosevelt

[Bakersfield, California]   August 15, 1934

Well — another day gone. A long day of driving about seeing things, with the chairman of the county board of supervisors and several relief people. The most interesting thing I saw was the little village of adobe houses built by Allan Hoover[1] on his ranch for his migratory workers.

A syndicate in which the former President is said to be a dominant figure, owns a ranch, four square miles, near here. They raise mostly cotton and alfalfa. Young Allan Hoover is managing the place.

One of the principal causes of the labor trouble in the Imperial and San Joaquin valleys last winter lay, as you may know, in the unspeakably bad housing provided for the seasonal, migratory workers, who come in to pick cotton and harvest the fruit and vegetable crops. Although the growers are supposed to provide decent housing and sanitary conditions for these people, they don't. Most of the workers live in tent colonies, with no water and no sanitation. Many of them live on the banks of the irrigated ditches and drink the ditch water. I saw some of those "ditch-bank" colonies in the Imperial Valley a few weeks ago.

Since the strikes, some of the more liberal growers have started a movement to provide better housing, but, so far, young Hoover is the only one who has actually done anything. I visited his ranch today. Fortunately he was away. I think we both might have been somewhat embarrassed had he been at home.

So far, he has built about 30 adobe houses, at about $400 each. They are white-painted, inside and out, with concrete floors, and electric lights. There is no running water in the houses, but outside each house is a tap. And in the center of the village are bathhouses, with modern toilets and showers, one house for men, the other for women. Very simple, but *so far superior* to anything else I've seen in the way of living accommodations for this seasonal farm labor. The houses are small, but new and clean. Most of them have sleeping porches. All screened in of course. They are really attractive looking — no two of them exactly alike — and trees have been set out and a start made toward landscaping the village. It really represents something of an investment — about $7,000 so far — and he is planning to build more. Of course, I'm wondering if it isn't the beginning of a "company town," although no rent is charged. But I wonder if company towns didn't get their start this way. And yet — there is such a need for it. Well —

It's funny, but ten miles away from the Hoover ranch, on the outskirts of Bakersfield, is a place called "Hoover City" — a jungle of tents, cardboard houses, built out of cartons, no sanitation whatever. In "Hoover City" live 100 families, wretchedly — itinerant farm workers, oil workers out of jobs, unemployed of all sorts. It's a terrible place, like thousands of other terrible places growing up on the outskirts of our towns. The tent colony in West Virginia really wasn't any worse, except that the winters are colder in West Virginia. What *are* we going to do with these people?

This country has gone one step toward solving it. Near the town of Shafter, twenty miles from here, they leased some land, put in running water and toilets, and let the people move their ragged tents and cardboard houses in there. It's at least better than "Hoover City" and the "ditch-bank" colonies in Imperial Valley. The chairman of the board of supervisors told me they wanted to put up cabins, but that opposition from the townspeople was so strong that they couldn't get away with it! . . .

1. Son of former President Herbert Hoover.

To Aubrey W. Williams

San Francisco, August 17, 1934

Dear Mr. Williams:

. . . People administering the relief show out here are quite enthusiastic about the production projects and are going at them with vim. In Bakersfield the county supervisors have acquired a large warehouse, where sewing and mattress projects will be under way in a few days. So far, the public doesn't know enough about the production idea so that it has any ideas, but when you explain it to people they seem to like it. My own feeling is that these production projects will take away some of the curse of trying to carry on public works projects without any equipment or material. I like the production idea. It is carrying out the idea of the cooperatives, but with better supervision and better chances of success.

One of the most intelligent of the group in Fresno was a chap named Kelly, head of the Unemployed Citizens' Council, which has some 3,000 members. It started last spring, about the time CWA went out, as a protest group. Undoubtedly, Kelly said, some of the Communist crowd were behind it. The crowd wanted to march on the courthouse and pull some riots. Kelly, himself unemployed, got control by using some old political tricks. What he actually did was to form the organization into a political club to wield over the heads of the county supervisors. This is an election year, and 3,000 votes are enough votes to elect or defeat a supervisor. Kelly set up two objectives: a reorganization of the relief set-up in the county, and a work program. He has achieved them both, and members of the Fresno Unemployed Citizens' Council are happy and reasonably contented. There have been no riots, either. * * * On first glance, Kelly's methods appear a bit questionable — dangerous, at any rate — forming the unemployed into groups as political clubs. But, dammit, how are you supposed to get things accomplished in this country except by use of the ballot? And I don't know that Kelly's organization is any worse than — say, the sugar lobby or the lobby of the American Federation of Labor in Washington. * * * The Council has as its objective now a subsistence homestead unit in the Bakersfield area, and they have written to Mrs. Roosevelt asking her support. Kelly said one thing that interested me a lot, representing, as he does, a large group of the unemployed.

"We, the unemployed, are fed up with relief," he said. "The Government has spent millions and millions of dollars on it, without much success. Suppose we clean out relief — drop it — put on an inflation program. Suppose the Government lends us money for housing, making it so that we actually can get the money. The money is too hard to get now. Most of us aren't going to be in a position to borrow a dime under the federal housing program. Suppose Mr. Roosevelt were to say: 'Tomorrow I'm going to start the printing presses if the banks don't loosen up.' I wonder if that wouldn't get results. And suppose the Government actually imposed a 30-hour week on industry and made it stick. I wonder if we might not get somewhere." . . .

One of the supervisors is a farmer — he termed himself a "small farmer" — and he was quite articulate on the troubles of the small farmer in California.

It is his feeling that farming generally will not get back until the big operator is more rigidly controlled. In California of course the big operator, raising thousands of acres of fruit or vegetables, is more of a problem than he is elsewhere in the country. That is one of the worst evils, for instance, in the Imperial Valley.

My farmer friend explained it this way:

Under the AAA cooperative marketing agreement, peach growers are getting this year $40 a ton for their peaches. They are limited on the amount they can sell. I believe they are permitted to sell some 70 per cent of the crop. Now while this price, he said, is better than last year's, the small peach grower's overhead is still high enough so that, being permitted to sell only 70 per cent of his crop, he is able barely to break even. If he could sell his whole crop at $40 a ton, he'd make a little money, but he can't sell his whole crop. On the other hand, the big operator can produce a ton of peaches quite a bit cheaper than the little fellow can. Hence he's able to make money under the cooperative agreement. And the little fellow is gradually being forced out of the picture. . . .

This farmer owns 50 acres of irrigated land and 300 acres of dry land, on which he raised some feed, small grains, and so on. His principal crop on his irrigated land has been raisins. He also has a dairy herd.

"A few years ago I had one of the best diversified farms in this community," he told me. "I used to get a gross income from it of about $5,000 a year — some $3,000 net. I used to get $150 a month out of my cows. I now get less than $60. I used to get 45 cents a pound for butter fat. I now get 24 cents. My gross income from that farm this year will be less than $2,000 — not enough to cover expenses. Certainly not enough to pay taxes or interest on my indebtedness. I'm putting up most of my supervisor's salary now, trying to save that farm. I'm probably going to lose it.

"Ten years ago my irrigated land was worth $1,000 an acre. Now I can't get a federal loan on it!"

He joined with Kelly, the Unemployed Council man, in saying that federal loans are "too hard to get." . . .

To Aubrey W. Williams

Reno, Nevada, August 20, 1934

Dear Mr. Williams:

. . . One of the most interesting things I saw in the San Joaquin Valley was a sort of model village set up on his ranch near Bakersfield by Allan Hoover, son of the former President. As you may know, much of the labor situation in the San Joaquin and Imperial valleys last autumn and winter grew out of extremely bad housing. I believe there is some sort of state law in California compelling growers to provide some sort of decent housing and sanitation for the seasonal workers they employ. If there is, it is disregarded. These laborers move in with their families, thousands and thousands of them, living in colonies of tents or shacks built of cardboard — it never rains down there, you know — with no sanitation whatever. Many of them live along the ditch banks in the irrigated section, drinking ditch water. I visited some of those colonies in the Imperial Valley a few weeks ago. . . . There was a good deal of sickness in some of the camps last winter. They were fertile territory for the Communists and the housing situation had a good deal to do with the strikes. Some of the more liberal-minded growers, it appears, have decided to remedy the housing condition. So far, however, young Hoover is the only one who has done anything. He and a partner — said not to be his father, although his father financed him — have bought a large alfalfa and cotton ranch — four square miles of it — near Bakersfield. And there, Allan Hoover, who is running the ranch, has put up some 30 adobe houses for his seasonal workers. I went out to see them with some county officials. They are pretty good little houses. Cost about $400 apiece. Electric lights, concrete floors, screened sleeping porches. There is no running water in the houses, but a tap outside each door and in the village community baths and toilets. Simple, but so far ahead of anything else I'd seen provided for the farm laborers! . . . One thing you wonder about, of course, is whether this is the beginning of a company town. I imagine that a great many company towns may have been started that way. Only young Hoover charges no rent. Whether he takes it out of the wages of the laborers I don't know. I was told not.

I had opportunity to observe in the San Joaquin and Sacramento valleys a problem that seems to be growing to terrific proportions out here in California. I suspect it may be growing elsewhere, too. It's partly due to unemployment, making it impossible for people to pay any rent, and partly due to lack of houses. I was told that some of these people probably could pay a little rent if they could find houses. At any rate, they are squatting on the outskirts of towns like Bakersfield and Stockton and Sacramento, with no sanitary facilities whatever, in the most miserable colonies of tattered tents, shacks built of pieces of tin and paper cartons, and crude shanties that you ever saw. Just why no epidemics have started in them no one seems to know. The local health departments are terribly worried about them. There are nearly 1,000 humans living in one of those colonies right on the outskirts of Bakersfield. Lord only knows how many there are around Sacramento. Some of them are living in caves there, along the river. Curiously enough, very few of them are on relief. They manage to scratch out a living some way.

The Kern county (Bakersfield) board of supervisors, one of the best I've seen, has tried to do something about those colonies. Local opposition is terrific. The townspeople object to the camps being cleaned up, because they think a clean camp will attract more of these people. However, near one town, the supervisors leased a piece of land, piped in some water, built some community toilets, and have let the people move in. They wanted to build some cabins, they told me, but the local people wouldn't stand for it. That camp certainly is an improvement over those other colonies. I shouldn't wonder if a lot of communities will have to do something of that sort before very long. Many of these people are of course seasonal farm laborers. Allan Hoover is trying one way. The supervisors are trying a different way. Either is an improvement over the usual thing. Many of these people aren't transients at all. Some of them have actually established legal residence by living a year in those wretched shacks. In most of them there isn't any sort of outhouse of any description. What happens to the ground and any streams nearby I leave to your imagination. And they also bathe in those streams and drink the water!

In the Sacramento Valley conditions were not so good as in the San Joaquin Valley. Oh, business is alright, and the people generally are contented enough, I gathered. But the relief business is awful, as described to me by one of the state field staff there. And the story of chiseling by everybody, politics, low relief standards, as given me, was damned depressing. I'll just go through my notes.

Here's some chiseling for you. Fruit canneries in Stockton, having canned their quotas under the code, are nevertheless taking on more help, some of them putting in another shift for a couple of weeks. Our relief people strongly suspect them of doing some bootlegging.

For years the fruit growers have given their surplus to the poor. Anybody could have them for the asking. This year they were turning them over to the relief administration to be dried or canned until some bright guy, an officer of the Grange, got the idea of having the Government buy all the surplus. Now you can't get any fruit free at all. They'll let it rot on the ground first. And it has raised Hell with the relief canning program.

In Yolo county, across the river from Sacramento, the farmers have fought any sort of relief program like blazes. "The reason," the field staff man explained, "is that they are getting highly skilled labor from the nearby towns — mechanics who used to work for as much as $8 a day — to run their tractors and keep up their machinery for $1 a day. Of course they don't want any relief in there."

Relief standards are shamefully low. In Sacramento county, on direct relief, administered by the county supervisors, the average is somewhere between $4 and $5 per month per family! All entirely on a political basis. I was told of one nearby county where relief funds were simply divided up among the supervisors, who handled it entirely on a patronage basis. This is, of course, not federal money, but in most counties money they have borrowed out of the state bond issue. Some of the counties have no records whatever of how the money is spent. In Sacramento county, the state staffer said, they don't even know how many people there are on relief!

Oh, it's all the damnedest mess! California is. Right now, apparently, the whole state staff is pretty badly demoralized because, in addition to fighting politicians on the outside, the state administration is itself honeycombed with internal politics. I heard rumors of it repeatedly. Apparently they're all after the job of state administrator, everybody knifing his neighbor and Vernon Northrop.[1] Combinations forming. Talk of this person and that person being "out." Gossip, gossip, gossip. And you can imagine the effect on the staff.

And a wretchedly inefficient business. In almost every county two set-ups — office staff, case workers, engineers, and all — at each others' throats! The county people in San Francisco charged that FIFTY-FOUR papers had to be signed before a man could be put to work on a relief work project. Frank McLaughlin, Los Angeles director, who is making an investigation of the San Francisco set-up . . . told me he had found it to be "only NINETEEN." Terribly high administrative cost. Northrop told me it was 25 percent in the state set-up. Engineers, case workers, supervisors, office help, administrative officers — all mixed up in one grand mess. Nobody knowing what he's doing or where he's going. It's funny the relief business hasn't a much worse reputation in California than it has! . . .

1. Acting FERA administrator for San Francisco.

To Aubrey W. Williams

Winnemucca, Nevada, August 23, 1934

Dear Mr. Williams:

I am now in Nevada, and a nice, quiet, simple place it is — after California. . . .

For one thing, they don't have in each county in this state two sets of social workers — or pseudo social workers — a SERA[1] set and a county set, at each others' throats! . . . But it strikes me sometimes that in California there are too many! An administration cost that runs up to 25 percent — and Northrop told me it was that high — indicates something must be wrong somewhere. . . . Anyway, the more I travel around, the more convinced I am that what we're going to have to do is to separate the employables from the unemployables, set up a real work

315

program for the employables, giving them enough to live on, apply a means test if we have to, and cut out all this infernal nonsense about case work and so on. We're getting top heavy. . . .

First of all, I find that, when you get away from the relief staff, relief committees, politicians, and big ranchers with the "gimmies," the people you meet along the road don't feel so hopeless. I am now referring to garage and filling station men, restaurant keepers, little storekeepers, and so on.

Oh, there isn't any doubt that Nevada is in bad shape. Big cattlemen will tell you that the cattle and sheep populations of the state will be reduced — by starvation and government purchasing — probably 50 per cent by the time winter sets in. They will tell you, too, that most of the cattle and sheep men don't own their stock anyway. All mortgaged for much more than it's worth. The feed situation is bad. In some parts of this state they've been having drouth for 11 years. I guess you'd cease to call it drouth after that many years. It's become a permanent condition. The price situation is bad, too. Yesterday, fatted steers were bringing 6 cents a pound in San Francisco — and housewives were paying 35 cents a pound for beefsteak!

But —

These little garage men, filling station people, restaurant keepers, storekeepers, all will tell you, too, that business is a little better than it was last year. They'll tell you they believe in the President and in what he is trying to do. They are feeling not so hopeless as they were a year ago. Sometime, somewhere, somehow, they feel the President will find a way out.

Now I think that is interesting.

Of course, someone remarked today that they'd never had anything anyway — these people out here, most of them, are poor — and that any sort of improvement looks big to them. But anyway they don't seem to be the downcast lot you'd expect them to be. . . .

The only person I've talked with for several days, of these inconspicuous little people, who told me things had not improved even a little was an Irish woman today. She runs a little restaurant in a very small town back down the line.

"No, I can't say things are any better," she told me. "Sometimes I don't take in even a dollar a day. Today, until you came in, my total receipts were 30 cents."

BUT — she added:

"We manage to get along, though. My husband has a bit of road work. I run the town switchboard. My boy picks up some work now and then. We're getting along alright. And we believe in Mr. Roosevelt and what he's trying to do."

Another interesting thing in Nevada is that, while the state as a whole is Godawful poor, there are spots in it where there is no unemployment at all!

One of these is famous old Virginia City. That town is having a mild boom. Gold and silver mining. Some sort of technique, it seems, has been developed for going back into the celebrated old gold mines and taking out what gold there was left behind. Something like "retreating," I believe they call it, in a coal mine. Anyway, the population of Virginia City has just about doubled in the last year, the Crystal Bar has moved its chandeliers and plate glass, its mahogany bar, and collection of old photographs into a less tumbledown location, and there is work for everybody who is able to work. The same is true in Silver City and one or two other places.

The third interesting thing is the situation down at Las Vegas and Boulder City. There's no unemployment down there either — not now. There are about 4,800 men now at work on the dam and allied projects. However, the dam is nearly finished, and, when it is, there WILL be a situation.

Our transient director down there — and transients, by the way, are now passing through there at the rate of about 7,000 per month — told me yesterday that they expect to start laying off men in a great big way about January 1. He himself expects that it will begin before that, probably in November.

Now here's the situation. You're going to have, he says, some 5,000 men — including some 1,500 heads of families — turned loose without a cent in the world. He predicts that 30 days after they are laid off they will be on relief! The single men will probably drift away and may end up in transient camps. But what about those 1,500 families, with children? What about school? Where are they to go?

Not only will they have no money, but no place to go! They are at present living on the government reservation. No one is permitted to live there unless he is working! And there aren't houses enough in Las Vegas to take care of them.

His prediction that they'll not have any money when they are laid off is based on two things — low wages paid at the dam and the high cost of living there. The highest skilled labor gets only 85 cents an hour, he said, while common labor gets $3.50 a day. I was told that the minimum for common labor elsewhere in the state is $4 a day.

Against that, you have families paying from $25 to $40 a month rent for shacks in company towns set up in Boulder City by the six companies engaged on the project. Boulder City, as a matter of fact, is just one big company town, operated by the six contractors. And food prices, he said, are terribly high.

317

He didn't seem to think there was actually much gyping done by the companies, at least on food prices — they operate company stores. Rents, he thought, were unreasonably high, and that the companies were getting away with it because they have a monopoly.

Food, he pointed out, would be higher in Boulder City because of the cost of getting supplies in. And the company stores grant credit — the curse of the American working man. At first, the companies had a monopoly on the food business, by paying their men in scrip on the company stores. This, however, was stopped. But of course, as he says, where credit is given, whether at a company store or any other store, people simply will buy more than if they paid cash. . . .

1. State Emergency Relief Administration.

To Aubrey W. Williams

Winnemucca, Nevada, August 24, 1934

Dear Mr. Williams:

. . . Now it may be that, if I have any value as an observer these days, it lies in the fact that in the last year I've been lots of places and seen lots of people. I can draw comparisons. And I wish to say most emphatically that, so far, I have seen nothing in Nevada in the way of drouth suffering that can be mentioned in the same breath with what I saw in the Dakotas almost a year ago! I have seen something of Nevada's drouth area, I've seen some of the stock, I've talked with a lot of people. I am willing to concede that I haven't seen it all, and that I haven't seen the worst, but from what I've seen and heard I'm damned sure that it isn't so bad as some of the other drouth areas. South Dakota, for instance.

I spent about five or six hours today bumping around through the brush with a county agricultural agent looking at some of the wells and springs we're opening up in our water development job. This is desert country, mind you. But the county agent pointed out to me half a dozen varieties of vegetation right there on the desert that the stock can eat, now that there is water there for them to drink. It had not been available before because of lack of water. The cattle had to go so far for water that the food did them no good. . . . Now, contrast this with range country I saw in Dakota last fall, where the grasshoppers had eaten the grass down so that it looked as though it had been run over with a lawn mower, and you get the idea. No rye grass or sand grass or edible kinds of brush on those ranges, as there are here.

I know, too, that most of these ranchers are in a bad way. The banks own their stock. They'll probably lose much of it.

But anyway they are better off than those poor devils in the Dakotas. I doubt very seriously if there are ANY ranchers in Nevada as badly off as some of those I saw in South Dakota. . . .

I asked the director just what he thought would be the needs of the cattlemen in his county this winter. Stock feed? Human food? Clothing? And so on.

Yes, he said, all those things would be needed. . . .

"These people are desperate!" he hotly declared. "Desperate!"

"Just what are they desperate about?" I asked him. "They've got roofs over their heads, haven't they?"

"Oh, yes."

"Have they no food in their houses? Are their cupboards empty?" I demanded.

"No, not now," he conceded. "Some of them have raised quite a bit of garden stuff this summer. And of course they can always go out and kill a calf." * * *

"Are their children without clothing?" I asked. "Will they have to go barefooted this winter?"

He replied that he didn't think they were that badly off.

"Well, then, just what are they so desperate about?" I asked.

"Why, they're going to lose their cattle. They're desperate about the future," he answered.

Whereupon I proceeded to tell that gentleman about the children I'd seen running about with bare feet in Bottineau county, North Dakota, in zero weather last autumn, about the farmers in South Dakota who were clawing mildewed Russian thistle out of the stacks they had cut for their cattle and making it into soup, about those absolutely dry ranges on the Rosebud reservation in South Dakota, about cattle I'd seen, so weak they could barely walk, about horses that dropped dead from starvation when they tried to work them on the roads, about stock that had died from eating so much dirt with the grass roots that they had to dig up out of the ground to get anything at all. Maybe I shouldn't have, but I was so damned mad. I thought perhaps I could drive into what he calls his head the idea that perhaps there were other parts of this country worse off than Humboldt county, Nevada, and that possibly in those parts of the country relief was going to cost quite a bit this winter, with the result that states like Nevada might not be able to have quite EVERYTHING they wanted. I don't think I succeeded. But I hope he is feeling a little calmer by now. And maybe he'll think about those things occasionally. That stuff about the cattle dying from mudballs in their stomachs seemed to make a little dent.

What a people we are! "Guv'ment easy money," as the Negroes used to say down around Savannah, Georgia, last winter. And from the politicians one grand chorus: "Let's get our slice of the pie!"

Well, as I said before, I spent a hot, dusty, bumpy morning out in the brush having a look at some of our water development projects. They are grand. And there are some cattlemen hereabouts who will tell you most enthusiastically that this water development program is the finest help anyone has ever given them. They haven't ALL got the "gimmies." Some of them are damned grateful.

What the water development program really is doing is to open up thousands of acres of fairly good range that couldn't be used before because of lack of water. You see, a cow, to keep in any sort of condition at all, must have water once a day. Six miles, to the water and back to the feeding ground, is about the most an animal can walk, and that's too much. This morning I was out in a great big valley, where, as I said before, the county agricultural agent pointed out to me several kinds of vegetation that the cattle can eat and thrive on until the snow — if there is any — gets so deep that they can't get at it. Some of it doesn't become edible until after the frost comes. It's late fall feeding, good after they come down out of the mountains. And NONE of that feed had been available before because of lack of water. This is what the water developmemt program is doing — opening up fairly good feeding places all over the state. Instead of a vast dry desert with no water at all or only a few mudholes, you have still a desert — but a desert with a fair amount of food on it and every few miles some troughs filled with clean, clear water that means the difference between life and death to those cattle. I can't help feeling that it is a grand idea, and more than one cattleman will tell you the same thing.

I think we're going to save money for the government by doing it, too. Incidentally, all of the wells are being dug on government property. Most of the range out here that isn't owned by the Southern Pacific railroad — which got every other section given it during, I believe, the Grant administration — is owned by the government. * * * Well, this is how we are going to save money. By opening up some of that range, we'll not have to start buying feed for that stock right away. Although the ranchers are holding them back in the mountains as long as they can, those cattle and sheep will have to come down pretty soon now. Before the first snow. Without that feeding ground opened up in the foothills and valleys, they'd have to be provided with other food right away. And it looks as though the government may have to buy most of that food. As it is, they'll be able to get along for several weeks without it — maybe up until the end of November. And your wells and springs aren't so expensive. A good well, with a windmill, costs $400 or less. A spring a whole lot less. And they'll last for years, most of them. So * * * it looks sensible to me. . . .

To Harry L. Hopkins

Salt Lake City, September 1, 1934

Dear Mr. Hopkins:

. . . I spent part of the afternoon with Mrs. May Stevens, one of the Salt Lake City case work supervisors. She is a trained social worker of considerable experience and has an excellent reputation. People in the state relief administration say she is one of the best in this part of the country. She impressed me as being an exceptionally broad-minded, intelligent, honest sort of person. . . .

The committee in charge of relief activities in Salt Lake City must be, from what I've been told, pretty hopeless. It apparently is stupid, not particularly in sympathy with the federal program, and utterly lacking in any imagination or social sense. There are strong indications that it is tied up with the political crowd. The original committee was appointed by one of the county commissioners, I was told. Since then, whenever there has been a vacancy, the members of the committee have themselves appointed someone to fill it. It has thus become a self-perpetuating body.

Here are some samples of the membership. The chairman was appointed because he had once been welfare director for one of the mining companies. I may be prejudiced, but my experience with welfare directors of mining companies has not given me any assurance that they fit into our picture at all. One of the members, a woman who lives in a suburb, organized sewing projects for women in her community and became so enthusiastic that she went out recruiting women to work in the sewing rooms, regardless of whether they needed the work or not! These are just samples!

The county relief director has held political jobs most of his life. His last, I believe, was superintendent of the state fair! The head of the works program, an architect, also has spent most of his life in political jobs. As Mrs. Stevens put it:

"He tried practicing his profession on his own, but failed, so they gave him this job." . . .

In Mrs. Stevens' district there are 1,169 cases — families and single persons. Of these, she says, only 300 are at work, far below the number of those qualified to work.

As another indication of political meddling, Mrs. Stevens cited the fact that clients who are at work continually come into her office complaining that they have been transferred from one job to another, apparently without any reason.

"They make the charge," she said, "that it's because of politics. Whatever I've been able to find out would indicate that this is true.

When a man is taken off a perfectly good project near his home and, for no reason whatever, is sent to a less desirable job away across the city, and his job given to someone else, it looks queer, doesn't it? And this happens very frequently — too often to be accidental, it seems to me."

They have in Salt Lake City a clothing warehouse. People up at the Capitol openly charge that this is purely a political set-up.

So far, the social service department has not been allowed to have anything to do with setting up budgets for the families in the work program. They were arbitrarily set up by the works director, Mrs. Stevens said, with resultant confusion and irritation on the part of the clients. Recently the social service division has been granted the privilege of SUGGESTING what a family's budget should be!

The standards on direct relief, Mrs. Stevens said, are lamentably low. For a single person, $1.50 worth of groceries every two weeks! For two persons, $3.50. And so on. They had a commissary here until the unemployed rose up in wrath and raided it a couple of times. Now they give them grocery orders.

"The disorder occurred mostly last summer," Mrs. Stevens said. "Things have been quieter this summer, largely, I think, because of surplus commodities, which have helped to keep these people from actually being hungry."

The committee in its work projects so far has shown no imagination whatever. The members apparently have no conception of what we're driving at. Until, I believe, last week, there wasn't a single project for white collar or professional people. All pick and shovel work. . . .

One of the rather delightful things Mrs. Stevens told me about relief clients is that, here in Salt Lake City at least, they have developed a slang of their own! They always refer to FERA, for instance, as "Santa Claus." And their identification cards are known as "dennies."

Next to the feeling that the whole show is being run politically, she said, they seem to mind most being "regimented." They hate like poison having certain days set when they may visit their case worker in her office. They loathe being investigated all the time. They want to be "on their own," with wages, however little, to spend as they see fit. Those at work are beginning to grumble about the pay — that it is woefully inadequate. Mrs. Stevens thinks this may be largely due to the fact that the budgets were arbitrarily set by the work director without any knowledge of the families' needs.

"Look at it from any angle you choose," she said, "these people will never be happy or contented until they are employed, on some basis other than relief. Their discontent is growing. They are beginning to feel that they never will get back to a normal, self-respecting existence. And I hate to think what may happen if this goes on much longer."

One thing that worries Mrs. Stevens is what is happening to the children. She cited this as an example of what she means:

"A school nurse reported to me one day that she had overheard two small boys boastfully arguing about whose father had been on relief longest! And later the principal of another school reported the same thing to one of my workers."

Mrs. Stevens also gave me my first report on how the young college graduates are making out in the social service department. Two girls, fresh out of the University of Nevada, were assigned to her this summer, one 21, the other 22. Both were "A" students in college, majoring in the required subjects. . . .

"One of them is pretty good," she said. "The other is bad. What they both lack, most woefully, is maturity. I have to watch them every minute. I seriously question the wisdom of turning these youngsters, no matter how excellent their technical training, loose on these people. Maturity, the judgment that comes with maturity, cannot be acquired in any classroom. The difference between the one who is pretty good and the one who is bad is entirely a matter of maturity. The better one seems older." . . .

Well — I feel that from Mrs. Stevens I did get a fairly good idea of what some of these clients are thinking about. Except for white collar people or the organized discontented, I find it rather difficult to get "next" to them myself, although I'm going to try very hard to get frank expressions out of some of them in the rural areas as I drive through Wyoming and Kansas these next two weeks.

She told me a couple of interesting stories about them.

One was about a young chap with a wife and several small children who had been sent to a CCC camp and came home on leave. He dropped into Mrs. Stevens' office one day while he was home. He was an exceptionally fine young fellow, she said, and instead of sending $25 home every month, he had been sending $29, keeping only $1 a month for himself.

"Oh, yes, I like it fine there," he told her, "only — sometimes I can't eat. The food is fine, but the trouble is they feed us so much better there than the folks get at home that I feel ashamed and it sort of chokes me."

And here's the other story:

One of the problems they have here in Utah is polygamy. It's a hangover from the old Mormon church. Out in some of the remote districts, I'm told, it is practised to a greater extent than anyone would believe. And all sorts of difficulties arise, such as incest. You see, Mormons believe — or Mormons used to believe, and some of the more ignorant of them apparently still do — that the air is just filled with little souls flying around waiting to be born, and that it doesn't matter how they're born, so long as they are born. The church, of course, has discarded polygamy and kicks anyone out who is known to practise it.

But little sects grow up, here and there, and return to the old way. Mrs. Stevens says they are usually started by men, but the women take it Godawful seriously. The law can do very little about it, apparently, for they don't take out marriage licenses, so, in the eyes of the law, no bigamy is committed. Really they are just common law marriages.

Among Mrs. Stevens' clients are three polygamists. One man has four wives and nine children, the eldest 9 years old. He has two wives living together in one house on one side of town, and two living together on the other side of town. All four families are on relief. Case workers report that the wives get on perfectly amicably, believe they are obeying the will of God, and are dead in earnest about it. The latest "bride" was a schoolteacher. And she presented the "community husband" with a house and lot and an automobile! And apparently there is nothing to stop him from going on and siring four children a year and marrying houses and lots and automobiles until he reaches senility! The man, Mrs. Stevens remarked, has had two years of college.

"What's his occupational background?" I asked.

"He gave his occupation as promoter," she replied, her eyes dancing with glee.

While we're on this subject of birth rates, I'll tell you another story. Yesterday, going through one of those big bundles of stuff the office sends out, I came upon "Confidential Research Bulletin (Not for Release) No. 3046," put out by the research section of the Division of Research and Statistics. It was carefully encased in a yellow cover, was dated August 13, and was entitled "Fertility of Relief and Non-Relief Families." It was based on a study made by Dr. S. A. Stouffer of the University of Wisconsin of 5,520 families in Milwaukee. The study indicated that between October 1, 1930, and December 31, 1933, there were 35 percent more confinements in the relief group than in the non-relief group.

Now this may not be the whole answer, but I think it deserves consideration.

A couple of weeks ago, while I was down in the San Joaquin Valley, California, several clients and former clients were brought in to tell me about working conditions in the cotton and fruit industry. Among them was a woman, rather above the average, who had gone out with her husband last year into the cotton fields. They didn't make enough even to support themselves while they were working, but that has nothing to do with this story.

The next morning the case worker who used to visit that family — the woman's husband is back at work now, temporarily at least, and they are off relief — called me up and said the woman wanted to see me, alone. So I went to see her.

Falteringly, terribly ill at ease at first, she told me she wanted to talk to me about something that had nearly driven her crazy when she and her husband were on relief and that she knew was one of the worst problems of women whose husbands were out of work.

"It's this thing of having babies," she said. "You've got no protection at all. And here you are, surrounded by young ones you can't support and never knowing when there's going to be another.

"You don't have any money, you see, to buy anything at the drugstore. All you have is a grocery order. I've known women to try to sell some of their groceries to get a little money to buy the things needed. But if they catch you at it, they'll take you off relief. Maybe they wouldn't really, but there's always that fear.

"Maybe you could tell your case worker, but lots of women don't like to talk about those things to outsiders. You understand, I'm not asking any help for myself. My husband's working now, and it's alright with us."

She looked at me timidly.

"I suppose you can say the easiest way would be not to do it. But it wouldn't be. You don't know what it's like when your husband's out of work. He's gloomy and unhappy all the time. Life is terrible. You must try all the time to keep him from going crazy. And many times — that's the only way."

Waiting for me in a car outside while I was talking with her was Stanley Abel, one of the best county commissioners I ever met. He is welfare commissioner, and they tell me he has nearly been run out of the county several times because he set up a rule that no pregnant woman, no matter where she came from, whether she was a resident of the county or not, can be turned away from the county hospital of which he is in charge.

Mr. Abel's county hospital operates a free prenatal clinic, too, but when I asked him if the clinic gave any birth control assistance, he looked terribly shocked and shook his head.

Before I close, even though this is a long letter, I must tell you about my session with the Mormon dignitaries this afternoon, before my session with Mrs. Stevens.

In three big, deep, soft chairs, in a dim and luxuriously furnished office in the Church Office building (right next to Brigham Young's Beehive) they sat — Heber Grant, Brother [Anthony Woodward] Ivins, and J. Reuben Clark. I believe all three have the title of "President." President Grant, nodding — he went to sleep a couple of times — showing life only when something was mentioned about banking and defaulting on interest payments. President Clark, round, impassive, for the most part silent. President Ivins, aged, apparently almost bloodless, doing most of the talking.

I was accompanied by Dean Brimhall, a member of the state relief staff. His grandfather was one of Brigham Young's right-hand men. His father was for years president of Brigham Young university. He calls himself an "apostate," or something of the sort, and informed me, with some glee, as we went in, that Warren Harding was the only man who ever had nerve enough to light a cigaret in that building. (I suspect him of warning me.) At any rate, Dean Brimhall is not exactly an enthusiastic supporter of the Church.

Said President Grant, before relapsing into his afternoon nap: "I can tell you one effect of your relief out here in Utah. People are defaulting on their interest payments and their mortgages so they can get Government relief."

Said President Clark: "The Government was going to build a new pipe to carry water down from the mountains into the little town where I live. There's been talk of putting in a new pipe for several years, but we've never got around to it. I guess maybe they felt it might be needed more this year on account of the drouth. It would cost $20,000. I asked if it was going to be a loan or a gift. They said it was going to be a gift. So I said, 'No—this town isn't going to rob the United States Treasury.' I guess we can get along without that pipe a few years more."

Said President Ivins, after defending the Relief administration, on the ground that "if we didn't give them relief, they'd come and take it": "Here's one message I wish you'd take back to Washington, to President Roosevelt. Tell him to rid this country of these aliens."

More was said, by me mostly, asking questions—politely, oh, so politely, you just wouldn't believe that I could be so polite! But it's hardly worth setting down.

And all the time, across the room, sat the grandson of one of Brigham Young's right-hand men, the son of a former president of Brigham Young university—literally writhing in a rage to which he dared not give expression!

After that conversation, I don't think the New Deal can count much on understanding or support from the Latter Day Saints of Utah!

To Harry L. Hopkins

Salt Lake City, September 2, 1934

Dear Mr. Hopkins:

Fairly briefly, I shall now conclude my observations on the state of Nevada.

I spent my last day in Nevada in Elko, in the heart of the sheep and cattle country, and sat around most of the afternoon talking with a small group of stock men. There are in that county some 125,000 head of cattle, said to be nearly half the cattle in the state, and about 345,000 head of sheep, more than a third of the sheep in the state. Twenty thousand of the sheep belong in Idaho and will go back there this winter. They will probably be alright, I was told, for there seems to be quite a bit more feed in Idaho than in Nevada. In fact, some of the Nevada sheep men are planning to winter their sheep in Idaho.

Removing the 20,000 Idaho sheep, you have left in Elko county 325,000 head. The Government, it is expected, will buy about 50,000 of them. There is in the county now enough hay to carry 20,000 of them through the winter. That leaves in the county some 270,000 sheep with no place to go this winter for feed.

"I guess we'll just have to send 'em South and let 'em starve," one sheep man said.

The cattle situation is better. After the Government takes out from 5,000 to 8,000 head, cattle men say they think they will be able, with the hay that is available, to get the rest through the winter.

It's the sheep men who are really worried.

Ordinarily these sheep would be driven down into the Southern part of the state late in October to graze through the winter. But stock men who had been down there looking things over told me there is nothing for them to eat down there this year.

One man, who said he had 40,000 head of sheep, told me he would feel safe in taking his sheep South if it rains between now and October 15. Another man, who had recently been in the South disagreed with him. It's too late now, he said, for rains to do any good. . . .

South of Elko county the condition of the stock is bad, although, I gathered, this is only a small portion of the state. I was told that a Government inspector killed 27 out of 52 head of cattle because they were too emaciated to be driven to the railroad for shipping. Incidentally, since I have been in Utah, I've heard that some of the cattle bought by the Government were in such poor condition that the meat on the carcasses refused to set after they were hung in the refrigerators. "Setting" is a kind of hardening process that is supposed to occur when the carcass is chilled.

"After four days in the ice house, it was so soft you could poke your finger right into it," one of the relief workers told me.

She had gone to one of the slaughter houses to see if she couldn't get some fat for a soap-making project. There wasn't a handful of fat on any of those carcasses, she said.

As I have said before, cattle men with whom I talked appeared to be fairly cheerful. As a matter of fact, after what I saw in the Dakotas a year ago, I swear I don't think these people out here know the meaning of the word "drouth." Normally, of course, it's drier out here. They say their drouth has lasted 11 years. But, honestly, in Nevada I neither saw nor heard anything that could touch what I saw and heard in South Dakota last fall.

And, in the light of that, I am a bit irritated — I can't help it — at the state of mind of some of the good people of Nevada. Dammit, they've got the "gimmies," that's all. It's Government money, and they want their share. They think only in terms of their own county. They aren't even state-minded, some of them, let alone being national-minded.

For instance, when I was there, a lively row was going on in adjoining Elko and Humboldt counties because Humboldt county felt that the forest service chief, in charge of water development in Humboldt National Forest, which lies in both counties, was having more wells dug in Elko county, where he lives, than in Humboldt county. They were spending hours fighting about it!

Some of the ranchers aren't even county-minded. There have been rows over locating some of the wells. The wells are all dug on Government property, which the ranchers have divided up among themselves, on some sort of "squatters' rights," as range country. They don't pay the Government a cent for the use of it — or haven't up until now — but they regard it as their own property. And you have the pretty picture of ranchers refusing to allow wells to be dug on Government property because they might attract cattle belonging to another owner onto range that the rancher regards as his own.

Their attitude toward our water development program is interesting. They regard it as a permanent improvement of their range, and they are jubilant about it, although now and then someone wonders what all this well-digging is going to do to the water table. They don't look on it so much as a drouth-relief measure as a means of increasing their profits in future years.

"Now this is something [we] like," one cattle man assured me. "All that CWA work was wasted, building parks and making skating rinks for kids."

It's just Government money, you see, and they're going to get all of it they can, for their future enrichment. It's getting for nothing something that's going to make a lot of money for them, they think, in the future. It's in no sense a partnership with the Government. It's just getting all they can out of the Government. . . .

Another thing they keep talking about is the possibility of a loss of "taxable wealth," if the herds are badly diminished. The idea is that the Federal Government, through income taxes, paid largely in the industrial East, shall save Nevada's state income.

Sometimes I get so damned mad when people start talking about chiseling and grasping instincts among the unemployed.

In Elko I got a rather unhappy impression of the transient business. I've got so I dodge every time anybody says "transient" to me, anyway. We're not solving this thing. Not that I think we could, as a matter of fact. All we're doing is supplying over-night free stops to them and herding a few of them into camps, where we beg them to remain. The trains out here are so thick with them that you could pick 'em off like bedbugs.

Near Elko is a transient camp, and the director — too young, too inexperienced, and too kind of sissified, in my humble opinion, to be any good at his job — wept on my shoulder.

"They're a lot of bums," he wailed. "We've found only one man in the camp who can be trusted in the commissary.

"They won't stay put. We send 'em home, and they come right back. We're simply encouraging them to travel. You can't make them stay in any camp. Fifty of them left our camp last week. A week ago Sunday we didn't have a ball game, and the next day half the team checked out."

I think the young man is something of a fool, perhaps — misplaced, at any rate — but you do hear much the same sort of thing all the time.

One thing he said did interest me. Very often, when they write to the place of residence of a transient — especially a transient family — they'll get a letter back, acknowledging the fact that the individual or the family belongs there, but refusing to authorize return. Seattle, he said, is one of the worst offenders. Very often, too, a man will bob up again after he's been sent home, saying he couldn't get work and they wouldn't give him relief.

It seems to me that, if we're ever going to get ANYWHERE with this transient business, we've got to have better cooperation between states and communities and better follow-up work on these people after we send them home. It seems to me that about the only constructive job I've seen is that in the boys' camps in California, where they don't send a boy home until there is assurance he will be looked after when he gets there. And at least in those camps they have separated the kids from the professional transients and are teaching them something. Mostly, however, I'm afraid the whole thing is a joke.

Several people have suggested the possibility of enlarging the CCC service to take in the transients. Others had added the suggestion that the younger men be taken into the CCC camps, and that other camps — sort of permanent camps — be established for the men who are too old to work. "National poor farms," you might call them. Another suggestion is that we set up camps around the country where men out of work can go and work for, say $30 a month, to save some money, so that when they do go hunting for jobs again they'll be able to pay their way. Then, if they can't get work, they can return to the camps, save some more, and try again.

I know one thing. Those work camps for unattached men in California are a flop. They can't get any work out of them — I've heard that over and over again — and here's why, according to the men themselves:

They can't get out of their heads the idea that they are expected to do the work of men in the CCC camps, but for $5 a month instead of $30.

329

You can tell them, until you're black in the face, that the CCC boys really get only $5 because they are required to send $25 home. They won't believe you.

And they also resent the camps because they feel they are shut off from all possibility of getting jobs. They're isolated. They admit they are more comfortable in the camps, and that the amount of work required doesn't over-tax their strength. But they don't want to live in camps all the rest of their lives. They want JOBS, and they want to get out and hunt for jobs. . . .

To Harry L. Hopkins

Cheyenne, Wyoming, September 9, 1934

Dear Mr. Hopkins:

Human patience is a beautiful — and terrible — thing.

Last Thursday on the way down here from Casper I went with the engineer in charge of the Wyoming work relief program to look at a project near Douglas. They are building a wooden bridge over the Platte river, tearing down the old one as they go.

A dozen men were at work, under the supervision of a foreman, who appeared worried and kept clucking at them like an old mother hen. He was constantly warning them to be careful. As a matter of fact, most of them acted as though they were not at all familiar with the kind of work they were doing, and the foreman told me he was afraid all the time that someone would get hurt.

While I stood by, listening, the engineer entered into a conversation with one of them, a husky, goodlooking fellow of about 30, who was prying away with a crowbar, trying to loosen some planks on the old bridge, patiently and so clumsily that I expected any moment to see him take a header into the river.

"How you making out on your budget?" the engineer asked.

"Fair," the man replied.

His budget, for himself, his wife, and two children, was somewhere around $30 a month, but last month he hadn't got all of it because a shortage of money had necessitated cutting the budgets of most of the workers.

"It ain't hardly enough to get by on," the man said mildly, "but I'm glad to have it, such as it is, and I guess the Government's doing all it can."

Prying around, trying to find a way of working the plank loose, he added quietly, almost apologetically:

330

"This ain't my kind of work, and I don't know much about it. I'm a plasterer by trade, but I haven't been able to get any work in that line to amount to anything for a long, long time." . . .

Wyoming and possibly Utah are the only states I've visited where I've had a chance to observe the state of mind of clients who have been on projects under our present work program long enough to realize that it isn't "just another kind of CWA." Most of these Western states seem to have started very late. Wyoming's work program has been in progress, however, since last April.

I'm sorry, but I haven't heard a good word for that budget system of ours since I've been in the state. The clients themselves, the engineers, foremen on the job, the social workers, members of the relief commit- tees — they're all against it. The mildest critics were, by and large, the clients themselves.

In Casper, a man at work on a high school stadium project said:

"I'd be better satisfied to work six days a week and get my check every Saturday night and know I was going to get it, no matter how little it was, than I am this way. This ain't a job. I don't know exactly what you'd call it, but it ain't no job — not when some case worker comes and tells you how much you need to live on, decides for you, and you only work two or three days a week, and then maybe you don't even get all the case worker says you should have. A man doesn't feel he's getting anywhere, somehow."

Two men working on a park project near Casper came over and asked the engineer:

"Say, when they going to bring CWA back?"

They, too, complained about the budget system — with some bitter- ness as to the inadequacy of the budgets.

"It's a funny thing," one of them said. "If our kids get run down because they don't get enough to eat, they start this nutrition business, or send 'em away to camps to feed 'em up. Wouldn't it be better to give us enough to live on right, so we can feed our kids ourselves? I wish they'd cut out a lot of this monkey business and just give us jobs and let us run our own affairs."

We visited a canning project at a little town called Wheatland. A woman dishing steaming corn out of a big kettle into tin cans said there were four in her family, and that in August she got $16. (Budgets were cut in that county in August because of lack of funds.) . . .

So much for the attitude of the clients. The more articulate of them go into the offices and kick, of course. Mostly, however, their attitude is one of patience — a rather terrible sort of patience, I think. And cer- tainly this program gives them no feeling of security whatever, no hope for the future. It is to them just a stop-gap, something they're getting by on — and barely getting by.

They can't go on on this basis forever. And even here in Wyoming, with its small and, for the most part widely scattered population — even on the main highways in this state I've driven darned nearly 100 miles at a stretch without seeing a human being or any sign of one — I've encountered the old story. People who apparently aren't ever going to get their jobs back in private industry.

When I was in the Beaumont-Port Arthur oil fields, in Texas, last spring, I was told that the oil refineries would not take back men who were over 35 years old. There are big oil refineries in this state (home of the Teapot Dome) . . . and up in the vicinity of Casper. And here, too, I've heard the same story. They don't want men over 35!

The head of the social service division up at Casper told me the other day that the superintendent of one refinery, I believe, at Midwest, had asked him to move 12 families out of the company town into Casper. The heads of none of these families, he said, would ever be employed in the refinery again. One or two had been involved in some labor dispute and were blacklisted, but the rest were all over the age limit — that is, they were over 35. . . .

More and more, some of them feel, there is growing among the clients and the general public a resistance to social work. I can see that, too.

For one thing — I hear more about this in the cities than in a thinly populated state like Wyoming — there is a feeling that, more and more, the really good social workers, experienced, mature, adequately trained, are being drawn away from contact with the clients into administrative jobs, their places being taken by those younger, less experienced, less mature, less adequately equipped. . . .

Aside from these things, you don't hear much kicking in Wyoming. There's been some difficulty over transients, but it's being ironed out. Cheyenne resented the presence of the transients in the shelter in the city, and they seem to have got themselves in bad by refusing, so I was told, to go out and work a few days, at $4 a day, repairing a railroad after a washout. There are undoubtedly two sides to that story. But transients simply aren't popular anywhere — except in Florence, Ala., where they built that marvelous park system. . . . I insist that the weak spot in the transient service lies in lack of cooperation between states and communities and lack of any sort of uniformity in standards in the various states.

The projects themselves in this state, aside from a feeling on the part of the public that too many airports were built, seem to have general approval. Especially those that have to do with drouth relief and conservation of water supply. There is a feeling that the Department of Commerce unloaded too many airports on the state under CWA. They tell me they built airports in places in Wyoming where there isn't a Chinaman's chance of a plane landing once a year. But, compared with all the other good work that is being done and has been done, that's a rather small matter.

Production units are just being set up. Not much public comment on them so far. The canning projects, of course, are nearly always popular. [Will] Metz[1] tells me he's planning to can enough beef so that every relief family in the state will have somewhere between 15 and 20 pounds of beef a month for the next year.

He has a tannery project, too, that sounds interesting. In the sheep buying program they are going to condemn and shoot, right on the range, thousands of head of sheep in the next few weeks. Metz is going to skin them and tan the hides. And to facilitate the skinning operations, he has taken on some Austrian who knows how to "blow them up." You insert the business end of a bicycle pump or automobile tire pump under the skin in the animal's leg and simply blow the skin away from the carcass. That way, he says, you can skin 'em mighty fast. I regret that I am not going to be able to see this operation myself — it doesn't start for about a week — but I warned Metz he'd better not get too close!

Metz has another project that I'm keen about, although he's a little bit in doubt because he says he can't find it in the rules. However, he believes in it himself and is going ahead with it, and I enclose a copy of the plan.

Briefly, it's this:

There are in drouth relief families in this state several hundred boys and girls of high school age who cannot go to high school this year because their families can't afford to pay their board in town, and work in the towns for room and board is mighty scarce because of the poverty of the townspeople. A trading center, like Douglas, for instance, is absolutely flat when the ranchers and farmers have no money.

Metz believes it will be a good thing to get these youngsters away from their homes this winter and into school, where they would normally be. They have to live in town, of course. Distances out here are tremendous, you know. So, under the general supervision of the Department of Education, he is setting up a system of dormitories in the towns where there are high schools. The communities are to cooperate, furnishing the houses and some of the equipment. Supervision, necessary repairs on buildings, and so on are to be made a work project. Most of the food will be out of surplus commodities. Whatever additional cost there is will be prorated among the families, the father to work it out. Metz expects to have some 300 or 400 boys and girls living in these dormitories and going to high school this winter. The thing is not really started yet. An outline of the plan and a questionnaire are going out to the communities this week. The plan was evolved in answer to a demand from several communities.

I believe he is planning to finance it out of drouth relief funds. Well, all the children involved will be from drouth relief families! . . .

This drouth business gets worse the further East you go. For instance, the sage brush is scantier and lower to the ground in Western Wyoming than it is in Nevada. As you drive across the state, it gets gradually worse. Driving down from Casper Thursday I saw for the first time — although I admit I didn't see the worst in Nevada or in Utah, perhaps — conditions that began to approach what I saw in the Dakotas last fall.

They've had grasshoppers as well as drouth in Wyoming this summer. And once more I saw range that looked as though it had been gone over with a safety razor and stacks of Russian thistle put up for winter feed. Apparently the grasshoppers hadn't been quite so bad as they were in Dakota, though. They hadn't eaten the corn. But the corn and a few potatoes had grown up only a few inches before the sun burned them up.

I didn't see many cattle on this side of the state. I spent most of last Tuesday morning, however, in the stockyards at Rock Springs looking over the stuff the Government was buying. Most of it had come down out of the mountains and not in such bad shape, either, I was told. But there won't be a damned thing for it to eat this winter, so the Government is buying it. From the standpoint of breeding, most of it is grand stuff. Pure bred Hereford. They tell me there is a law in this state penalizing a man who turns a scrub bull loose on the range! Certainly these are much finer range cattle than you see in the Dakotas.

Incidentally, most of those cattle had been trucked into Rock Springs. They couldn't be driven. No water holes at all.

By and large, the cattle men appear to be deeply appreciative of what the Government is doing to help them out.

"Many of us are desperate," one of them told me. "I think we'd just pack up and move out and leave our stock to starve if the Government hadn't stepped in. This gives us new hope, to try again."

They are all, of course, praying for a good hard winter out here, with lots of snow. It's the only thing that will save them. And if it comes, as they hope it will, our expense for human relief is going to mount terrifically. Many of these people — and that must include parts of other surrounding states — haven't had any cash for a long time. Their clothes, their bedding, things like that are worn out.

On that intangible thing, what people are thinking about, I have some more rather interesting dope. I still get, more and more, that impression that they are expecting a big change in our whole economic system. They seem to think it's coming — socialism, many of them say — and that the President couldn't stop it if he tried! . . .

1. Wyoming FERA administrator.

To Eleanor Roosevelt

Topeka, Kansas   September 14, 1934

Dear You:

. . . Tonight we went out to the Kansas Free State Fair with Mary Smith, assistant to the administrator and herself a native Kansan. And where they all came from I don't know, but you never saw so many apples in your life. The whole show — fruit, grain, livestock, everything — Miss Smith said, compared very favorably with former years. And yet the whole state of Kansas has been included in the primary drouth area! Furthermore, the place was packed. You never saw so many new Chevrolets in your life. One man had sold eight or ten "electric" refrigerators, operated by natural gas or kerosene, to farmers' wives! And Mary Smith wound up the evening by telling me this one:

Julius Stone, representing Lawrence Westbrook, came out here recently to start plans for a rural rehabilitation program. He went out into Western Kansas, in the real drouth area, and came back and told her with a puzzled air, she said, that the farmers told him:

"All we need is a little rain!"

They didn't want to be "rehabilitated." They didn't want to be transplanted. There is something pathetic in that story. But tonight the humor of it hit me right in the stomach. I laughed and laughed. Dammit, I wonder if we don't need a little more humor injected into this business. I wonder if we aren't rather losing our perspective. Maybe I'm the only one who is taking it so seriously, though. But I think not. Certainly I'm no more deadly serious — and no more unconsciously funny — than most of the people I talk with. . . .

To Harry L. Hopkins

Kansas City [Mo.], September 15, 1934

Dear Mr. Hopkins:

. . . Kansas is a funny state. Oh, I always thought it was funny, but it is funny, I find, in a way quite different than I had imagined.

Here's what I mean:

There's no doubt at all about there having been a drouth in Kansas this year. All you've got to do to realize that is to drive through the state. You drive for miles through country where you know they couldn't have harvested a peck of anything this year. Miles and miles of burnt brown pastures. Here and there a cornfield that burned up before the stuff ever got much above knee-high. Fields of scant, ragged wheat stubble with pathetically little piles of straw. Russian thistle piled up for stock feed.

335

They're selling the stuff in Western Kansas now — from $6 to $8 a ton. We also have several work projects for cutting and stacking Russian thistle. Everywhere, terribly thin cattle. All the evidence of drouth, certainly.

That's one side of the picture.

Last night in Topeka we went to the Kansas Free State Fair. And, dammit, judging by the exhibits at that fair, you wouldn't have known there had been a drouth in Kansas at all! It seemed to me I'd never seen so many apples in my life before! And all out of Northeastern Kansas, where wells that hadn't gone dry in 60 years went dry this summer! All kinds of grain. Alfalfa. Hay, although I swear I drove two days without ever seeing a haystack. That fair would give you the idea that the whole state of Kansas was a garden spot!

Plenty of evidences of prosperity, too. Big crowds. Literally hundreds of new Chevrolets. Ten thousand people in the grand stand for the night show Thursday night. Hot dog sellers, peanut vendors, church supper pavilions — all doing a rushing business. One "electric" refrigerator salesman — the contraption operates with natural gas or kerosene — told me he'd sold ten during the week, at prices ranging from $200 to $295. * * * The hotels in Topeka had done a grand business all summer. Not especially tourist trade, either, they said. "Just business — traveling salesmen." . . . And, to top it all off, Grace Falke went shopping here in Kansas City this afternoon and came back and reported that the department stores were jammed to the doors, and that salespeople told her the stores were getting right now the best business they'd seen in five years! * * * Where's all the money coming from? It's too much for me.

Of course, there are spots in Kansas where there was no drouth this year, and farmers who have any crop are getting good money for it, or expect to. Probably a lot of this buying is being done on credit. Big, heavy farm machinery. Automobiles. All sorts of gadgets. * * * For instance, in the washroom of an office building in Topeka, I saw something I'd never encountered before. A hot-air drier for your hands, taking the place of towels, roller or paper. It operates like a hair-drier in a shampoo parlor, by electricity. You step on a pedal and it turns on the hot air, which dries your hands. As Grace Falke remarked:

"Wouldn't you just know they'd have it in Topeka, Kansas?"

We drove into Kansas Tuesday, from Colorado. All that day and until late Thursday afternoon all we saw, except for now and then a field or two, everything looked burnt up. They'd had a few showers, but they were scattered. And when there had been rain there had been only enough to bring a light tinge of green to the pasture lands.

We were told that showers in the Southwestern part of the state had been more general and heavier. They are all planting winter wheat down there, expecting to turn the cattle into the fields to eat it as it comes up.

We were in the worst drouth section in the state, we were told. We visited one county where, out of 1,800 families, 1,036 are on relief, and applications are piling up. Nothing growing there at all save a few fields of badly stunted cane, planted for forage. When this stuff is stunted, prussic acid develops in the leaves and stalks. If a cow happens to get hold of any of it, she'll walk four or five steps and drop dead. * * * One farmer's wife in that county told me she had taken their cows down by a creek bed to graze. "They ate all the leaves off the trees," she said.

Thursday afternoon late we drove into Salina, and just before we got there, the country began to get green. No evidences of crop. Field after field of withered, yellow cornstalks. It hadn't even been worth cutting. But there had been enough rain so that the pastures looked green. The cane crop looked a little better. Everybody was planting winter wheat.

From Salina on, the country got greener and greener, until, in the rolling country 25 or 30 miles out of Kansas City, you might have thought you were in New England. Still, no evidences of any crop to speak of.

Our first conversation in Kansas was with a filling station operator at Sharon Springs, away over by the Colorado border. He said just about what we expected. Just a kind of wail. ("We are the best screamers you ever saw, out here in Kansas," Mary Smith, a member of the state relief staff and a native Kansan, remarked last night.) Everything was all wrong. The Government was spending too much money on the farmers. He had apparently never heard of the processing tax. The Government was spending too much money on relief. The postmaster's daughter had a job as stenographer in the relief office. And who's going to pay for all this? Oh, yes, of course, the wheat and corn checks were a big help to the community. And many of the people on relief needed help. And business had been pretty good this summer in spite of the drouth. BUT * * * and so on.

There were several more like that before we actually had a chance to sit down and talk with any farmers.

We had our first chance at them in Oakley, a little town about 85 miles from the Colorado line. Two came in, one of them an old fellow who had come out here from Connecticut 35 or 40 years ago. They had no kick at all to register against AAA or the relief program. They did complain about the high price of feed — cotton seed cake now costs $45 a ton in Kansas, a little more than $5 less than in Wyoming and Nevada — and about "suitcase farmers." A suitcase farmer is a man from the city, who buys up a lot of virgin land, cheap, comes out in the fall, plows it up — thereby destroying good buffalo grass — puts in some winter wheat, goes back to a nice, comfortable winter in the city, and comes back next summer and harvests his crop. They said they found it difficult to compete with that kind of farming. They said, too, that those fellows were chiseling in on the AAA program. Some of them have had tenants on some of their land heretofore. Now they're getting rid of them, so they can grab off more wheat allotment money. * * * They had little or no comment to make on the relief program.

We went down to Gove, about 25 miles South and East of Oakley. Here we talked to a dozen or more farmers, taking 'em as they came, around the courthouse. Among these were several who were handling the wheat and corn program, with the county commissioners.

"We were not very keen for Triple-A," one of them said, "until we sweated through it. Now we understand it, and we're for it."

He said he thought not all of the farmers understood it thoroughly, however, and that a little "missionary work" of some kind might help.

None of these farmers had any crop this year, they said. Most of them had no feed for their stock. But they felt that somehow, with the Government's help, they'd pull through the winter. And they all had hopes for next year. Optimists-plus, these people. But, you see, they've been through drouth before. Farming has never been such a cinch out in Western Kansas. And when they do get a crop, usually it brings in the money. They say they can raise wheat at somewhere around 25 cents a bushel out there — "25 cents a bushel if you're a good farmer, all the way up to 50 cents a bushel if you ain't." It costs somewhere around 70 cents a bushel to raise winter wheat in the Red River valley in North Dakota. So, you see, low prices don't worry Kansas wheat growers so much as they do wheat growers in North Dakota. We talked to some farmers who weren't on the committee.

"Well, you see, we wasn't so enthusiastic at first about the program," one of them said, "because we just couldn't believe we were going to get anything out of it. We thought there must be a string tied to it somewhere."

Here again we heard complaints about "suitcase farmers" — wheat speculators. You hear that pretty much everywhere in Kansas.

"We speculated in land out here," said Mary Smith last night, "just as city people in the East speculated in General Motors."

Up in Graham county — the county where 1,036 famlies out of 1,800 are on relief — the high cost of feed and an apparent inadequacy of relief, both our own and the "credit relief" of the Farm Credit Administration, were worrying people.

Our situation there is not so good. This month the families will get only 53 percent of their budgets. Last month they got only 40 percent. And those budgets are none too adequate, running about $35 per family, that amount including stock feed. This month the average family will get a little more than half of that $35. Last month they got only 40 percent.

Feed loans to families not on relief, we were told, were too low, and there was no assurance that a family would be able to get a loan next

338

month, after getting one this month. The loans, they said, averaged around $3 per head of cattle. They said that, with feed prices up as they are and still mounting, that was too little. It doesn't sound like much.

The result of these facts, we were most earnestly informed, is that many of these people are selling off too much of their stock. Milch cows, for instance, that have provided the only cash income of most of those families in the last three years of drouth. They will go into the spring with no resources to carry them if they cut their herds down too low. Some of them are even selling all their chickens, we were told, because they had nothing to feed them. . . .

"Our farmers," said the banker in Hill City, "are in the position of knowing they can borrow money for feed, but only a month at a time. They aren't sure they will be able to borrow next month. They lack any sense of security. And they are worried about feed prices going up all the time. Anyway, they don't like the idea of buying a little at a time, this way, especially when prices are going up. They don't like the idea of driving into town and carrying home a couple of bales of hay on the back of the automobile. They don't like the idea of being able to see the bottom of the grain bin this early in the fall.

"The result if that they're afraid to take a chance and are selling off their stock. Out of six or eight people selling milk in this town, only one is selling now. Milk was 8 cents a quart here in Hill City in August. It costs 10 cents a quart now."

Several people up there thought it would "make better sense" if the relief administration would give clients more feed for their cows, so they would continue to give milk, and less for themselves. They said it would cost $8 a month to keep a cow in production through the winter, but pointed out that a cow that was giving milk would provide milk, butter, and cream — prices of all of which are rising — for the client's table, thereby cutting down his need for "human relief." And where there were several cows, keeping them in production through the winter would provide a weekly cream check.

The last assessor's report placed the cattle population of Graham county at 23,000 head. The population, we are told, is actually about 30,000 head. Of these, 8,000 have already been sold, and 14,000 are listed for sale.

"This is the worst thing that ever happened to Graham county," remarked one of the case workers, daughter of a farmer who "homesteaded" in the county and sent nine children through college on the proceeds of his farm. "If these people lose their cattle, they lose their last reserve. They won't have anything to bring in any cash should there be another drouth next year."

Another thing we'll have to watch out for in sections of Kansas this winter is a need for clothing and bedding for the clients. In parts of the state where they have had drouth for three years or longer, these people haven't had cash to replace worn out bedding and clothing. It's a situation somewhat like that in Bottineau county, North Dakota, last October. We certainly ought not let these families go into the winter without doing something about it. One case worker, in Graham county, told me that more than 50 percent of her people were in need of clothing and bedding right now. I suggested that some of those counties take a census of quilts and blankets. . . .

"Some of my folks came out to visit us from the East," one farmer told me today, "and before they came I went to town and bought one towel so they'd have one to use. We hadn't been able to buy any for years. Ours was all wore out."

But what optimists! And this optimism is going to make it difficult, I'm afraid, to launch any sort of rural rehabilitation program out here. And, as you may have heard, they are somewhat violently opposed to any move to transplant them. They just don't want rehabilitating or transplanting, that's all.

I think this story is as pathetic as it is amusing. Miss Smith told us that a few weeks ago Julius Stone, out here on a trip, went into Western Kansas. He evidently asked them about possibilities of a rural rehabilitation program and transplanting some of them to better country. He came back to Topeka, Miss Smith said, and reported that the farmers had replied in a good deal of bewilderment:

"But all we need is a little bit of rain!"

Here's a fairly typical story of Western Kansas:

In heavily patched overalls, faded almost white on the worn spots from many washings, he came in to talk with us at the courthouse down in Gove — a squat, sturdy fellow, about 35, red-headed, with a couple of days' stubble on his chin. He is married and the father of three children, the eldest a girl of 9, the youngest a boy a little over a year old.

For four years he's been living on a farm that he is buying Southwest of Gove, and during those four years he hasn't "taken a wagon load of crop off the place." He finally came on relief about a month ago.

But is he discouraged about that farm? He is not! You'd have one heck of a time convincing him he could never make a go of it. It's just been drouth, that's all. Next year will be better.

"I was rentin' up until four years ago," he said. "But I always figured I'd like to have a farm of my own, a place to raise up my family. So four years ago we sold out and began looking around for a farm to buy.

"We went over to Colorado and looked around, but I figured the land and rainfall was better over here. Finally I found this place. It's good land, all right — nuthin' the matter with it. Has an oil lease on it, which helps carry the payments. Is near a pretty good school. Has a good house on it. Give me some rain, and I'll be all right."

340

I asked him about his bedding, household equipment, clothing for the children. He was a bit reticent.

"Give me enough work, and I'll get along all right until next year," he said.

"What do you use for fuel?" I asked.

"Cow chips," he replied.

"They don't give much heat, do they?" I asked.

"Well, they do burn up pretty fast," he replied with a grin.

"How does your wife feel about the whole situation?" I asked.

"Well — she don't exactly appreciate it all the time," he replied, "but she's a 'short-grass gal,' just as I'm a 'short-grass boy' — that's what they call us out here in Western Kansas. She was born here, and she knows this country and likes it, like I do myself."

Now what are you going to do with a guy like that?

Yes, this is an interesting state. Even the Republican candiate for governor,[1] running for reelection, is a sort of New Dealer. I read an account of one of his campaign speeches the other night, and I'll swear I'd have thought it was the Democrat talking! The Democratic candidate,[2] they tell me, is having a tough time of it, because the Republican has grabbed all his campaign material!

Well — that's Kansas. . . .

1. Alfred M. Landon.
2. Omar B. Ketchum.

To Harry L. Hopkins

Washington [D.C.]   November 13, 1934

Dear Mr. Hopkins:

. . . I spent some time with two men who do contacts for the Baltimore office of the National Reemployment Service. Their assignment is to go out and get jobs for the unemployed, both relief and non-relief, who are registered with NRS in Baltimore. These two men — [H.T.] Bahnsen, a young Lutheran clergyman from St. Louis, on leave, he told me, from his church, and a middle-aged coal dealer, once worth well over $100,000, I was told, but now broke and glad to work for NRS for probably $20 a week — visit every employer in Baltimore of any consequence at all, making 15 or 20 calls a day. They certainly should know what they are talking about on this employment situation. * * * I got in touch with them, with the idea of finding out, with as many figures as possible, just what the situation looked like in the various Baltimore industrial concerns. We never got that far, because I became so much interested in their general observations. I'm not through with them yet, however. Some day next week, we are going to sit down together again and go over the whole town, payroll by payroll.

Baltimore, as you probably know, is quite diversified as to industries. There is only one really large payroll — out at the Sparrows Point plant of Bethlehem Steel. In normal times — or, let us say, previous to the depression — there were employed there, according to Findlay French, director of the industrial bureau of the Baltimore Association of Commerce, between 8,000 and 13,000 men. Mr. French said 12,000 were working there for a short time in June and July this year. The payroll was down under 7,000 in September, I was told, and apparently it was dropping.

Some of the other industries are: the Glenn Martin airplane factory, where, in the technical departments at least, things seem to be picking up a little just now, due to army contracts; soap manufacturing, Gold Dust and Procter & Gamble; a Western Electric plant; one or two fairly large plants where they manufacture bathroom fixtures; a fairly large clothing industry; a tin can factory; a number of canneries and other food processing plants that afford seasonal employment; and the usual run of small concerns.

The picture presented by my two NRS contact men — and it goes, too, for everybody in the NRS setup in Baltimore, from Oliver C. Short, state NRS director, and Mr. [H. Norman] Milburn, head of the Baltimore office, down — is not very bright. . . .

Messrs. Bahnsen and [George] Smith see no considerable increase in employment in private industry in the next few months in Baltimore. Most of the work offered now is seasonal, they say — AND AT WAGES SO LOW THAT PEOPLE ON RELIEF REFUSE TO TAKE THE JOBS BECAUSE THE WAGES OFFERED ARE LOWER THAN RELIEF.

Relief for a family of slightly under five in Baltimore now averages a little over $8 a week. The most a family of slightly under five can possibly get in Baltimore now is $12.69 a week, and darned few are getting anywhere near that amount.

"You'd be astounded at the low wages offered around here," Bahnsen told me. And he gave me some specific instances.

Stenographers work for as little as $3 a week, he said, $6 or $7 a week is average, and $13.50 top.

"There are plenty of stenographers working in the Equitable building for attorneys who get $3 a week," he said. . . .

He mentioned an iron and metal company "who want to pay men $1.50 for a 10-hour day WHENEVER THEY NEED THEM — and let them shift for themselves whenever they DON'T need them, which is most of the time."

He cited a chemical company who hired three electric crane

342

operators from NRS at 40 cents an hour, whereas the usual rate was 70 to 80 cents an hour—and then kicked because the operators sent were not skilled enough.

There is only one hotel in Baltimore, for instance, where the maids get as much as $9 a week—cleaning from 15 to 20 rooms a day and getting no tips.

In the cafeterias they pay the help 25 cents an hours, no tips, and the girls must keep their own uniforms laundered.

In other restaurants, he said, wages for waitresses average around $6 - $7 a week—and employers seeking girls from NRS insist on good looking girls, stress the amount they'll make out of tips, and frequently refer to them as "nothing but dirty little streetwalkers, anyway." * * * Mr. Bahnsen says there is one restaurant proprietor in Baltimore who employs 87 girls on these terms. Food prices in his restaurant have gone up—as wages came down. And that gentleman, Mr. Bahnsen told me, is a member of the restaurant code authority and spends a lot of time here in Washington.

He mentioned Montgomery Ward and Butler Brothers, this last a wholesale house, as having employed several stenographers, billing machine operators, and so on from NRS—at $12.50 to $13.50 a week.

"And anybody to get one of those jobs," he added, "has got to be GOOD. In stenographers generally, whether they are paying $12.50 a week or $3 a week, it is expected that they shall be able to type 60 words a minute."

The standards set up for these people—especially when you get into the garment industry and Baltimore's one or two textile mills—are, to quote my NRS people, "beyond human endurance." . . .

The vast majority of the employers have made the code minimum wage their maximum wage. In fact there is hardly an employer who pays ANYBODY more than the minimum.

"We find most employers," Bahnsen said, "strongly opposed to the codes because, they say, their employees can't make the minimum wage." Now here's the trick. If a workman can't make the minimum wage, the employer must make it up out of his own pocket. In other words, the employer has set up a more than maximum—a super-maximum speed—to earn a minimum wage, and, if a workman can't live up to it, and the employer has to take on another workman to help him, his cost of production goes up, and he writes it down as loss.

"Take the clothing industry, for instance. Clothing prices have gone up, presumably to keep the manufacturer from taking too great a loss due to processing taxes, minimum wage, shorter hours, and so on. But what does the employer do? He grabs every cent out of the increased profit from higher prices and pockets it. And he takes it out of his labor.

343

What he has done has been to increase standards of efficiency to take up increased cost of production. If he accepted normal standards of efficiency, his cost of production would go up, thereby cutting into the increased profit he is getting out of higher prices." . . .

The clothing industry, on a piece-work basis, and the textile mills, using the stretch-out system, are the worst offenders, Bahnsen and Smith said.

"I doubt if the human system can stand the pace they've set," Smith remarked. "They are simply making nervous wrecks out of their workmen. It's not at all uncommon for a girl operating a machine in one of these garment factories to throw up her arms and scream." . . .

Having set these standards to which one must live up to in order to get the minimum wage, which is the maximum, they — especially in the garment manufacturers — are having a hard time finding "experienced operators."

"Of course, they've set a pace so fast that only a super-operator could keep up with it," Bahnsen said, "but they don't see it. And they keep yelling for 'experienced' help. The garment industry is even thinking of setting up its own training school for machine operators!" . . .

And as requirements to get even the minimum code wage go higher and higher, more and more exacting, they pointed out, opportunities for learning a trade diminish.

The unions don't want apprentices, the NRS men say. I've heard that elsewhere. They make it practically impossible for even their own members to get back if they've let their dues lapse while out of work.

An unemployed carpenter in Baltimore last week told me it would cost him $85 to get back into his union. An unemployed tile-setter said it would cost him $50 — and he never expected to have the money. Neither could tell me why, nor could the NRS people, who said they had heard similar stories again and again.

"Whatever pickup in private industry there may be," Bahnsen said, "THERE IS — THERE WILL BE — NO CHANCE FOR THE INEXPERIENCED TO GET BACK TO WORK. AND MOST OF OUR PEOPLE ARE INEXPERIENCED, WITH NO OPPORTUNITY TO BECOME EXPERIENCED."

The situation for young people in the industrial scheme is simply hopeless. They've no chance to learn any trade. There are no apprenticeships open to them. Smith said he had talked recently to an 18-year-old boy who had never had a chance to work — at ANYTHING. As for high school graduates — they're "simply out in the cold," to quote Bahnsen. And college graduates are in just about as bad a situation.

Said Mr. Smith:

"There's no use kidding ourselves. Industry, as it's now managed,

344

with its present idea of the sacredness of profit, can't absorb this unemployment load. It might eventually take in the majority of those between the ages of 20 and 40, but that leaves out two groups that cause the most worry — boys and girls under 20 and men, with half grown families, between 40 and 50. The youngsters can't qualify because they have no chance to acquire trades, and the older men, who have experience, can't keep up the pace demanded."

From what these gentlemen tell me, I get this impression of Baltimore employers:

"We've got to speed up our workmen so that the minimum wage (which they have also made the maximum wage) won't eat into our profits."

And:

"With all this unemployment around, a man ought to be GLAD to have a job at ANY wage and under ANY sort of working conditions we may wish to impose. A man ought to be so damned glad to GET a job that we can pay him as little as we please and overload him as much as we like."

You hear it over and over again, as a matter of fact.

These employers are by no means consistent. Even as they chisel their profit out of labor — and naively tell Bahnsen and Smith about it — many of them tell Bahnsen and Smith they think the present economic system is doomed. They are scared stiff at the prospect of the Government taking over their business — and have no idea on how to meet the present situation.

You might think that their tendency would be to blame present conditions on the Roosevelt Administration — on the New Deal, with its codes. But quite generally they don't.

They are beginning, I was told, to feel that industry itself has made the mistakes that led up to this situation. Just now, according to the NRS men, many of them are questioning the advisability of so much technological improvement. "Apparently, it's just occurred to them," Smith said. "Every day or so someone says:

"'Now you take out there at the Bethlehem plant at Sparrows Point. They're constantly installing new machinery — and every time they install a new machine, they throw a couple of hundred men out of work — for good.' "

Bahnsen and Smith both encounter among employers a decided prejudice against taking on relief clients.

"Don't send me anybody who's been on relief," they say. "Those guys don't want to work."

People on relief, Bahnsen and Smith say, whether deservedly or not, are rapidly acquiring the reputation of being chiselers. . . . There is a

345

story of a man given a job in a dry-cleaning establishment, who worked two days and then quit, announcing that he could get more out of life on relief than by work for $15 a week. . . .

To Eleanor Roosevelt

Baltimore, MD.   November 21 [1934]

Dearest:
   . . . This has been a busy day. Most of it spent with school people. I quote the principal of a school in one of the most poverty-stricken sections of Baltimore:

"We give free lunches to the children here — only to those who are the worst off, because we haven't enough money to feed all those who may be hungry. (One child they're feeding is 8 *years* old and *twelve* pounds underweight!) The food we give them is very plain — soup, cocoa, or milk, and bread without any butter. You know you've got to be really hungry to eat dry bread and like it. It makes you heartsick to see these children grab that food. We feed about 100. Never have we had enough bread — just plain, dry bread — so that there was enough for each child to have all it could eat! Never has there been even a crust left. They just gulp it down. It's all gone in five minutes."

Only the children who otherwise wouldn't have any lunch at all are fed, she said. Those who can get even so little as bread and lard or bread and coffee at home don't get fed at school.

She has been principal of that school, in a terribly poor district, for five years, and *never once, in all those five years,* she said, *has there been a case of thievery in the school.* Aren't children swell?

I spent two hours in the late afternoon with Joseph P. McCurdy, head of the A.F. of L. in Maryland. He's grand — the most intelligent and, it seemed to me, thoroughly honorable leader I've met. I found him deeply discouraged, though. He sits on various boards and meets plenty of businessmen in capacities other than that of head of the unions. Corporation lawyers generally, he says, are advising them to ignore NRA and the other New Deal regulations, on the ground that they are unconstitutional, and that industry can go to court and "beat the gavel." Not five percent of the employers who have been forced to accept 7A[1] are living up to it, he says, and none has accepted it without being forced. "So far," he says, "NRA has made about as much dent on industry as a sparrow's bill could make on an alligator's back!" He cites as typical the remark which he says a department store proprietor made to him: "Hell, NRA don't mean a thing!" . . .

1. The provision in the NIRA that allowed workers to join the union that the majority of them favored.

To Harry L. Hopkins

[Washington, D.C.]   December 6, 1934

Dear Mr. Hopkins:

This report is based on several trips of several days each to Baltimore in the last six weeks. It was the only field work I was able to manage during the special autumn survey.

On these trips I have concentrated on the employment picture rather than on the relief show. I have tried to find out just what the chances are of getting any appreciable portion of Baltimore's relief load of around 28,000 cases absorbed in private industry in the next few months: what jobs there are, what they pay, what the attitude of employers is toward our relief clients, and what the attitude of the relief clients is toward whatever jobs there may be.

The relief and employment situation in Baltimore is particularly interesting because the Baltimore Emergency Relief Commission, following an investigation last summer and a 20 per cent cut in Maryland's grant, 85 per cent of which goes into Baltimore, is now straining every nerve to get these people back to work.

My own feeling is that they may be straining a little too hard! A young woman who places unemployed women, both relief and non-relief for the Baltimore office of the National Reemployment Service, told me, for instance, that she was constantly driven to put relief clients to work, no matter what the wages or how bad the working conditions. She was told, she said, that, if the wages were below the minimum subsistence level, the Relief Commission would supplement them. . . .

I heard a good deal in Baltimore of this business of supplementing wages with relief. I was unable to get figures on just how many workers on full time are receiving supplementary relief, but casework supervisors believed it was too large. The administrator said the commission had set up $5 a week as the minimum to be paid for domestic service, and that no one was to be taken off relief for refusing to work for less, but the young woman down at NRS said she had received no such instructions.

At any rate, by one means or another, they are managing to hold the relief load down in Baltimore and cutting it some.

On May 4 the case load was 38,564. On October 31 it was 26,882. That isn't a net drop, however, for during that same period they had a total intake slightly over 6,000.

C. Howard Beck, Jr., the administrator, was very proud of the fact that he had gone $100,000 below his budget in September and $125,000 in October. Some of this saving was due to cutting down administrative cost. Mostly, I believe, it was the result of rigid investigation, pressure on the clients to get back into industry, demands on relatives, and, possibly, holding down the clients' budgets.

Of some 17,000 cases closed between June 1 and September 30, 7,988 were closed because of ineligibility. Among these were people who were removed because they had turned down jobs in private industry, refused to undergo a new investigation — whereby in many cases it meant calling on their relatives for aid — were referred as non-emergency cases to another social agency, were guilty of misrepresentation (several of these were taken into court and prosecuted), and many families that were "adjusted financially." Being "adjusted financially" meant, in the majority of cases, that relatives were made to take over the burden. More than anything else in Baltimore's relief cutting, I found this aroused resentment. I'm wondering myself if it isn't really worse for a man's morale to make his relatives — who don't want to do it and many times can't do it without materially cutting their own standards of living — contribute to his support. . . .

Among the cases closed between June 1 and September 30, there were 6,503 in which some member of the family got a job. That doesn't mean they got permanent jobs, though. Nor at living wages. One casework supervisor estimated that two-thirds of those jobs were temporary, running from one week to six. Wages ran from a couple of dollars a week to $16, for white collar people. * * * On the other hand, take one day's figures from the National Reemployment Service and they look better. On November 15, for instance, the Baltimore office of NRS put 40 people, relief and non-relief, to work. They listed 36 of those jobs as "Regular," not "Temporary." But 22 of the 36 jobs went to bricklayers to be employed on a PWA building job (Fifth Regiment Armory) which certainly can't last more than a few weeks. If there isn't another big building job, private or PWA, underway when that one is finished, these people will all be out of work again. Wages *look* better, too, on the NRS report. Those 22 bricklayers were to be paid $33 a week. Of their other "Regular" placements for that day, a fireman, third grade, was to get $15 a week; a sheet metal helper, $15 a week; a machine operator, $13 a week; a sail-maker, 3rd class, for the U.S. Coast Guard, $26.70 a week; an asphalt raker (which certainly doesn't sound like a permanent job to me), $13.50; a floor layer (and that doesn't sound permanent these days, either), $33; some laborers (report doesn't specify what they were to do), $13.20 and $13.50; a baker's helper, $16; a couple of housemaids, $5. * * * The two principal flaws in the NRS reports are, I think, that they list, as permanent, jobs that really aren't permanent at all and they list a weekly wage which THEIR OWN CONTACT PEOPLE tell me isn't actually paid because of the practice on the part of employers of breaking it down into an HOURLY rate and then paying the workmen ONLY for the time they are actually WORKING. This is pretty prevalent, I gather. Department stores are said to be among the worst offenders — breaking the salaries of their clerks down into hourly rates and sending them home during the quieter hours — and Arthur Hungerford, head of the NRA compliance board, says this is in violation of the code.

Honestly, I can't see anything to get very hopeful about in the employment picture in Baltimore. We'll grant that Baltimore always has been a "low wage" town. I still feel that the attitude of the industrial crowd over there — from Bethlehem Steel's Sparrows Point plant, with a "payroll," more or less mythical as nearly as I could find out, of 13,000, down to the housewife who wants a maid-of-all work for her "keep" — can't be much different from that of the rest of the country.

Their big idea — their WHOLE idea — is this: "There are a lot of people out of work. Therefore, we ought to get help for very low wages." And they get resentful as the devil because relief makes it possible — however little it may amount to — for people to refuse to take jobs at less than a living wage.

I've heard it said too often for me to doubt it — by NRS contact people, labor people, social workers — that they are trying to make the relief budget, which was never supposed to be anything more than a temporary, minimum subsistence budget, the actual BASIS for wages.

It's hard to get figures. But my impression most certainly is that the only people who are getting anything like the wages they got before this depression are the union members, and they've got an awful fight on their hands. As for the rest of the workers — they are helpless and hopeless.

Whatever NRA may have done to improve this situation you could hardly see with the naked eye. Sure, there's a minimum wage. It's also the MAXIMUM wage. And, legally or illegally, it's broken down into an hourly rate so that it doesn't MEAN anything. What's the use of working, I ask you, if you can't even earn enough to live on? Might as well be on relief.

Listen to some of the troubles of Arthur Hungerford, head of NEC[1] and the NRA compliance board in Maryland:

Two firms recently in Baltimore — one of them the Glenn Martin airplane company, with a lot of army contracts — announced they were going to raise wages. Whereupon, they were REQUESTED by the Baltimore Association of Commerce NOT to do it. Mr. Hungerford says he has this straight. He has reported it to Mr. [Donald] Richberg.[2]

Some months ago Hungerford got, about the same time, evidence involving labor practices against a certain small merchant in Baltimore and against Montgomery Ward, from all I hear about the worst employer in Baltimore. Baltimore businessmen, he said, hounded the life out of him trying to get him to crush the little guy, but managed to get Montgomery Ward off with only a warning — over here in Washington — on the plea that they had been misinformed. And recently an order came through that from now on all complaints against Montgom-

349

ery Ward involving labor were to be handled in Chicago! You can just figure out how much reason Montgomery Ward has to be afraid of the NRA compliance board in Chicago!

Not so very long ago Hungerford had a case against one employer who had made his employees sign falsified payrolls for four months, the payrolls indicating they got more than they actually did get. The fellow got off because some federal trade commissioner went out there and meekly accepted the falsified payrolls at their face value and declared there had been no violation!

Back in the summer he had a complaint, apparently well backed up, against a fairly large garment manufacturer. The fellow came into his office, looked Hungerford right in the eye, and said: "How about me paying a $10,000 personal fine to get this thing cleared up? You know what I mean." He got off merely by paying restitution to his employees, because when they had the hearing over here in Washington the man who knew all the details was absent.

I went down to see Hungerford boiling mad. I had just had lunch with Miss [Tressa] Solomon, the girl who places women in jobs for NRS. She had told me about Montgomery Ward sending down there for waitresses who were supposed to work three hours a day for 25 cents an hour. That's 75 cents a day, mister, and their carfare would cost them 20! Mr. Hungerford was out when I got there. To his assistant I stormed: "How about NRA? How about your code?" His assistant calmly replied: "Oh, that's legal under the restaurant code. They wrote their own code. Childs[3] also hire waitresses for 25 cents an hour, three hours a day, all the time!"

Yet in spite of all this kind of thing, Hungerford thinks we're getting somewhere, slowly moving ahead. The NRS contact people, fellows who go out, day after day, seeing 15 or 20 employers a day, going back to the same employers again and again, trying to get jobs for people, don't feel so optimistic. . . .

I talked with a number of Negro caseworkers, including one who had for three years been in the placement bureau at the YWCA. There isn't much use repeating what they said. I suppose they could be accused of bias. I attended a committee meeting of businessmen, considering the problem! The gentleman who presided—he says he pays his own servants $12 a week—thought that all women who refused to take living-in housemaid jobs at $3 a week should be cut off relief. Someone suggested that many of these women couldn't live-in because they had small children to look after at home nights.

"We-e-ell," he said, "I don't believe ordinarily in separating mothers from children, but we've GOT to think of the taxpayers' money. And if we can institutionalize these children—for the time being, anyway—take care of them cheaper than we're doing it now and put their mothers to work, I think we owe it to the taxpayers, etc."* * *

My own feeling was, after several sessions on the subject, that what the good housewives of Baltimore really want is a flock of Negro Mammies who will work for their room and board.

This thing is too long. It certainly is more than enough for one sitting. But what I've honestly tried to do — and I'm terribly in earnest about it — is to give you an idea of what these unemployed are up against as we try to shove 'em back into private industry. And, as I said before, admitting that Baltimore has always been a "low wage town," I can't believe that the attitude of Baltimore employers is so VERY much different from that of employers elsewhere.

I know I've not been consistent in my thinking about this wage business. Well, after all, I didn't know a darned thing about relief or any of the rest of it when you started me traveling around the country. I was critical of CWA because I thought the wages were too high. I still think that they shouldn't have exceeded what an employer was SUPPOSED to pay under the code. But now, dammit, I'm wondering if the only way to get employers to pay people enough to live on won't have to be for the government to treat the unemployed as labor surplus, take them all out of the market, pay them living wages, and let industry howl.

I keep thinking of a labor leader I met in Baltimore — the only fairly high-up leader I ever met whom I really liked much. This chap was honest, I thought, and intelligent. He was also deeply discouraged.

"How in God's name," he said, "are you going to inculcate into people the desire to do the right thing? You can't legislate it into them."

And he wound up his conversation with me this way:

"There's hardly a day passes without some worker coming in here, all red and sore as Hell, saying: 'I'm going to kill that bastard!' I keep hushing them, smoothing them down, but — I wonder what's the use." . . .

1 National Economic Council.
2. NRA administrator.
3. A restaurant chain.

To Harry L. Hopkins

REPORT SUMMARY   [Washington, D.C.,   January 1, 1935]

Relief on a nationwide scale will be indispensable during the coming fiscal year. This is true even though a business upswing should take place. A little figuring from available data will show that it would require a boom exceeding that of 1929 for the millions at present out of work to be reabsorbed into employment.

It must not be overlooked that since 1929 our population has increased by several millions, and that the number of persons in our population for whom gainful employment would normally have to be provided in 1935-1936 has correspondingly grown.

The extent to which available work has been "spread" during the last five years of diminished employment is itself a factor militating against the taking back into industry of more than a small percentage of those now unemployed. In view of the limited volume of business, few industries in the United States are at present working the maximum hours authorized by their NRA codes. Speaking generally, American industry would be able to turn out a considerably increased volume of product by merely building up to the code maximum (40 hours in the majority of industries) the working hours of those at present employed.

The following basic industries may be cited from among the large number to emphasize the phenomenal increase in demand which would have to take place before employment could be given to approximately the same number of persons as gained a livelihood in industrial occupations during the boom year of 1929.

The lumber industry (logging camps, saw mills, planing mills, and box factories) which in 1929 provided employment for approximately 500,000 wage earners, had approximately 400,000 at work when 1934 ended, and these employees were working approximately 30 hours per week as against the allowed code maximum of 40. The lumber industry did not profit from the prosperity of 1926-1929. In fact, the industry had experienced a steady decline for several years prior to 1929, and lumber production that year was actually 20 per cent under that of 1919. Just before the adoption of the lumber code in the late summer of 1933, the industry was at the lowest ebb in over sixty years. Although 1934 will show an increase of about 15 per cent in production of lumber over 1933, it would take an increase in the consumption of lumber during 1935 that could only be termed miraculous for half a million persons to have steady employment in the industry. A considerable increase in the demand for lumber could be met merely by building up to 40 hours per week the working time of those at present on part time. In the logging camps and saw mills of the South, the Southwest, and Northwest, local relief administrators tell us it would be folly to expect the lumber industry to enjoy such a degree of prosperity as would make relief unnecessary. It is estimated that close to 100,000 logging and saw mill employees are still totally unemployed.

The blast furnaces, steel works, and rolling mills of the United States in 1929 provided employment for approximately 550,000 persons. However, during that boom year, nearly 15 per cent of the country's steel-making capacity stood idle for want of demand. As the year 1935 opens, the industry is operating at about 40 per cent of capacity, or double the rate of operation four months previously. However, the number of wage earners employed during November, 1934, was less than 400,000, or only 10 per cent more than were employed in September,

1934. This indicates how an increase in output can be handled without any corresponding increase in total number of employees. During the last quarter of 1934, employees in the steel industry worked an average of fewer than 30 hours per week. The code maximum is 40. It will be obvious, therefore, that steel output could be still further increased without any large number of new employees being taken on. One has to be exceedingly optimistic to believe that 450,000 persons will receive steady employment in the steel industry of the United States during 1935. On the contrary, it appears certain that in the neighborhood of 50,000 persons, able bodied and employable, who look upon the local steel industry as their most logical chance of a livelihood, will have to be cared for by public relief. Investigations by FERA field workers who made special visits to steel towns of the United States during November, 1934, support the foregoing prediction of the inability of the steel industry to provide for anything like the total population dependent upon it. For anything like 450,000 persons to be given steady employment in the steel industry during 1935 (say 2,000 hours per employee) it would be necessary for half as much more steel products to be marketed than were turned out in 1934.

The coal industry gave employment to something like 600,000 persons in 1929. (460,000 in bituminous; 140,000 in anthracite.) As 1934 ended the soft coal mines of the Appalachian region were working four days a week in an effort to meet the increased demand for coal brought about by the sudden onslaught of winter weather. However, in spite of the relatively good demand, less than 390,000 miners were at work. Another 70,000 were reported by the United Mine Workers of America as idle in several thousand mining communities in the country over. In the boom year 1929, it required an output of 530 million tons of bituminous coal to provide employment for approximately 460,000 persons. Under the Soft Coal Code, five days of seven hours each constitute the working week. It is estimated that in order for 460,000 persons to be steadily employed (and allowing for the reduced number of hours per week), approximately the same quantity of bituminous coal would have to be marketed in 1935 as was sold in 1929. This means an increase of 50 per cent over 1934 production of approximately 350 million tons. Relief officials in thousands of coal communities tell us there is no possibility of coal mining activity reaching a level during 1935 where relief could be dispensed with. The anthracite industry in Northeastern Pennsylvania is in a grave situation, and fully 35,000 miners are totally unemployed.

Agriculture, it must be remembered, is an employing industry. In addition to the owners and tenants operating farms, there were over 2,000,000 persons working for wages on American farms according to the Census of 1930. The curtailment of the farmer's income has not only deprived him of the power to purchase things needed on the farm; it has made it impossible for him to hire his customary "help." Until the farmer is once more in a position to employ labor to assist him, the Nation must accept the responsibility for providing relief to the able-bodied farm laborer. If he is not aided through relief given in the community in which he normally resides, he will migrate to the city and swell the ranks of the unemployed there.

The building industries provided employment for 2,500,000 persons in 1929 and should take care of a considerable number more if the increase in the number of those for whom gainful employment must normally be provided is taken into account. The depressed state of the construction industries and the activities dependent on building is too well known to require extended comment here. But does any thoughtful person seriously believe that within the next eighteen months anything like 2,500,000 men and women can find employment in the building construction industries? Although accurate figures are not available as to the total number of persons at present out of work in the building industries, reports from relief administrators in cities and towns from one coast to the other testify to the distress among this large group of workers. The labor unions connected with the construction industry confirm evidence received by relief headquarters as to the need for continued relief for many thousands of artisans and laborers who must await a resumption of building construction in their respective communities before they can do without relief.

The importance of the transportation and communications industries of the United States in providing employment is likely to be lost sight of. During 1929-1930, water, rail, highway, and air transportation, telephone, telegraph, etc. provided employment for nearly 4,500,000 persons. Railroad employees have been especially hard hit by the prolonged depression. In 1930 over 1,500,000 persons were employed on steam railroads alone. By the middle of 1932, this number had declined by nearly 500,000. During recent months there has been an improvement in railroad employment. But is anyone prepared to say when and under what conditions the steam railroads of the country will again be able to employ 1,500,000 persons? The answer to this question is not in sight, but in the meantime, and making full allowance for the pickup in railroad traffic that would inevitably follow an improvement in general business, provision must be made for the continuance of aid to many thousands of able-bodied railroaders who cannot find employment in their regular occupation.

The decline in freight and passenger traffic on our railroads and their unsatisfactory financial condition have worked a hardship on many thousands of workers dependent upon railroad repair shops and independent locomotive and car building plants. The low volume of freight and passenger traffic during the last four years has made it possible for railroads to get along with fewer cars and locomotives. As a result there is less repair work to do in the railroad shops; many of them are working only a few days a month. The same thing holds good for the industrial plants specializing in the construction of new locomotives and freight and passenger cars. A recent report showed only 60 per cent of the pullman cars of the country in service, and the output of new freight and passenger cars during the last four years has been negligible. Only a restoration of the purchasing power of the steam railroads of the country will bring about a revival of purchasing of locomotives and cars to replace the large proportion of existing rolling stock that is admittedly obsolescent. In 1929-1930, railroad repair shops and locomotive and car building plants accounted for 450,000 employees. The number working part time at present probably does not exceed 150,000. Until this industry recovers, some reasonably adequate provision must be made for the thousands dependent on it for a livelihood, who, under present circumstances, are unable to find employment.

The copper industry presents a particularly difficult problem from the standpoint of reemployment. While copper mines and smelters do not account for a relatively large number of persons in our total working population, these industries are carried on in places in which there is no other important occupation. Until the capital industries stage a comeback, the outlook for the return of prosperity to the communities in Michigan, Montana, Utah, New Mexico, Arizona, and Nevada that are entirely dependent on copper is anything but bright.

American copper has been one of our chief exports, but the expansion of copper production in Canada and South Africa and the ability of producers in those countries to sell copper to our former European customers at less than it costs to make it in the United States is a serious barrier to reemployment in the copper industry. Unemployment is especially severe in the copper camps and smelter towns of the Far West, and until some at present unforeseen demand for copper arises there is nothing for the Government to do but make sure that the families who legitimately look to copper for a livelihood are taken care of.

The automobile industry should be mentioned in connection with any discussion of the prospects of reemployment. In this industry, fortunately, the outlook is for a greatly increased output of cars during 1935. It must be remembered, however, that the production of automobiles is highly seasonal in character, and that the bulk of employment ends with the month of May. The leading manufacturers are endeavoring this year to "stagger" the output of cars, in the hope that employment may thus be spread more evenly over the year, instead of being concentrated, as at present, in the first five months.

However, the towns of the Middlewest that largely depend on the manufacture of automotive parts and accessories and on the production of cars have had such bitter experience with the up-and-down nature of employment in these industries that they are unwilling to assume the risk that the promised improvement in the demand for automobiles in 1935 will enable them to get along without relief. The relief administration must take a realistic view of the prospects for the automotive industries employing anything like the large number of persons who look to them for employment and must be ready with relief for many thousands of families in the Middlewestern communities who will certainly fail to find a livelihood this year in any of the industries connected with the production of automobiles.

The foregoing instances will suffice to call attention to the magnitude of the employment problem confronting the United States during 1935-1936. What has been said about these particular industries could be said (with certain modifications and with greater or less emphasis) about practically every industry in the United States.

If the estimated output of the industries of the country for 1934 is compared with the output of 1929, the distance the country has to go before again attaining the 1929 volume of quantity production will be apparent. This is particularly true of basic industries like railroad transportation, steel, coal, and lumber.

Another factor working against the probability of any large number of those now unemployed getting steady jobs during 1935-1936 is the progress of mechanization of industrial processes. As is well known, this trend was steadily at work in most American industries up to the crash of November, 1929. Between 1919 and 1929 the industrial output per wage earner rose by almost one third. When the Federal census was taken, in April, 1930, and before the downward trend in employment had really become severe, there were between 2,000,000 and 2,500,000 employable men and women out of work. There is every reason to believe that the trend toward the replacement of human labor by machinery will be resumed, once a business revival gets under way and capital for new mechanical installations becomes available to the enterprising industrialist. The desire on his part to cut production costs in order to maintain what he considers a normal profit will encourage the search for more economical production processes that will enable him to turn out an increased volume of product without a corresponding increase in payroll. During the depression industrial engineers have had the leisure and the incentive to work out methods of cutting production costs by the "rationalization" of industrial organizations, equipment, and methods.

In steel manufacture (again to take this basic industry as illustration) the installation of "continuous" sheet mills is now under way in many plants in an effort to capture the business in automobile sheets. These installations will greatly reduce the number of men required to turn out a given tonnage. In the soft coal industry the elimination of loading labor underground, through the installation of mechanical loaders, is reported as likely to resume, once the volume of business in sight justifies the necessary capital outlay. In the textile industry the question of the "multiple loom" system (what the workers call the "stretch-out"), i.e., the system by which one operative tends a large number of looms, is once more to the fore. The extension of this system, even with the consent of the workers, cannot do otherwise than reduce the number of operatives required to turn out a given quantity of cloth. In the agricultural industry, the ability of farmers to employ anything like the 2,500,000 who worked on farms for wages in 1929-1930 is doubtful, for in this industry likewise mechanization is a potent factor. The improvement in farm income during 1934 means a renewal of purchasing of farm machinery, and the farm implement makers are looking forward to a good year. However, this good news has a sombre aspect, when viewed from the side of employment of farm labor.

In case 1935-1936 should be characterized by a marked improvement in business, the Nation will in all probability be faced with the paradox of increasing industrial employment without any corresponding reduction in the volume of unemployment.

Entering the Winter of 1934-1935, the Nation's relief load has been increasing, with promise of a continued rise. In some cities there have been predictions that by late Winter it will have reached a new peak. From New York, from Chicago, where the closing of the World's Fair threw thousands out of work, from the Pennsylvania coal and steel towns, from industrial Ohio and Indiana, expecting a rise of 10 to 15 per cent by the end of February, from New Jersey, facing "heavily increased relief rolls and a serious problem by Spring," from New England all the way to Texas, the story is the same — a general upward trend. In Detroit a few weeks ago, optimistic statements by Henry Ford and other automobile men were followed by a drop in relief applications, but still they came in, only fewer of them.

Weekly reports from 15 FERA investigators covering the industrial areas in November and early December indicated that industry, except for a few sporadic spurts, has so far failed even to catch up with the relief intake, let alone reducing the load. * * * "More people are reaching the point where relief is their only recourse," comes the report from Kansas City. "Industry is not absorbing the unemployed as rapidly as the number of those whose resources are exhausted is increasing." * * * In Schenectady, N.Y., there were in November 2,000 more employees on the General Electric payroll than a year ago. "But," observes an FERA investigator, "it must be remembered that in August, 1929, General Electric had 28,000 employees. Today it has 11,500. Thousands represented in that difference have been out of work so long that they have used up their savings and their credit, have ex-

357

hausted the help of friends and relatives, and will have to come on relief if they don't get work soon."

A great "back-log" of the unemployed is, as a matter of fact, represented in those thousands who used to work for General Electric in Schenectady, but who are now still jobless even though the company has taken back 2,000 in the last year. In Chicago in November, in addition to the 130,000 already on relief, there were 200,000 unemployed, potential candidates for relief.

In this group are our best people, the last to lose their jobs because they were the best workmen, the last to come on relief because they were thrifty, had credit, were able to care for themselves. They will be the first to get their jobs back, too — when there are any jobs. In Dallas, Texas, last Spring one large bank had taken back more than 50 of its former employees, not one of whom had ever been on relief.

But now the jobs are not coming back fast enough, and these people, too, are coming on relief, in increasing numbers, filled with despair, timidly slipping into relief offices to ask for "jobs." Out of 252 applications in Elmira, N.Y., one month this fall, 45 had never asked for help before, and "ten of these belonged to a strata that even in their wildest nightmares had never dreamed there was anything but solid ground under their feet." * * * In Dallas, Texas: "More applications are coming from the upper middle-class. Applications for work relief have been received from 300 unemployed teachers." * * * A factory executive in Troy, N.Y.: "In spite of the pickup we show for a certain class of labor, the white collar class is worse off than ever, and there is no employment in sight for them." * * * In Providence, R.I.: "Even when the mills are hiring new hands, the relief loads go up. This is because every winter more people who have been holding their own must at last give up. The Winter clients are new ones, finally hopeless."

One hears a good deal about "relief psychology" these days — that if it were all direct relief, with no work, thousands would never apply. No social worker out in the field would deny this. Through work the stigma has to some extent been removed from relief. Into every relief office in the country have come applicants, not for relief, but for jobs. More of them than you would perhaps believe have shaken their heads and turned away when informed that it was really relief. Without doubt there are many thousands of families on work relief in this country who would not have applied had they not been able to call it — to themselves, at any rate — "a job." But when one hears the testimony of clinical doctors, school nurses, teachers, and social workers that the "marginal families" — those who haven't yet come on relief — are really worse off than those on relief, one wonders how long these people could have held out after all. * * * This from a doctor in a mental hygiene clinic in Providence, R.I.: "Most of the people we see are not on relief, but are starving. Many of these are white collar people and people in the skilled labor class who avoid relief, whose pride remains stronger than hunger. The result on the children is malnutrition and a neurotic condition produced by hearing and being constantly part of parental fear. The child grows obsessed with the material problems of the home and mentally shoulders them, and the nervous system cracks."

Much of this winter increase is of course seasonal. In one district in Gary, Indiana, 4,100 families, mostly of former employees of the Illinois Steel Company, now employing less than 25 per cent of its normal payroll and on part time, were on relief in November. Last summer that district had only 1,500 cases. "The jump to 4,100," reports an investigator, "was due to the fact that during the warm months they had been living in tents or shacks. They could get by with little food and clothing then, no rent, no fuel. Finding themselves worse off than they were a year ago, these jobless people are now rushing to the relief station with appeals for shoes for the children, fuel, rent, warm clothes, food."

There is another seasonal angle this year to the rise in the relief load. Many thousands have come back on the rolls after working during the summer — at wages so low that they could barely feed themselves, let alone save anything. In beet sugar fields these people have been working, in cotton fields, in orchards, lumber camps, truck gardens, canning factories. A Baltimore case work supervisor estimated that two thirds of her people who worked last Summer had jobs that lasted from one week to six, at pay ranging from $2 a week to a very occasional $16. * * * A school principal in a district where there are a number of canning factories said: "When a load of vegetables comes in they blow a whistle. It's as much as your life is worth to be down in the street then — everybody running to get there first. But the most they ever earn is a dollar or two."

You say: "Well, most of these people were always seasonal workers. They used to manage to get through the Winter on what they earned in the Summer." Some of them did — at wages higher than they got this year. Many more "managed to get through the winter" on credit, now withheld by landlords and employers. "Relief psychology" works two ways. * * * Probably no class of labor has suffered more from reduced wages than have these seasonal workers. No other class of employers, except possibly housewives, is so irresponsible. Their attitude has been almost universally: "There are lots of people out of work. I can therefore get all the help I need for next to nothing." * * * Some classic examples: New Mexico sheep growers publicly howling that they couldn't get herders for $40 a month, but secretly trying to get them for $25; South Carolina truck gardeners highly incensed at relief and CWA because Negresses were unwilling to work in their truck gardens for 25 cents a day whenever they happened to need them; an Up-State New York apple grower, who blamed it all on relief when he was unable to persuade men to come out from Niagara Falls to pick his apples, providing their own transportation at a cost which would have exceeded their earnings!

To work under conditions only a little better than these, thousands of families did go off relief last Summer. They are coming back now. Even when they did have anything left, there was clothing to buy — relief officials generally acknowledge that we have never given enough clothing — household equipment to be replaced, debts to pay. Failure to withhold from creditors those few dollars undoubtedly has brought many families back on relief sooner than if they had held onto them. "He trusted me when I didn't have any money," they patiently explain. "I couldn't hold out when I had the cash." Creditors aren't always so good to them. From industrial centers like Detroit you get frequent reports of men losing the jobs they finally got back, because they were garnisheed. Employers haven't much patience with that sort of thing. And in one Middlewestern city an association of credit men actually applied at the relief office for information on how to garnishee a man's work relief check! * * * Relief clients are often tempted not to report these temporary, poorly paid jobs. That is called "chiseling," and people have been arrested for it. But again — heads of families, ashamed and defiant, have led investigators into their homes and have pointed out to them where those few, pathetic dollars went. Dishes, towels, clothing, badly needed bits of furniture, drugstore supplies, "things you can't get on relief."

So goes the Nation's relief load — up, down a bit, up again perhaps higher than ever before — while the newspapers and the business leaders are filled with optimism, and the country, bored with relief, wonders why these people don't get back to work. * * * Their chances of getting them back within the next six months certainly looked anything but bright this Winter. * * * NEW YORK CITY: "No private jobs in sight. From Public Welfare Commissioner [William] Hodson down to the case workers there was unanimity on this point. Relief workers report a complete lack of confidence in the majority of clients that jobs are coming back. My talks with clients brought the same reaction." * * * In CHICAGO only the farm implement people predicted any appreciable pickup in jobs. Retail stores and mail order houses were cutting down their payrolls. Thousands of packing house workers were being let out as the companies completed their Government orders. By the middle of November 2,000 who had lost their jobs when the World Fair closed had applied for work at the National Reemployment Service. The Pullman Company was employing about 10 per cent of its normal payroll, with the prospect of raising it temporarily to 25 per cent while doing some air conditioning, which, according to George A. Kelly, vice president, would be "negligible in relation to our capacity." Of the 125,000 members of the Chicago Building Trades Council, only 10,000 were regularly employed. * * * GARY, Indiana, was "dotted with silent factory buildings." Universal Atlas Cement Company was operating four of its 40 kilns, producing 150,000 barrels a month, compared with a normal 750,000, had 10 or 15 trucks instead of 300, and employed 350 men instead of 1,600. "We do not anticipate that we shall ever again hire as many men as we did in 1929," the manager said. * * * PHILADELPHIA: "I have talked to officers of some 25 concerns, employing from 75,000 to 100,000 hands. If you are looking to them to shoulder a substantial part of the relief load in the near future, you are bound to be let down. The best I can see is that there will be no more wholesale firings in the next few months. Most plants are so geared today that an increase of 25 per cent in output would not mean much more than a 10 per cent rise in employment." * * * UP-STATE NEW YORK: "I have visited seven industrial cities in Central and Western New York: Buffalo, Rochester, Syracuse, Schenectady, Jamestown, Olean, and Dunkirk. Their industrial products vary from locomotives to spectacles, from concrete sewer pipes to silk ribbons. In all of them important industries which formerly employed many people have been discontinued, and the industries that remain have substituted machines for men during the depression, so that each city has a body of unemployed, many on relief, who can never get their jobs back because those jobs have vanished." * * * ST. LOUIS: "Some employers may increase the number of hours worked — they have been working only 24 — but they will not add more employees." * * * HOUSTON, Texas: "Nobody at present thinks there will be an appreciable increase in the demand for labor in the near future. There is now an abundant supply of skilled labor in all trades, and so much common labor has drifted in from the country that there is a large surplus." * * * In DETROIT "all the big automobile concerns have their own preferential lists for reemployment," and very few of the men on those lists, the observer pointed out, are on relief.

That report from Detroit touches a condition that is reflected in many parts of the country. Through loss of skill, through mental and physical deterioration due to long enforced idleness, the relief clients, the people who have been longest without work, are gradually being forced into the class of unemployables — rusty tools, abandoned, not worth using any more. * * * "The man who has been used to earning his living by physical labor," writes the chairman of the citizens' relief committee in a Southern city, "has been out of a job for a long time. For the last four years he has been living on scant rations. He is soft, and it takes him some time to get back in trim to do a real day's work." * * * "Idleness," notes an observer in Chicago, "is doing something fundamental to these people which is destructive to their capacity for work. They become nervous, muscularly soft, unconfident of their ability to do work they formerly did, and when they finally obtain jobs they are so fearful of making mistakes that they actually do make mistakes and are fired. One firm hired 100 men and within a week dismissed 25. Their muscles had become too flabby to do the work required of them, and the employer was unwilling to keep them on until they had recaptured their physical strength and their confidence." * * * Welfare workers in Wilmington, Del., estimate that 25 per cent of their relief clients "will never be worth much in a competitive world again." * * * The head of the Ohio Employment Service believes that in Akron alone 30,000 of the 70,000 unemployed will never get jobs in the present industrial setup. * * * "They can't seem to adjust themselves to the rhythm of the plant," explained one employer in Endicott, N.Y., where a large shoe factory and a plant making office machines had had enough business so that practically every relief client who had ever worked for either concern was called back, but only a few lasted on the job. * * * List among those made unemployable by the depression one whole stranded generation! Men over 40, with half-grown families. Because of group insurance policies, which make them "bad risks," because of the crowding of the desperate younger generation, because they "can't keep up the pace" set by a newly high-geared industry, they are through. And they are beginning to realize it. The result is a kind of bitter apathy. "A man over 40 might as well go out and shoot himself," one of them said honestly out in Chicago a few weeks ago.

Do these relief clients want work? Listen to this, from Homestead, Pa.: "Everybody talks work, work, work and feels it would solve their problems." * * * And from New York City: "Jobs is the cry everywhere, and I can't over-emphasize this point." * * * "The pleas, the subterfuges resorted to in desperate efforts to get jobs is ample answer to critics who say that people don't want to work." * * * A well known settlement worker in Chicago believes 90 per cent of those on relief would rather have jobs in private industry. * * * "I have seen my first tears," writes an observer from Joplin, Mo. "A woman of middle age, the wife of a skilled workman, with daughters in high school, wept as she said: 'This will be our last week on relief. Next week we shall be able to take care of ourselves again. I do not think you know quite what it is like to have gone through this.'" * * * In Detroit a class was organized to teach young girls how to apply for jobs. "Are there any questions?" the teacher asked. One girl asked this question, and the other girls also found it important: "How can you go up and apply for a job without crying?"

They are willing to work, thousands and thousands of them, at wages even below relief standards. Relief officials and employment agencies report generally a tendency on the part of employers to make the relief minimum subsistence budget the basis for wages. "Deep down in my

362

heart I'm ashamed of the jobs I send many women and girls to," said a placement director in the National Reemployment Service in Baltimore, where housewives demand maids for $2.50 a week out of which they are expected to pay 20 cents a day carfare, where restaurants ask for "goodlooking" girls to work three hours a day for 25 cents an hour and keep their own uniforms laundered; where a stenographer to get a job for $7 a week must be able to type 60 words a minute. * * * One FERA investigator spent considerable time in Baltimore in November talking with vocational counselors in the high schools, labor leaders, heads of private and public employment agencies, the NRA compliance board, "contact men" for the National Reemployment Service who tramp the streets, day in and day out, talking to employers, getting jobs for people. The picture they presented of the attitudes and practices of employers was appalling. Department stores putting their clerks on a commission basis; automobile dealers paying their salesmen a minimum weekly wage of $17.50 and holding out each week $5, charged to "deterioration of the demonstrator car"; automobile mechanics, required to hang around the garage all day, but actually paid for only the time they are working on cars, sometimes only a couple of hours a day. "And these people are considered employed!" remarked one of the contact men. * * * Combine this attitude with the "spread-of-work" policy and you have a situation like that in Scranton, Pa., where employment in 1934 was up 12 per cent over 1933, but the total of wages paid out was 22 per cent smaller!

The effect of these low wages and of the uncertain tenure of jobs is bound to be insecurity — among the employed, as well as among the unemployed. That sense of insecurity is growing. * * * "Unconsciously," writes an observer from Detroit, "a large number of the relief clients have made Government relief a seasonal unemployment insurance." * * * They work a few weeks at reduced wages — the owner of a large woolen mill in Gloversville, N.Y., said, "I know skilled workers who used to make $40 and $50 a week, who are now getting $10 — are unable to save anything, and come right back on relief." * * * From Providence, R.I., comes this statement: "Right now a man on relief is a good deal better off than a part-time worker in private industry. He gets more, and he is sure of his future, whereas the industrial worker doesn't know from day to day when his part-time is going to evaporate into nothing. I still believe they want to work and don't want to stay on relief. But if you have the choice between two evils, you take the lesser one."

And so they go on — the gaunt, ragged legion of the industrially damned. Bewildered, apathetic, many of them terrifyingly patient. Protest groups have made little headway among them. "There are no organized protest groups here," wrote an observer from a Massachusetts mill town. "Only decay. Each family in its own miserable home, going to pieces. But I wonder if some day, crazed and despairing, they won't revolt without organization. It seem incredible that they should go on like this, patiently waiting for — nothing." * * * From a Pennsylvania steel town: "The appearance of the best of them is distinctly reminiscent of good troops who had been left too long in the lines. There are the same drawn features, the same look about the eyes of having seen too much, the same disciplined self-control."

Only among the young is there evidence of revolt, apparently. These young people are growing restive. Out of some 15 weekly reports from industrial centers all over the country, hardly one omitted a paragraph pointing out that these young people may not tolerate much longer a condition that prevents them from starting normal, active, self-respecting lives, that will not let them marry and raise families, that condemns them to idleness and want. At present there is no leadership among them. College men are shoveling sand, checking freight cars, working in filling stations. High school graduates are offering themselves to industry "for nothing, just experience" — and are being accepted. Boys who normally would be apprentices in the trades are tramping the pavements, riding the freights back and forth across the country, hanging about on street corners. One day in November a 21-year-old boy in Baltimore walked 20 miles, looking for work. "I just stopped at every place," he said, "but mostly they wouldn't even talk to me." * * * "There's going to be trouble as sure as you're sitting here," predicts the junior placement director in the New York State Employment Service. "There are no leaders in the group between 17 and 20, but these kids would gladly follow a leader of the next age level." * * * "There seems to be a general acceptance," wrote a FERA investigator from Homestead, Pa., "of the fact that leadership will develop among the educated young people who are mingling on the only jobs they can get with embittered unskilled laborers and absorbing their point of view." * * * Here are remarks from several young people to a FERA investigator in Providence, R.I.: A 20-year-old boy: "Why the Hell should I get up in the morning, lady? What am I going to do with all these days? I've been looking for a job for four years. I've had two. Five months I've worked, in all. After a while you just know it ain't getting you anywhere. There's nothing for us!" Another boy: "I'd steal if I had the guts." A pretty 21-year-old girl: "I'm young. It seems to me I got a right to something, if it's only one new dress a year." A 19-year-old boy: "It's funny. A lot of times I get offered a drink. It seems like people don't want to drink alone. But no one ever offers me a meal. Most of the time when I take a drink it makes me sick. My stomach's too empty." * * * This, from Wilmington, Delaware: "The worst that will come out of the depression is the breaking down in the morale of present day youth. Those maturing in the lean years. The schools, it seems, have not tempered their bright promise to the facts of the times. These youngsters come out feeling that the world is still easy, for them — that it's their elders who are the weak sisters. Soon they lose confidence. Then all sense of responsibility or respect for anyone. By the time work eventually turns up, they won't be able to hold a job. They have no experience and no chance of getting any. Their juniors will be first choice in a short time, and our present day crop will constitute a lost generation, sold out by a depression they didn't make."

With the comment that the case worker who gave it to him believed it expressed the feeling of many of her younger clients, a FERA investigator a few weeks ago sent in this poem from a town in Ohio. It was written by an 18-year-old boy.

Prayer of Bitter Men

We are the men who ride the swaying freights,
We are the men whom Life has beaten down,
Leaving for Death nought but the final pain
Of degradation. Men who stand in line
An hour for a bowl of watered soup,
Grudgingly given, savagely received.
We are the Ishmaels, outcasts of the earth,
Who shrink before the sordidness of Life
And cringe before the filthiness of Death.

Will there not come a great, a glittering Man,
A radiant leader with a heavier sword
To crush to earth the enemies who crush
Those who seek food and freedom on the roads?
We care not if Thy flag be white or red,
Come, ruthless Savior, messenger of God,
Lenin or Christ, we follow Thy bright sword.

Index

368

A Note on the Editors

RICHARD LOWITT is chairman of the department of history at Iowa State University, Ames. Born in New York City, he received his master's degree and Ph.D. from Columbia University. He is the author of a three-volume biography of the progressive George W. Norris.

MAURINE BEASLEY is an associate professor at the College of Journalism, University of Maryland, College Park. She received a M.S. in journalism from Columbia University and a Ph.D. in American Civilization from George Washington University. She is the co-author of *Women in Media: A Documentary Source Book* (with Sheila Gibbons).